ADDICTION
ENTRIES AND EXITS

ADDICTION
ENTRIES AND EXITS

JON ELSTER

EDITOR

Russell Sage Foundation • New York

The Russell Sage Foundation

The Russell Sage Foundation, one of the oldest of America's general purpose foundations, was established in 1907 by Mrs. Margaret Olivia Sage for "the improvement of social and living conditions in the United States." The Foundation seeks to fulfill this mandate by fostering the development and dissemination of knowledge about the country's political, social, and economic problems. While the Foundation endeavors to assure the accuracy and objectivity of each book it publishes, the conclusions and interpretations in Russell Sage Foundation publications are those of the authors and not of the Foundation, its Trustees, or its staff. Publication by Russell Sage, therefore, does not imply Foundation endorsement.

Library of Congress Cataloging-in-Publication Data

Addiction : entries and exits / edited by Jon Elster.
   p.   cm.
   Includes bibliographical references and index.
   ISBN 0-87154-235-8
   1. Addicts—Psychology. 2. Substance abuse—Etiology. 3. Self-control.
   I. Elster, Jon, 1940– .
RC564.A282   1999
  616.86—DC21   99-31479
                                        CIP

RUSSELL SAGE FOUNDATION
112 East 64th Street, New York, New York 10021
10 9 8 7 6 5 4 3 2 1

Contents

Contributors

Jon Elster is Robert K. Merton Professor of Sociology at Columbia University.

Caroline Jean Acker is assistant professor of history at Carnegie Mellon University.

George Ainslie is chief psychiatrist at Veterans Affairs Medical Center, Coatesville, Pennsylvania, and clinical professor of psychiatry at Temple Medical College.

Eliot L. Gardner is professor of psychiatry and neuroscience and director of the Division of Basic Research in the Department of Psychiatry at the Albert Einstein College of Medicine.

Olav Gjelsvik is professor of philosophy and chairman of the Department of Philosophy at the University of Oslo.

Jørg Mørland is director of the National Institute of Forensic Toxicology and professor of toxicology at the University of Oslo.

Ted O'Donoghue is assistant professor of economics at Cornell University.

Matthew Rabin is professor of economics at the University of California, Berkeley.

Ole-Jørgen Skog is professor of sociology at the University of Oslo.

Helge Waal is director of the national center for Methadone Assisted Rehabilitation in Oslo.

Gary Watson is professor of philosophy at the University of California, Riverside.

Acknowledgments

The chapters of this book were first presented at a conference on addiction at the Russell Sage Foundation in June 1997. The conference marked the end of a five-year project on addiction, generously funded by the Norwegian Research Council and supported also by the Norwegian Institute for Alcohol and Drug Research, the Norwegian Directorate for the Prevention of Alcohol and Drug Problems, and the Russell Sage Foundation. An earlier publication from the project, *Getting Hooked* (edited by Jon Elster and Ole-Jørgen Skog), was published by Cambridge University Press in 1999.

Introduction

Jon Elster

A COMMON image of addiction is captured in the following thumb-nail sketch of rats who have been trained to stimulate the plea-sure circuits in their brains by pressing a lever:

> The rat rapidly acquires the lever-pressing "habit"—giving itself approximately 5,000–10,000 pleasure/reward "hits" during each one-hour daily test session. During these test sessions, the rat is totally focused on obtaining the desired electrical stimulation—lever-pressing at maximum speed and completely ignoring other attractions within the test chamber (food, water, playthings, sexually receptive rats of the opposite sex). After several weeks, the rat suddenly faces a new and unexpected behavioral contingency. An electrified metal floor grid has been placed in the test chamber, between the entrance and the wall-mounted lever. This floor grid delivers intensely painful footshocks. The rat enters the chamber, received a footshock, and jumps back off the floor grid. It stands in the entrance, looking alternately at the aversive floor grid and the appealing wall-mounted lever. After some minutes of indecision, it crosses the floor-grid, receiving intensely painful footshocks with every step (and flinching and squealing in pain), to reach the lever and once again self-administer the pleasurable brain stimulation (Gardner and David 1999, 94).

We may or may not want to say that the rat is *addicted* to brain stimulation, which produces craving but not tolerance and withdrawal symptoms. Yet the syndrome described in the passage is one that matches a widespread view of the behavior of addicts. Compare, for instance, the rat in front of the aversive grid with a habitual drunkard as described by a nineteenth-century pioneer in the study of alcohol, Benjamin Rush: "When strongly urged, by one of his friends, to leave off drinking, he said, 'Were a keg of rum in one corner of a room, and were a cannon constantly discharging balls between me and it, I could not refrain from passing before that cannon, in order to get at the rum' " (cited in Levine 1978, 152). A common pretheoretical view of human addiction does in fact suggest that the behavior of the addict is based on an irresistible craving: compulsive, mechanical, and insensitive to all other rewards and punishments. At least this is supposed to be true for the most strongly addictive drugs, such as crack cocaine. In their use of these drugs, human beings allegedly do not differ from rats in their tendency to ignore all other considerations for the sake of the euphoria of consumption or relief from the dysphoria of abstinence.

The essays collected in this volume challenge this commonsensical view of addiction. Most simply stated, they show that addiction in humans differs from addiction in animals because of various specific properties of human beings. Unlike animals, which mostly behave like simple reinforcement machines, they can make *choices* on the basis of long-term consequences of present behavior. Unlike animals, which do not seem capable of introspection, they can have *awareness* of their addiction, deplore it, and fight it. Unlike animals, which lack beliefs and values of the requisite complexity, they are embedded in a *culture* that shapes cognition and motivation in ways that matter for drug consumption. This being said, the contributors also emphasize the commonalities of animal and human behavior. No contributor defends the view that drug consumption is simply a matter of rational choice or the view that addiction is simply a cultural construction. The neurophysiological facts about drug use—which are essentially the same in animals and humans—provide hard constraints on any choice-based or culture-based account of addiction. Even more obviously, no *treatment* of addiction can ignore these constraints.

Because of the many facets of human addiction, an interdisciplinary approach is called for. Whereas the study of addiction in animals is confined within the biological sciences, human addiction must be understood in light of the cognitive, moral, and cultural capacities of human beings, whence the need to draw on the humanities as well as the social sciences. In this volume, Gary Watson (a philosopher) shows that phrases such as "overpowering desire" and "irresistible desire" are intrinsically confused, at least when applied to human behavior. Olav Gjelsvik (also a philosopher) argues in his chapter that because humans typically internalize certain normative attitudes toward choice over time, a purely naturalistic account of addiction is insufficient. From a choice-theoretic perspective, the chapter by Ted O'Donoghue and Matthew Rabin (two economists) and the one by Ole-Jørgen Skog (a sociologist) show that once an addict becomes aware of his predicament, he can take action to deal strategically with his future selves. In their chapter, Helge Waal and Jørg Mørland (a psychiatrist and a neurophysiologist) stage a systematic confrontation between three choice-theoretic approaches on the one hand

and neurophysiological and clinical data on the other. Their analysis is neatly supplemented by George Ainslie's chapter, which contrasts one of these approaches (his own) with another (George Loewenstein's theory of visceral motivations). In the chapters by Caroline Acker (an anthropologist) and myself (a philosopher), a central argument is that socially prevailing beliefs about addiction can shape the behavior of addicts and of the doctors who treat them. Eliot Gardner's chapter provides a state-of-the-art summary of the neurophysiology of addiction, with emphasis on genetic predispositions to addiction and potential techniques for neutralizing them.

The Becker-Murphy Causal Model of Addiction

In an influential article, Gary Becker and Kevin Murphy (1988) present a model of rational addiction. The model has two main aspects. On the one hand, it offers a simple causal model of the consequences of consuming addictive substances. On the other hand, it offers a standard belief-desire account of how people might choose to engage in such consumption.

The Becker-Murphy causal model offers a valuable bridge between economics and neurophysiology. This creation of a common language is perhaps their most important contribution to the analysis of addiction. The causal model is in fact retained by several writers in this volume who do not share the belief-desire account of addiction.

In the causal model, addiction is characterized in terms of habit formation and negative internalities. (See notably the chapter by O'Donoghue and Rabin for an explanation of these two properties and the relation between them and Skog's chapter for a diagrammatic illustration.) The first feature, habit formation, implies that the more one consumes of the addictive drug now, the more one wants to consume in the future; or more technically, that past consumption increases the instantaneous *marginal* utility from current consumption. The second feature, negative internalities, implies that past consumption decreases the instantaneous *total* utility from current consumption. Intuitively, the first feature reflects the production of withdrawal symptoms and the second the emergence of tolerance phenomena.

The representation of important properties of addiction in the economist's language of utility functions is a considerable achievement. Yet the mapping is not perfect. As argued by Skog (1999), the two properties could also derive from other features of addictive drugs. Moreover, Becker's model does not incorporate the important phenomenon of cue-dependent cravings (but see Laibson 1996a for a Becker-type model of this feature of addiction). Also, as Gardner emphasizes in his chapter, the implicit assumption in the Becker-Murphy model—that people crave drugs mainly for relief from abstinence symptoms—ignores the basic fact that "recreational and addiction-producing drugs act on . . . brain mechanisms to produce the subjective reward, or high, sought by drug users." Craving is due not only to the push from dysphoria but also to the pull from euphoria. In particular, the *memory* of euphoria seems to be a very important aspect of the phenomenon of relapse, which the Becker-Murphy model is ill equipped to handle. Finally, as Waal and Mørland explain in their chapter, the importance of tolerance and withdrawal phenomena vary greatly from drug to drug. They also emphasize that drug effects that take place outside the dopaminergic system of the brain, where euphoria or dysphoria are encoded, also have an important place in explaining the addictive properties of drugs.

The Belief-Desire Models of Addiction

The mechanics of addiction is obviously an important part of explaining addictive behavior. Yet it is, equally obviously, insufficient. To understand why people start using addictive drugs, why some of the users become addicted, and why some of the addicted users eventually quit, we also need to model the beliefs and the motivations or desires of the users.

Consider first the *beliefs* of the users. Becker and Murphy (1988) assume, heroically, that people embark on a life of addiction with full knowledge about the harmful consequences of the behavior. At the other extreme of the spectrum, there is the "primrose path" model of addiction proposed by Richard Herrnstein and Drazen Prelec (1992), according to which people get trapped into addiction because they ignore the negative internalities. An intermediate position is argued by Athanasios Orphanides and David Zervos (1995). In their model, people know that they might be at risk if they start using addictive drugs but also know that there is a possibility that they might be able to consume without any harmful consequences. The contributors to the present volume do not emphasize this cognitive dimension of drug use. They assume, by and large, that people have accurate beliefs about the harmful consequences of drug use. (The chapter by Waal and Mørland is an exception.)

The contributors place more emphasis on another cognitive dimension, referred to as naiveté versus sophistication. To explain what that issue is, I first have to say something about the *motivations* of the users. Assuming for simplicity that people are motivated only by the desire for hedonic satisfaction, the question arises whether future hedonic experiences have the same motivational power as present ones. In more technical language, this is the issue of *time discounting*, which has a prominent place in many of the chapters of this volume. In Gjelsvik's chapter, the question is addressed from a normative point of view. Gjelsvik belongs to a long line of philosophers who question the rationality of very high rates of time discounting. He argues that some discounting is consistent with rational self-governance (just as some risk taking is consistent with a rational life) but that very high discounting is not (any more than extreme degrees of risk taking).

In the chapters by O'Donoghue-Rabin, Skog, and Ainslie, the issue of time discounting is addressed from an explanatory point of view. Exactly how do people discount the future? And what are the behavioral implications of discounting? Before 1955, it was generally assumed by those who thought systematically about the matter that the future is discounted *exponentially*. Simply put, this assumption means that the *relative* motivational force of any two future hedonic experiences remains constant as one moves closer to them in time. (Because of the discounting phenomenon, their *absolute* value or motivational force, compared to consumption in the present, increases as one moves closer to them.) An implication is that an exponentially discounting agent who wants to allocate consumption over time never has to reconsider his decision. Exponential discounting is *time consistent* because the relative value of consumption in any two periods remains constant. In his work on addiction, Becker assumes that people discount exponentially. Except for a brief remark (in Becker 1996, 120), he also assumes that the discounting function involved in addiction is *constant*.

The assumptions of exponential and constant rates of discounting can both be challenged. In a pioneering article, Robert Strotz (1955) argues that people discount the future hyperbolically rather than exponentially. One implication of his argument is that the relative motivational force of an early compared to a later hedonic experience increases as one moves closer to them in time. Intuitively, the value of the present relative to the near future is higher than the value of the near future relative to the more distant future. Another implication is that of time inconsistency: a hyperbolically discounting agent may have to reconsider his plan as he moves closer to the time when he has to implement it. Seen from a distance, a delayed greater reward may seem better than a smaller earlier reward, but as the agent approaches the moment when the early reward becomes available, his preferences may be reversed. Over the years, George Ainslie (see notably Ainslie 1992) has explored the properties of hyperbolic discounting in a number of domains, including addiction. The reader is referred to his chapter as well as to Skog's chapter for details.

Later, Edmund Phelps and Robert Pollak (1968) offered a different approach to nonexponential time discounting. In their model, discounted utility is a sum of utility from consumption in the current period and some fraction of exponentially discounted utility from consumption in future periods. If the fraction is equal to one, this reduces to the exponential case. If it is less than one, we obtain a discounting function that differs from both the exponential and hyperbolic forms. Following David Laibson (1996b), we may refer to this as quasi-hyperbolic discounting. When the fraction is less than one, it is qualitatively quite similar to hyperbolic discounting, in the sense that both implications mentioned in the previous paragraph also obtain under this model. The reader is referred to the chapter by O'Donoghue and Rabin for details.

The idea that discounting functions—whether exponential, hyperbolic, or quasi-hyperbolic—might not stay constant over time is a more recent development. It comes in two versions. The most ambitious version is offered by Gary Becker and Casey Mulligan (1997), who argue that people can choose their rate of time discounting. I argue against this idea in Elster (1997). A less ambitious claim is that rates of time discounting, like other aspects of the person, undergo causal, unplanned processes of change. In their chapter, O'Donoghue and Rabin explore this idea under the rubric "variable myopia," including the important case of consumption-induced myopia. Related arguments are found in Skog (1997) and Orphanides and Zervos (1998).

Both time inconsistency and changes in discounting functions may cause people to deviate from their plans. The person who decides to abstain from drinking on the weekend may, because of hyperbolic discounting, reverse his preferences when Saturday approaches. The person who decides to limit himself to two glasses of whisky may, because of consumption-induced myopia, go on to a third, fourth, and fifth glass. Either of these reversal experiences can give rise to learning. Once the person observes himself reversing his decisions time and again, he will come to know that this is just the way he behaves under these circumstances. In the language of O'Donoghue and Rabin, he is no longer naive, but sophisticated. In the language of the belief-desire model, he has *a new belief about his future desire* that is capable of modifying his behavior in the present.

Once a person knows that he is likely to react in a certain way to specific circumstances, that knowledge becomes part of his decision problem. To use a metaphor—which should not be taken too seriously—his future selves may then appear as constraints on the decision of his current self. He cannot lay plans for later periods and blithely assume that his future selves will implement them. Instead, if he would like to take two drinks at the party but knows that if he does he is likely to take five, he might decide to limit himself to one drink if that will leave his rate of time discounting unaffected. This example supports the commonsense idea that sophistication about one's own undesirable tendencies can help one keep them in check. O'Donoghue and Rabin show, however, that in the simplest case sophistication is harmful rather than helpful. In their three-period example, a naive person who is unaware of his inconsistent discounting will *plan* to abstain in the first and the second periods and consume in the third but will *in fact* abstain in the first and consume in the second and third. A sophisticated person will correctly expect that he will consume in all three periods. This result does not obtain under more complex conditions. O'Donoghue and Rabin show that when either the benefits from drug use or rates of time discounting vary over time, the naive person typically consumes more than the sophisticated one.

This strategy—taking one's future decisions as parameters for one's current decision—is not the only strategy available to a person who is subject to time inconsistency. As Ainslie (1992) shows, the agent may also try to overcome the problem by looking at the current decision as part of a series of identical future choices. On each occasion, one can choose between an impulsive decision (for example, smoking) and a more prudent decision (for example, abstaining from smoking). Well ahead of each occasion one intends to abstain, but because of a preference reversal induced by the hyperbolic discounting one makes the impulsive choice on each occasion. If, however, one can frame the problem as one in which the options are "always smoke" and "never smoke," one may prefer the latter option. This framing depends on the earlier choice being seen as a predictor of later choices: "If not now, when?"

There is no doubt that the strategy of bunching successive choices together often helps people to overcome their tendency to behave in a time-inconsistent manner. The setting up of an intrapsychic domino effect can be very effective in resisting temptation. Two of the chapters in the present volume cast some doubt, however, on the rationality and universal efficacy of the strategy. Following Michael Bratman (1995), Gjelsvik argues that Ainslie does not show the belief in the efficacy of precedent, "If not now, when?" to be *rational*. Skog, by contrast, questions the statement that bunching will invariably be *effective* in overcoming inconsistency and shows that the effect of bunching depends on the time horizon of the addict. If he sees an imminent decision to consume as a predictor of a very long string of later decisions to consume, he will decide to abstain and stick to his decision; if he sees it as predicting only a few later decisions, he will decide to consume and stick to the decision; whereas an addict with a horizon of intermediate length will decide to abstain and then change his or her mind.

The reader should study the chapters by O'Donoghue-Rabin and Skog to appreciate the force of their arguments. Here, I only want to observe that despite some differences, these two chapters represent a common—

and pioneering—effort. On the one hand, both chapters rely on the basic causal model offered by Becker, defining addiction in terms of habit formation and internalities. On the other hand, both replace Becker's assumption of exponential discounting with one of nonexponential discounting. The main differences are, first, that the chapters use different models of nonexponential discounting and, second, that they make different assumptions about how a sophisticated nonexponential discounter would behave. Note, however, that these two differences are entirely unrelated. As argued by Strotz (1955) and corrected in Pollak (1968), someone who discounts the future hyperbolically might well respond by taking his or her future choices as parameters for the current decision problem. Conversely, the strategy of bunching would presumably also be feasible for someone who discounts the future in a quasi-hyperbolic way. I am unaware, however, of any attempt to explore that issue.

Self-Control and Treatment

In his chapter, Watson argues against the common view that addicts are unable to control themselves because of an overpowering or compulsive desire for the drug. He does not exclude that addicts can find it hard to resist temptation but places the emphasis "not on the power of addictive desires to defeat our best efforts but on its tendency to impair our capacity to make those efforts." As he also notes, in yielding to temptation "we are not so much overpowered by brute force as seduced." I might add that the seduction operates in part through the belief that the desire is overpowering, so that any resistance will be fruitless.

Watson makes a compelling case against the argument that addicts cannot overcome their problem by sheer, unassisted willpower. Yet as a matter of fact, most addicts do not quit just by making a decision to stop consuming. Naive addicts may think they can achieve abstinence in this way, but they typically slip into relapse. They may then resort to more complicated cognitive or behavioral strategies—or seek treatment. Earlier, I mention two cognitive strategies available to sophisticated addicts: (1) treating one's future decisions as parameters for one's current problem and (2) bunching successive choices together in one overall choice between always consuming and always abstaining. These strategies, as noted, may not always work and could even make things worse.

Behavioral strategies include a number of precommitment devices: making the drug physically unavailable or available only with a delay, imposing additional costs on its use, and avoiding environments that might trigger a cue-dependent relapse. Addicts can also enlist other people as agents to protect them against themselves. In Colorado, a physician may write a letter to the State Board of Medical Examiners, to be sent in case he tests positive for cocaine, confessing that he has administered cocaine to himself in violation of the laws of Colorado and requests that his license to practice be revoked (Schelling 1992).

These cognitive or behavioral strategies of self-control may not work, however, either because of the intrinsic problems just discussed or because they are too fragile to cope with sudden and intense drug cravings. In that case, treatment may be an alternative. There is a wide range of drug treatments. The main thing they have in common is that they rarely work. In my chapter, I suggest that some of them may even make things worse. In her chapter, Acker shows the moralizing middle-class biases in early twentieth-century opiate treatment, one doctor comparing addicts to "little men who endeavor to lift themselves into greatness by wearing 'loud' clothes or by otherwise making themselves conspicuous, when effacement would be more becoming."

In his chapter, Gardner discusses the conceptual possibility and plausible realization of a drug-based form of treatment. He draws on work suggesting that parts of the population have an inborn or acquired reward-deficiency syndrome, which induces novelty seeking and sensation seeking, in general, and drug taking more specifically. To counteract this deficiency he suggests the technique of *dopamine substitution,* by which brain reward in individuals with naturally low levels of dopamine could be enhanced artificially by a nonaddicting drug. The crucial idea is to find a drug that (like cocaine) blocks the dopamine reuptake transporter but that has "a much slower onset of action and much longer duration of action" and hence does not produce the sudden rush that makes cocaine so attractive.

Beyond Addiction

Some of the contributions to the present volume go beyond addiction to discuss appetites, emotions, and visceral factors more generally. In my own chapter I attempt a systematic comparison of addiction and emotion, arguing that both should be seen in the triple perspective of neurobiology, culture, and choice. If taken in isolation, each of these approaches can give rise to a dangerous form of reductionism. If combined, they allow us to see these phenomena as partly shaped by individual choice and social pressure but always within hard neurophysiological constraints. I also discuss some salient differences and similarities between the phenomena of addiction and emotion. Let me highlight only one difference. To the extent that addictive cravings are triggered by encounters with the external world, they depend mainly on perceptual cues. Emotions, by contrast, depend much more heavily on beliefs.

In Ainslie's chapter he defends a view he develops at greater length elsewhere (Ainslie 1992) against a rival theory offered by George Loewenstein (1996, 1999). Both theories go beyond addiction to include other visceral motivations, such as emotions, hunger, and even pain. Roughly speaking, Loewenstein argues that these states are triggered by external cues, whereas Ainslie argues that they are triggered by the prospect of reward. In my opinion, there is no question that Loewenstein's theory captures important features of addiction, emotion, and the like. The issue is whether it also provides an explanation of these phenomena or, as Ainslie argues, merely a redescription of them. The fact that, phenomenologically, pain, hunger, anger, and addictive cravings are experienced as involuntary rather than chosen does not exclude, Ainslie argues, that they are ultimately governed by reward.

Ainslie's theory is satisfying because of its coherence and parsimoniousness. It is, however, vulnerable to the objection of being speculative and based on inferences and extrapolations rather than on direct empirical evidence. Rather than taking a side on that issue, I only adduce some empirical illustrations that may help to bring the debate into clearer focus.

The question of whether cravings are in fact shaped by reward or by exposure to cues might be amenable to empirical resolution, by considering Ainslie's example of Jewish smokers who are able to abstain on the Sabbath. In principle, one should be able to determine whether the craving subsides because of the lack of exposure to other smokers who might trigger it or because of the belief that the craving, were it to arise, would not be satisfied. Cravings can, in fact, be cue dependent as well as belief dependent, as illustrated by two stories told by Avram Goldstein (1994, 222). The first is

> a convincing story from a colleague who had been a nicotine addict but hadn't smoked for years. He had abstained from cigarettes in a variety of situations where he had smoked in the past, and thus he had desensitized himself to a variety of conditioned associations—cigarettes at parties, cigarettes at morning coffee, cigarettes at the desk, and so on. One day he went to the beach and was suddenly overwhelmed by an intense craving to smoke. He found this beyond understanding until he realized that smoking on the beach had been an important pattern at one time in his life, and that he had not had the opportunity to eliminate that particular conditioned association.

The second story concerns "the nicotine addict who goes skiing for a whole day, leaving cigarettes behind. No thought is given to cigarettes—they are simply unavailable. Then back at the lodge, where nicotine is available again, intense craving strikes, and the addict lights up." Although Goldstein does not specify whether cigarettes were *visible* or merely *known to be available* at the lodge, the first couple of sentences suggest the latter. In that case, we are close to Ainslie's interpretation of the Sabbath phenomenon.

The disagreement between Ainslie and Loewenstein can also be stated in terms of cue-dependent craving versus hyperbolic discounting. Ainslie writes in his chapter that "both people and animals have a robust tendency to discount the future hyperbolically. In that case, external stimuli should not be needed to either impose or release emotions. A small amount of immediate reward will be enough to lure someone into a process that is quite unrewarding over time." The difference between the two views may be illustrated by an example suggested by Loewenstein (personal communication). Suppose I have a tendency, which I deplore— to order rich desserts at restaurants. To control myself, I can choose my restaurant according to one of two precommitment strategies. On the one hand, I can decide to go to a restaurant where I have to order dessert at the beginning of the meal. This would help me overcome my problem of time inconsistency, if that is what I am fighting. On the other hand, I can opt for a restaurant in which they do not go around with the dessert trolley but in which dessert instead has to be ordered from the menu. This would help me overcome my problem of cue-dependent craving, if that is what I am fighting.

Ultimately, however, the disagreement between Ainslie and Loewenstein cannot be resolved at this level. Examples may be suggestive, but they cannot substitute for demonstration. Whether pain, hunger, anger, and cravings are reward-governed behaviors or arise involuntarily from cues in the environment is a question that can be settled only by examining the reward circuits in the brain. One of the lessons we can draw from Gardner's chapter is that the complexity of those circuits is such that the debate will not be resolved any time soon.

References

Ainslie, George. 1992. *Picoeconomics.* Cambridge: Cambridge University Press.
Becker, Gary. 1996. *Accounting for Tastes.* Cambridge, Mass.: Harvard University Press.
Becker, Gary, and Casey Mulligan. 1997. "The Endogenous Determination of Time Preference." *Quarterly Journal of Economics* 112: 729–58.
Becker, Gary, and Kevin Murphy. 1988. "A Theory of Rational Addiction." *Journal of Political Economy* 96: 675–700.
Bratman, Michael. 1995. "Planning and Temptation." In *Mind and Morals,* edited by L. May, M. Friedman, and A. Clark. Cambridge, Mass.: MIT Press.
Elster, Jon. 1997. "Review of Becker (1996)." *University of Chicago Law Review* 64: 749–64.

Gardner, Eliot, and James David. 1999. "The Neurobiology of Chemical Addiction." In *Getting Hooked: Rationality and the Addictions*, edited by Jon Elster and Ole-Jørgen Skog. Cambridge: Cambridge University Press.

Goldstein, Avram. 1994. *Addiction*. New York: Freeman.

Herrnstein, Richard, and Drazen Prelec. 1992. "A Theory of Addiction." In *Choice over Time*, edited by George Loewenstein and Jon Elster. New York: Russell Sage Foundation.

Laibson, David. 1996a. "A Cue Theory of Consumption." Manuscript, Department of Economics, Harvard University.

———. 1996b. "Hyperbolic Discount Functions, Undersaving, and Savings Policy." NBER Working Paper 5635. Cambridge: National Bureau of Economic Research.

Levine, Harry. 1978. "The Discovery of Addiction." *Journal of Studies on Alcohol* 39: 143–74.

Loewenstein, George. 1996. "Out of Control: Visceral Influences on Behavior." *Organizational Behavior and Human Decision Processes* 65: 272–92.

———. 1999. "A Visceral Theory of Addiction." In *Getting Hooked: Rationality and the Addictions*, edited by Jon Elster and Ole-Jørgen Skog. Cambridge: Cambridge University Press.

Orphanides, Athanasios, and David Zervos. 1995. "Rational Addiction with Learning and Regret." *Journal of Political Economy* 103: 739–58.

———. 1998. "Myopia and Addictive Behavior." *Economic Journal* 108: 75–91.

Phelps, Edmund, and Robert Pollak. 1968. "On Second-Best National Saving and Game-Theoretic Equilibrium Growth." *Review of Economic Studies* 35: 185–99.

Pollak, Robert. 1968. "Consistent Planning." *Review of Economic Studies* 35: 210–18.

Schelling, Thomas. 1992. "Self-Control." In *Choice over Time*, edited by George Loewenstein and Jon Elster. New York: Russell Sage Foundation.

Skog, Ole-Jørgen 1997. "The Strength of Weak Will." *Rationality and Society* 9: 245–71.

———. 1999. "Rationality, Irrationality, and Addiction: Notes on Becker and Murphy's Theory of Addiction." In *Getting Hooked: Rationality and the Addictions*, edited by Jon Elster and Ole-Jørgen Skog. Cambridge: Cambridge University Press.

Strotz, R. 1955. "Myopia and Inconsistency in Dynamic Utility Maximization." *Review of Economic Studies* 23: 165–80.

PART I

PHILOSOPHICAL PERSPECTIVES ON ADDICTION

Chapter 1

Disordered Appetites: Addiction, Compulsion, and Dependence

GARY WATSON

IN BOTH POPULAR and technical discussion, addictive behavior is said to be in some sense *out of control*. However, this description does not distinguish addiction from various forms of moral weakness. The excessive indulgence of appetites, for example, gluttony and promiscuity, are excesses for which we still hold one another responsible. The loss of control in addiction seems different: Addiction appears to be a source of compulsive desire, desire too strong for the agent to resist.[1]

The World Health Organization expresses this view in its 1969 definition of "dependence" (a term that replaced the use of "addiction" in its earlier declarations). Dependence is defined as

> a state, psychic and sometimes also physical, resulting from the interaction between a living organism and a drug, characterized by behavioral and other responses that always include a compulsion to take the drug on a continuous or periodic basis in order to experience its psychic effects, and sometimes to avoid the discomfort of its absence. (Grinspoon and Bakular 1976, 177)

Nonetheless, talk of compulsion remains controversial among theorists and practitioners as well as among nonprofessionals in their dealings with addictive behavior.[2] In part, the controversy is due to moral ambivalence. If addiction is compulsive, then addicts might be absolved from responsibility. To some, this implication is a necessary step to a more humane policy ("Addicts need help, not blame"). Others find this way of thinking

3

morally evasive—indeed, countertherapeutic. Moreover, thinking of addiction in this way encourages a dangerous paternalistic public policy.[3] The controversy about compulsion is also conceptual. It is far from clear how the notion of motivational compulsion is to be analyzed. The moral and conceptual concerns interact with one another. Insofar as talk of compulsion is ill defined, it is liable to abuse. As Grinspoon and Bakular (1976, 191) skeptically put it, "What we know so far is only that sometimes some people intensely desire to consume certain substances called psychoactive drugs." They suspected that

> words like *compulsion, craving,* and *overpowering need,* that are used to explicate *dependence* in the WHO definitions, apply just as often to love of chocolate cake, or for that matter to love of another human being, as to desire to take the drug; or else they are merely scare rhetoric to incite punitive campaigns. (Grinspoon and Bakular 1976, 186)

With the recent appearance of twelve-step programs not only for food and relationship junkies but also for those hooked on debt or on the internet, perhaps these words have lost some of their rhetorical force. Still, the caveat is well taken; we should remain wary of the tendency to conflate devotion and addiction, temptation and compulsion.

My focus in this essay is mainly on the conceptual issues, though I touch on some normative questions at the end. I have two main aims. First, I want to explore some of the analytical difficulties arising from talk of motivational compulsion. Second, I try to propose an account of addiction that avoids problematic notions of compulsion and clarifies some of the differences between addictions and other forms of dependency.

Motivational Compulsion

The kind of compulsion under consideration here is *intrapersonal;* you, or your behavior, is in some sense compelled by your own desires. Let's consider how this notion is related to the interpersonal paradigm.

When the bouncer compels you to leave the room by literally picking you up and tossing you into the alley, the movement of your body is explained by another's purposes, rather than your own. In interpersonal compulsion, one is subject to the intentions of someone else. This is not enough to constitute compulsion, however. Suppose you allow someone to move your arm along the table. To be a case of compulsion, the explanation must entail your inability to resist.[4] A third feature is typically present as well: As in the case of the bouncer, you are guided by the other's aims not only independently of your will but *against* it.[5] When that condition is in place, you are moved, helplessly, by someone else's desires, contrary to your own.[6]

The question about "motivational compulsion" (as I call it) is this: Could I have a relation to (some of) my own desires that is sufficiently parallel to my relation to the bouncer's intentions to warrant non-metaphorical talk of compulsion?

One phenomenon that leads us to take the notion of intrapersonal compulsion seriously is a certain kind of motivational conflict. Just as the bouncer can force you out of the room contrary to your will, so your appetites and impulses might lead you where you do not "really" want to be. This form of conflict reflects a kind of duality that is analogous to the two-person case. Here the opposition is not between you and another but between you—that is, your evaluative judgment—and your other desires. Here, the "other" is your own motivation. This kind of conflict presents an issue of self-control rather than deliberation because here insubordinate desires are *to be resisted*. In these circumstances, their claims lack authority.[7]

Doubts About Compulsion as Irresistibility

Does this this sort of duality warrant serious talk of motivational compulsion? A strong case can be made for a negative answer to this question. Consider Joel Feinberg's claim about the notion of irresistible desire:

> Strictly speaking no impulse is irresistible; for every case of giving in to a desire . . . it will be true that, if the person had tried harder, he would have resisted it successfully. The psychological situation is never—or hardly ever—like that of the man who hangs from a windowsill by his fingernails until the sheer physical force of gravity rips his nails off and sends him plummeting to the ground, or like that of the man who dives from a sinking ship in the middle of the ocean and swims until he is exhausted and then drowns. Human endurance puts a severe limit on how long one can stay afloat in an ocean; but there is no comparable limit to our ability to resist temptation. (Feinberg 1970, 282–83)[8]

Now we do speak of some recalcitrant desires being stronger than others and of some being very hard to resist. Unless we call into question the notion of strength of desire altogether, on what grounds can we deny that some desires are so strong that they are *too* hard to resist, quite beyond the limits of one's capacities?[9] Would this denial mean that we are all endowed with unlimited willpower? If so, the capacity to resist temptation would surely be extraordinary among human powers.

Feinberg appeals in this passage to a conditional criterion of resistibility: If one had tried harder, then one would have resisted. The adequacy of this test is suspect because it does not address whether one *could* have tried harder, in which case one may still not have been able to resist. Still, it seems right to say that failure to satisfy Feinberg's criterion is a sufficient condition of *ir*resistibility. If one's utmost efforts do not prevail, surely one is up against an irresistible force. Feinberg's insight is that this negative test has no clear application in the motivational case, for circumstances of temptation necessarily involve motivational conflict, which precludes wholehearted effort.[10]

To satisfy the wholehearted attempt criterion, a desire would have to be an internal pressure that might be opposed, successfully or not, with all one's might—as one might attempt to counter the gravitational force of a slab of stone. This conception of desire, however, is of questionable coherence. Perhaps examples that come close to this are the felt stress of a full bladder, the urge to release one's breath after holding it for a while, or to ejaculate. Significantly, each of these cases involves material in tubes or sacs under pressure. These pressures can be felt in extreme cases as nearly unconquerable hydraulic forces inextricable from desire.

Perhaps one could so transcend the pain and discomfort caused by such pressure that one could be described as wholeheartedly resisting these forces (successfully or not). In this case, if it is intelligible, one would have succeeded in externalizing the desire, thereby transmuting it from a source of attraction or temptation into a physical tension. To be defeated in this case would no more be a misdirection of the will than would be the failure of the wholehearted attempt to resist the force of the boulder. Yielding to pressure would not in this instance be voluntary movement.[11] If this example as described makes sense at all, however, it is hardly the typical case in which we tend to speak of compulsive desire.

The circumstance described would certainly not be one of temptation. Recalcitrant cravings for nicotine or heroin are not like internal tensions, sometimes mounting to a breaking point. The circumstances of the seriously unwilling addict seem rather more like those of the exhausted climber. The discomfort both inclines one to give up the project and leads one not (in the end) to resist the desire to do so. Unlike external obstacles (or internal pressures), motivational obstacles work in part not by defeating one's best efforts but by diverting one from effective resistance. One's behavior remains in these cases in an important sense voluntary.

That is the crucial difference between the mass of the boulder and the motivational force of a desire. The mass of the boulder can overpower me by bypassing my will, whereas desire cannot. Being overpowered by the hunk of stone means that full, unconflicted use of one's powers are insufficient to resist its force. Being defeated by a desire means that one's capacities to resist are not unconflictedly employed. Hence, one who is defeated by appetite is more like a collaborationist than an unsuccessful freedom fighter. This explains why it can feel especially shameful; to one degree or another, it seems to compromise one's integrity. A parallel point holds for addictions. For self-reflexive beings, the ambivalence of addiction is built into its mechanism: It enslaves by appeal, rather than by brute force.

Thus Feinberg's doubts about irresistibility call attention to a conceptual point about desire rather than to an awesome volitional power of human beings. It is not that there are certain forces that, remarkably, are no match for human determination; rather, we do not stand to our desires as to slabs of stone. For this reason, desires cannot be said to be irresistible by the same criterion, and perhaps in the same sense, as forces of nature. The corollary for the concept of motivational ability is this: In Feinberg's words again, that "there is no . . . limit to our ability to resist temptation" that is comparable to the limits of our physical capacities: not, again, because of an unusual omnipotence in this region of life, but because ability means something quite different in the motivational case.

To sum up: Feinberg's observations point to an important disanalogy between the interpersonal and intrapersonal notions of compulsion. The forces that defeat us in motivational compulsion do so not by opposing our wills but by directing them. Does this disanalogy mean that talk of motivational irresistibility is hyperbole or that putative cases of compulsion are after all cases of weakness? Or can we make sense of the phenomena in some other way?

Resistibility as Reasons Responsiveness

A number of philosophers have proposed to identify the capacity for self-control with sensitivity to countervailing reasons. John Fischer, who analyzes motivational compulsion in terms of the absence of "guidance control,"[12] applies this idea to addiction in the following passage:

> When a [drug addict] acts from a literally irresistible urge, he is undergoing a kind of physical process that is not reasons responsive, and it is this lack of reasons responsiveness of the actual physical process that rules out guidance control and moral responsibility. (Fischer 1994, 174)

Jonathan Glover's notion of unalterable intention is basically the same idea:

The test for self-control, which differentiates between my intention and that of the alcoholic, is that my intention can be altered by providing reasons that give me a sufficiently strong motive, while his can only be altered, if at all, by some form of manipulation such as behavior therapy or drugs.[13]

"Where we have evidence of an unalterable intention of this kind," Glover goes on to say, "it is reasonable to say that the person who acts on it cannot help what he does" (Glover 1970, 99; for a related analysis, see Duggan and Gert 1979). One difficulty here is that the susceptibility to counterincentives might not be responsiveness to them qua reasons. If motivated behavior can be insensitive to reasons, as compulsion must be on this view, then it is no good appealing to susceptibility to countermotivation as a criterion of control unless that motivation would be operating in a reason-responsive manner rather than compulsively. One's response to what is in fact a reason might not be an instance of sensitivity to reasons.[14] That my desire to shoot up would be overpowered by my dread of punishment (or of rats) might only prove that I am doubly enslaved.[15] Freedom cannot be understood as subjection to countervailing compulsions.[16]

This point parallels the objection to the "cop at your shoulder" standard sometimes invoked in discussions of criminal responsibility. That the accused would have resisted if they had had that kind of incentive is supposed to show that they possessed powers of self-restraint sufficient for legal responsibility. Similarly, if you knew your drug taking was subject to immediate punishment, then you would have had a certain kind of reason to abstain. If that knowledge would have led you to abstain, then you are at least minimally responsive to reasons.[17] My objection is that the counterfactual incentive might be compulsive as well.

Although this objection helps itself to an unexplained notion of compulsion, it is valuable, nonetheless. If we can make sense of motivational compulsion at all, then susceptibility to different motivation does not prove voluntary control. Hence, no serious test of compulsion in terms of susceptibility to counterincentives will work.

Perhaps these worries can be met by suitable refinements. Another, even more obvious, concern comes to the fore in Glover's discussion: to avoid conflating incapacity and incontinence. How is unalterability to be distinguished from weakness of will?[18]

Here is Glover's suggestion:

If, like the alcoholic or drug addict, he is not open to persuasion by himself or by other people, then he does have a psychological incapacity.

Yet, if a reasonable amount of persuasion would alter his intentions, but he himself chooses to avert his attention from the reasons in question, his is then a case of moral weakness without psychological incapacity. (Glover 1970, 100)

It is not clear why Glover is so confident that those we call addicts do *not* "choose to avert their attention from reasons." The philosophical worry, however, is that the appeal to such a choice returns us to our starting point. For the choice to avert one's attention is itself not reasons responsive. If it is not on that account unalterable, then self-control is not just a matter of reasons responsiveness. If the choice not to be responsive to reasons is noncompulsive, as it must be if Glover is to distinguish weakness from addiction, then we must supplement sensitivity to reasons with an independent notion of control. We are left in the end, then, with an unanalyzed appeal to what is in the agent's power and, hence, with the question: Is it within the agent's power to resist the temptation to go against reason?

The appeal to choice suggests a further complication. An intention might be unalterable because it expresses a determination to close off further consideration. Such resolution might be a kind of strength, if not a virtue, or it might just be stubbornness—but it should not count as compulsive. (Nor, indeed, as weakness of will.)

Fischer distinguishes incontinence from incapacity by defining guidance control in terms of *weak responsiveness:* In contrast to the compulsive agent, the weak-willed agent is sensitive to *at least some* sufficient reasons to do otherwise. But, I doubt that any clearly intentional behavior fails to meet this condition. Certainly, the paradigm cases of severe and desperate addictions are not literally irresistible in this sense. Few if any addicts are beyond the reach of one counterincentive or another.[19]

The case of Ben Sanderson, the drunken character in the film *Leaving Las Vegas,* might be instructive here. Initially, Sanderson might strike one as an example of someone whose alcoholic behavior is unalterable, but this example is complicated. What is unwavering here, if anything, is not Sanderson's intention to drink *simpliciter* but his mission to drink himself to death to escape a shattered existence. Much of the dramatic tension in the film centers on the question whether the loving ministrations of Sera, the prostitute, will call him back to life. In the end, they do not; but it is not clear that nothing could have deflected him from his suicidal course: for example, that he would have been unmoved by a vivid and immediate threat to kill his children (for whom he appears still to have some attachment) unless he remained in the detox center for three months.

Of course, Sanderson's determination reflects not stubbornness but despair. He cannot see a way to go on with his life. (This might remain so even if he had pulled himself together for a bit to save his child.) The problem is not that his intention to put an end to his life is unalterable but that he sees no reason to alter it. He can see no future for himself that makes sense. This might indeed point to a sense in which Sanderson is motivationally disabled; but the incapacity here is not the incapacity to resist desire but to care.

Compulsion and Disruption

I suspect, then, that no reasons responsiveness theory will by itself provide a satisfactory account of motivational compulsion or enable us to preserve a plausible and significant distinction between compulsive and weak-willed behavior. (I discuss this distinction in Watson 1977.) Nothing in these criticisms shows that the relevant notion of control cannot be identified with the *capacity* for sensitivity to reasons (or normative competence). They do show, however, that this capacity cannot be understood solely in terms of susceptibility to counterincentives.

Just the same, the idea that addiction involves a diminishment of the sensitivity to reasons has a good deal of plausibility. Characteristically, addicts have difficulty in bringing reason effectively to bear on their choices in a certain region of deliberation, at least under some circumstances. We will do well, I think, to abandon the interpersonal model, which features the power of addictive desire to defeat our best efforts and, instead, to understand the relevant notion of compulsion in terms of the tendency of certain incentives to impair our capacity to make those efforts. We are not so much overpowered by brute force as seduced.

One feature of desires experienced as compulsive is their power to capture one's attention. It is in this sense that we speak of a musical rhythm, or a literary plot, as compelling. This quality is generally desirable in a tune or drama but can be quite unwanted in other contexts. Desires can be more or less compelling in this sense. One measure of the strength of desires is their capacity to claim one's consciousness, direct one's fantasies, break one's concentration on other things. One finds it difficult to keep one's mind on one's work because one keeps thinking of one's lover, or of the chocolate cake in the pantry, or of the cigarettes at the market. The objects of these desires tend to demand or dominate one's attention, despite oneself.

These desires are sources of a good deal of "noise"—like a party next door. The clamor of appetite directs one's attention to its object as something to be enjoyed. This feature of desire, it seems to me, accounts both for the potential irrationality and the power of desires we experience as compulsive. The efforts involved in various techniques of resistance require a focus (or redirection) of consciousness that is hard to achieve in the midst of much appetitive noise. Again, this is the source of what might be called the predicament of self-control. Techniques of self-control often work by maintaining one's focus against such distractions, and yet employing those resources already takes an amount of focus that tends to dissolve precisely when it is needed.[20] This fragmentation of consciousness is one of the familiar elements of practical irrationality (Elster 1999a).

Understood in this way, compelling desires are often implicated in a kind of impairment of normative competence.[21] This impairment admits of degrees and does not entail complete incapacity. I am inclined to see the distinction between weakness and compulsion as a normative one: Roughly, individuals we describe as weakly giving into temptation are those who reasonably could be expected to have resisted or to have developed the capacities to resist. This view locates compulsion toward one end of a continuum that includes weakness of will; those at this end of the continuum are subject to such strong desires that it is unreasonable to expect even a strong-willed person to hold out.[22]

I do not have the space to develop and assess this proposal here. I am sure it is unsatisfactory as it stands, but it does have some appeal. The concept it identifies is an important one, and makes sense of many of our practical concerns. Compulsive behavior tends to disrupt one's life in ways that are very difficult to control without help. It is this characteristic that elicits sympathy. It is this characteristic that is of interest to the therapeutic community. (Indeed, this is what *creates* that community.)

The overall effect of this proposal is to give up on the understanding of addictive compulsions as forms of necessitation. Anyway, addictions are not necessarily compulsive, even in the proposed sense. Some addictive conditions are relatively mild; others are terribly difficult to break; but if enough is at stake in someone's life, it might not be unreasonable to expect, or indeed demand, that she (genuinely seek help to) overcome the problem.

Addiction and Dependency

I have, among other things, been presenting some grounds for dissatisfaction with talk about motivational compulsion, understood on the model of irresistible desire. Although addiction is commonly described (if not always strictly defined) in these terms, we need not be skeptical about the concept itself. For the crucial notion here, I suggest, is the idea of an *acquired appetite*. It is this notion that explains the stereotypical or symptomatic characteristics of addiction, including its association with compulsion. I develop this idea in what follows.

It is important to distinguish three levels of dependency. The first level I call *physical dependency*. Very roughly, individuals are physically or chemically dependent on some substance if consuming that substance has made them prone to suffer withdrawal symptoms—discomfort, agitation, restlessness, illness—when deprived of the substance for a period of time and, usually, to find the ingestion of the substance highly pleasurable.

Whether or not physical dependency is necessary for addiction, it is clearly not sufficient. Imagine you have been given morphine for pain control while in the hospital.[23] Suppose upon withdrawal you have no idea of the cause of your malaise. Although you no doubt desire relief, you have no desire, overpowering or not, to take the drug. Once you learn the cause of your discontent, probably you will come to want, and want badly, some morphine (or anything else) to avoid the discomfort. Clearly, *this* instrumental desire for the drug would not be the craving that is constitutive of addiction. One could have this sort of desire for morphine without ever having ingested the stuff—to relieve a toothache, say. So a desire for the drug (overwhelming or not) that is motivated by the discomfort resulting from this physical dependency is not on that account addictive.[24]

When infants are said to be born addicted, what must be meant is a condition of narcotic dependence that does not involve cravings or addictive behavior. To call this addiction without qualification seems to me misleading, since it need not involve addictive craving and corresponding patterns of behavior. Nor need it involve the propensity to irrational thought and desire.

To be addicted, in the sense in which infants and those who become aware of their chemically dependent states cannot (yet) be, involves a dependency of a further kind. It requires a history of behavior that forges a cognitive link and motivational link between that kind of substance and behavior and pleasure and relief. The fact that behavior of a certain kind (drug-taking behavior) has certain effects (dependent on the individual's chemical dependency) generates a periodic craving. The physical dependency increases one's tendency to be (more or less intensely) rewarded by the behavior and to be more or less acutely uncomfortable without this substance (or behavior). These withdrawal symptoms might secondarily reinforce behavior that leads to ingestion of the substance. Only then does one acquire, not only a dependency on but an *appetite* for the substance or behavior in question.[25]

This further condition is sometimes satisfied by nonhuman animals. In experimental conditions, rats can become chemically dependent on opiates and stimulants. They learn to do various things to get more. They thereby acquire something structurally similar to their natural needs for water and food. They come to enjoy taking in opiates as they do food. When they are deprived of these things, they are distressed.

Since nonhuman animals lack a capacity for critical evaluation, they are not even prima facie candidates for either motivational compulsion or weakness. Addictions may move them contrary to their own good but not contrary to their own conceptions of the good. Nevertheless, when their addictive behavior displaces their natural appetites, they suffer from what might be called an appetitive impairment.

To become addicted is to acquire an appetite, an appetite that, typically, is caused and sustained by the regular ingestion of certain substances. To acquire an appetite is to acquire a felt need, a source of pleasure and pain, that has a periodic motivational force that is independent of one's capacity for critical judgment. Hence, for creatures with such a capacity, to acquire an appetite is to become vulnerable to temptation.

Appetites involve positive and negative inclinations. We are naturally hooked on food and drink. When I am hungry, I typically become more or less uncomfortable. That is distracting. I desire to various degrees to relieve this discomfort, but that is not all. More positively, the distinction between the edible and the nonedible in my environment becomes highly salient to me. Depending on experience, certain sorts of food are especially alluring and their consumption intensely enjoyable. It can be more or less difficult to resist eating, or seeking, food, primarily because it becomes more or less difficult to keep my mind off the subject. We do not call these ordinary food dependencies addictions. Indeed, lack of interest in food or drink after a period of abstinence is a sign of disordered appetite.

An addiction is a nonnatural or acquired appetite. The ingestion of nicotine or caffeine can induce a periodic craving for these substances. Although addictions tend to be in some measure compelling, in the sense we discussed earlier, nothing in this conception implies straightaway that the addicted person is subject to cravings that are irresistible.[26] When temporary abstinence is the result of a deliberate, wholehearted plan (say, for the observance of a religious holiday), smokers often get by without much difficulty—just as some people fast for quite a while without being subject to great temptation. The strategies and techniques of self-control are similar for natural and nonnatural appetites.

Nor does the conception of addiction as acquired appetite imply that this condition is necessarily harmful, all things considered. Certain addictions can be regulated without interference with a person's physical or mental health or with productive social relations.[27] Opiate dependency can be a reasonable price to pay for control of acute or chronic pain.[28] Just the same, acquiring appetites is a hazardous business. Natural appetites are grounded in natural needs, and the health of an animal depends in general upon their satisfaction. We tend to do poorly when our natural appetites are suppressed or disordered. Insofar as addictions exhibit the phenomenon of tolerance (which, apparently, not all of them do), the appetites in which they consist are more difficult to regulate and tend toward an unhealthy insatiability.

As we have seen, addictions involve a tendency to various kinds of irrationality—but so do the appetites generally. There may be nothing distinctive about addictions in this respect; hunger, thirst, and sexual attraction create similar liabilities. On the other hand, possibly certain addictions are linked to special or especially serious distortions of judgment and reasoning. For all I know, certain addictive substances have distinctive effects on parts of the brain that govern cognitive functions.[29] If deprivation of food or water, for example, were shown not to have similar effects, then that would support the idea that (some) addictions made us especially liable to distortions of rationality.[30] For my purposes, it suffices to note our general susceptibilities as appetitive beings.

One advantage of characterizing addiction primarily in terms of its effects on rationality rather than in terms of irresistibility is that this conception readily makes sense of the idea of mild addictions, for the disorder it identifies has different degrees and dimensions. Caffeine addiction rarely if ever leads to fundamental changes in personality or to severe distortions in practical thought. Even here, there are familiar distortions—for example, a professor who risks being late to lecture in order to stop by Starbucks on the way to class. ("It will just take a minute.") Note that one might do this for pastry, as well, without having what some call a food disorder. On this view, again, addictions are continuous with ordinary appetites, such as one's craving for croissants (to go with that latte).

Further Questions

The conception of addictions as acquired appetites raises difficult questions about both of its constitutive concepts. What should be comprised under the heading of appetite? How exactly can we distinguish between appetites that are acquired and those that are original? Here, I can only touch on these issues.

I have been working with a paradigm list of natural appetites—hunger, thirst, and sex—but I have no precise account of the criteria of membership. The natural appetites have to do with what is needed for the health or flourishing of the individual, I said, but sexual appetite is anomalous in a number of respects. Sexual attraction often exhibits a periodic appetitive structure, tied to hormonal activity; but unlike nutrition, sexual activity is not required for the survival of the individual. To be sure, many of us find abstinence distressing, but this effect depends somewhat on individual circumstance, age, and culture. As difficult as it may be for others to understand, some physically normal individuals manage to flourish in celibacy.

Moreover, unlike hunger and thirst, sexual appetite is fulfilled by behavior without the ingestion of substances into the body. To be sure, natural reproduction in human beings occurs by the literal incorporation of certain substances into the body of female sexual partners. This brings out a deep biological parallel with the other appetites.[31] For evolutionary reasons, human beings tend periodically to find specific activities more or less intensely pleasurable and to be discomfited by their frustration. Nonetheless, a significant contrast with hunger and thirst remains. The satisfactions and fulfillment of sexual desire, and the discomfort resulting from nonfulfillment, have nothing to do with the ingestion of substances. If so, and if addictions are acquired appetites, then there is room for the possibility of acquired behavioral appetites, as many people think. In any case, beyond (male?) adolescence, sexual desire is connected only loosely with appetitive periodicity. It has much richer emotional and interpersonal content than hunger and thirst.[32] Erotic responsiveness is often evoked by the perceived sexual interest of others in us. This would be an unexpected feature of the other appetites: as though I were aroused to hunger by the recognition of the desire of the blueberry muffin to be eaten by me.

Furthermore, not all natural needs for substances are appetitive. Oxygen is essential to individual survival; we feel extreme discomfort when deprived of it for even a moment or two; and a felt need to breathe exhibits a (very short) periodic structure. Why, then, is the need to breathe not appetitive?[33]

This question deserves a fuller treatment than I can give it here. The answer, I think, is connected with the fact that breathing is an automatic response, controlled by the autonomic nervous system. Appetites, acquired and unacquired, are sustained by reward.[34] In contrast, I suppose, the desire to breathe and the discomfort of not breathing do not involve the brain's reward system in the same way, but I am not sure how to incorporate these observations into a satisfactory definition of the appetitive.

These are questions about what an appetite is. Another set of issues concerns the contrast between acquired and original appetites. I said earlier that we are naturally hooked on food and drink, but of course what is edible and drinkable (or sexually appealing) is largely a cultural matter. The appetites are not just for indeterminate food or drink or physical contact. What an individual who is hungry or thirsty or sexually aroused thereby desires depends upon specific training and experience. One wants this or that culturally available form of satisfaction.

In one sense, then, all appetites are acquired. Beyond early infancy, the ways we satisfy our appetites are virtually always mediated by acculturated tastes. On the other hand, addictions are in a sense perfectly natural. Our constitution is such that many of us are prone to become physically dependent when exposed to certain substances (or activities?) and to acquire appetitive desires for these. The idea that natural appetites (in contrast to addictions) are unacquired has to be interpreted in a way that is consistent with these truths.

Nevertheless, I think the distinction marks a real difference. Its defense depends on the fact that the social construction of the appetites takes place on a biological foundation of culturally independent needs. This point certainly requires careful formulation and development. Until then, a certain amount of skepticism is admittedly in order.

Dependence and Attachment

Addiction often involves what some writers call *existential dependence* (Seeburger 1993); that is, the development of an identity to which the addictive practices are crucial. In this way, devotion to the relevant behavior becomes bound up with the meaning of one's life. Pete Hamill (1994) describes his relation to drinking in this way:

> I had entered the drinking life. Drinking was part of being a man. Drinking was an integral part of sexuality, easing entrance to its dark and mysterious treasure chambers. Drinking was the sacramental binder of friendships. Drinking was the reward for work, fuel for celebration, the consolation for death or defeat. Drinking gave one strength, confidence, ease, laughter; it made me believe that dreams really could come true. (146–47)

Breaking the addiction thus requires fashioning a new sense of what one's life is about. Herbert Fingarette (1988) emphasizes this kind of dependence as a feature of alcoholism (though he scrupulously avoids the language of addiction):

> For a heavy drinker to make a major change in his drinking patterns requires a reconstruction of his way of life. The drinker must learn over time to see the world in different terms, to cultivate new values and interests, to find or create new physical or social settings, to develop new relationships, to devise new ways of behaving in those new relationships and settings. (110)

Existential dependency is surely one of the most disturbing features of paradigmatic addictions. One's existence might come to be more or less centered around the satisfaction of this appetite, in such a way that one's sense of what is most important in (one's) life is defined by one's addiction, and life without it would seem significantly diminished in meaning. This explains what is often so demeaning about that condition: One becomes *devoted* to what is unworthy of devotion.[35] Still, I see no reason to think that addictive appetites are necessarily bound up with a distinctive way of life.[36] Existential dependence is a matter of degree. Acquired appetites (like natural ones) might lead to such dependence but they need not to any notable extent. We should not be misled by sensational examples into thinking of this level as a feature of all addiction.[37] It is rarely if ever reached by those who are hooked on caffeine or even nicotine. (But, consider the remarkable example of the literary critic, Mikhail Bakhtin, who reportedly used up the only copy of his book manuscript for cigarette paper.)

For something to be bound up importantly in my way of life, I need not see myself as strictly unable to do without it. It is enough that its absence would leave, as we say, a very big hole. Individuals in this third stage of dependency have an especially difficult time changing. In the extreme case, I might find another form of life unthinkable—I cannot imagine my life without it.[38]

It is useful to see this stage of dependence as involving *attachment* to one's addiction. Life without one's addiction presents itself to one as a grave loss. The prospect of a change is at least daunting, sometimes even terrifying. The sense that one otherwise lacks the resources to cope with everyday life might induce panic. In extreme cases, this sense might amount to an attachment disorder.

Dependence and Autonomy

The difficulties presented by addictive dependency are not necessarily different in kind or degree from other dependencies that we would not want to count as addictions. Attachments that are central to human flourishing make us vulnerable to losses of a similar magnitude.[39] It is not just a question of wanted versus unwanted addictions. Unwise attachments are not on that account addictions.

Existential dependence is not necessarily regrettable. Most of our lives are structured around the appetites in one way or another. They and their expression tend to be dear to us. The pains and perplexities of this devotion sometimes tempt us to ideals of detachment; but on reflection our appetitive lives matter to most of us in ways that we do not regret.

The same goes for attachment to acquired appetites. As we have seen, some people can manage their addictions. Addiction is in principle compatible with temperance.[40] We cannot dismiss a regulated devotion to tobacco or drink as demeaning or enslaving just on the grounds that it involves dependence. That would presuppose an ideal of self-mastery that would condemn much of what we value in human life.

Let me press this point a bit further. I am told that it is possible for a well-supplied heroin addict to live an otherwise healthy and productive life. (It appears to be otherwise with cocaine and amphetamines.) In any case, imagine that this is so for a certain severely addictive substance, S, and that in a certain culture, otherwise similar to ours, the use of S is not only tolerated but respected as highly spiritually beneficial. This culture regards the dependency on this substance, which is to say, the vulnerability to various kinds of diminished self-control, as a small price to pay for the enrichment of human life provided by S. Fortunately, S is easily obtainable, perhaps even subsidized by the society for religious reasons.

This fantasy makes it clear that the moral significance of an individual's volitional vulnerability depends not only on individual responsibility and the limits of human endurance but also on judgments about the meaning and value of the behavior and relationships that they make possible. In our imagined society, both the use of and dependency on S are regarded as entirely fitting and normal, on a par with the appetites for food and drink. The unfortunate minority who cannot tolerate S are thought to be missing something. To become addicted to S is not thereby to infringe any social or legal norms of self-control. The content of such norms is not determined by an abstract standard of self-control but by a sense of what is worth pursuing in human life. The threat of being deprived of one's S is here on a par with the prospect of imminent starvation.

The assessment of addiction as a form of slavery depends as much on norms regarding the value of addictive dependencies as from concerns about self-control per se. We tend to see them as demeaning or destructive rather than as possible sources of worthwhile human activity. For this reason, we tend to expect people to avoid those conditions and see the plight created by those conditions as the individual's own fault.

I know of no substance in our culture that has the role of S exactly, but there are instructive examples of parallel acquired dependencies which we encourage and honor. I have in mind the various relationship attachments exemplified by parenting or being in love. Like addictions, to be attached in these ways is to be vulnerable to diminished control of certain kinds.

I am not arguing that addictions of any kind should be valued in the way we value the attachments just mentioned. Perhaps we are right as a culture to disrespect addiction. That deserves a separate discussion. My point is that these forms of dependency cannot be disparaged *solely* on the grounds that they diminish self-control, that is, simply because they *are* dependencies. Addictions must be shown in some further way to reduce the value of human experience or agency. Obviously, countless lives have been ruined by devotion to drugs. On the other hand, addictive substances help many of us to endure what would otherwise be rather bleak prospects.

Conclusion

The concepts of appetite and of addiction are both highly indeterminate. Therefore, any proposed analysis is perforce somewhat regimentary. Hence it would be wrongheaded to object that those who would speak of curiosity as an appetite for learning or of obsessions with chess or music as addictions are misusing the terms. Similarly, those who define the term "addiction" as involving uncontrollable impulses or self-destructive behavior can find a lot of support in both popular and technical discussions. The issue for us is theoretical: What regimentation is most illuminating? Even the answer to this question is partly relative to purposes. It is quite natural for the therapeutic community to work with a normative conception according to which the addicted individual is one who needs help, but these broader and normative conceptions seem to me to obscure connections and differences among the phenomena that the conception of addiction as acquired appetite highlights. This narrower conception enables us to see structural similarities between the clear cases of addiction and natural appetites.[41] These similarities illuminate the connection of addiction with various forms of irrationality (and in extreme cases motivational impairment) and suggest common neurophysical processes.[42]

By itself, this conception leaves it open whether and to what extent addiction is a bad thing in particular cases. That seems to me desirable. The issues raised by addiction are not sharply distinct from the issues raised by the appetites in general. In part, these concern our notorious troubles in dealing well with the pleasures of life. Addictions dispose us to be led on and distracted by pleasure, as though it were our master. In extreme cases, they can even corrupt our sense of what evil is, but they can also figure as part of the meaning of a life well enough lived, at least compared to the alternatives. In this respect, too, addictions lie on a continuum with the other appetites.

I am grateful to the other participants in the conference on addiction for comments, especially to my commentator on that occasion, Michael Bratman. I also thank Jon Elster for convening and moderating the conference as well as for his insightful work on virtually all aspects of this topic. This chapter has also benefited from discussions with Teresa Chandler, Michael Hudson, Sara Lundquist, and audiences at various colloquia.

Notes

1. In the scattered allusions to addiction in my own writing, I have certainly tended, uncritically, to take it as exemplary of motivational compulsion.

2. The authors of later editions of *Diagnostic and Statistical Manual of Mental Disorders* of the American Psychiatric Association depart from the second edition by dropping the reference to the "compelling desire to use a substance" in its definition of dependency. This change was apparently prompted by the goal of appealing only to "patterns of pathological use that can be objectively quantified." This goal does not prevent the third and fourth editions from using the "ability to cut down or stop use" as a criterion. See Kuehule and Spitzer (1992, 22–23).

3. The list of skeptics includes Fingarette (1988); Grinspoon and Bakular (1976); Peele (1985). Peele insists that "people are not passive victims of the addictive urges or cues that occur in their bodies or in their lives; they select not only the settings in which to live nonaddicted lives but also the reactions they have to the urges they experience to return to their addictions. The methods they use are in keeping with their values and the people they see themselves as having become" (191).

4. In the bouncer case, we should distinguish two possible moments of resistance. Perhaps you could have resisted the efforts to throw you out. Once thrown, however, you are powerless to counteract the forces that move you. This distinction has a possible counterpart in the case of addiction. It may be within one's power to resist taking the drug up to a certain point but not beyond it. So one might be responsible for getting to that point and, therefore, for not allowing oneself to reach the point of powerlessness.

5. What seems crucial here is independence rather than actual conflict. To continue with the parallel, just as the bouncer might compel me to go exactly where I want to be (perhaps even in the same manner), an impulse might have an overpowering force without actually going against the agent's aims. In both the interpersonal and intrapersonal cases, actual conflict is a manifestation, but not a criterion, of independence. This is what Frankfurt (1971) has in mind by "willing addicts," whose compulsive desires to take the drug agree with their critical evaluations. Frankfurt would not agree, by the way, that in these cases the individuals' agency is entirely undermined. If the behavior is performed not only

because it is compulsive but also because of their critical evaluation, then the actors are responsible for what they do.

6. This formulation is based on examples of forced movement. Of course, someone might *prevent* you from moving, instead. The bouncer might immobilize you by pinning you to the ground. We could take intrapersonal compulsion to comprise both cases, as well. This would be to treat agoraphobic panic, say, as an irresistible aversion to leaving the house. I doubt that this is the best approach to these cases, but this question is not central to the purposes of this chapter.

7. Plato was concerned with these issues in *The Republic,* where he comments on the case of Leontius, who

> became aware of dead bodies that lay at the place of public execution, at the same time felt a desire to see them and a repugnance and aversion, and . . . for a time he resisted and veiled his head, but overpowered in despite of all by his desire, with wide staring eyes he rushed up to the corpses and cried, There, ye wretches, take your fill of the fine spectacle! (439e–40a)

The sources of desires, Plato concludes, are multiple. Appetites per se are desires, for food and drink, not for good food or good drink (438–39). The hunger for french fries is one thing; the concern to eat what is good for me to eat is another. The latter has its source in the agent's evaluative judgment; the former arises from appetite. Judgments of the good belong to reason:

> [S]ome men sometimes though thirsty refuse to drink . . . Is it not that there is a something in the soul that bids them drink and a something that forbids, a different something that masters that which bids? . . . And is it not the fact that that which inhibits such actions arises when it arises from the calculations of reason?

[439e, following. The foregoing translations are Paul Shorey's (Hamilton and Cairns 1989).] For a searching discussion of Plato's doctrine see Terry Penner (Vlastos 1971, 96–118).

8. I discussed this passage less appreciatively in Watson (1977).

9. "For months, Rafael Ramos [a recovering heroin addict] lived in fear of catching a glimpse of bare arms, his own or someone else's. Whenever he did, he remembers, he would be seized by a nearly unbearable urge to find a drug-filled syringe" (Nash, 1997, 72). Would it not be strange if there were motivational forces that were nearly unbearable but none unqualifiedly so?

10. The parallel point holds for inability. As Hampshire (1965) says: "When we definitely, and without qualification or conflict, want to do something at a particular moment, sincerely make the attempt in normal conditions, and yet fail, we know as surely as we can ever know that at that moment we

could not do it" (3). This criterion is central to our attributions of powers, but it does not give us a handle on the notion of motivational inability, since the antecedent conditions are never, in those cases, satisfied.

11. In his critical discussion of the idea that free will (as distinct from free action) might be compromised by compulsive desire, Albritton (1985) remarks that compulsive sexual desire would have to be "like being thrown into bed." However, then "there's no unfreedom of will in it, for you haven't in the relevant sense done anything" (248). For a discussion of Albritton, see Hoffman (1995) and Watson (1995).

12. "An agent exhibits guidance control of an action insofar as the mechanism that actually issues in the action is reasons-responsive" (Fischer 1994, 163). See also Fischer 1987; Fischer and Ravizza 1991.

13. But, suppose that the agent's intentions are alterable by self-administered behavior modification therapy and that the agent knows how to do this. (I suppress here some worries about the coherence of putting some of Glover's points in terms of intention.)

14. What is more, such accounts must block the possibility that the circumstance of the counterfactual incentive (even when that incentive operates rationally) somehow renders one responsive to reasons (by somehow bringing one to one's senses, as it were). My criticisms show that the capacity for reasons responsiveness cannot be understood purely dispositionally. Fischer (1994, 164–68) would try to provide for this and some of the worries in the text by appealing to a requirement that the actual mechanism that issues in the action be held fixed in the counterfactual situation. The operation of the counterfactual incentive would show that one's action is actually reasons responsive only if the same mechanism is at work in the actual and counterfactual circumstances. This idea meets the requirement, formally, but I am skeptical about the possibility of filling out its content in a satisfactory way.

15. Consider the possibility of an individual with competing addictions; that is, sources of potentially incompatible compulsive desires. The only thing that will lead me not to take a drink, suppose, is the belief that drinking now would require me to forgo heroin for a long while. Or perhaps I would resist taking the heroin only if the supply were guarded by rats, to which I am highly phobic.

16. Taken as a sufficient condition, Feinberg's (1970) test is open to a similar objection. If I tried harder, I would resist. Perhaps the presence of a counterincentive would *enable* me to try harder than I could in its absence. If my capacity to try were in some way impaired in certain contexts of temptation, my susceptibility to deterrent incentives under certain circumstances would not show that the desire is under my control (here and now). There is some plausibility to the idea that addictions tend to have this effect; I return to this point later.

17. In terms of learning theory, of course, all aversive consequences are tantamount to punishment. So the restriction by the "cop at one's shoulder" stan-

dard to this one counterincentive seems arbitrary. If this standard reflects a deterrent or regulative conception of criminal law, however, the restriction is intelligible. If you are susceptible to the prospect of deterrence by legal threats, then it makes sense to subject you to them.

18. Glover (1970) points out two different ways in which an intention might be unalterable: It is independent of reasons one takes to be sufficient, or one would see contrary considerations to be sufficient if one were to "reason properly, or were not in some way deluded" (100). My worry concerns the first way. The second kind of unresponsiveness to reasons might well involve an incapacity, but it is not a case of irresistible desire.

19. James (1950, 2:543) quotes a report "of a man who, while under treatment for inebriety, during four weeks secretly drank the alcohol from six jars containing morbid specimens. On asking him why he committed this loathsome act, he replied, 'Sir, it is as impossible for me to control this diseased appetite as it is for me to control the pulsations of my heart.' " James also tells us of a "dipsomaniac" who claimed, "Were a keg of rum in one corner of a room and were a cannon constantly discharging balls between me and it, I could not refrain from passing before that cannon in order to get the rum." I remain skeptical. (I thank George Loewenstein for this reference.)

20. Consider the remarks of a former heavy drinker: "It seems to me that a person needs to have it within himself, be strong enough to handle his own problems. . . . You have got to have some inner strength, some of your own strength in resources that you can call up in yourself" (Peele 1985, 194).

21. For this term, see Wolf (1990, 129). In Wolf's terms, the addict's will is less intelligent than it would be in the absence of addiction. Addictions can impair normative competence not only by distorting probabilistic judgment or instrumental rationality, but also by affecting our fundamental values and projects—what we find meaningful in life.

22. A normative account is developed in Greenspan (1986). Her discussion focuses on those who are subjected to aversive behavioral control (such as the character Alex in Anthony Burgess's *Clockwork Orange*). The victim of compulsion is "unfree because he is faced with a kind of threat, like a robbery victim coerced at gunpoint, with intense discomfort as his only option to compliance. This means that the actions he is compelled to take will be reasonable—reasonable in the light of an *un*reasonable threat" (Greenspan 1986, 196). In Watson (1977), I suggest a normative account of a different kind. Whereas Greenspan suggests that we can account for compulsion without assuming that the compulsive cannot do otherwise, I argue there that we can account for the difference between compulsion and weakness without assuming that the weak agent *can* at the time do otherwise. The idea is that weakness is the manifestation of a vice; someone is a victim of compulsion if she is subject to motivation that even a person of exemplary self-control could not resist. My discussion there presumes (though it does not require) what I have been questioning here: that motivational compulsion in the sense of irresistibility makes sense.

23. This example, and the point it supports, come from Seeburger (1993, 46): "Hospital patients who are given morphine or other narcotics for relief from pain can develop tolerance and can show withdrawal symptoms, once the administration of the drug is discontinued. Nevertheless, they rarely become addicted. Most have no difficulty getting off the drug and are often grateful to be able to do so."

24. Portenoy and Payne (1997) insist upon a distinction between physical dependence and addiction. What they mean by physical dependence is roughly what I mean, but they define addiction as a condition in which one is unable to abstain: "Use of the term 'addiction' to describe patients who are merely physically dependent reinforces the stigma associated with opioid therapy and should be abandoned. If the clinician wishes to describe a patient who is believed to have the capacity for abstinence, the term physical dependency must be used' (564). Since my second level of dependency, which I consider to be addiction proper, need not involve this inability, Portenoy and Payne are marking a different distinction.

25. Spelling out these cognitive and motivational links is complicated. One of the complications concerns the relation between the object of one's appetite and what one is addicted to. Rats and people become addicted to cocaine. Should we say that a rat or a person craves or wants cocaine even if it or she has no conception of that substance? (I am grateful to John Christman for raising this issue with me.) Suppose you have a completely false belief about the object of your appetite. Suppose you are regularly but unknowingly exposed to certain addictive "fumes" when and only when at a certain villa in Italy. When you are away for awhile, you find yourself "craving" another visit; when you return you are deeply gratified, and you find that you need to return more frequently, for longer visits. You might imagine that you have developed an attachment to the place. You are in fact addicted to the "gas"; what is your appetite for? (I am indebted to Lee Overton for suggesting to me an example like this.)

26. This is contrary to Halikas et al. (1997, 85), who define craving as "an irresistible urge to use a substance that compels drug-seeking behavior."

27. This is the goal of methadone maintenance programs. Apparently, when properly administered, these have had considerable worldwide success in countering the adverse effects of heroin addiction. Nevertheless, as a matter of public policy, they have been controversial in the United States partly because they are thought merely to replace one addiction with another (Lowinson et al. 1997; Kreek and Reisinger 1997).

28. Portenoy and Payne (1997) observe that physical dependency as a result of prolonged use of opiates in programs of pain management does not reliably lead to addiction. "A reasonable hypothesis is that addiction results from the interaction between the reinforcing properties of opioid drugs and any number of characteristics . . . specific to the individual . . . such as the capacity for euphoria from an opioid and psychopathy" (582).

29. Of course, extreme intake of alcohol (or speed or LSD) can induce psychosis and cause brain damage. So can eating lead paint or, for that matter, I suppose, a great deal of carrot juice.

30. It is important to distinguish the effects on rationality of the dependency itself from the more direct effects of the ingestion of certain addictive substances. As dependencies, all addictions create liabilities to irrationalities when one is deprived (or threatened with deprivation) of the substance. Addictive substances differ, however, in their intoxicating properties. Being "high" may itself diminish rationality. I suspect these differences are linked to the different capacities of substances to lead to what I call existential dependency; some of these impairments of consciousness are precisely what one comes to "need." (Here, I am indebted to discussion with Susan Neiman.)

31. Here, I am indebted to discussions with Michael Hudson.

32. I am grateful to Sharon Lloyd for emphasizing this point.

33. The desire to sleep (from sleepiness) is periodic and naturally connected with the individual's health. Why isn't it appetitive? (See Watson 1977; I am grateful to Laurie Piper for pressing this question on me again.) I do not have an adequate answer. My hunch is that this desire does not constitute a craving that arises from and is focused on voluntary behavior in the relevant way— but this is too obscurely put for me to have much confidence in it.

34. Ainslie (1998) summarizes neurophysiological work since the 1950s in this way: Researchers "have found that most or all recreational substances . . . exert their rewarding effect by stimulating dopamine release in one small part of the midbrain, the nucleus accumbens, which is the same site where normal rewards like food and sex occur" (16). That both addictions and appetites involve in some way a subsystem of the brain's dopamine system is supported by Gardner and Lowinson (1993). According to them, "more than three decades of neuroanatomical, neurochemical, neuropharmacological, neurophysiological, and neurobehavioural studies have converged to indicate that brain stimulation reward is largely mediated by a portion of the mesotelencephalic dopamine system of the ventral limbic forebrain" (360). This reward system "is strongly implicated in the pleasures produced by natural rewards (for example, food and sex)." See also Gardner (1997); Gold and Miller (1997), note that dopamine "antagonists block the rewarding effects of food and water just as they block the self-administration of stimulants such as cocaine" (174).

35. Seeburger (1993, 50–51) endorses William Burroughs's remark that "junk is not a kick. It is a way of life. . . . You become a narcotics addict because you do not have strong motivations in any other directions." Addiction either supplants whatever had provided meaning to the individual before, or it supplies meaning to an otherwise empty life.

36. If being addicted to alcohol means having acquired an appetite in virtue of one's chemical dependency, and if being an alcoholic means coming to

center the meaning of one's life around the consumption of alcohol, then we ought to distinguish alcoholism from alcohol addiction *simpliciter*. More generally, we should distinguish being addicted to this or that from *being an addict*.

37. Elster (1999b) refers to this kind of dependency as "crowding out." Elster rightly rejects it as a necessary condition of addiction.

38. This, again, is a different form of motivational incapacity from irresistible desire. This is an instance of what Frankfurt calls volitional necessity; see "Rationality and the Unthinkable" in Frankfurt (1988).

39. Seeburger (1993) ignores this point: "What counts in addiction is that one relates to something, whether a substance, a process, a relationship, or whatever, in such a way that one experiences oneself as unable to do without it" (58–59). So much for grand passion (for Vronsky and Anna Karenina) as well as the ideals and attachments of everyday life.

40. Or at least with continence, which Aristotle distinguishes from virtue proper (*Nicomachean Ethics*, 1152). If addictive cravings are inherently sources of temptation, then addiction is incompatible with the virtue of temperance, as Aristotle conceives it. That would sharply distinguish addictive appetites from natural ones, for the virtuous woman or man will, in Aristotle's picture, have and enjoy the natural appetites. My claim is that a virtuous person could have the same relation to his or her acquired appetites.

41. The closest relative of this account that I have found in the empirical literature is Loewenstein's (1999) visceral theory. Loewenstein identifies addictions with conditional cravings. Like the proposed account, this view emphasizes the similarities between addictions and appetites and other visceral factors. Loewenstein also emphasizes the importance of cue conditioning for craving. I am not clear enough about the author's conception of craving to venture a more detailed comparison and contrast here.

42. Elster (1999b, 6) critically discusses accounts of addiction that focus on "phenomenological similarities rather than causal commonalities."

References

Ainslie, George. 1998. "A Research-Based Theory of Addictive Motivation." Paper prepared for National Humanities Center Workshop on Addiction.

Albritton, Rogers. 1985. "Freedom of the Will and Freedom of Action." *Proceedings and Addresses of the American Philosophical Association*. 59: 248.

Aristotle. 1985. *Nicomachean Ethics*. Translated by Terence Irwin. Indianapolis, Ind.: Hackett Publishing.

Duggan, Timothy, and Bernard Gert. 1979. "Free Will as the Ability to Will." *Noûs* 13: 197–217.

Elster, Jon. 1999a. "Rationality and Addiction." In *Getting Hooked: Rationality and the Addictions*, edited by Jon Elster and Ole-Jørgen Skog. Cambridge: Cambridge University Press.

———. 1999b. *Ulysses Unbound*. Cambridge: Cambridge University Press.

Feinberg, Joel. 1970. "What Is So Special About Mental Illness?" In *Doing and Deserving*. Princeton: Princeton University Press.

Fingarette, Herbert. 1988. *Heavy Drinking*. Berkeley: University of California Press.

Fischer, John Martin. 1987. "Responsiveness and Moral Responsibility." In *Responsibility, Character, and the Emotions*, edited by F. Schoeman. Cambridge: Cambridge University Press.

———. 1994. *The Metaphysics of Free Will*. London: Blackwell.

Fischer, John Martin, and Mark Ravizza. 1991. "Responsibility and Inevitability." *Ethics* 101: 258–78.

Frankfurt, Harry. 1971. "Freedom of the Will and the Concept of a Person." *Journal of Philosophy* 63: 5–20.

———. 1988. *The Importance of What We Care About*. New York: Cambridge University Press.

Gardner, Eliot L. 1997. "Brain Reward Mechanisms." In *Substance Abuse: A Comprehensive Textbook*, edited by Joyce H. Lowinson, Pedro Ruiz, Robert B. Millman, and John G. Langrod. Baltimore, Md.: Williams and Wilkins.

Gardner, Eliot L., and Joyce H. Lowinson. 1993. "Drug Craving and Positive/Negative Hedonic Brain Substrates Activated by Addicting Drugs." *The Neurosciences* 5: 359–68.

Glover, Jonathan. 1970. *Responsibility*. London: Routledge and Kegan Paul.

Gold, Mark S., and Norman S. Miller. 1997. "Cocaine (and Crack): Neurobiology." In *Substance Abuse: A Comprehensive Textbook*, edited by Joyce H. Lowinson, Pedro Ruiz, Robert B. Millman, and John G. Langrod. Baltimore, Md.: Williams and Wilkins.

Greenspan, Patricia. 1986. In *Moral Responsibility*, edited by John Fischer. Ithaca, N.Y.: Cornell University Press.

Grinspoon, Lester, and James Bakular. 1976. *Cocaine*. New York: Basic Books.

Halikas, James, et al. 1997. "Craving." In *Substance Abuse: A Comprehensive Textbook*, edited by Joyce H. Lowinson, Pedro Ruiz, Robert B. Millman, and John G. Langrod. Baltimore, Md.: Williams and Wilkins.

Hamill, Pete. 1994. *A Drinking Life*. Boston: Little, Brown.

Hamilton, Edith, and Huntington Cairns, eds. 1989. *Plato: The Collected Dialogues*. Princeton, N.J.: Princeton University Press.

Hampshire, Stuart. 1965. *Freedom of the Individual*. New York: Harper and Row.

Hoffman, Paul. 1995. "Freedom and Strength of Will: Descartes and Albritton." *Philosophical Studies* 77: 241.

James, William. 1950. *The Principles of Psychology*. New York: Dover.

Kreek, Jeanne, and Marc Reisinger. 1997. "The Addict as Patient." In *Substance Abuse: A Comprehensive Textbook*, edited by Joyce H. Lowinson, Pedro Ruiz, Robert B. Millman, and John G. Langrod. Baltimore, Md.: Williams and Wilkins.

Kuehule, John, and Robert Spitzer. 1992. "DSM III Classification of Substance Use Disorders." In *Substance Abuse: A Comprehensive Textbook*, edited by Joyce H. Lowinson and Pedro Ruiz. Baltimore, Md.: Williams and Wilkins.

Loewenstein, George. 1999. "The Visceral Account of Addiction." In *Getting Hooked: Rationality and the Addictions*, edited by Jon Elster and Ole-Jørgen Skog. Cambridge: Cambridge University Press.

Lowinson, Joyce H., I. J. Marion, H. Joseph, V. P. Dole. 1997. "Methadone Maintenance." In *Substance Abuse*, edited by Joyce H. Lowinson, Pedro Ruiz, Robert B. Millman, and John G. Langrod. Baltimore, Md.: Williams and Wilkins.

Nash, J. Madeleine. 1997. "Addicts." *Time*, May 5.

Peele, Stanton. 1985. *The Meaning of Addiction*. New York: Heath.

———. 1989. *The Diseasing of America*. New York: Heath.

Portenoy, Russell K., and Richard Payne. 1997. "Acute and Chronic Pain." In *Substance Abuse: A Comprehensive Textbook*, edited by Joyce H. Lowinson, Pedro Ruiz, Robert B. Millman, and John G. Langrod. Baltimore, Md.: Williams and Wilkins.

Seeburger, F. 1993. *Responsibility and Addiction*. New York: Crossroads.

Vlastos, Gregory, ed. 1971. *Plato: A Collection of Critical Essays*, Vol. II. Garden City, N.J.: Anchor.

Watson, Gary. 1977. "Skepticism About Weakness of Will." *Philosophical Review* (April): 316–39.

———. 1995. "Freedom and Strength of Will in Hoffman and Albritton." *Philosophical Studies* 77: 261–71.

Wolf, Susan. 1990. *Freedom Within Reason*. New York: Oxford University Press.

Chapter 2

Freedom of the Will and Addiction

OLAV GJELSVIK

"LIKE MY CAT, I often simply do what I want to do. I am then not using an ability that only persons have" (Parfit 1984, ix). I concur. The quoted writer, and possibly his cat, enjoy what I call freedom of action: Acts are free when agents simply do what they want to do.

Whether writers and cats enjoy freedom of the will is a different and complex question. The capacity for free will is here approached this way: Let us think of our desire, D, which effectively produces behavior, B, at a time, t, as the content of our will at that time. We might, at t, dislike the fact that D is the content of our will at this time.[1] All those who care about the content of their wills, and at particular times have a reflectively based desire for their will to have a specific content, possess a capacity that I think of as the capacity for free will. Persons care in this way about the content of their wills, and the capacity for doing that seems to be distinctive of persons. Such (reflectively based) second-order desires directed toward the content of our wills are often called second-order volitions. When, at a time, the content of the second-order volition corresponds to the actual content of the will, the will is free.

There are thus two freedoms, one of them distinctive of persons. We enjoy freedom of action when we do what we want to do, and we enjoy freedom of the will when we have the will we want to have. It follows that acting freely and intentionally need not be an exercise of a free will.

Addictive behavior is here seen as free, intentional action. Not all addictive behavior is of this sort, but addictive behavior exhibited by persons often is. There are sophisticated, rational, choice-based, explanatory approaches to such addictive behavior. Addicts might be

29

seen as myopic and as continuing their addictive behavior because that behavior maximizes utility for the addicts at each time of choice, even if the addictive behavior is the inferior option in the long run. As long as we do what we want when we act, we clearly enjoy freedom of action. Addicts do what they want and are free in the sense in which a cat is free. Of course, addicts may also have the will they want to have when they engage in addictive behavior. But, they need not have that. They might intensely want the content of their will to be different from what it actually is. They might even have many desperate failed attempts at quitting behind them.

Addicts might therefore in an important sense be unfree. Freedom to act, however, seems not to be what they lack: Their taking of the drug is by assumption free action and not compulsion. This assumption I share with rational choice approaches. Many cases of addiction—smoking, drinking, and even the taking of cocaine—are clearly free actions in this sense. (I am not speaking about choices done "under the influence" but sober choices to affect that one is going to consume a substance.) The freedom that addicts lack seems clearly to be freedom of the will.

Addiction can be thought of as a specific change in some neural pathways. This approach, important as it is, is silent about whether the addictive behavior can be explained as rational behavior or not. Likewise, the explanatory approaches of rational choice theory are silent about whether our wills are unfree when we are addicted but desperately want to quit. Freedom of the will is not a concept placed within rational choice theory; that theory explains free action, actions wherein we do what we want. This leaves room for a different sort of theorist, that is, a philosopher.

This chapter is in this sense philosophical. My aim is to account for how uncompelled and therefore free addictive behavior might exemplify a limitation upon our freedom of the will. This aim requires a clarification of two basic notions, addiction and freedom of the will. I start with the latter and move on to the former. The reason for starting here is simply that we are not even sure we can make precise, or precise enough, sense of the concept of freedom of the will. If we cannot do that, this route to the elucidation of addiction is not available.

The most controversial positive claim I make about freedom of the will comes toward the end of that discussion. I argue that a capacity for critical, reflective, rational self-governance is essential for free will and that only a negligible discounting of value over time is compatible with having that capacity. On this background I discuss the two main decision-theoretic approaches to addiction and try to settle whether they are capable of capturing, in the right way, the unfreedom that stems from being addicted.

Freedom of the Will

The conception of freedom of the will I allude to raises many problems.[2] Obvious questions concern the understanding of the phrase "to have the will one wants to have." I believe there are two related but distinct questions here. One question concerns what it is to possess freedom of the will, to be a free and responsible person. A second question concerns what state one is in when one fails to have the will one wants to have. The approach to freedom of the will I briefly presented earlier may collapse these two questions into one.

Accounting for the Will I Want to Have

I look at the second question first, the question about the state one is in when one fails to have the will one wants to have. The view under scrutiny says that in these cases there is a conflict between the reflectively based second-order volition and the content of one's will. That is promising. Second-order volitions are reflectively based attitudes toward first-order desires that might produce action. Formally speaking, they are second-order desires that have first-order desires as their objects; that is, they are desires about which among one's first-order desires should produce action. This account of what it is to fail to have the will one wants to have necessarily sees second-order desires of this particular sort as expressive of what one wants one's will to be. First-order desires that effectively produce action are not, in these cases of conflict between the levels, seen as expressing this.[3]

This necessitates further clarification. We use the term "what we desire" in two senses. On a particular occasion we might desire many things, while we can have only one. We desire an apple and also an orange and would much prefer those to a banana or a pear. Both an orange and an apple are then among the things we *desire*, as the other fruits might also be. The first sense of desire denotes things we have a positive attitude toward having. (We prefer them to options we are indifferent about.) Let us then imagine the situation in which we have to choose one and only one piece of fruit and are asked about what we desire. We might then say, an orange. When we say in this situation that we desire an orange, we use desire to denote what we *desire most* among the things we can choose from. This is the second sense of desire. To get the use of desire in second-order volition clear, we have to extend this second use of desire (as desire most) from the first order to the second order.[4]

How can the formal order of desire be relevant to determining or settling which desire is expressive of what I want my will to be? My first-order desire, which produces action, expresses what I desire most on the ground level. Why is that not expressive of what I want my will to be? Why is the second-order desire the favored one for this task? If this cannot be accounted for, we do not have available an explanation of why these desires are expressive of what I want my will to be. It is hard to see how order of desire in itself can settle a substantial issue like this one.[5]

The challenge at this point concerns, among other things, how to identify the set of desires expressive of what I want my will to be. One might try to meet this challenge by distinguishing between the motivational system and the valuational system of the agent (Watson 1982). The latter system, grounded in one's conception of what is good, is then supposed to be expressive of what I want my will to be. The picture this move gives rise to might easily seem too rationalistic. There is a deep difference between the attitude of valuing, on the one hand, and cognitively based evaluations, on the other. One might think that something is good without valuing it. Thinking something is good is not, as such, a motivational state (for example, I know that listening to opera would be very good for me, but I do not want to). For this reason we cannot simply use our conception of what is good at this point. What we value is nevertheless a possible candidate for making up the desired subset of our desires. We lack, however, an account of valuing (a conative, and not a cognitive, attitude) that can identify a subset of our desires in the right way.

Answering this second question is hard. Perhaps we first should approach the substantial question of what freedom of the will is and not try directly for an identification of the subset of desires that is expressive of what we want our will to be. It can surely be true that in typical cases in which one wants one's will to be different from what it is, one's will is unfree. The approach discussed here, introducing second-order volitions, may be seen as giving a sufficient condition for an unfree will. This condition is satisfied when we have a frustrated second-order volition and when this second-order volition is expressive of what we want our will to be. I take it that we might in particular cases be confident that such a second-order volition is expressive of what we want our will to be, even in the absence of a satisfactory general account of a favored subset of desires. We might get this confidence from the way we answer the first question, about what freedom of the will is. I now turn to this question.

The Reactive Attitude View

Here is my view on what freedom of the will is (the first question above).[6] I see our practices and interactions with others, in which our reactive attitudes like resentment have their place, as basic to answering this question. These practices make sense only if people are seen as free and responsible. Practices of this sort do not stand in need of an external justification. Intellectually convincing arguments to the effect that freedom of the will is not compatible with causal determination or determinism cannot really bring about changes in these basic human practices and reactions. This reflects the deeper truth that justification comes to an end somewhere: Looking outside these practices for a justification of them is looking for a type of justification that cannot be had in such cases. Against this background we can see unfreedom of the will as specified by the excusing conditions we generally recognize or should recognize in a reflective equilibrium in which our reactive attitudes are input and epistemic conditions are optimal.

We must ask whether this approach to freedom of the will is challenged by the thesis that actions are linked to antecedent events by laws as deterministic as all causal laws governing the universe.[7] A challenge may arise if or as long as the excusing conditions indicate that people cannot be blamed for what they do when what they do is the result of outside causes. This is because all actions seem in a sense to be the results of outside causes. This might support skepticism about free will from premises rooted in the excusing conditions themselves. Perhaps this approach to free will has no good argument against this skeptic.

We should meet this reasoning by an account of the significance of choice that explains both why the commonly accepted excusing conditions point to cases in which choice is undermined and why the significance of choice cannot be undermined everywhere even if all actions are caused by outside events in the sense invoked by the skeptic (Scanlon 1987). If acceptable, such a line might deprive skeptics of their roots in common sense and in our practices. That is what this approach to free will needs.[8]

The ability to live out normative or moral judgments seems fundamental to freedom of the will. Normative judgments are reached through critical reflection under the pressure provided by the desire to be able to justify one's actions to others on grounds they could not reasonably reject. Normative considerations lead to conclusions about what the contents of our wills ought to be. One component of the ability that underlies free will is the ability to reason morally and to reach normative conclusions. When we care about the content of our wills, this caring also has a moral background.

To have free will, however, we also need to be able to translate normative conclusions into action. Therefore, the ability that underlies free will has another component, and that is the general capacity through which the results of normative and nonnormative reasoning make a difference to what one does. This capacity has been called the capacity for critical, reflective, rational self-governance (Scanlon 1987). I see this idea—of two components in the ability that underlies free will—a further working out of this reactive attitude program. I am very interested in the second component. Understanding what this capacity involves is crucial for the rest of this chapter.

Critical, Reflective, Rational Self-Governance

How can we spell out this nonmoral component of the ability that is crucial to freedom of the will? It is clear that it is a capacity that a being who is not concerned with morality at all could have. Morality is addressed to people who are assumed to have the capacity, and it tells them how the capacity should be exercised. The capacity is assumed to make a difference to how one acts. One clear necessary condition has been stated in the literature: To have this capacity, one must have a certain coherence through time (Scanlon 1987). Conclusions reached at one time must be seen as relevant to later reflections, unless specifically overruled.

Our views about the limits of blame are sensitive to views about the limits of this capacity in a particular person. Children lack the full capacity, and some forms of mental illness exhibit limitations in this capacity. People who exhibit such limitations are not blamed or resented in the same way as others. What has to be impaired for the person not to be blamed, however, is this general nonmoral capacity. If a person simply lacks concern for others, then we are facing a moral fault.[9]

I believe we should try to give this capacity more substance. It is a capacity we acquire through normal upbringing and that we might, for instance, see exhibited by "planning agents" (Bratman 1987). Generally, it is a capacity to critically assess options, reason about them, and make rational evaluations. Second, it is the ability to translate conclusions into intentional action. I look into what this means in two dimensions, first for a person at a particular moment in time and then (in the next section) for a person in and through time.

Rational Self-Governance at One Point in Time   Here are some conceptual connections applying to a person at a moment in time. I call them the backward and forward connections (Pears 1984; Gjelsvik, forthcoming). I take these principles to be true descriptions of those of us who possess this capacity for critical, reflective, rational self-governance on the occasions we exercise it. It articulates rational self-governance at a particular moment in time.

The following describes the *backward connection* principles:

1. When we act intentionally and with a free will, what we do is what we want most to do among the things we can do and believe we can do.

2. What we want most to do is what we judge best to do.

These two principles put constraints on *how we might reason given how we act (when we act with a free will)*. The following are the principles describing the *forward connection*, from reasoning to intentional free-willed action:

3. Practical reasoning is aimed at establishing what course of action is best, and the reasoning about this takes place in the context of settling what to do.

4. Intentional action, done with a free will, involves the conclusion of a piece of practical reasoning in the sense that the intention in acting is or corresponds to the practical conclusion.

Principle 3 gives the point of practical reasoning, and principle 4 connects conclusion in practical reasoning and free-willed intentional action. Together, principles 3 and 4 put constraints on *what we can intentionally do with a free will, given how we reason.*

It seems right to take these four principles linking the forward and backward connections as a package. The backward and forward connections are like the beginnings of a tunnel from each side of a mountain: They must connect in the middle. I shall not here give an argument for the need to see them as a package but only point out that, by taking the four principles as a package, we can thereby see them as jointly providing criteria for whether something is an intentional action produced by a free will. Something is a free-willed intentional action in this sense when what we do is what we are most motivated to do among the things we can do and believe we can do; what we do corresponds to a practical conclusion; and this practical conclusion corresponds to a judgment about what is best.[10]

Rational Self-Governance in and Through Time   A necessary condition for having the capacity required for free will is that one has a certain coherence over time. We may ask, what type of coherence? Are there rationality constraints on attitudes to value over time? The relation between discounting of value over time and freedom of the will must be discussed here. Writers on rational choice tend to see discounting of value over time as fully rational and the degree of discounting a matter of taste. Temporal inconsistencies are mostly seen as irrational. Many central moral philosophers see all discounting of value over time as irrational.[11]

If we see discounting of future value simply as irrational, and if the capacity for critical, reflective, rational self-governance requires rationality, then it follows that people who discount value over time have a limitation in the capacity that underlies freedom of the will. The question is whether we ought to see time discounting simply as a taste, something that cannot be rationally disputed, or as something irrational. This seems at least to be true: There is no way of rationally convincing dynamically consistent discounters that they should discount future value less than they do.[12] There is in this sense no way of arguing convincingly from the point of view of someone who does not discount value over time against those who do discount value over time.[13]

The important point for my argument is that those who possess the complex capacity required for freedom of the will—that is, normal, reflective, and mature human beings—see extreme discounting of value as irrational or as not fully rational. Speaking for such human beings, I say that our practices and reactive attitudes in the case of people who totally fail to care about tomorrow typically express the belief that extremely myopic people need help in various ways, that they are not fully responsible for their actions, that we should not blame them as we blame others, and so on. This way of thinking is natural for adult humans who are exposed to the sort of upbringing we are exposed to. It has become our point of view. We see this point of view as more than a taste. We see it as right and rational. Still, it is not a point of view one can cognitively achieve by standard rational persuasion if one starts out as a strong discounter. This is a feature that this view on time discounting has in common with tastes. The neat division of everything into tastes and things that can be rationally justified will not do.

The observations about excusing conditions therefore support the view that, as discounting increases substantially, our capacity for rational self-governance diminishes.[14] The reduction amounts to a reduction in freedom; it is a reduction in a capacity necessary for freedom. It goes without saying that variable discount rates, or hyperbolic discounting with the following dynamic inconsistencies, are deeply at odds with the view, which goes back to Plato and today is shared by for instance John Rawls (1972), that sees all discounting of value over time as irrational. (Hyperbolic discounting can be seen as a case in which you discount more per time unit as you get closer to an object in time.)

If this Platonic-Rawlsian view on discounting, shared by most moral philosophers, is right and is part of our thick conception of rationality, then all substantial discounting of value over time may be at odds with the capacity for critical, reflective, rational self-governance. We might say that we are immersed in time but are more free when we are less immersed in the now and able to act on the conclusions we reach. If we are less disposed to discount, we are better able to satisfy the necessary preconditions for being able to reason from a point of view that is extended in time and thus sees our lives as wholes, wherein all temporal parts have their rightful claims.[15] (I do not mean to suggest that it is a requirement of rationality that we distribute goods equally between equal-sized temporal parts of our future selves—only that, to be able to answer questions about distribution between temporal parts of ourselves in the right way at a particular time, discounting ought to be negligible or nonexistent. Whether there are further rationality constraints on choices among different distributions between temporal parts—which through time might add up to different total sums—is a different issue, which I do not go into here.)[16]

It seems to me that the Platonic-Rawlsian view, or a softened version of it, reflects our practices, our reactive attitudes, and the reflections we might entertain in this connection. There is no forceful argument in support of a precise conclusion. The observations about excusing conditions can only in an imprecise way be brought to bear on the question of how much discounting we tolerate before we come to think of people as impaired in their capacity for rational self-governance. I shall pass that by. I want to point out that this view links up with the discussion about limitations in the capacity at one point in time: There might be quite different ways in which our exercise of free will is impaired. Merely to discount value over time very much might not conflict at all with the four principles discussed earlier. Still, the freedom of the will is restricted due to the impairment of this general capacity that the discounting of value constitutes. We might not think of this as weakness of the will, even if Plato did. Be that as it may: Weakness of the will might represent a failure to exercise the general capacity at a time and need not reflect that the capacity is generally impaired. In the case in which there is no general impairment of the capacity, there is no reason to hold back blame or resentment. (The weak-willed also typically blame themselves.)

Discounting of value over time is an impairment in the general capacity that underlies freedom of the will. There are probably many other ways of having this capacity impaired, too; and there might be further rationality constraints that are often considered to be matters of taste. I conclude my discussion of the nonmoral component underlying freedom of the will and turn to addiction.

Addiction: Two Explanatory Perspectives

I look at two rival decision-theoretic approaches to addiction and discuss them in the perspective of whether they can be said to represent addiction as a reduction in our ability to exercise of free will. These theories typically use time discounting as the central explanatory mechanism, and in that sense they use something we might see as an impairment in the capacity for rational self-governance to explain addiction. The state of being addicted should, however, represent a further reduction in freedom compared with the state before being addicted. This further reduction would be clearly demonstrated if the theory made room for the emergence of the possibility of a second-order volition to the effect that one wants to have a different will from the will one actually has, a second-order volition that expresses the will the person wants to have. This I see as an intuitive constraint on the adequacy of such explanatory theories. These theories must also be theoretically and empirically adequate in other ways. To really be satisfactory, they need good accounts of the way into addiction, attempts at quitting (occasionally successful), and finally the propensity to relapse.

"Rational" Addiction

Let me first turn to Gary Becker and Kevin Murphy's (1988) theory of rational addiction.[17] I do this not because I think they give a full view of the state of addicts but because they present a plausible structure for a part of addicts' beliefs and desires when in the addicted state. Their theory simply put is this:

Consider a consumer good with two basic properties:

- The higher the consumption of the good in the past, the smaller the welfare (value utility) that can be obtained from the consumption of one unit in the present. (This can be thought of as tolerance but can also be seen as delayed harmful effects of past consumption.)

- The higher the consumption of the good in the past, the larger the gain by consuming one more unit in the present. (The mechanism can be thought of as relief from withdrawal symptoms.)

Consider a choice whether to consume a good with these properties. The combination of properties is such that a rational consumer of the good faces a dilemma about how to weigh the short-term effects of consuming the good against the long-term effects of consuming the good. Simply put, present high consumption will lead to future high consumption with a lower overall welfare level. One has to weigh this future negative effect against present benefits. How much one discounts value over time will determine one's consumption level. If one does not discount future value very much, one might settle for a modest consumption, whereas if one discounts future value substantially, the balance will tip in favor of high consumption.

Becker and Murphy (1988) exhibit rational addicts as rational consumers of a good with these properties. In their theory, rational addicts find themselves trapped in a state of high consumption of the good and with a considerably lower overall welfare level than they would have in a state of low consumption. (By trapped I mean that addicts, being rational, and with their present rate of discounting, would not start high consumption again if they were to start from scratch.)

How does this entrapment come about? It cannot come about if all choices are done with full information about all the future consequences of one's choices and with a stable exponential discount factor. Both of these requirements can, however, be relaxed. (Becker and Murphy do not discuss this point.)

By considering consumers with quite different exponential discount factors, we can complete our picture. There are scenarios wherein this basic model entails that consumers who discount the future heavily will start consuming the good and will consume permanently at a very high level in spite of a reduction in the longer run in their overall welfare level. The cause of the continued high consumption is the rise in marginal utility of the good, given high past consumption. These are willing addicts who care little about the future and for whom it is rational to start consuming a lot even with perfect foresight of the effects.

There is an intermediate level of discounting of future value, in which rational consumers with perfect foresight will not start to consume the good in large quantities. Even if they will not start such consumption from scratch, they will not stop consuming at a high level if past consumption level is high enough. These people, if attuned to high consumption, are unwilling big consumers. They realize that they are worse off than they would have been had they not started high consumption. They would have chosen to consume only small quantities if they had started from scratch (no consumption in the past, no consumption capital, with the given discount factor).

Rational consumers who discount future value *fairly little* will not start to consume much of the good. People who discount future value *very little*, less than intermediate discounters, might be able to cut down from a high level of consumption (if they find themselves there) if the long-term reduction in welfare matters more to them than the short-term gain (for instance, in relief from withdrawal symptoms).

The group of interest in this theory of addiction is the intermediate group, the consumers who will not start high consumption but who are unable to reduce consumption if they have consumed much in the past: A rational agent from this group with perfect foresight and a stable discount rate cannot be trapped in the envisaged way.

Becker and Murphy consider a life crisis with an increase in consumption capital as a causal explanatory background for rational addiction. A significant increase in consumption over a certain period can surely land a person from this intermediate group in the described entrapment. Still, that leaves us with questions about how the increase in consumption capital comes about; consumption capital is typically a consequence of past choices, in the Becker-Murphy view. I like this explanatory background for rational addiction (and for the increase in consumption capital): Consider the possibility that addicts' discount factor is not fully stable through time; perhaps they care less about the future during a certain period. A temporary reduction of the discount factor due to a life crisis might turn a person into a willing addict, who, when the discount factor again increases, becomes a trapped, unwilling addict. A further increase in the discount factor might lead to drastic reductions in consumption.

The question to be answered is whether the Becker-Murphy view really captures addicts' reduction in freedom in the right way.[18] Assume that we accept the view that the more addicts discount, the less free they are. The picture we then get, when reflecting on Becker and Murphy's theory of rational addiction, is that addiction can occur when addicts *gain* freedom, in the sense that addicts then discount less. However, their consumption pattern from the time when they were less free prevents them from enjoying the freedom they gain. If the change to less discounting occurs sooner, then past consumption might not have this effect. In this case, their past catches up with them. If they never discount less (and never in this sense gain freedom), they may remain ordinary consumers of the addictive drug without being rationally addicted.

The view that time discounting is irrational is ours, not that of the addicts. Becker-Murphy addicts can nevertheless make the judgment that they would have been better off today if they had a different past from the one they have. Their past choices are not to be rationally regretted by them, though, as long as each choice is seen as rational when it was made. By assumption, they did what was reasonable in order to get information about the consequences of consuming the substance in question, and they took all information into account.

The question is whether being able to judge that they would have been better off today if they had a different past from the one they have is good enough for our purpose: to supply a basis for a second-order volition to the effect that they would like their will to be different from what it is. Does this judgment result in their really wanting their will to be different from what it is? Does it only result in a simple wish or a fancy that they be a different person with a different past, thus being able to enjoy their newly gained freedom better? Wishes of that kind come cheap. We can also have an intellectual recognition of the fact that we would have a richer or better life if we learned to appreciate literature and opera, without being motivated to do so. (We can, as previously stated, cognitively hold something to be good without wanting it or valuing it.)

Becker and Murphy's addicts did nothing in their past they need to regret; all of their choices were rational by the standards they had when they made them. Athanasios Orphanides and David Zervos (1995) seem to me to describe rational choice under uncertainty as a way into addiction, and so in that case there is nothing to regret (even if they claim otherwise), since all choices are rational when made. We all know that we do not choose our preferences, that they might be partly determined by our past choices, and that we might wish them to be different from what they are. The presence of such a wish is not what we are after to ground a second-order volition. Rather, it has to be grounded in what we desire most on the reflectively based second-order level.

The grounds for a second-order volition of the right sort are thin in the Becker-Murphy approach as long as there is nothing to regret in past choices. Imagine now a new situation wherein something is added on to the Becker-type picture—the addicts also endorse a theoretical-cognitive judgment to the effect that discounting as such is wrong. Then they might see the entrapment they are in in a different light: They would have available, in theory at least, a point of view in which their present continuation of the consumption of the drug becomes something bad and objectionable. From such a point of view, they have good theoretical grounds for wanting a different desire than the desire for the drug to be the content of their will. People who have gone through the sort of upbringing we go through tend to have such a theoretical view about discounting of value available, or so I claim. There is a very big difficulty here in understanding how we can have this perspective without living it out. That is an instance of the general phenomenon that we do not always value what we think is good.[19]

Still, even if we and the addicts share this theoretical view in the imagined situation, there is some doubt that this can give rise to what we need. We are so far speaking about a theoretical view that addicts endorse, not about something that they actually value. We know that addicts need more than a second-order desire for having a different will; they need to desire most (on the second-order level) that they have a different will on the first-order level. In cases in which there is a second-order desire matching the theoretical view in question, there will be a competing second-order desire, fighting this one, in support of the will we actually have. It is not clear to me how we can have much of a second-order desire for having a different will as long as we do not value what we endorse as a theoretical view. On the other hand, if we do value it, we would probably act differently as well. So there is genuine doubt about whether the Becker model can allow for a second-order *volition* of the right sort in support of not taking the drug even when we let in a theoretical recognition of the normative view that discounting is wrong.

My conclusion is that if we can ascribe to addicts a theoretical acceptance of the Platonic-Rawlsian normative view on discounting, then we are closer to meeting this crucial adequacy condition on a theory of addiction. Without admitting a perspective like that on discounting on addicts' behalf, the Becker-type theory seems to me to fail badly to meet the condition that those in the addicted state can fail to have the will they want to have; it is unable to represent the state of being addicted as a state in which the will in free action is contrary to what addicts want their will to be. On the other hand, allowing this Platonic-Rawlsian perspective is problematic. First, because we would then bring into the Becker-type picture elements that are really foreign to the explanatory theory we are here dealing with. We may nevertheless keep the explanatory machinery going as long as we just allow in the theoretical view that time discounting is wrong but not the full internalization of that norm. Unfortunately, it is not clear that that is sufficient for a second-order volition of the right sort.

Hyperbolic Discounting of Value and Addiction

George Ainslie's work on addiction seems to me in many ways much more promising than Becker and Murphy's, both theoretically and empirically (Ainslie 1985, 1992; Ainslie and Haslam 1992a, 1992b). The basic explanatory mechanism is hyperbolic discounting of value. Our state of nature, according to Ainslie, is to fail to have consistent preferences through time. Having consistent preferences through time is the exception rather than the rule. Still, at the end of the day, human adults seem to control their impulsiveness. The former exception is now the rule. We need an account of how this comes about when the basic picture is that dynamic inconsistencies make up the state of nature. To achieve consistency, or to achieve it in the right way, we can see as achieving willpower, that is, the ability to resist temptations. This may not be all there is to willpower, but it is part of it.

I now introduce an example discussed by Michael Bratman (1995). (This is not an example of addiction.) I have a choice between drinking wine in the afternoon and playing the piano well at night. I am a piano player who is very fond of wine, and I face this repeated choice. I may take the thirty coming days into consideration when making my present choice of whether I shall accept today's offer of wine. I ignore nice issues about backward induction; the basic case can also be stated without giving it a structure that invites the special issue of backward induction.

I am offered wine at six in the evening. At that time I choose between drinking the wine (the *drink* alternative) and not drinking the wine (the *abstain* alternative). At six o'clock I prefer the *drink* alternative, even if until half past five I preferred *abstain*. At six o'clock we can also compare the following possibilities: my drinking the wine today and on the next thirty occasions (the *always drink* alternative) and my not drinking the wine today nor on the next thirty occasions (the *never drink* alternative). In this case, my preference is clearly *never drink*, since after discounting *never drink* has a much larger utility than *always drink*.

If we were able to simply choose sequences of thirty actions instead of one after the other, it seems as if we would be much better off than when we choose each day at six o'clock. To choose to live by a rule of not drinking wine until after I have played the piano would solve the present problem. A choice of rule to live by is equivalent to choosing a very long, perhaps infinite, sequence of actions. (See Ole-Jørgen Skog's chapter in this volume for the importance of the length of the sequence.)

Ainslie's working assumption is that the action that is carried out at any point in time is the action that is supported by maximizing considerations at that point in time. It is obvious that when we bring in the next thirty occasions and discount the value of those occasions to present value, then, relative to maximizing considerations, the best strategy at six o'clock is to drink today and abstain on the next thirty occasions. So let us include these options as well: drink today and abstain on the next thirty occasions (the *drink now, abstain later* alternative); and abstain today and drink on the next thirty occasions (the *abstain now, drink later* alternative).

When *drink now, abstain later* and *abstain now, drink later* alternatives are included, we can sum up. In the morning of each day the preference ordering of sequences is never drink > drink now, abstain later > abstain now, drink later > always drink, but at six o'clock my preferences reverse to *drink now, abstain later* > *never drink* > *always drink* > *abstain now, drink later*. The situation is that I have to choose whether to drink or not at six o'clock. What do I choose? If I, at six o'clock, see the choice as a choice between single acts, I will drink the wine. If I see the choice as a choice of a sequence, the best sequence involves drinking today and then abstention. If I believe that what I do today has no consequences for my choice tomorrow, I will choose to drink.

If, however, I see what I do today as influencing what I will do on the next occasion, then this might alter my choice. Imagine the belief that if I do not drink today I will not drink on the next thirty days. Let us call this the belief in precedence, belief *p*. This belief is a simple indicative conditional. If I believe *p*, then *never drink* might be my preferred option. It will be my preferred option if I believe that, without choosing to act on this belief p, I will as a matter of fact drink on all these thirty occasions. If I believe I can drink today and then abstain, I will drink today even if I believe p.

Are abstentions correctly seen as precedents? Does p have a rational foundation? It seems clear that if we do not believe p, we will as a matter of fact drink at six o'clock on all days, even if we have a stable preference for *never drink* > *always drink* through time and believe that we will drink tomorrow if we drink today. This follows from the payoff structure. Without a belief in p, we will implement the strategy *always drink*, although we have a stable preference for *never drink* > *always drink*. We can see our drinking as giving in to temptation but being able to act upon the stable preference *never drink* > *always drink* as having willpower.

It is easily seen that if we adopt the rule to abstain in the afternoon and thereby gain willpower, we would be much better off in terms of total welfare in the long run than without such a rule; we would realize our preference for *never drink*. If we were able to believe p, that would make us adopt the rule in question. The question of whether this rule can be adopted by rational means boils down to whether we can give a rational foundation for p. Ainslie argues that a rational foundation for seeing actions as precedents in the required way can be found if we see the situation as a repeated prisoner's dilemma in a noncooperative game between successive person stages, or successive motivational states within the person. We choose to play tit for tat or a similar strategy with tomorrow's self. We make a cooperative move. As in the game with two people, tomorrow's self will have reason to cooperate in the same way with the self of the day after tomorrow, and so on. The net result is to our overall gain.

Put simply like this, it needs much detailed backing. The hard problem in Ainslie's positive approach is the analogy to the two-person game. There is no other person with whom we interact through time. I believe that Ainslie's critics (especially Bratman) are right and that this analogy to two-person games cannot be sustained. If so, then the belief in p might not have a rational basis of this sort. Individual abstentions are rational when we have enough confidence in p to make abstention the best option and when these abstentions can, when repeated, come to be seen as confirmations of p, thereby making p more subjectively probable and abstentions even more worthwhile. If, however, we are confident in our belief in p and believe that one exception cannot really shake this confidence, then why not consume today and abstain again tomorrow? Abstention suddenly seems unstable again.

Theories of addiction within the Ainsliean hyperbolic framework need, in my judgment, to account for the change that occurs when we enter the state of being addicted. It is natural and plausible to see, as

Becker does, the continued consumption of the addictive drug as bringing about changes in our perception of utilities, and herein might lie a clue about how to represent this important change. We also need to account for relapse in a plausible way.

Here is a way of dealing with these theoretical needs. We start out in the example we use above and introduce the change that past drinking slowly raises the utility of drinking relative to the utility of abstaining. Everything else remains the same. As the past contains more and more drinking, and when we then add up the sums of discounted future consumptions (in the example, there are always thirty such occasions), we sooner or later reach a point at which the preference *never drink > always drink* is no longer stable. At this point, the preference *never drink > always drink* is still in place most of the time; but for a very brief period of time, namely at the time of consumption choice, there is the preference *always drink > never drink*. This period is a much briefer than the period when *drink* is preferred to *abstain*.[20] Still, it implies that with this new perception of the utilities, simply coming to believe *p* is not sufficient to overcome the temptation. In this case, we need to employ additional precommitment techniques to succeed in resisting the temptation at the point in time when consumption would be rational if we did not employ these additional techniques.

I suggest that we think of this possible change as the change that occurs when people become addicted. Ainslie has no representation of the point at which people change from not being addicted to being addicted. We do, however, need to address the issue of a proper theoretical representation of when people have undergone the change by virtue of which they have become addicted. To represent it this way has other advantages than being plausible in itself. It is well suited as a representation of why abstaining now (in the addicted state) is more difficult than it used to be in the past, when there was little drinking; it also makes the explanation of relapse much easier (Gjelsvik 1999).

It is clear that the hyperbolic discounter who is addicted in this sense fails badly in enjoying fully what I call the capacity for critical, reflective, rational self-governance that is essential for freedom of the will. In the case of hyperbolic discounting, we have irrational discounting of value in time, and we also have dynamic inconsistency. The question is, however, whether we have a reflective basis for a second-order volition to the effect that we want a different desire than the desire for the drug to be the desire that produces action. There is a stable preference *never drink > always drink* through time in the situation Ainslie concentrates upon. This Ainsliean agent fails to translate into action this general preference for *never drink* and, in fact, implements *always drink*. There is a sense in which we fail to do what we think best and, relative to this sense, a failure to satisfy the conditions for free-willed action at a moment in time. This forms the basis for a desire for not being motivated by the desire for the drug at the time of action. Is it enough for a reflectively based second-order volition?

At each moment of choice, Ainsliean agents choose what they see as best at that moment. There will naturally be a second-order desire in support of the desire behind the *never drink* strategy. There will, however, also be a second-order desire in support of the desire that effectively produces action. (Agents generally want to realize the option they find best at the time of choice, and in second-order reflection, the first-order desire, which produces action, will be supported by a corresponding second-order desire in these cases. This second-order desire can of course be weaker than other second-order desires, even if its corresponding first-order desire produces action and is the strongest desire on the basic level.) Is there, in this case, a reflectively based reasoning that favors the one second-order desire over and above the other conflicting second-order desire? People know that they in fact implement the strategy *always drink* when they prefer *never drink*, and they might wish that was different. The desire not to drink is the strongest most of the time, both on the first-order level and on the second-order level. Second-order volitions are assumed to be reflectively based, and one might think that they are stable through time in a way quite different from that of first-order preferences, especially in cases of dynamic inconsistencies. The question concerns the grounds on which we can attribute this stability to the second-order volitions of a hyperbolic discounter.

What this seems to imply is that there is no knockdown argument that an Ainsliean hyperbolic discounter should come out differently when it concerns conflicts between desires on the second-order level, as opposed to the first-order level, and thus form second-order volitions that conflict with first-order volitions. As long as we do not have resources beyond those described by hyperbolic discounting, we might not get a different result by moving one level up, and the conflict at the second-order level might remain a reflection of the first-order conflict. There will be a sense in which people think that what they do when they act is not best, and in this sense they will conflict with the requirements for freedom of the will at a particular moment in time. We might have a dynamic conflict reflecting the first-order dynamic conflict also on the second-order level in a pure Ainsliean case.

Let us now consider the same move I introduced in the Becker-Murphy case and introduce a theoretical recognition of the Platonic-Rawlsian view that both dynamic inconsistencies and substantial discounting of value in time is wrong. It is one thing to accept theoretically the view that this is a good norm and another thing to accept and internalize the norm. The theoretical acceptance of the norm automatically contributes to the existing conflict. It has no immediate consequence at the first-order level, since we assume no internalization of this norm. Still it might matter on the reflective second-order level. Here, we have a conflict between the desire for being motivated by the desire for drinking and the desire for being motivated to abstain, and the last desire dominates most of the time even before the introduction of this norm.

The Platonic-Rawlsian view both condemns the dynamic inconsistencies and the strong discounting. We now imagine that addicts like this view: Even if it is not internalized as a norm, it is in a theoretical way considered right or good. The belief in the Platonic-Rawlsian view obviously favors the interests of the second-order desire for not being moved into action by the desire for the drug. This second-order desire will, on reflection (and reflection is here assumed), be strengthened in various ways by the introduction of the Platonic-Rawlsian view, and all of these ways will reduce the strength of the second-order desire in support of being moved to action by the desire for the drug. It therefore seems that, with the introduction of this belief into the Platonic-Rawlsian view on behalf of the addict, we clear the way for the potential conflict between the second-order volition and the first-order volition that characterizes unfreedom of the will even in the presence of freedom of action. In this case, we know why the second-order volition and the first-order volition conflict, and we have no difficulty in seeing the second-order volition as expressive of what we want our will to be. Thus we are strikingly unfree.

The difference between Ainslie and my amended theory is in this respect not fundamental. Further, in my view, agents have the same grounds for a second-order volition as they do in Ainslie's view. The difference between Ainslie's view and mine is that in my view agents have a real preference for *never drink > always drink* almost all the time, in contrast to Ainslie, for whom this preference is stable through time. There are, however, advantages in my amended theory on this point, or so I claim. One such advantage is that we ought, in any case, to see dynamic inconsistency as an impairment in the capacity necessary for freedom of the will. By amending Ainslie's theory the way I suggest, we get a further reduction in our freedom exactly in the situation in which we believe in precedences (hold p). This limitation in freedom is additional to limitations in freedom in Ainslie's unamended view, and it is brought about by past consumption. It is a specific change and reduction of our freedom brought about by consumption of the addictive drug itself. I claim that an adequate theory ought to make room for some such change. Ainslie's unamended theory does not seem able to do that.

There is also in this explanatory approach to addiction (which Ainslie and I share) a need to make room for a perspective, perhaps a theoretical judgment, that transcends the point of view that explains actions. This is, I believe, a need that will arise anyway. Grown-up humans find actions explained by hyperbolic discounting puzzling and disturbing. When we succumb to them ourselves, we tend to be irritated and angry with ourselves and, in some cases, even ashamed. In other words, we have self-directed reactive attitudes as well as reactive attitudes directed toward others. These self-directed reactive attitudes I take as evidence for an internalization of norms about time discounting that probably are of a Platonic kind. We have in fact deep emotional attachments to these norms. Self-directed reactive attitudes need explaining, and I see no good way of explaining them except by an ascription of internalized Platonic-Rawlsian norms.[21]

It also seems that it is here that we should seek an explanation of why we come to look like someone who believes strongly in precedence (the belief in p) even if there is no rational explanation of how we come to believe in p, and it looks like magic that we leave the dynamically inconsistent states and become stable if we start out in Ainslie's basic picture. I believe the naturalistic perspective Ainslie here has is too limited. We are beings with an underlying tendency toward hyperbolic discounting, but we are also beings who react to a normal moral upbringing and habituation in such a way that we come to see something like the Platonic-Rawlsian view on discounting as the right, or rational, view. The less firm or stable the internalization of this Platonic-Rawlsian view, the more we need to support it with beliefs in precedences. Most grown-up humans manage without relying on beliefs in precedences, but far from all, and for these the belief in precedence is what they use to achieve the result others achieve without it. As a side effect, these precedence-relying people either develop very rigid natures, with an overly strong will, or they start to give in to temptation a lot (appearing reckless) as their belief in precedence fails. These people are much more prone to addictions as explained by Ainslie-type theories, since the theories apply to them much better and more directly than to the people who acquire a solid Platonic view.[22]

Conclusions

I distinguish between freedom of action and freedom of the will, and I argue that freedom of the will requires critical, reflective, rational self-governance. To possess critical, reflective, rational self-governance, we need to satisfy strong requirements upon attitudes to value in time.

Explanatory approaches to addiction typically concentrate on attitudes to value over time in order to get the explanatory machinery going. The upshot is that people who are prone to addiction are in a way not fully free to begin with. Still, becoming addicted should be represented as a further reduction in freedom, a reduction that does not occur in those who do not consume enough to become addicted.

Becker's theory can be seen as an attempt to deal with this requirement, but it has many problems. Ainslie's theory does not really satisfy this requirement. I suggest that a specific amendment of Ainslie's theory can exhibit the loss of freedom that results from becoming addicted in a way that cannot otherwise be clearly shown in Ainslie's view. Addiction is partly caused by an impairment in the general capacity for rational self-governance, and the state of being addicted ought to represent a further impairment in this general capacity.

The state of being addicted is also a state in which it should be possible for us to have second-order volitions directed against continued consumption of the addictive substance. I argue that the Becker-type theory has great difficulty in coming to terms with this requirement and that an Ainslie-type approach with hyperbolic discounting fares better on this count. It is, however, somewhat unclear how well it fares. By introducing on addicts' behalf the theoretical insight about the goodness of the norm whose internalization is a prerequisite for enjoying the full capacity for rational self-governance, we get a quite different picture. It is still not clear that a Becker-type view can accommodate a second-order volition that is sufficient for enjoying freedom of the will. It seems much clearer that the Ainslian addict can. Thus, in this latter case, the recognition of the rightness of the norm whose internalization is necessary for freedom of the will makes room for the required second-order volition. This second-order volition is a genuine expression of what we want our will to be, and thus we are unfree if we are addicted.

For comments on this material, I thank all the participants at the conference on addiction at the Russell Sage Foundation in June 1997, especially Jon Elster; Bjørn Ramberg, Jennifer Whiting, and Tim Williamson; and an anonymous referee.

Notes

1. The account I give of free will is developed by Harry Frankfurt (1982). I see Frankfurt as identifying a sufficient condition for being unfree, a condition I believe an unwilling addict should satisfy. I do not see Frankfurt as giving a satisfactory positive account of what having a free will is.

2. For an illuminating overview of much of this discussion, see Gary Watson (1987).

3. Desires expressive of what one wants one's will to be also are said to express the "real self." See Susan Wolf (1990).

4. This is a natural way to read Frankfurt, but it perhaps not fully explicit in his writings. I came to this conclusion and find it nicely confirmed in Eleanore Stump (1993).

5. To my mind, and to Frankfurt's I believe, this is convincingly argued in Gary Watson (1982).

6. In my judgment, Peter Strawson's influential essay (1982) gets much of the picture absolutely right.

7. I aim with this formulation to remain neutral about the extent to which these laws governing the universe are deterministic.

8. Susan Wolf (1990) argues that acting out one's second-order volitions is not sufficient for freedom of the will or responsibility. A free subject must satisfy further constraints, and we must focus on these. Autonomy, understood by her as a capacity to act radically at odds with reason, will not do either. Wolf champions what she calls the reason view, which sees a person as free and responsible when the person at the time of performance possesses the ability to act in accordance with the true and the good. This is explicitly a normative view of what freedom is, and the question of whether a person possesses this ability is seen as prior to and independent of the question of whether the ability is exercised on a specific occasion. I accept this view as long as the further specifications of what this ability comes to are given within a Strawson-type framework.

9. Thomas Scanlon (without giving any details) also links the possession of this capacity with Frankfurt's view of the integration of higher-order and first-order desires in a person who enjoys freedom of the will.

10. Another point is that, by accepting these four principles jointly and by seeing them as on a par, we might create very big difficulties for the most promising accounts of weak-willed, free action. In a way, this is as it should general capacity that makes up the nonmoral component in free will. Weak-willed, or acratic, actions, when they occur, cannot be seen as exercises of this capacity. In my view, weak-willed action is free action but is not an exercise of free will. Most writers on weak will do not operate with two senses of freedom here. I think one should be able to fully appreciate the issue of acrasia, or weak will. If the frequency of weak-willed actions grows, it becomes questionable how firmly we possess the capacity required for free will and responsibility. If we no longer possess this capacity, we probably should not think of ourselves as capable of weak-willed action. To be so capable requires having a free will. Davidson's theory of weak will starts with principles 1 and 2 but faces severe difficulties if we accept principles 3 and 4 as on a par with 1 and 2 (Davidson 1980, 1982,

1985). Michael Bratman's approach starts with principles 3 and 4 but faces difficulties if we already accept principles 1 and 2 as on a par with 3 and 4 (Bratman 1979, 1985, 1987, 1995). I argue this in detail in Olav Gjelsvik (forthcoming).

11. The view goes back to Plato, who saw time discounting as acrasia in the dialogue "Protagoras." For a nice discussion of Plato's view, see John Cooper (1984). John Rawls (1972, chap. 64) endorses the view that discounting is irrational but refers us to Henry Sidgwick (1884) for argument. There is, however, no real argument in Sidgwick for this view on discounting of value in time—for instance, directed against Jeremy Bentham. Bentham (1970) saw distance in time as a relevant parameter for the determination of present value of a temporally distant good, and only present value matters, in his view.

12. Gary Becker and Casey Mulligan (1997) discuss endogenous change of time preference and basically see time discounting as arising out of weak presence in the mind regarding goods in the future. They believe we can invest in better representations of future goods in our minds and thus reduce time discounting and work out how big an investment is optimal. Note that this time discounting is derived from "inferior" representations in the mind about future goods. There are, however, conceptual problems raised by the fact that it is the myopic self that has to make the investments and to decide what is inferior and what is not.

13. There is, however, an argument directed at people who do not discount to the effect that a limited discounting might be rational for them in order to take care of future change of preferences. I do not assess this argument here but only point out that it can rationalize only a very limited discounting, if any at all (see Hurley 1989, chap. 8).

14. It might also be that time is not the heart of the matter and that it all should be traced back to how we learn to deal with pleasures that just present themselves to our senses and become salient. To be temporally much closer than another pleasure is just one way of becoming salient.

15. Persons are of course extended in time. I do not go further into this matter here, but I am in sympathy with J. David Velleman's (1993) complaint that a belief-desire-based account of practical reasoning does not give a proper role to the temporally extended agent. I disagree, however, with the positive views that Velleman presents.

16. I owe this to points made by Jon Elster, in comments on my chapter, and to George Loewenstein, at the conference on addiction.

17. My presentation of the Becker-Murphy view is much indebted to the discussion in Ole-Jørgen Skog (1999).

18. I am interested in the state they describe as the addicted state, and I believe that there are realistic paths into this state. Those paths are not really given in Becker and Murphy, but such a path can easily be demonstrated by dropping the assumption that agents have perfect foresight or information

about the delayed price they have to pay for high consumption in the present. The lives of many addicts testify to much wishful thinking and self-deception at such crucial points.

19. This relates to a point in Aristotle's account of weak will: There are things we know in a sense without really knowing them.

20. As the relative value of drinking increases, *drink* is preferred for a longer and longer period, and at the time of drinking the net difference between drinking and abstaining increases. *Always drink* is *drink* plus (*drink the next twenty-nine times*). *Never drink* is *abstain* plus (*abstain the next twenty-nine times*). There is in our example a stable preference for *abstain the next twenty-nine times* > *drink the next twenty-nine times*. The discounted difference between these latter two sums needs to be smaller than the net difference between *drink* and *abstain* if we are to have the preference *always drink* > *never drink* at the time of drinking. It should be clear that when we, after much drinking, reach the point when *never drink* > *always drink* is no longer stable, the preference *always drink* > *never drink* occurs for a very brief period indeed, a period briefer than the period when *drink* is preferred to *abstain*.

21. Jon Elster has also pointed out the need to explain these phenomena and the difficulties Ainslie faces at this point.

22. Ole-Jørgen Skog asked at the conference on addiction whether, in my view, one could choose to be spontaneous. I answer that one cannot, even though the fully rational person I envisage does the spontaneous thing when that is the right thing to do. Imagine a hyperbolic discounter who relies heavily on belief in precedences and who would otherwise be unable to go to bed. One occasion arrives when staying up is of great value. This person, with an overly strong will, is unable to break his normal pattern of going to bed, because staying up in his perception might lead to always staying up, and that cost would be too high. The rational person who does not discount and who does not rely on precedences to achieve dynamic consistency stays up and is spontaneous on this occasion. He is also, for this reason, more free than a person who is unable to make an exception to his normal pattern. Still, one cannot choose to be spontaneous.

References

Ainslie, George. 1985. "Beyond Microeconomics." In *The Multiple Self*, edited by Jon Elster. Cambridge: Cambridge University Press.

———. 1992. *The Strategic Interaction of Successive Motivational States Within the Person*. Cambridge: Cambridge University Press.

———. 1993. "Where There's a Will There's a Won't." Paper prepared for the symposium, Contemporary Perspectives on Self-Control and Drug Dependence, Chicago.

Ainslie, George, and Nick Haslam. 1992a. "Hyperbolic Discounting." In *Choices over Time*, edited by George Loewenstein and Jon Elster. New York: Russell Sage Foundation.

——. 1992b. "Self-Control." In *Choices over Time*, edited by George Loewenstein and Jon Elster. New York: Russell Sage Foundation.

Becker, Gary, and Casey Mulligan. 1997. "On the Endogenous Determination of Time Preferences." *Quarterly Journal of Economics* 112: 729–58.

Becker, Gary, and Kevin Murphy. 1988. "A Theory of Rational Addiction." *Journal of Political Economy* 96: 675–700.

Bentham, Jeremy. 1970. *Introduction to the Principles of Morals and Legislation.* London: Athlone.

Bratman, Michael. 1979. "Practical Reason and Weakness of the Will." *Nous* 13: 153–71.

——. 1985. "Davidson's Theory of Intention." In *Actions and Events: Perspectives on the Philosophy of Donald Davidson*, edited by Ernest LePore and Brian McLaughlin. Oxford: Blackwell.

——. 1987. *Intentions, Plans, and Practical Reason.* Cambridge, Mass.: Harvard University Press.

——. 1995. "Planning and Temptation." In *Mind and Morals*, edited by Larry May, Marilyn Friedman, and Andy Clark. Cambridge: Cambridge University Press.

Cooper, John. 1984. "Plato's Theory of Human Motivation." *History of Philosophy Quarterly* 1: 3–22.

Davidson, Donald. 1980. *Essays on Actions and Events.* Oxford: Oxford University Press.

——. 1982. "Paradoxes of Irrationality." In *Philosophical Essays on Freud*, edited by Richard Wollheim and James Hopkins. Cambridge: Cambridge University Press.

——. 1985. "Deception and Division." In *The Multiple Self*, edited by Jon Elster. Cambridge: Cambridge University Press.

Frankfurt, Harry. 1982. "Freedom of the Will and the Concept of a Person." In *Free Will*, edited by Gary Watson. Oxford: Oxford University Press.

Gjelsvik, Olav. 1999. "Addiction, Weakness of the Will, and Relapse." In *Getting Hooked: Rationality and the Addictions*, edited by Jon Elster and Ole-Jørgen Skog. Cambridge: Cambridge University Press.

——. Forthcoming. "The Epistemology of Decision-Making Naturalised." In *Knowledge, Language, and Logic: Questions for Quine*, edited by Alex Orenstein and Peter Kotatko. Dordrecht: Kluwer.

Hurley, Susan. 1989. *Natural Reasons.* Oxford: Oxford University Press.

Orphanides, Athanasios, and David Zervos. 1995. "Rational Addiction with Learning and Regret." *Journal of Political Economy* 103: 739–58.

Parfit, Derek. 1984. *Reasons and Persons.* Oxford: Oxford University Press.

Pears, David. 1984. *Motivated Irrationality.* Oxford: Oxford University Press.

Rawls, John. 1972. *A Theory of Justice.* Oxford: Oxford University Press.

Scanlon, Thomas. 1987. *The Significance of Choice.* Tanner Lectures on Human Values, vol. 8. Cambridge: Cambridge University Press.

Sidgwick, Henry. 1884. *Methods of Ethics.* London: Macmillan.

Skog, Ole-Jørgen. 1999. "Rationality, Irrationality, and Addiction: Notes on Becker and Murphy's Theory of Addiction." In *Getting Hooked: Rationality and the Addictions,* edited by Jon Elster and Ole-Jørgen Skog. Cambridge: Cambridge University Press.

Strawson, Peter. 1982. "Freedom and Resentment." In *Free Will,* edited by Gary Watson. Oxford: Oxford University Press.

Stump, Eleanore. 1993. "Sanctification, Hardening of the Heart, and Frankfurt's Conception of Free Will." In *Perspectives on Moral Responsibility,* edited by John Martin Fischer and Mark Ravizza. Ithaca: Cornell University Press.

Velleman, J. David. 1993. "What Happens When Someone Acts." In *Perspectives on Moral Responsibility,* edited by John Martin Fischer and Mark Ravizza. Ithaca: Cornell University Press.

Watson, Gary. 1982. "Free Agency." In *Free Will,* edited by Gary Watson. Oxford: Oxford University Press.

———. 1987. "Free Action and Free Will." *Mind* 96: 145–72.

Wolf, Susan. 1990. *Freedom Within Reason.* Oxford: Oxford University Press.

PART II

THE NEUROBIOLOGY OF ADDICTION

Chapter 3

The Neurobiology and Genetics of Addiction: Implications of the "Reward Deficiency Syndrome" for Therapeutic Strategies in Chemical Dependency

ELIOT L. GARDNER

IN SPITE OF decades of research into the underlying determinants of drug addiction and chemical dependence, no clearly efficacious therapeutic modality has emerged (Kleber 1992, 1994; O'Brien 1997). Group therapy and support on the Alcoholics Anonymous twelve-step program model, "therapeutic communities," cognitive and behavioral therapies, various pharmacotherapies (methadone maintenance, nicotine patch, Antabuse, naltrexone), and other therapeutic modalities all claim varying degrees of success (Lowinson et al. 1977; O'Brien 1997), yet careful epidemiological studies (including the National Household Survey on Drug Abuse) reveal that more than five million Americans continue to suffer from severe drug addiction (Woodward et al. 1997; Epstein and Gfroerer 1998). Approximately 40 percent of this severely afflicted population do receive treatment (Woodward et al. 1997; Epstein and Gfroerer 1998), yet relapse and recidivism severely compromise therapeutic outcome even among such treatment-receiving patients (Vaillant 1966; Hunt, Barnett, and Branch 1971; Thombs 1994).

Although some claim that drug and alcohol addictions have high spontaneous recovery rates and short durations (for example, Heyman 1998), the preponderance of evidence is that drug and alcohol addictions are chronic, relapsing, progressive, and often fatal (Vaillant 1998); that abstinence does not occur by chance or by maturation (ibid.); that while initial drug use is virtually always voluntary, many drug users lose the voluntary ability to control their use and then proceed to outright addiction (O'Brien and McLellan 1998); and that after this progression has taken place there is a compulsive, often overwhelmingly involuntary aspect to continued drug use and to relapse after a period of abstinence (ibid.).

It is well-accepted clinical knowledge that short-term detoxification and behavioral extinction of drug taking are easy to accomplish; but craving and vulnerability to drug-triggered relapse, cue-triggered relapse, and stress-triggered relapse persist for months, years, and even decades. Although some question either the existence of craving as a distinct psychological state (Shiffman 1987) or the importance of craving to relapse (Tiffany and Carter 1998) or criticize the concept of craving as a useless tautology (Marlatt 1985a), it seems clear that, when defined in terms of cognitive theory and positive incentive motivational value (Marlatt 1985b), craving is a useful intervening cognitive construct. Thus defined (as an expectancy or anticipation that precedes the behavioral "urge" to reuse drugs; Marlatt 1987), a strong case can be made for causal links among cravings, urges, and relapses to drug taking (Marlatt 1985b; Shiffman et al. 1997). In much of the addiction literature, "craving" is clearly used interchangeably with behavioral "urge," which tends to reduce criticisms of the importance of craving in the addictive process to a purely semantic level. For such highly addicting drugs as cocaine, the craving (or behavioral urge to use) can be "so intense and intrusive that it disrupts concentration, interferes with performance . . . and controls subsequent actions. In short, craving is an irresistible urge to use a substance that compels drug-seeking behavior" (Halikas et al. 1991, 22; Halikas 1997, 85).

As long ago as the early nineteenth century, Jean Etienne Dominique Esquirol (1838) suggested that drug addiction is a form of impulse control disorder: "Voluntary control is profoundly impaired: the patient is compelled to perform acts which are dictated neither by his reason nor his emotions—acts which his conscience disapproves of, but over which he no longer has willful control; the actions are involuntary, irresistible, and monomaniacal."[1] In recent years, Charles P. O'Brien and Anna Rose Childress have contributed enormously to the literature on drug craving (for example, Childress et al. 1988; O'Brien et al. 1988, 1992), have shown that desensitization of craving-eliciting environmental cues is therapeutically beneficial to the recovering addict (Childress, McLellan, and O'Brien 1986; O'Brien et al. 1990), and that—during successful pharmacotherapy for drug addiction—decreased drug craving precedes and predicts decreased drug use (Volpicelli et al. 1992). In short, whether called cravings, urges, desires, or appetites, the strong yearning for drugs shown by truly dependent addicts is widely accepted as a major component of drug addiction and as a major contributor to drug read-ministration (see also Dackis and Gold 1985; Gawin and Kleber 1986; Vaillant 1988; Jaffe 1992; O'Brien et al. 1992; Kreek 1992; Hoffman and Miller 1993).

Recent advances in understanding the neurobiological and neuro-genetic substrates of drug addiction give rise to unifying and interlock-ing hypotheses regarding vulnerability to drug addiction, craving, and relapse that yield concrete suggestions regarding the development of new pharmacotherapies for addiction based on the model of remediat-ing a fundamental neurochemical deficiency in crucial pleasure-reward brain circuits. Based on this model, a new class of potential pharmaco-therapies for cocaine addiction has been developed, with encouraging preliminary preclinical results.

Actions of Addicting Drugs (Acute Administration) on Brain Reward Mechanisms

The concept that reinforcement produced by addicting drugs results from direct neuropharmacological enhancement of brain reward cir-cuits has become central and seminal in recent years (Wise 1980; Wise and Bozarth 1981; Kornetsky 1985; Engel and Oreland 1987; Gardner 1989, 1997), with much supporting evidence. Virtually all well-studied addicting drugs (including opiates, stimulants, sedative-hypnotics, anxiolytics, cannabinoids, ethanol, nicotine, and anesthetics) enhance brain stimulation reward (Wise 1980, 1984; Wise and Bozarth 1981; Kor-netsky 1985; Wise and Rompré 1989; Gardner 1997) and enhance neu-ronal firing or neurotransmitter release in brain reward loci (Gysling and Wang 1983; Hommer and Pert 1983; Kalivas et al. 1983; Di Chiara and Imperato 1986; Imperato and Di Chiara 1986; Imperato, Mulas, and Di Chiara 1986; Westerink et al. 1987; Hernandez and Hoebel 1988; Kalivas et al. 1988; Wise and Rompré 1989; Chen, Paredes, and Gard-ner 1993; Gardner 1997). Animals self-inject addicting drugs into brain reward loci but not into other brain loci (Phillips and LePiane 1980; Bozarth and Wise 1981a; Goeders and Smith 1983; Goeders, Lane, and Smith 1984; Hoebel et al. 1983; Gardner 1997), and lesions and phar-macological blockade of brain reward circuits markedly inhibit the rewarding properties of systemically administered addictive drugs (Bozarth and Wise 1981b; Spyraki, Fibiger, and Phillips 1983). Thus, acute enhancement of brain reward mechanisms is an important com-monality of addicting drugs, including both alcohol (De Witte and Bada 1983; Kornetsky et al. 1988; Lewis and June 1990, 1994; Moolten and Kornetsky 1990; Gardner 1997; but compare Routtenberg 1981) and nicotine (Huston-Lyons and Kornetsky 1992; Huston-Lyons, Sarkar, and Kornetsky 1993; Wise 1996; Gardner 1997; Yeomans and Baptista 1997; Wise, Marcangione, and Bauco 1998). The hypothesis that recreational and addiction-producing drugs act on these brain mechanisms to produce the subjective reward, or high, sought by drug users is a principal hypothesis on the neurobiology of drug addiction (Kornetsky et al. 1979; Wise 1980, 1984; Bozarth and Wise 1981a; Wise and Bozarth 1984; Kornetsky 1985; Wise and Rompré 1989; Gardner 1997).

Persuasive to the view that addicting drugs act by facilitating a common brain reward substrate is the finding that addicting drugs of different pharmacological classes (for example, opiates and stimulants) have synergistic effects on brain reward when coadministered (Seeger and Carlson 1981; Hubner et al. 1987). Persuasive to the view that brain reward facilitation is related to addictive potential are findings with opiate mixed agonist-antagonists, some of which are addicting and some of which are not (Jaffe and Martin 1985). Among these drugs, action on brain reward discriminates between those having addictive potential and those devoid of it. For example, the addictive opiate mixed agonist-antagonist pentazocine lowers brain reward thresholds while other mixed agonist-antagonists lacking addictive potential (for example, cyclazocine, nalorphine) do not (Kornetsky and Esposito 1979). From more than forty years of work, it is known that the reward substrates of the mammalian brain primarily involve the medial forebrain bundle (MFB) and its dopamine (DA) nuclei (for example, ventral tegmental area [VTA]) and DA terminal loci (for example, nucleus accumbens [Acb]) (Gardner 1997). It is further known that brain reward is critically dependent on the functional integrity of DA neurotransmission within this system (Corbett and Wise 1980; Wise 1981; Wise and Bozarth 1981; Fray et al. 1983; Fibiger and Phillips 1988; Wise and Rompré 1989; Gardner 1997). DA neurons in this system form a crucial second-stage anatomic convergence, upon which the first-stage neurons (Gallistel et al. 1981) synapse to form an in-series neural reward circuit (Wise 1980; Wise and Bozarth 1984; Gardner 1997).

It is in this second-stage DA convergence that addicting drugs act to enhance brain reward (Wise 1980, 1984; Wise and Bozarth 1981; Wise and Rompré 1989; Yeomans 1989; Gardner 1997), including both alcohol (see, for example, Di Chiara and Imperato 1986, 1988; Imperato and Di Chiara 1986; Gardner and Chen 1992; McBride et al. 1993a; Benjamin et al. 1993) and nicotine (see, for example, Imperato et al. 1986; Nisell et al. 1994a, 1994b; Gardner 1997; Pontieri et al. 1997; Schilstrom et al. 1998; Dewey et al. 1999). Emphasizing the importance of these DA brain reward mechanisms to drug-taking behavior are findings from studies in which animals are allowed to self-administer intravenous cocaine or heroin and in-vivo DA neurochemistry is concomitantly monitored in Acb by brief-sampling-time microdialysis (Wise 1993; Wise et al. 1995a, 1995b).

In these studies, both tonic and phasic alterations in Acb DA levels were observed as a function of drug self-administration. At the beginning of each self-administration session, an enormous tonic elevation in Acb DA occurred after the first loading doses of self-administered drug. This tonic DA elevation quickly reached a plateau and was followed by small but significant phasic fluctuations that correlate very tightly with voluntary self-administration. Acb DA decreased before—and appeared to predict—each drug self-administration, whereas Acb DA increased immediately after each drug self-administration and appears to correlate with behavioral indexes of satiation.

The assumption that the effects on brain reward mechanisms in animals produced by acute administration of addictive drugs (the brain reward enhancement measured electrophysiologically and the DA enhancement measured neurochemically in Acb) has relevance to self-reported euphoria at the human level is supported by real-time, in-vivo, positron emission tomography studies of DA transporter occupancy in human brain loci following acute cocaine administration (Volkow et al. 1997). The purpose of these studies was to determine what level of DA transporter occupancy (and thus what level of synaptic DA) is required to produce a subjective cocaine high in human volunteers who regularly abuse cocaine. It was found that intravenous cocaine (exogenously administered and placebo controlled) at doses commonly abused by humans blocked between 60 percent and 77 percent of DA transporter sites in vivo. Compellingly, the magnitude of the self-reported high was significantly correlated with the degree of local brain DA transporter occupancy and thus of synaptic DA, and the time course of the high paralleled that of the cocaine concentration. These studies confirm and extend previous, and somewhat more inferential, ones (Fowler et al. 1989). Thus, a unifying hypothesis is that reward euphoria constitutes a primary positive reinforcing property of addicting drugs and that this reward euphoria is referable to neuropharmacological facilitation of VTA-MFB-Acb DA brain reward mechanisms.

The Relationship Between Drug-Induced Reward and Nucleus Accumbens Dopaminergic Mechanisms: Some Caveats

Cautions concerning a direct or simple relationship between drug-induced enhancements of brain reward and forebrain (especially Acb)

DA mechanisms have been raised by several workers. The first general caution centers on studies in which in-vivo voltammetric electrochemistry (see Gardner, Chen, and Paredes, 1993) has been used to monitor Acb DA in laboratory animals during self-administered heroin, cocaine, or electrical brain stimulation reward. In the heroin and cocaine self-administration experiments, the voltammetrically detected Acb DA signal was found to rise before each self-administration of drug and to fall immediately upon receipt of the self-administered intravenous heroin or cocaine hit (Kiyatkin, Wise, and Gratton 1993; Gratton and Wise 1994; Gratton 1996). This pattern is 180 degrees out of phase with Acb DA responses to self-administered opiates or cocaine when the DA is measured by brief-sampling-time in-vivo brain microdialysis (Wise 1993; Wise et al. 1995a, 1995b). These exactly opposite findings are extremely difficult to reconcile, especially as they all (both the in-vivo electrochemistry findings and the in-vivo microdialysis findings) come from the same laboratories and group of investigators.

Faced with this conundrum, I am forced to place more reliance upon the microdialysis findings, in view of the possible contamination of the electrochemical DA signal by other chemical species that oxidize at the same voltage as DA (for example, 3,4-dihydroxyphenylacetic acid [DOPAC], ascorbic acid, uric acid) (see Gardner, Chen, and Paredes 1993). With voltammetry, the best that one can say is that the observed electrochemical signal is DA-like (in spite of ascorbate-rejecting and DOPAC-rejecting coatings on the recording electrode, high oxidation-reduction ratios, DA-like cyclic voltammogram footprints, and other stratagems). In contrast, with microdialysis one is sure that the observed signal is due to DA, because of the excellent separation of chemical species afforded by the chromatography columns (Gardner, Chen, and Paredes 1993).

Another, and quite different, interpretation of these in-vivo voltammetric electrochemistry findings is that functional heterogeneity exists within the VTA-MFB-Acb reward system, with some DA neurons firing to signal drug-induced satisfaction while other DA neurons within the reward circuitry firing to signal drug abstinence-induced craving (Gardner and Lowinson 1993).

Another caution centers on studies combining in-vivo voltammetric electrochemistry with self-administered electrical brain stimulation reward in laboratory animals (Wightman and Garris 1996; Kruk et al. 1998). Using this combination of techniques, Zygmunt Kruk and colleagues (1998) found no elevations in Acb DA during self-administered rewarding electrical brain stimulation in laboratory rats. R. Mark Wightman and Paul Garris (1996) did observe an elevated Acb DA electrochemical signal during self-administered rewarding electrical brain stimulation in laboratory rats, but it disappeared after the first few self-stimulations and never reappeared for the duration of the testing session, in spite of the continued avid self-delivery of the rewarding electrical stimulation by the animals. On the other hand, exogenous administration of the same trains of electrical brain stimulation that animals voluntarily self-administer have been reported to enhance forebrain DA voltammetric signals—but only when the voltammetric electrode was very carefully positioned to be extremely close to a synaptic site of DA release, so that diffusional distortion was eliminated and the DA molecules were detected before their rapid clearance from the extracellular space by the highly efficient DA reuptake carrier in the presynaptic membrane (Young and Michael 1993). To my mind, these studies—like those that paired in-vivo voltammetry with intravenous drug self-administration—must be interpreted with caution, due to the concerns about chemical identification with in-vivo voltammetric electrochemistry.

Another caution centers on studies using various reward paradigms in animals in which the DA transporter gene has been deleted from the animal's genome (so-called DA transporter knockout animals). Intravenous cocaine self-administration is unimpaired in DA transporter knockout mice (Rocha et al. 1998), and conditioned cue (place) preference to psychostimulants can be readily established in DA transporter knockout mice (Sora et al. 1998). Although such rewarding effects are undiminished, the locomotor effects of cocaine and amphetamine were completely abolished in such animals (Giros et al. 1996). However, as appealing as the knockout technology may be, interpretations are hampered by the fact that, from the time of gene deletion to the time of behavioral testing in adulthood, an entire life span exists during which neural compensations may take place by which other mechanisms take over the reward functions mediated in the normal animal by DA mechanisms (for example, the serotonergic system taking over some of the reward-mediating functions normally handled by the DA system).

Yet another caution centers on the fact that stress (presumably aversive to the animal) has been clearly shown to enhance Acb DA (Kalivas and Duffy 1995; Tidey and Miczek 1997). However, upon further examination, the relationship between environmental stress and Acb DA appears neither simple nor straightforward. First, the effect of environmental stress on forebrain DA is far more pronounced in the DA terminal fields of the prefrontal cortex than in Acb (Abercrombie et al. 1989; Cenci et al. 1992). Second, Acb DA and prefrontal cortex DA respond differently to different amounts of stress. That is, a small degree of stress elevates DA in both Acb and medial prefrontal cortex, while higher amounts of stress decrease Acb DA while further elevating prefrontal cortex DA (Kurata et al. 1993). Third, while Acb DA is elevated by stress, it is also elevated by relief from stress, and the stress-induced Acb DA elevation shows rapid tolerance while the relief from stress-induced Acb DA elevation shows no tolerance (Imperato et al. 1992a). Also, stress-induced Acb DA release shows a biphasic response elevation upon presentation of stress followed by DA depletion during prolonged stress (Puglisi-Allegra et al. 1991). On this basis, these workers postulate that the initial Acb DA elevation to stress may mediate an arousal or orienting function, while the subsequent Acb DA depletion may mediate a coping failure and the markedly diminished hedonic tone that is presumed to result from such failure. They also conclude that rewarding and aversive experiences are mediated by different DA neural systems. Fourth, addictive drug-induced Acb DA elevations are more pronounced than stress-induced Acb DA elevations (Shaham and Stewart 1996). Fifth, it has been known for decades that members of many mammalian species, including humans, deliberately seek out mild to moderate stress-inducing environmental stimuli. Roller coasters, automobile racing, skydiving, and giant slalom ski races are all testimonial to this tendency at the human level. Some individuals openly characterize their motives for participating in such potentially dangerous sports with comments such as "you haven't really lived until you get your adrenaline pumping," implying that (at least at some level) such stress-inducing pastimes are rewarding to their participants. Thus, while it is true that stress elevates Acb DA, the simplistic extrapolation that Acb DA therefore cannot mediate reward per se does not seem supportable.

Yet another caution centers on the mismatch observed between the effects of some drugs on electrical brain stimulation reward and on Acb DA levels as measured by in-vivo brain microdialysis (Gardner and Lowinson 1993). My colleagues and I have studied the effects of the addicting drugs phencyclidine and ketamine on brain reward thresholds in laboratory animals (Nazzaro, Seeger, and Gardner 1980; Gardner 1992) and observed dose-dependent bidirectional effects. At low doses, phencyclidine and ketamine enhance brain reward, whereas at higher doses they inhibit brain reward. We have observed a similar dose-dependent bidirectional effect on electrical brain reward thresholds with benzodiazepines and barbiturates and have suggested that this low-dose brain reward enhancement, high-dose brain reward inhibition is the laboratory animal homolog of the "low dose, good trip," "high dose, bad trip" phenomenon reported by both addicts and recreational users of these drugs. If a simple one-to-one correlation holds between enhanced brain reward and enhanced Acb DA, one would expect to find enhanced Acb DA as a result of phencyclidine doses that yield enhanced brain reward and decreased Acb DA as a result of phencyclidine doses that yield inhibited brain reward—but this is not what one sees. Using in-vivo brain microdialysis, both my group (Chen, Paredes, and Gardner 1993) and others (Carboni et al. 1989) find that phencyclidine produces only a dose-orderly increase in extracellular DA in forebrain reward loci, extending even to very high doses (for example, twenty mg. per kg.) that yield inhibited electrical brain stimulation reward (and are thus inferentially dysphorigenic).

A final caution centers on the fact that VTA-MFB-Acb DA reward-related mechanisms seem to encode a much more complex array of reward-related phenomena than the mere set point of hedonic tone (Schultz et al. 1992, 1993; Schultz, Apicella, and Ljungberg 1993; Chang et al. 1994; Mirenowicz and Schultz 1994; Schultz 1994).

Brain Reward Mechanisms During Chronic Drug Administration and Withdrawal

In contrast to the effects of acute administration of addicting drugs on brain reward mechanisms, the effects of chronic administration of addiction-producing drugs on reward mechanisms are even more complex. With respect to neurochemical indexes (in-vivo brain microdialysis measures of DA overflow in forebrain reward loci), a clear difference appears to exist between the effects of chronic intermittent versus chronic continuous administration (or chronic intermittent treatment involving high doses, which presumably produces continuous intoxication). With chronic intermittent low doses of psychostimulants (cocaine, amphetamines), reverse tolerance, or sensitization of DA overflow in the forebrain reward loci, is seen upon subsequent psychostimulant rechallenge (Akimoto, Hamamura, and Otsuki 1989; Horger et al. 1994; Kalivas and Duffy 1993; Parsons and Justice 1993; Paulson and Robinson 1995; Pettit and Pettit 1994; Pettit et al. 1990; Robinson et al. 1988; Wolf et al. 1993; Wolf et al. 1994). Similar psychostimulant neurochemical sensitization has been reported with self-administered, rather than exogenous, dosing (Hooks et al. 1994).

This sensitization may extend to basal DA overflow as well as drug challenge-evoked DA overflow (Weiss et al. 1992a; Parsons and Justice 1993). Similar sensitization of DA overflow in forebrain reward loci has been reported for opiates (Schrater et al. 1993; Spanagel and Shippenberg 1993). With chronic continuous administration (or chronic intermittent treatment involving high doses) of psychostimulants, there is decreased DA synthesis (Brock, Ng, and Justice 1990), and—in withdrawal from such dosing regimens—depletion of basal extracellular DA in such brain reward loci as Acb (Parsons et al. 1991; Robertson,

Leslie, and Bennett 1991; Imperato et al. 1992b; Weiss et al. 1992b). When cocaine is administered to emulate human binges, decreased basal and cocaine stimulated DA levels are reported (Maisonneuve and Kreek 1994). Reward-related functional and behavioral sequelae have also been reported.

With continuous treatment or intermittent treatment with high doses, acute tolerance to cocaine's rewarding effects develops (Fischman et al. 1985; Emmett-Oglesby and Lane 1992), and withdrawal from the continuous intoxication produced by frequent low-dose cocaine or amphetamine produces elevations in brain stimulation reward thresholds (functional inhibition of brain reward functions, or dysphoric effects) (Leith and Barrett 1976; Simpson and Annau 1977; Barrett and White 1980; Kokkinidis, Zacharko, and Predy 1980; Cassens et al. 1981; Frank, Martz, and Pommering 1988; Kokkinidis and McCarter 1990; Wise and Munn 1995). In opiate withdrawal from chronic dosing regimens (either abstinence withdrawal or precipitated withdrawal), a pattern of decreased DA levels in forebrain reward loci (particularly Acb) similar to that seen in withdrawal from continuous or high-dose intermittent psychostimulant administration is seen (Pothos et al. 1991; Acquas and Di Chiara 1992; Rossetti, Hmaidan, and Gessa 1992; Crippens and Robinson 1994; Spanagel et al. 1994). Clear reward-related functional and behavioral sequelae are also seen in opiate withdrawal (elevations in electrical brain reward thresholds, or dysphoric effects [Schaefer and Michael 1986; Schulteis et al. 1994]). Also, opiate withdrawal produces conditioned cue aversion (Mucha 1987; Koob et al. 1989a; Stinus, Le Moal, and Koob 1990; Higgins et al. 1991; Harris and Aston-Jones 1993; Higgins, Nguyen, and Sellers 1992; Schulteis et al. 1994; Spanagel et al. 1994; Kelsey and Arnold 1994; Kosten 1994; Nader et al. 1994).

Self-administered opiate intake increases significantly in withdrawal, and the degree of increase correlates with severity of withdrawal (Young et al. 1977; Dai et al. 1989; Shaham 1993). Significantly, the neural mechanisms underlying this withdrawal-produced presumptive negative hedonic tone or dysphoria may involve the Acb (Koob et al. 1989a; Koob, Wall, and Bloom 1989b; Stinus, Le Moal, and Koob 1990), just as the acute drug-induced positive hedonic tone does. Congruent with these findings from a variety of paradigms, DA depletion in Acb and elevation in brain reward thresholds have been proposed as neural substrates for post-drug-use anhedonia and drug craving (Dackis and Gold 1985; Koob et al. 1989a; Markou and Koob 1991). Since DA depletion, unlike other withdrawal symptoms (Kalant 1977), offers a withdrawal symptom common to psychostimulants, opiates, and ethanol, it may offer a long-sought common denominator for addiction (Wise 1987a). Adding credence to this possibility are findings from the studies in which animals are allowed to self-administer intravenous cocaine or heroin and in-vivo DA neurochemistry is concomitantly monitored in Acb by brief sampling time microdialysis (Wise 1993; Wise et al. 1995a, 1995b). These studies show that Acb DA decreases before—and appears to predict—each drug self-administration, whereas Acb DA increases immediately after each drug self-administration and appears to correlate with behavioral indexes of satiation.

Brain Reward Mechanisms and Drug Craving

From the aforementioned evidence, and from the opponent process theory (Solomon and Corbit 1974; Solomon 1980), George Koob and colleagues have proposed an opponent process theory of the motivation for drug taking (Koob and Bloom 1988; Koob et al. 1989a, 1993; Markou and Koob 1991). This theory is based upon the negative reinforcement (relief from aversive stimuli) that drug taking produces in the face of the dysphoria and anhedonia imputed from the evidence. The theory holds that drug reinforcers arouse both positive (appetitive, pleasurable) and negative (aversive, dysphoric) hedonic processes in the brain, and that these processes oppose one another in a simple dynamic system. The time dynamics and tolerance patterns of the two processes are hypothesized to differ. The positive hedonic processes are hypothesized to be simple, stable, and of short latency and duration, to follow the reinforcer closely, and to develop tolerance rapidly. The negative hedonic processes are hypothesized to be of longer latency and duration (thus, they build up strength and decay more slowly) and to be resistant to the development of tolerance.

Thus, if self-administration of an addictive drug is frequently repeated, two correlated changes in hedonic tone are postulated to occur. Tolerance to the euphoric effects of the drug develops, while at the same time the withdrawal or abstinence syndrome becomes more intense and of longer duration (Koob and Bloom 1988; Koob et al. 1989a, 1993; Markou and Koob 1991). Thus, the positive reinforcing properties of the drug diminish, while the negative reinforcing properties (relief of withdrawal-induced anhedonia) strengthen. It is proposed that not only are the positive reinforcing properties of addicting drugs mediated by drug effects in Acb but that opponent processes within these same brain reward circuits become sensitized during the development of dependence. These opponent processes become responsible for the aversive stimulus properties of drug withdrawal and, therefore, ultimately for the negative reinforcement processes that come, in this view, to dominate the motivation for chronic drug addiction. Thus, brain reward mechanisms, and the regulatory neural mechanisms controlling them, are conceptualized to dominate not only the positively reinforcing acute hit, rush, or high resulting from early administration but also the negatively reinforcing properties that develop with chronic drug use and that are important in the maintenance of drug habits. George Koob and colleagues have postulated that endogenous opioid peptide mechanisms intrinsic to, and synaptically interacting with, the DA reward circuitry of the forebrain are critically involved in this opponent process motivation for drug dependence and addiction. (Such negative hedonic processes within the reward-encoding circuitry of the brain must differ from the aversive physical abstinence symptoms produced by drug withdrawal, which are mediated by non-reward-related neural circuitry involving the periaqueductal gray, locus coeruleus, medial thalamus, and the diencephalic-mesencephalic juncture [Wei, Loh, and Way 1973; Bozarth and Wise 1984; De Vry, Donselaar, and Van Ree 1989; Bozarth 1994]).

Congruent with this concept, my co-workers and I have gathered evidence, using both in-vivo electrical brain stimulation reward and in-vivo brain voltammetric electrochemistry, suggesting that drug administration does evoke both positive and negative affective hedonic processes within the pleasure-reward DA circuitry of the forebrain (Nazzaro, Seeger, and Gardner 1980, 1981; Gardner 1992; Gardner and Lowinson 1993). Medial brain reward DA circuitry, originating in VTA and projecting through the medial portions of MFB to Acb, appears uniquely sensitive to the brain reward-enhancing properties of addicting drugs. With electrodes in the lateral portions of the reward circuitry, opiates inhibited brain stimulation reward (were dysphorigenic), this inhibition dissipated as time passed following each daily injection, and a progressive augmentation of this brain reward inhibition developed with repeated daily injections. Both the medial and lateral loci are DA-mediated (Eichler, Antelman, and Fisher 1976; Ettenberg and Wise 1976; Seeger and Gardner 1979; Gardner, Walker, and Paredes 1993). Thus, these two anatomic domains (medial and lateral) within the DA reward circuitry of the ventromedial forebrain respond to drug administration in a manner consistent with the predicted behavior of the positive hedonic processes and negative hedonic processes (Koob and Bloom 1988; Koob et al. 1989a, 1993; Markou and Koob 1991).

Using in-vivo voltammetric electrochemistry, my colleagues and I found that some DA reward neurons responded to drug administration by inhibition of DA overflow while other DA neurons within the same circuitry (but anatomically distinct) responded to drug administration by enhancement of DA overflow (Broderick 1985; Gardner 1992; Gardner and Lowinson 1993). Congruent with these observations are electrophysiological data showing that some DA reward neurons respond to opiate administration by inhibiting their firing (Ostrowski et al. 1982) rather than by the enhanced firing (Gysling and Wang 1983; Matthews and German 1984; Gardner 1997) normally seen. This, in turn, is congruent with reports from Donald Woodward (Chang et al. 1994) and Wolfram Schultz (Mirenowicz and Schultz 1994; Schultz et al. 1992, 1993; Schultz, Apicella, and Ljungberg 1993; Schultz 1994) concerning the heterogeneity of response patterns of reward-related DA neurons in Acb.

A closely related concept to this opponent process anhedonia is that of craving. Craving is experienced by chronic drug addicts when they have been drug deprived for a period of time and is often elicited by sensory stimuli previously associated with drug taking. Conditioning paradigms have been used to model craving in laboratory animals, especially conditioned cue (place) preference (Bozarth 1987; Phillips and Fibiger 1987; van der Kooy 1987). In this paradigm, animals are tested (when free of drug) to determine whether they prefer an environment in which they previously received drug as compared to an environment in which they previously received saline or vehicle. If the animal, in the drug-free state, consistently chooses the environment previously associated with drug delivery, the inference is drawn not only that the drug was appetitive but also that the appetitive hedonic value was coded in the brain and is accessible during the drug-free state, which, if not craving per se, would appear to be closely related to craving. The questions arise: Is craving coded in the same neural circuitry as drug-induced reward? Do pharmacological manipulations or lesions of the reward-relevant DA circuitry alter conditioned cue preferences induced by addicting drugs?

Many postulate that craving is coded in the reward circuitry and results directly from functional deficiency of DA in the reward DA circuitry (Dackis and Gold 1985). It is also clear that DA pharmacological manipulations or lesions profoundly alter place conditioning for addicting drugs and that the DA system serves as an important substrate for the central encoding of the hedonic value imparted by addicting drugs (Phillips and Fibiger 1987). Further, Norman White and Noboru Hiroi have shown (Hiroi 1990; Hiroi and White 1990; Hiroi, McDonald, and White 1990; White and Hiroi 1993) that different aspects of conditioned hedonic value appear to depend upon different neurochemically specific DA substrates. Specifically, in amphetamine cue conditioning, the newly synthesized DA pool appears to subserve the neural encoding of hedonic value, while the vesicular DA pool appears crucial for the behavioral expression, or readout, of that previously encoded hedonic value. Also, while systemically administered D1 and D2 DA receptor antagonists block both the acquisition and the expression of conditioned cue preference, selective D1 antagonism is more effective at blocking the behavioral expression of previously encoded hedonic value than D2 antagonists. Also, preconditioning and postconditioning lesions of the lateral amygdaloid nucleus impair amphetamine-conditioned cue preference. Thus, behavioral expression of conditioned incentive stimuli for amphetamine (the animal homolog of amphetamine craving) is mediated by a DA neural system involving the vesicular DA pool and the D1 DA receptor in Acb and the lateral amygdaloid nucleus (Hiroi 1990; Hiroi and White 1990; Hiroi, McDonald, and White 1990; White and Hiroi 1993).

I have argued (Gardner and Lowinson 1993) that drug craving is functionally modulated by a complex interaction between multiple DA systems within the pleasure-reward DA circuitry of the forebrain and that some (but not all) drug craving is referable to DA hypofunctionality in brain reward systems. Additionally, with respect to DA function in forebrain pleasure-reward circuitry and its relation to drug craving or drug-taking vulnerability, the work of Eric Nestler and colleagues should be noted (Beitner-Johnson, Guitart, and Nestler 1991; Guitart et al. 1992, 1993; Beitner-Johnson and Nestler 1993; Nestler 1993, 1994; Kosten et al. 1994; Nestler et al. 1994; Self et al. 1994; Self and Nestler 1995), as they have found that—in addition to other neurobiological changes at the level of DA-stimulated receptor-linked G proteins, second messengers, and protein kinases—animals rendered vulnerable to the rewarding effects of addicting drugs (by either genetic inbreeding or repeated administration of addicting drugs) show marked deficiencies in DA precursor transport, tyrosine hydroxylase activity, and DA release from axon terminals of reward-related DA neurons in Acb.

The Relationship Between Dopaminergic Hypofunctionality and Drug Craving: Some Caveats

Cautions concerning a simple relationship between DA hypofunctionality and drug craving are warranted. First, clinical observations and subjective self-reports suggest that there are many subjectively different craving states—some dysphoric, some hedonically neutral, and some pleasurable. Second, from both human and animal studies, there appears to be a wide variety of stimuli capable of triggering drug craving, including sensory stimuli previously associated with drug taking, stress, and small, priming drug doses. For present purposes, it is important simply to note that the two most robust stimuli for triggering reinstatement of drug self-administration in animals (such reinstatement being operationally taken as the animal homolog of craving) are stimuli (stress or a priming drug dose) that increase rather than decrease DA function within the brain's reward circuitry (Gardner 1997).

Thus, the reinstatement phenomenon appears inconsistent with the hypo-DA hypothesis of craving. Equally inconsistent with the hypo-DA hypothesis is the mismatch between the time course of craving and the time course of synaptic DA function after cocaine administration. Frank Gawin and Herbert Kleber (1986) have rated the duration and intensity of symptoms, including cocaine craving, following cocaine self-administration binges in chronic cocaine users. They found that following a cocaine binge a period of essentially immediate high cocaine craving occurs, with typical onset within fifteen to thirty minutes of the last cocaine administration and typical waning duration of a few hours. There then ensues a period of intense dysphoria (the crash), initially consisting of dysphoric agitation, which yields within hours to dysphoric lethargy and anergia, lasting for three to six days and characterized by no cocaine craving or even cocaine abhorrence. After the crash, a period of one to five days of near-normal mood and functioning occurs, during which there is either no or very little cocaine craving. There then ensues a period, lasting from one to ten weeks, of fluctuating mood with substantial anhedonia, dysphoria, and anxiety, coupled with high cocaine craving. An indefinite period of normal hedonic functioning then follows, coupled with episodic cocaine craving (often triggered by conditioned cues).

In broad outline, this description of the time course and associated clinical phenomena of the cocaine binge, crash, and postcrash periods is congruent with other published descriptions (Siegel 1982; Dackis, Gold, and Sweeney 1987; Jaffe et al. 1989). If any simple interpretation of the hypo-DA hypothesis of cocaine craving were correct, extracellular synaptic Acb DA levels should correlate temporally with the waxing and waning of cocaine craving, but they appear not to do so (Roy et al. 1978; Pettit et al. 1990; Parsons et al. 1991).

Brain Reward Mechanisms and Expectancy of Reward

Complicating this picture even more is evidence (Chang et al. 1994; Mirenowicz and Schultz 1994; Schultz et al. 1992; Schultz et al. 1993; Schultz, Apicella, and Ljungberg 1993; Schultz 1994; Richardson and Gratton 1996) that these DA reward-related neurons may be functionally heterogeneous, with some neurons encoding reward magnitude per se while others encode expectancy of reward, errors in reward-prediction, prioritized reward, and other more complex aspects of reward-driven learning, memory, and incentive motivation. While these complexities of function within the reward substrates of the forebrain do appear to exist, it seems equally clear (on the basis of evidence cited previously and also that of Wise and Rompré 1989; Wise 1996; Gardner 1997; Shizgal 1997) that one of the primary functions of those reward substrates is to compute hedonic tone and neural payoffs, that this computation takes place in large measure within the MFB-associated circuits delineated earlier, that the second-stage DA component is the common site of action for addicting drugs and crucial to their addictive features, that drug reward per se and drug potentiation of electrical brain stimulation reward have common mechanisms, and that electrical brain stimulation reward and the pharmacological rewards of addicting drugs are habit forming because they act in the brain circuits that subserve more natural, biologically significant rewards (Kornetsky and Bain 1992; Kornetsky and Duvauchelle 1994; Wise 1996; Shizgal 1997).

The fact that some DA neurons encode expectancy of reward is especially provocative, as it implies that dysfunctions within these circuits may give rise to erroneous computations of reward expectancy, which may in turn relate to the aberrant drug cravings observed so commonly in drug addiction. Satisfying such aberrant neural expectancies, then, may be a necessary component of any successful pharmacotherapy for addiction.

Emotional Memory, Drug Craving, and Drug Seeking

The brain structure known as the amygdala has been implicated in the behavioral expression, or readout, of conditioned incentive stimuli for amphetamine (amphetamine-induced place preference, an animal homolog of amphetamine craving). This is exceedingly provocative. The amygdala is a large subcortical structure located deep within each temporal lobe and has long been implicated in the neural substrates of emotion (Papez 1937; MacLean 1955; Kupfermann 1991). Ample evidence exists that the amygdala is strongly involved in mediating neural substrates of fear and anxiety (LeDoux et al. 1988; Davis 1992), and recent evidence suggests that elevations of corticotropin-releasing factor (CRF) in the central nucleus of the amygdala may be a common feature of withdrawal from addicting drugs and may mediate the dysphoric subjective state associated with drug withdrawal (Koob et al. 1993; Merlo Pich et al. 1995; Koob 1996). In recent years, the amygdala has been specifically implicated in subserving emotional learning and memory. For example, damage to the central nucleus of the amygdala interferes with the ability to form a conditioned emotional response (LeDoux 1989), and single-neuron electrical recording studies have shown that amygdaloid neurons become selectively active when emotionally relevant stimuli, such as the sight of a device previously used to squirt a sweet solution into the animal's mouth, are presented (O'Keefe and Bouma 1969).

Work by a number of research groups has convincingly demonstrated that portions of the amygdala constitute the neural substrates of an emotional memory system that functions to facilitate stimulus-reward learning (Cador, Robbins, and Everitt 1989; Everitt, Cador, and Robbins 1989; Gaffan 1992) and drug-seeking behavior (Hiroi and White 1991; White and Hiroi 1993). Since the amygdala interacts closely with the Acb to form stimulus-reward associations (Cador, Robbins, and Everitt 1989; Everitt, Cador, and Robbins 1989), it is highly probable that amygdala-encoded emotional memories regulate (in homeostatic fashion) the set point for hedonic tone. Indeed, I have presented evidence (from electrical brain stimulation reward studies in monkeys in which VTA-MFB-Acb brain reward thresholds were significantly modulated by concurrent electrical stimulation of the amygdala) that this is so (Jackson and Gardner 1974). Thus, we may well be on the way to understanding the neural basis for the strong drug cravings evoked by drug-associated environmental cues and the translation of the emotional memories encoded in the brain by such cues into drug-seeking behavior.

Brain Reward Mechanisms and the Reinstatement of Drug Taking (Relapse)

The phenomenon of drug priming—the ability of a priming drug dose to reinstate previously extinguished drug taking—has been studied in laboratory animals as a model of relapse to drug taking (Gerber and Stretch 1975; de Wit and Stewart 1981, 1983; Stewart 1983; Stewart and de Wit 1987). In this paradigm, the ability of drugs (or other stimuli, including stressors [Shaham and Stewart 1995, 1996; Erb et al. 1996; Shaham et al. 1996] and drug-associated sensory stimuli) to reestablish extinguished drug-taking habits in laboratory animals is measured. As noted by Jane Stewart and Roy Wise (1992), "the most potent stimulus for renewed responding that has been demonstrated in this model is a free 'priming' injection of the training drug; a priming injection of the training drug can reestablish extinguished habits much as a single drink, cigarette, or injection are thought to reestablish such habits in detoxified ex-addicts" (Stewart and Wise 1992, 80).

Provocatively, such priming injections can be successfully given intravenously or directly into component parts of the brain reward circuitry, such as VTA or Acb. The pleasure-reward reinforcement circuitry is crucial for this triggered relapse. Priming microinjections into non-reward-related brain loci do not produce reinstatement of intravenous drug taking. Equally provocatively, successful cross-priming has been demonstrated. For example, priming doses of morphine reinstate cocaine self-administration (Stewart 1984) and priming doses of amphetamine or of the DA agonist bromocriptine reinstate heroin-trained responding (Stewart and Vezina 1988; Wise, Murray, and Bozarth 1990). Such cross-priming between drugs of different classes speaks to the existence of common neurobiological substrates within the DA reward circuitry of the brain, and the drugs and doses known to reinitiate drug self-administration in both humans and animals are drugs and doses known to increase DA function within the brain's reward circuitry (Gardner 1997). Thus, acute administration of either strong DA-mimetic compounds or stress (which enhances Acb DA) precipitates relapse to drug taking, just as acute heroin precipitates clinical relapse in human opiate addicts. Equally important, though, the drugs and doses that successfully trigger relapse are those with short-acting pharmacodynamic profiles.

Genetic Contributions to Vulnerability to Drug Taking

For many addictive drugs, genetic differences influence both drug preferences and propensity for drug self-administration (Li and Lumeng 1984; Ritz et al. 1986; Cannon and Carrell 1987; George 1987; Suzuki, George, and Meisch 1988). For example, mouse strains that show high ethanol preference and high ethanol self-administration appear to generalize this increased vulnerability to other addicting drugs such as nicotine and opiates (George and Meisch 1984; Khodzhagel'diev 1986; George 1987). This suggests that some inbred animal strains may have a generalized vulnerability to the rewarding effects of addictive drugs. The Lewis rat strain is particularly interesting in this regard. Lewis strain rats have a high vulnerability for both ethanol and cocaine oral self-administration (George and Meisch 1984; George and Goldberg 1989). Furthermore, Lewis rats also learn cocaine or opiate self-administration more readily, work harder for cocaine or opiate self-administration, and cue condition for cocaine or opiates more readily, all in comparison to other rat strains (George and Goldberg 1989; Nestler 1993; Kosten et al. 1994). My own research group has reported that the brain reward-enhancing property of Δ^9-tetrahydrocannabinol, the addictive substance in marijuana and hashish, is much more pronounced in Lewis rats than in other strains, as measured both by direct electrical brain stimulation reward and by in-vivo brain microdialysis of synaptic DA overflow in

Acb DA reward loci (Gardner et al. 1988; Gardner and Lowinson 1991; Chen et al. 1991; Lepore et al. 1996). These findings suggest that a basal dysfunction in DA regulation within the DA forebrain reward system may constitute a genetic vulnerability to the phenotypic polydrug preferences shown by Lewis rats (Lepore et al. 1996).

Congruent with this hypothesis, Nestler and colleagues have reported basal differences in DA neurotransmitter synthesis, transport, and release as well as DA-dependent receptor, second messenger, and immediate early gene function in DA reward neurons in Lewis as compared to other rat strains (Nestler 1993; Guitart et al. 1992). Compellingly, the same dysfunctional differences in DA neurotransmitter synthesis, transport, and release, as well as DA-dependent receptor, second messenger, and immediate early gene function in DA reward neurons can be induced by chronic cocaine administration in genetically nonvulnerable rats, and this results in the same behavioral phenotype of polydrug preference as seen in the genetically vulnerable rats (Nestler 1993; Lepore and Gardner 1995). Genetic contributions also appear to play a role in vulnerability to drug addiction at the human level (George and Goldberg 1989). Family, twin, and adoption studies all support a substantial genetic component in vulnerability to drug addiction and ongoing drug dependence (reviewed in Uhl et al. 1995).

Identifying genetic factors in vulnerability to drug addiction is crucial to understanding addiction and, possibly, to identifying clinical subpopulations who may respond differently to potential pharmacotherapies. Linkage analysis in well-defined pedigrees is a powerful approach for studying single gene disorders (Krugylak and Lander 1995). However, for complex inherited traits, association studies, which are statistical correlations between an inherited condition and polymorphisms occurring in strong candidate genes, may be a superior approach (Lander and Schork 1994; Elston 1995). As vulnerability to drug addiction does not follow clear Mendelian patterns of inheritance, most genetic studies on drug addiction have been association studies. Considering the wealth of preclinical data demonstrating the importance of DA in brain reward mechanisms, polymorphisms in genes that regulate DA neurotransmission are candidates as genetic vulnerability factors for drug addiction (Koob and Bloom 1988).

The genes for the DA D2 and D4 receptors and the DA transporter are some of the candidate genes that have been analyzed. An allelic association to Taq I restriction fragment length polymorphisms (RFLPs) located in the D2 receptor gene has been found in alcoholics and drug addicts in some studies (Blum et al. 1990; Smith et al. 1992; Noble 1993; Uhl et al. 1994). These results are controversial, as negative association and linkage studies have also been reported (Bolos et al. 1990; Suarez et al. 1994).

However, a meta-analysis conducted on published studies supports a positive association to the D2 Taq A1 and B1 alleles (Uhl et al. 1994). Also, an association of nicotine dependent behavior to the D2 Taq A1 allele has been reported (Comings et al. 1996a). One problem with these polymorphisms is that they are generated by nonfunctional intronic mutations. Thus, if the D2 gene is involved in vulnerability to drug addiction, the Taq polymorphisms must be in linkage disequilibrium with functional alterations located elsewhere in the gene. So far, none have been found.

An additional DA D2 receptor polymorphism—involving the Taq A4 allelic site—in drug addiction and alcoholism has also been reported (Persico et al. 1993). A VNTR polymorphism in the 3' untranslated region of the DA transporter (DAT) gene, which has been linked to attention deficit hyperactivity disorder (ADHD), has shown a weak association in alcoholics who have specific aldehyde dehydrogenase-2 genotypes and in cocaine-induced paranoia (Vandenbergh et al. 1992; Gelernter et al. 1994; Cook et al. 1995; Muramatsu and Higuchi 1995). However, another association study in polydrug addicts was negative (Persico et al. 1993). An association with ADHD would be interesting, since a high percentage of children and adolescents with this condition become drug addicts. However, the VNTR polymorphism is nonfunctional, and so far no significant alterations in the gene have been found that explain the positive linkage and association findings. A VNTR in the third cytoplasmic loop of the D4 gene has been reported to be associated with both alcoholism and novelty seeking behavior (Benjamin et al. 1996; Ebstein et al. 1996). The D4 gene differs from other candidate genes analyzed so far in that the polymorphism has been shown to be functionally significant, in vitro, as differences in atypical neuroleptic binding have been found in the four and seven repeat polymorphisms (Van Tol et al. 1992).

There is also evidence that the D4 polymorphism is functionally significant, in vivo, since it is associated with the behavioral trait of thrill seeking (Benjamin et al. 1996; Ebstein et al. 1996). No association to D4 was detected in a study conducted on alcoholics (Adamson et al. 1995). The DA D3 receptor gene has been found to have a common missense mutation that leads to a serine-glycine substitution (Lannfelt et al. 1992). Thus far, no significant association has been reported in drug or alcohol addicts (Rietschel et al. 1993). Another possible DA-related candidate gene for drug addiction vulnerability is that for catechol-O-methyltransferase (COMT). COMT plays an important role in regulating DA neurotransmission by inactivating synaptic DA (Axelrod and Tomchick 1958). A common COMT polymorphism exists in humans that results in a threefold to fourfold variation in COMT (Weinshilboum and Raymond 1977; Scanlon, Raymond, and Weinshilboum 1979; Spielman and Weinshilboum 1981; Boudikova et al. 1990; Aksoy, Kleiner, and Weinshilboum 1993). Approximately 25 percent of Caucasians express a low activity form of COMT, another 25 percent have a high activity variant, and 50 percent display an intermediate level of activity (Boudikova et al. 1990; Aksoy, Kleiner, and Weinshilboum 1993).

To identify the genetic basis of this enzyme activity variability, Lachman and colleagues at the Albert Einstein College of Medicine systematically screened the COMT gene by DNA sequence analysis of PCR-amplified genomic fragments, to identify allelic forms of the gene. A G → A transition was found at codon 158 of MB-COMT (corresponding to codon 108 of S-COMT) that results in a valine to methionine substitution. In retrospect, the two alleles are evident from a comparison of the two COMT cDNA sequences published several years ago (Bertocci et al. 1991; Lundstrom et al. 1991). For reasons outlined above, it was felt that an analysis of the COMT functional polymorphism in drug addiction vulnerability would be of interest. Lachman and co-workers have recently completed such an analysis, finding a significant increase in the frequency of COMT158[val], the high activity allele, in drug addicts. Approximately 40 percent of drug addicts were homozygous for COMT158[val] compared with 25 percent of controls (Vandenbergh et al. 1997a). This genetic association correlates with polydrug addiction, being found in both opiate-preferring and cocaine-preferring addicts. This finding is consistent with the hypothesis that blunted DA reward systems enhance vulnerability to drug addiction, as Schuckitt (1994) has found for ethanol responsiveness in alcoholics and sons of alcoholics, since expression of the high activity COMT variant would magnify the decrease in DA.

Behavioral (Nonchemical) Addictions and DA Brain Reward Substrates

It has become increasingly obvious that significant associations may exist between the chemical (drug, alcohol) addictions and certain repetitive compulsive behavioral syndromes such as compulsive or pathological gambling, compulsive overeating, compulsive sexual behavior, and even compulsive shopping. Such behavioral syndromes are, in fact, now being referred to as behavioral addictions or addictive spectrum disorders by some authorities (Bayle et al. 1996), in large measure because of such similarities.

First, there is the sometimes striking similarity in behavioral morphology and cognitive set between such behavioral addictions and the chemical addictions—including the all-encompassing, driven, compulsive, repetitious quality of the behavioral acts themselves and the obsessional thought processes therewith associated, plus the craving for the addictive behavioral pattern that is often reported when the individual is deprived of it. Second, it has become increasingly evident that substantial comorbidity exists between drug or alcohol addiction and at least some of the behavioral addictions, most especially pathological gambling (Feigelman et al. 1995; Spunt et al. 1995; Bayle et al. 1996; Comings et al. 1996b; Daghestani, Elenz, and Crayton 1996; Rupcich, Frisch, and Govoni 1997). Less compelling, though still provocative, is evidence for comorbidity among the behavioral addictions (Specker et al. 1995), evidence that behavioral addictions respond to the same twelve-step psychosocial therapeutic modalities found useful in treating the chemical addictions (Lopez Viets and Miller 1997), and the high comorbidity between the behavioral addictions and impulse control disorder (similar to the comorbidity between the chemical addictions and impulse control disorder) (Hollander and Wong 1995; Knecht 1995; Specker et al. 1995; Blaszczynski, Steele, and McConaghy 1997).

Given these commonalities, it may well be wondered whether any evidence exists for an involvement of abnormalities in DA brain reward substrates in the behavioral addictions. Although far from conclusive, the preliminary evidence—from several laboratory groups—appears to be in the affirmative. In pathological gambling, Kenneth Blum, David Comings, and colleagues have reported significant DA D2 receptor allelic variants congruent with a net decrease in overall DA function (Blum et al. 1995, 1996a, 1996b; Comings et al. 1996b) and a significant DA D1 receptor polymorphism (Comings et al. 1997). A Swedish research group has reported decreased cerebrospinal DA in pathological gamblers (Bergh et al. 1997), and a Spanish group has reported a significant association between genetic variants at a DA D4 receptor gene polymorphism and pathological gambling (Perez de Castro et al. 1997).

Another Spanish group has reported decreased monoamine oxidase (that catabolizes DA) activity in pathological gamblers (Carrasco et al. 1994; Blanco et al. 1996), which could be interpreted as a compensation for decreased basal DA function. In compulsive overeating, David Comings and colleagues have reported DA D2 receptor allelic variants (Comings et al. 1993; Blum et al. 1995) and a significant DA D1 receptor polymorphism (Comings et al. 1997). In compulsive shopping, the same group found a significant DA D1 receptor polymorphism (Comings et al. 1997). However, in compulsive sexual behavior, a single report exists of significantly increased serum and urinary levels of DA and the DA metabolite 3,4-dihydroxyphenylacetic acid (DOPAC) (Kogan et al. 1995). Provocatively, patients with ADHD or conduct disorder are reported to possess the D2 A1 receptor allele, congruent with a net reduction in overall basal DA neural activity (Comings et al. 1991, 1996c; Blum et al.

1995; Comings 1995, 1997). This is interesting, as ADHD and conduct disorder have been unequivocally identified as major adolescent risk factors for drug and alcohol addiction (see, for example, Whitmore et al. 1997; Crowley et al. 1998).

The Reward Deficiency Syndrome: A Possible Generalized DA Hypofunctionality Syndrome Subsuming Drug Addiction, Nonchemical (Behavioral) Addictions, and Cocaine Dependence

Kenneth Blum and his colleagues (Blum et al. 1995, 1996a, 1996b) have postulated the existence of a generalized reward deficiency syndrome, subsuming a large class of addictive, impulsive, and compulsive disorders under a common rubric and positing that they have a common genetic basis. They postulate that all these disorders are connected by a common biological substrate—an alteration in a hard-wired system in the brain that provides positive reinforcement (positive hedonic tone) for specific behaviors. They further postulate that reward deficiency syndrome results from a basal dysfunction of DA brain reward mechanisms.

Evidence cited in support of this hypothesis includes:

1. All addicting drugs, which produce augmented hedonic tone, have one major commonality: They augment DA function as a final common neuropharmacological action (via different specific sites and mechanisms of action), particularly in the VTA-MFB-Acb DA mesolimbic system so important in reward (Koob and Bloom 1988; Gardner 1997).

2. As my colleagues (Minabe, Emori, and Ashby 1995) and others (Beitner-Johnson, Guitart, and Nestler 1991) have shown, using both electrophysiological and molecular biological approaches, considerable differences exist in the DA reward systems of drug-preferring versus nonpreferring genetic strains of rats.

3. Alcoholics, cocaine addicts, compulsive gamblers, and patients with obesity (a majority being compulsive eaters) or ADHD are reported to possess the A1 D2 receptor allele (Comings et al. 1991; Noble et al. 1991, 1993, 1994; Comings et al. 1996b). The number of D2 receptors in A1 carriers may be 20 to 30 percent lower than those lacking the A1 genotype (Noble et al. 1991). Also, the likelihood that an individual possesses the A1 genotype increases dramatically when two or more of the clinical conditions are found to coexist.

4. Animal studies have shown that DA agonists can decrease the consumption or self-administration of various addictive drugs or reduce drug seeking (Dyr et al. 1993; McBride et al. 1993b; Pulvirenti and Koob 1994). The results of studies in humans regarding the efficacy of DA agonists in the treatment of drug addiction and symptoms of drug withdrawal have been mixed, with many negative reports. However, it has been postulated that this may be related to genotype, as alcoholics possessing the A1-A1 genotype are more responsive to the DA agonist bromocriptine for treatment of alcohol craving than matched alcoholics lacking the A1-A1 genotype (Lawford et al. 1995).

Provocatively, a predictive model based on Bayes's theorem of probability suggests that an individual with the A1 allele for the D2 receptor has a 74 percent chance of developing one of the disorders that compose reward deficiency syndrome (Blum et al. 1996a). Genetic mapping suggests that a possible locus for one of the genes that confer susceptibility to this syndrome—and more specifically for present purposes, to cocaine addiction—may be on the q22–q23 region of human chromosome 11 (Noble et al. 1993). In sum, the reward deficiency syndrome theory holds that addictive, impulsive, and compulsive disorders may have a common genetic basis—DA hypoactivity in reward pathways. Based on this, one would predict that DA substitution (direct or indirect) might decrease drug taking or craving, perhaps only (or more markedly) in genetically vulnerable subjects (either animal or human).

Personality and Temperament Traits that Predispose to Drug Addiction and Their Relation to DA Brain Reward Substrates

If, as predicted by the reward deficiency syndrome hypothesis, individuals with vulnerability to addictions suffer from a basal functional DA deficit in central brain reward circuits, it would not be unreasonable to inquire about the possible existence of temperamental or behavioral compensations that might serve to augment brain reward functions. Although this leap from neurogenetics and cellular neurobiology to temperament and personality characteristics may seem enormous, evidence has accumulated in recent years to suggest that such correlations may well exist.

A crucial concept in this area is that of novelty seeking. The mammalian nervous system appears to be biologically programmed to attend to novel information more readily than to familiar information. For example, human subjects respond more rapidly to novel auditory stimuli than to familiar repetitive stimuli (Tiitinen et al. 1994). In the

1950s, Harry Harlow and colleagues showed that nonhuman primates are intensely attracted to novel environmental stimuli (Harlow 1950). In fact, novel environmental stimuli can serve as effective behavioral reinforcers in rhesus moneys (Butler 1957a), and the rewarding effect of such stimuli is enhanced by being deprived of such stimuli (Butler 1957b), in much the same way that the reward value of other natural reinforcers (for example, food) is strengthened by deprivation. In rodents, too, novelty is a clear reinforcer (Berlyne 1955; Hughes 1968).

At the human level, the personality theorist Hans Eysenck observed in the early 1950s that marked interindividual differences in novelty seeking appear to exist (Eysenck 1953). Building upon that observation, research psychologists have devised a number of rating scales to measure this trait. Two that have been widely used for research purposes are the Zuckerman Sensation Seeking Scale (Zuckerman 1979, 1994), and the Cloninger Novelty Seeking Scale (Cloninger 1987a, 1987b; Cloninger et al. 1994). The Zuckerman scale has four subscales: thrill and adventure seeking, involving physically risky activities and novel experiences; experience seeking, involving unconventional lifestyles, friends, art, music, and travel; disinhibition, involving frequent social interactions, parties, and multiple sex partners; and boredom susceptibility, involving aversion to unchanging situations. The Zuckerman scale correlates significantly with the Cloninger scale (McCourt, Gurrera, and Cutter 1993). Both correlate highly with overt novelty-seeking behaviors and even with such overtly risky behaviors as mountain climbing, skydiving, and automobile racing. High scores on either the Zuckerman sensation-seeking dimension or the Cloninger novelty-seeking dimension are highly predictive of drug or alcohol abuse and addiction, as are high scores on two subscales (activity and approach) of a totally independently derived temperament-ranking (Wills, Windle, and Cleary 1998), which in turn correlate with the Cloninger novelty-seeking dimension. Strikingly, the subscales on the temperament-ranking instrument are highly predictive of adolescent drug abuse years in advance of first drug use.

In recent years, a growing body of evidence has accumulated to suggest that novelty-seeking behavior may be mediated by the VTA-MFB-Acb mesolimbic DA system (Bardo, Donahew, and Harrington 1996). For example, novelty-provoked locomotor behavior in rodents is blocked by Acb microinjections of DA antagonists (Hooks and Kalivas 1995). The volitional preference of rodents for novel as opposed to familiar environments (as measured using place preference testing) is similarly blocked by DA antagonist administration (Misslin, Ropartz, and Jung 1984; Bardo, Neisewander, and Pierce 1989). Also, novelty-seeking behavior in rodents (but not locomotion per se) is blocked by ultralow dose apomorphine—doses low enough to be selective for the presynaptic DA autoreceptor and, thus, to inhibit VTA-MFB-Acb DA tone (Bardo, Lacey, and Mattingly 1990). Interestingly, the DA D1 receptor seems more implicated in novelty seeking behavior in animals than the D2 receptor, as the selective D1 receptor antagonist selectively blocks novelty-seeking behavior at doses that do not impair other behaviors, while the D2 receptor antagonists sulpiride and eticlopride block novelty seeking only at doses that nonselectively impair other behaviors such as simple locomotion (Bardo et al. 1993; Misslin and Ropartz 1981). Novelty seeking is also inhibited by DA-selective microinjections of the neuronal cytotoxin 6-hydroxydopamine into the VTA-MFB-Acb mesolimbic DA system (Fink and Smith 1979a, 1979b). Provocatively, when the DA agonist apomorphine (at high enough doses to produce a direct postsynaptic DA stimulatory effect) was administered to these DA-denervated animals, investigatory behavior was increased toward novel, but not familiar, objects (Fink and Smith 1980).

Taking this work all together, it may be hypothesized that the integrity of the VTA-MFB-Acb mesolimbic DA system is essential for novelty seeking and, further, that exposure to novel stimuli may provoke presynaptic DA release in Acb. This latter presumption has actually been tested, both by in-vivo single-neuron electrophysiological recording studies in VTA (Fabre et al. 1983) and by in-vivo voltammetric electrochemical recording studies of DA release in Acb (Rebec et al. 1997a, 1997b). In the former experiments, the firing rates of VTA neurons was increased by the presentation of novel stimuli. In the latter experiments, fast-scan Acb cyclic voltammetry was combined with free-choice entry into a novel environment. Entry into novel, but not familiar, surroundings produced a sharp increase in DA efflux in the Acb shell (with abrupt onset and brief duration), together with a less rapid and more long-lasting DA increase in the Acb shell-core transition zone (Rebec et al. 1997a, 1997b). These results indicate that novelty mimics the Acb DA-enhancing effects of other positively reinforcing stimuli, including addicting drugs. It might not be unreasonable, then, that individuals with reward deficiency syndrome might actively seek out not only addicting drugs but also environmental novelty and sensation as a type of behavioral remediation of reward deficiency.

Obviously, novelty seeking and sensation seeking vary considerably from individual to individual within a given species, and equally obviously such variations may confer selective survival advantages or disadvantages depending upon environmental circumstances. In times of famine, drought, or prolonged climate changes, high novelty seekers may have advantage over low novelty seekers in locating new food or water sources, healthier or more agreeable climates, richer grazing or pasture areas, more arable land, or ocean regions with richer fish stocks.

At the same time, excessive novelty seeking or sensation seeking may be patently disadvantageous where behavioral inhibition is necessary to avoid predation or other dangerous circumstances.

It has become clear that such interindividual variations in novelty seeking or sensation seeking may correlate with differences in vulnerability to addicting drugs. Pier Vincenzo Piazza and colleagues have found that high novelty-seeking rats acquire intravenous amphetamine self-administration more readily than low novelty-seeking rats (Piazza et al. 1989) (an interpretational caution is warranted, though, in that high novelty-seeking rats do not differ from low novelty-seeking rats in terms of amphetamine-conditioned place preference [Erb and Parker 1994], although this may relate to subtle methodological peculiarities of the place-preference paradigm [Wise 1987b]). In-vivo brain microdialysis studies have further elucidated some relations between novelty seeking and addictive drug vulnerability. In these studies, high novelty-seeking rats have been shown to display augmented Acb DA responses to both amphetamine (Bradberry et al. 1991) and cocaine (Hooks et al. 1992), in much the same fashion as the drug addiction-vulnerable Lewis strain rats do. Genetic studies with inbred mouse strains are also relevant to these issues. The C57BL/6J inbred strain is inherently more novelty seeking than the DBA/2J inbred strain, and provocatively, novelty-seeking C57BL/6J mice acquire intravenous cocaine self-administration more readily (Carney et al. 1991) and consume more amphetamine, alcohol, and nicotine (Meliska et al. 1995) than novelty-avoidant DBA/2J mice.

In humans, high sensation seekers (as identified by the Zuckerman scale) have lower levels of platelet monoamine oxidase than low sensation seekers (Murphy et al. 1977; Schooler et al. 1978; Fowler, von Knorring, and Oreland 1980), a finding that has parallels with low monoamine oxidase levels found in alcoholics. In the study with alcoholics (von Knorring et al. 1991), it was found that both Type I alcoholics (later onset, no family history) and Type II alcoholics (early onset, family history) display lower monoamine oxidase levels than control subjects. A possibly related finding is that increased risk and lower onset age for alcoholism and drug addiction in males are both significantly correlated with the presence of a recently discovered dinucleotide repeat length polymorphism in the gene for monoamine oxidase A, with male drug and alcohol addicts disproportionately possessing a long allele (Vanyukov et al. 1995a). Given that conduct disorder constitutes a major risk factor for early adolescent onset of drug and alcohol addiction (Whitmore et al. 1997; Crowley et al. 1998), it is provocative that adolescents with conduct disorder tested before the average age of onset for drug or alcohol abuse also show the same polymorphism (Vanyukov et al. 1995b), suggesting that it may constitute a genetic risk factor for behavior or character traits that may confer vulnerability to addiction.

A great deal of interest has been aroused by several reports that novelty seeking (as identified by the Cloninger scale and other personality assessment scales) is associated with a long allele form (represented chiefly by a 7-repeat) of the DA D4 receptor gene exon III polymorphism. If true, this would be very provocative, because the long allelic forms of this receptor have been shown to mediate a blunted intracellular response to DA (LaHoste et al. 1996), which could theoretically mediate some aspects of a reward deficiency syndrome. The two original independent reports (one from an American cohort of subjects, one from an Israeli cohort) of this association between a DA D4 receptor gene polymorphism and the personality-temperament trait of novelty seeking (Benjamin et al. 1996; Ebstein et al. 1996; see also Benjamin, Ebstein, and Belmaker 1997; Ebstein and Belmaker 1997) have now been independently replicated in a Japanese cohort (Ono et al. 1997), an additional Israeli cohort (Ebstein et al. 1997a), and somewhat equivocally (tendency for an association, but not statistically significant) in a Swedish cohort (Jonsson et al. 1997). However, failures to replicate have also been reported (Malhotra et al. 1996; Gelernter et al. 1997; Vandenbergh et al. 1997b). On the other hand, the DA D4 receptor gene exon III seven repeat polymorphism has also been reported to be significantly associated with opiate addiction (Kotler et al. 1997), ADHD (which confers vulnerability to drug addiction) (LaHoste et al. 1996), and the additional addiction vulnerability-conferring personality trait of reward dependence (Ebstein et al. 1997b). In sum, suggestive and provocative—but not yet compelling at the human level—evidence exists for associations between genetic regulation of the VTA-MFB-Acb DA reward system, reward deficiency syndrome, drug-taking behavior, and behavior, personality, and temperament traits that may confer vulnerability to drug addiction.

DA Substitution Therapy as a Therapeutic Strategy in Cocaine Dependence

It has been suggested that DA substitution therapy is a rational pharmacotherapeutic strategy in cocaine addiction or dependence (for example, Dackis and Gold 1985). However, in view of published criticisms of the hypo-DA hypothesis of anhedonia and of drug craving, one may ask: Given the present state of knowledge and theory in the field, how rational is the DA substitution hypothesis? I believe it is rational and offer the following summary arguments in evidence:

1. Many studies have shown that DA neurons in the mesocortico-
    limbic system play an important role in mediating the reinforcing
    actions of cocaine. DA lesions in VTA or Acb markedly attenuate
    cocaine self-administration of cocaine in animal models. DA antag-
    onists diminish the reinforcing action of cocaine. DA agonists (espe-
    cially at the D1 or D2 receptors) will substitute for cocaine. Animals
    (and humans) will self-administer certain DA agonists.

2. It has been reported that after withdrawal from twelve-to-twenty-
    four-hour binges of intravenous cocaine self-administration, current
    thresholds for electrical brain stimulation reward are elevated in
    animals (Markou and Koob 1991, 1992). In addition, levels of extra-
    cellular DA are decreased in Acb following withdrawal from pro-
    longed cocaine self-administration (Weiss et al. 1992b). Long-term
    cocaine use can decrease tyrosine hydroxylase levels, leading to
    decreased DA synthesis (Trulson et al. 1987).

3. In preliminary experiments, my colleagues have seen that, follow-
    ing a forty-eight-hour withdrawal period from repeated cocaine
    use, the number of spontaneously active VTA DA neurons is signif-
    icantly decreased. Furthermore, the number of VTA DA neurons
    exhibiting a burst firing pattern is also decreased (Charles R. Ashby
    Jr. and Yoshio Minabe, personal communication). This is important
    since DA neurons that fire in a bursting pattern release four to six
    times more DA than those firing in a regular, single spiking mode
    (Gonon 1988).

4. Prolonged cocaine use in humans produces hyperprolactinemia
    (Mendelson et al. 1987) and decreased homovanillic acid (a major
    metabolite of DA), consistent with functional DA depletion (Extein,
    Gross, and Gold 1989; Extein and Gold 1993).

5. The effects of DA receptor agonists on cocaine self-administration
    have been examined, with some success—bromocriptine, lisuride,
    and SDZ 208911 have been reported to lower intravenous self-admin-
    istration of cocaine (Pulvirenti and Koob 1994).

6. Clinical data have shown that 52 percent of a sample of cocaine
    addicts possess the A1 D2 receptor allele compared to 20 percent in
    nonaddicted individuals; this is provocative, as individuals with the
    A1 allele are reported to have a lower number of D2 receptors
    (Noble et al. 1993).

Thus, based on many considerations, one could postulate that treatments that augment or supplement DA neurotransmission may be useful in attenuating or ameliorating either vulnerability to cocaine use or

the anhedonic processes associated with cocaine withdrawal. The rationale for this approach is supported by the success of methadone and l-alpha-acetylmethadol (LAAM) for heroin addiction and the nicotine patch for addiction to tobacco. However, the results from studies that have used DA agonists to treat cocaine dependence and withdrawal have been mixed. Many factors may be adduced in explanation, including the low number of subjects used in many studies; the limited range of doses used in most studies; the mixed patient populations used in some studies; and the mixed genotypes of individuals being tested. This latter factor may be important, as one study on alcoholics has demonstrated that bromocriptine was more effective in reducing craving and anxiety in individuals that possessed the A1/A1 compared to the A1/A2 or A2/A2 genotype for D2 receptors (Lawford et al. 1995). Perhaps most important, none of the DA agonist strategies attempted to date have used extremely slow-onset, long-acting strategies, to avoid the abrupt phasic changes in Acb DA levels that are known to trigger relapse in the "reinstatement" drug self-administration paradigm. Such abrupt phasic Acb DA changes would obviously militate against a therapeutic effect.

Direct Manipulation of DA Synaptic Substrates to Achieve DA Substitution Pharmacotherapy

Given recent advances in understanding the synaptic and receptor mechanisms subserving DA neurotransmission, a relatively large number of pharmacologic strategies present themselves as plausible options for attempting to achieve DA substitution therapy for anticocaine treatment efficacy. These strategies include the use of both direct and indirect DA agonists as well as transsynaptic modulation of DA tone by drugs that act on any one of a wide variety of neuronal systems and circuits (including serotonergic, GABAergic, and opioid peptidergic circuits) that synaptically interconnect with the DA pleasure reward reinforcement system (Gardner 1977) and exert strong modulatory action on that system (Chen, van Praag, and Gardner 1991; Klitenick, De Witte, and Kalivas 1992; Sesack and Pickel 1992; Suaud-Chagny et al. 1992; Benloucif, Keegan, and Galloway 1993; Devine et al. 1993; Willick and Kokkinidis 1995).

However, among the many possibilities that present themselves, compounds that directly block the DA reuptake transporter but that have a much slower onset of action and much longer duration of action seem plausible candidates, by analogy to cocaine's action as a DA reuptake transporter or carrier blocker. My colleagues and I hypothesize that slower onset and longer duration of action are critical features of such potential pharmacotherapeutic candidates, since the extremely rapid onset, brief duration, and rapid diminution of cocaine's DA reuptake transporter blocking action appear to be essential to the rapidity and subjective quality of its euphorigenic high and to the rapidity and intensity of post-cocaine-use craving (Gardner 1997; Gardner and David 1999), and obviously a potential pharmacotherapeutic agent for cocaine addiction and dependence that turns out upon both preclinical and clinical evaluation to be just as potently addicting as cocaine would constitute no advance in the search for effective anticocaine treatments.

Slow-Onset, Long-Acting DA Substitution Strategy: An Analogy to Methadone and LAAM for Opiate Substitution Therapy and to Slow-Onset Long-Acting Electrical Brain Stimulation Reward

A strategy for treating cocaine addiction and dependence that presents itself as attractive is that of DA substitution. Of extreme importance, though, is the parallel strategy of using prodrugs for very slow onset of action, very prolonged action, and very slow diminution of action. The analogy of this strategy is that of methadone and LAAM for opiate substitution therapy. With respect to the actions of methadone and LAAM on brain reward, much of the existing literature is comparatively old and is unsatisfactory on methodological grounds. For example, Khazan and colleagues in the 1970s demonstrated that morphine, methadone, and LAAM all support intravenous self-administration and that methadone and LAAM will substitute for morphine intravenous self-administration (Moreton et al. 1976; Young et al. 1978; Young et al. 1979), but the substitution studies were carried out in physically dependent rats, and the methods used did not allow a comparison of degree of appetitiveness among the three opiates.

More satisfactory are studies using progressive-ratio reinforcement schedules of drug self-administration (Hoffmeister 1979; Werner, Smith, and Davis 1976). In these, methadone was shown to produce an equal break point to that of morphine on progressive-ratio reinforced intravenous self-administration (Hoffmeister 1979). However, an ED_{50} dose of methadone produced a consistently lower reinforcement rate than an ED_{50} dose of morphine (Werner, Smith, and Davis 1976), supporting the hypothesis that distribution kinetics, duration of action, and elimination half-life do contribute to reward potency. However, the interpretation of such studies is hampered by the fact that methadone is metabolized much more rapidly in rats than in humans, making its pharmacokinetic profile more analogous to that of morphine (Ling, Umans, and Inturrisi 1981).

A more rigorous and satisfactory approach, to my mind, is work on modeling the drug kinetics of addicting drugs with electrical brain stimulation reward (Lepore and Franklin 1992; Lepore 1993). By using electrical brain stimulation reward instead of drug-induced reward, it was possible to avoid drug-to-drug variation in intrinsic reward efficacy and limit the examination very precisely to the role that kinetics plays in altering reward potency. It was found (Lepore and Franklin 1992; Lepore 1993) that electrical brain stimulation reward trains with very slow decay parameters produced a decrease in response rate, analogous to the previously-noted findings with a methadone-morphine comparison (Werner, Smith, and Davis 1976). Even more provocatively, it was found that electrical brain stimulation reward trains with very slow onsets and very slow rise times produced a decrease in break point on a progressive-ratio reinforcement schedule (Lepore 1993), showing clearly that brain reward of equivalent efficacy loses substantial appetitiveness when its kinetics are altered to produce slow onset and slow rise time to peak effect. It would appear convincing that these intriguing findings validate the strategy of prodrug development to produce very slow onset, long-acting compounds for DA substitution pharmacotherapy.

Preliminary Drug Design, Synthesis, and Preclinical Evaluation of a Series of Novel Slow-Onset, Long-Acting DA Substitution Medications as Potential Treatments for Cocaine Addiction

Based upon all the considerations presented above, I have been actively engaged during the last several years in a multidisciplinary, multisite, collaborative research program to design, synthesize, and test novel molecules that could fulfill the requirements for slow-onset, long-acting DA agonist pharmacotherapeutic agents to remediate reward deficiency syndrome and cocaine craving. To date, several dozen compounds have been designed using molecular modeling and computer-assisted molecular drug design principles and have been synthesized in sufficient milligram quantities to undergo in-vitro receptor binding and DA reuptake carrier binding tests and in-vivo testing in brain reward-related and cocaine self-administration test paradigms in laboratory animals (rats and monkeys).

Preliminarily, the data seem highly promising that this may be a useful approach to the previously intractable problem of efficacious pharmacotherapies for cocaine addiction. In in-vitro receptor binding studies and in-vitro DA reuptake carrier binding studies (Froimowitz, Wu, and Spealman 1996), compounds from the first chemical series designed and synthesized display high affinity for the DA receptor in brain and high affinity for the DA reuptake transporter (DAT), at which they potently inhibit DA reuptake into the presynaptic neuron, thus effectively enhancing synaptic DA levels. In in-vivo locomotor behavior studies in rodents, these first-series compounds dose-dependently produce significant augmentation of locomotor activity, with a slow onset of action and prolonged duration of action following a single injection (Froimowitz, Wu, and Spealman 1996). In monkeys, the prolonged time course of action was remarkable, peak effects occurring forty-eight to seventy-two hours after a single injection and lasting from four to six days.

For the in-vivo electrical brain stimulation reward studies with these first-series compounds, we used the rate-frequency curve-shift quantitative electrophysiological paradigm of electrical brain stimulation reward (Lepore et al. 1996). In this paradigm, cocaine produced its usual intense but extremely brief enhancement of brain reward functions, peaking at fifteen minutes after injection (Gardner et al. 1997). The lead first-series compound, CTDP-30,640, produced an enhancement of brain reward functions similar to that of cocaine at five milligrams per kilogram, amounting to an approximate 30 percent decrease in brain reward thresholds (Gardner et al. 1997, 1998a). The brain stimulation reward effect was characterized by a pronounced slow-onset, long-acting profile. No significant effect was detectable at thirty minutes postinjection, while peak enhancement of brain reward functions was seen four hours postinjection. Progressively diminishing brain reward enhancement was seen at eight, twenty-four, and forty-eight hours following the single injection.

To obtain a more precise picture of the time course of CTDP-30,640's enhancement of brain reward functions, animals were injected with three milligrams per kilogram and tested in the brain stimulation reward paradigm at two-to-three-hour intervals over a twenty-four-hour test period. CTDP-30,640 produced marked enhancement of brain reward functions (approximately 30 percent enhancement at five and a half hours postinjection, the time of peak effect), but with a pronounced slow-onset, long-acting profile. Brain reward functions did not return to baseline until approximately twenty-seven and a half hours postinjection. CTDP-30,640's enhancing action on brain reward functions was additive with that of cocaine but only when the cocaine was given many hours after it, to coincide with CTDP-30,640's slow-onset peak effect. When tested using in-vivo brain microdialysis procedures, CTDP-30,640 produced greatly enhanced Acb DA, with a slow-onset, long-acting profile (Froimowitz et al. 1997). Acb DA levels increased gradually over the eighteen-hour collection period, reaching an augmentation of approximately 400 percent over pre-CTDP-30,640 baseline levels at eighteen hours postdrug.

These first-series compounds also appeared very promising when tested in the in-vivo intravenous drug self-administration paradigm (Froimowitz et al. 1997). When given to stable experienced cocaine self-administering rats, CTDP-30,640 significantly attenuated cocaine self-administration. With a single injection of two and a half milligrams per kilogram CTDP-30,640, inhibition of cocaine self-administration was evident at four and a half hours but had disappeared at twenty-eight and a half hours. Peak (~60 percent) inhibition of cocaine self-administration was seen at five milligrams per kilogram CTDP-30,640, with peak effect at four and a half hours. The inhibitory effect was still evident twenty-eight and a half hours but was gone at fifty-two and a half hours. At ten milligrams per kilogram, CTDP-30,640's action was extremely prolonged, not disappearing until ninety and a half hours. A second chemical series of slow-onset, long-acting DAT blockers has been designed and synthesized, and preliminary results with these compounds in the in-vitro receptor binding and DAT binding assays, and in the in-vivo locomotor, electrical brain stimulation reward, brain microdialysis, and intravenous drug self-administration assays appear equally, if not more, promising than with the first-series compounds (Froimowitz et al. 1998; Gardner et al. 1998b; Hayes et al. 1998).

Conclusions

With the exceptions of methadone maintenance, LAAM maintenance, and nicotine substitution therapy (and probably naltrexone for alcohol addiction and bupropion for nicotine addiction), no clearly effective pharmacotherapy for drug addiction exists. Certainly, no broadly effective pharmacotherapy exists (effective for addictions to drugs of different chemical classes and pharmacological categories). Therapeutic strategies based on psychotherapy, group therapy, behavior modification, economic incentives, and aversion deconditioning have proven limited.

Considerations of the actions of addictive drugs on brain pleasure, reward, and reinforcement mechanisms suggest that direct DA substitution therapy may be a promising approach. This suggestion is supported by evidence that vulnerability to drug craving and relapse may be referable to a basal DA hypofunctionality at DA-mediated pleasure-reward synapses in the brain, especially in Acb. This suggestion is further supported by considerations of the genetic basis for drug addiction and by the suggestion that drug addiction is a subset of a broader reward deficiency syndrome referable to genetically imparted deficiencies in brain reward DA function. DA substitution therapy is further supported by analogy to the success of methadone and LAAM substitution treatment for opiate craving and addiction. The development and trial of several series of slow-onset, long-acting DA-mimetic pharmacotherapeutic agents is in process. Their use in both preclinical and clinical trials will reveal the merits or demerits of this conceptual approach to addiction, craving, and relapse.

Work from my laboratory cited in this chapter was supported by the U.S. Public Health Service under research grants DA-01560, DA-02089, and DA-03622 from the National Institute on Drug Abuse, research grant NS-09649 from the National Institute of Neurological Disorders and Stroke, research grant AA-09547 from the National Institute on Alcohol Abuse and Alcoholism, and research grant RR-05397 (Biomedical Research Support Grant) from the National Institutes of Health; by U.S. National Science Foundation research grant BNS-86-09351; by the U.S. Air Force Aeromedical Division, under research projects 6893-02-005 and 6893-02-039; by a research grant from the Natural Sciences and Engineering Research Council of Canada; by very generous research grant and fellowship support from the Aaron Diamond Foundation of New York City; and by a research grant from the Julia Sullivan Medical Research Fund. Preparation of the chapter was supported by the New York State Office of Alcoholism and Substance Abuse Services and by the Julia Sullivan Medical Research Fund. I am indebted to Dr. T. Byram Karasu, Silverman Professor and Chairman, Department of Psychiatry and Behavioral Sciences, Albert Einstein College of Medicine, and Dr. Dominick P. Purpura, Dean, Albert Einstein College of Medicine, for their support.

Note

1. Translation by the author from the original *Traite Des Maladies Mentales,* written by Jean Etienne Dominique Esquirol and published, in Paris, by Bailliere in 1838. A translation into English by Ebenezer K. Hunt, entitled *Mental Maladies: A Treatise on Insanity,* was published, in Philadelphia, by Lea and Blanchard in 1845. The 1845 translation was reprinted under the auspices of the New York Academy of Medicine in 1965 by Hafner Publishing Company, New York. The cited passage can be found, in the somewhat stilted language of 1845, on page 320 of the 1965 reprint edition.

References

Abercrombie, Elizabeth D., Kristen A. Keefe, Daniel S. DiFrischia, and Michael J. Zigmond. 1989. "Differential Effect of Stress on In-Vivo Dopamine Release in Striatum, Nucleus Accumbens, and Medial Frontal Cortex." *Journal of Neurochemistry* 52: 1655–58.

Acquas, Elio, and Gaetano Di Chiara. 1992. "Depression of Mesolimbic Dopamine Transmission and Sensitization to Morphine During Opiate Abstinence." *Journal of Neurochemistry* 58: 1620–25.

Adamson, M.D., J. Kennedy, A. Petronis, M. Dean, M. Virkkunen, M. Linnoila, and D. Goldman. 1995. "DRD4 Dopamine Receptor Genotype and CSF Monoamine Metabolites in Finnish Alcoholics and Controls." *American Journal of Medical Genetics* 60: 199–205.

Akimoto, Kiyoshi, Takashi Hamamura, and Sabuko Otsuki. 1989. "Subchronic Cocaine Treatment Enhances Cocaine-Induced Dopamine Efflux, Studied by In Vivo Intracerebral Dialysis." *Brain Research* 490: 339–44.

Aksoy, S., J. Klener, and Richard M. Weinshilboum. 1993. "Catechol-O-Methyltransferase Pharmacogenetics: Photoaffinity Labelling and Western Blot Analysis of Human Liver Samples." *Pharmacogenetics* 3: 116–22.

Axelrod, Julius, and Robert Tomchick. 1958. "Enzymatic O-Methylation of Epinephrine and Other Catechols." *Journal of Biological Chemistry* 233: 702–5.

Bardo, Michael T., Shana L. Bowling, Patricia M. Robinet, James K. Rowlett, Margaret Lacey, and Bruce A. Mattingly. 1993. "Role of Dopamine D_1 and D_2 Receptors in Novelty-Maintained Place Preference." *Experimental and Clinical Psychopharmacology* 1: 101–19.

Bardo, Michael T., Robert L. Donohew, and Nancy G. Harrington. 1996. "Psychobiology of Novelty-Seeking and Drug-Seeking Behavior." *Behavioural Brain Research* 77: 23–43.

Bardo, Michael T., Margaret Lacey, and Bruce A. Mattingly. 1990. "Effects of Apomorphine on Novelty-Induced Place Preference Behavior in Rats." *Pharmacology Biochemistry and Behavior* 37: 89–93.

Bardo, Michael T., Janet L. Neisewander, and Robert C. Pierce. 1989. "Novelty-Induced Place Preference Behavior in Rats: Effects of Opiate and Dopaminergic Drugs." *Pharmacology Biochemistry and Behavior* 32: 683–69.

Barrett, Robert J., and David K. White. 1980. "Reward System Depression Following Chronic Amphetamine: Antagonism by Haloperidol." *Pharmacology Biochemistry and Behavior* 13: 555–59.

Bayle, F. J., J. M. Chignon, J. Ades, and H. Loo. 1996. "Addictions Alternantes: À Propos de Trois Cas. [Alternative Addictions: Three Cases]" *Encéphale* 22: 293–97.

Beitner-Johnson, Dana, Xavier Guitart, and Eric J. Nestler. 1991. "Dopaminergic Brain Reward Regions of Lewis and Fischer Rats Display Different Levels of Tyrosine Hydroxylase and Other Morphine- and Cocaine-Regulated Phosphoproteins." *Brain Research* 561: 147–50.

Beitner-Johnson, Dana, and Eric J. Nestler. 1993. "Chronic Morphine Impairs Axoplasmic Transport in the Rat Mesolimbic Dopamine System." *Neuroreport* 5: 57–60.

Benjamin, Daniel, Elfrida R. Grant, and Larissa A. Pohorecky. 1993. "Naltrexone Reverses Ethanol-Induced Dopamine Release in the Nucleus Accumbens in Awake, Freely Moving Rats." *Brain Research* 621: 137–40.

Benjamin, Joathon, Richard P. Ebstein, and Robert H. Belmaker. 1997. "Personality Genetics." *Israel Journal of Psychiatry and Related Sciences* 34: 270–80.

Benjamin, Joathon, Lin Li, Chavis Patterson, Benjamin D. Greenberg, Dennis L. Murphy, and Dean H. Hamer. 1996. "Population and Familial Association Between the D4 Dopamine Receptor Gene and Measures of Novelty Seeking." *Nature Genetics* 12: 81–84.

Benloucif, Susan, Michael J. Keegan, and Matthew P. Galloway. 1993. "Serotonin-Facilitated Dopamine Release in Vivo: Pharmacological Characterization." *Journal of Pharmacology and Experimental Therapeutics* 265: 373–77.

Bergh, Cecilia, Tomas Eklund, Per Sodersten, and Conrad Nordin. 1997. "Altered Dopamine Function in Pathological Gambling." *Psychological Medicine* 27: 473–75.

Berlyne, Daniel E. 1955. "The Arousal and Satiation of Perceptual Curiosity in the Rat." *Journal of Comparative and Physiological Psychology* 48: 238–46.

Bertocci, B., V. Miggiano, M. Da Prada, Z. Dembric, H.-W. Lahm, and P. Malherbe. 1991. "Human Catechol-O-Methyltransferase: Cloning and Expression of the Membrane-Associated Form." *Proceedings of the National Academy of Sciences of the United States of America* 88: 1416–20.

Blanco, C., L. Orensanz-Munoz, C. Blanco-Jerez, and J. Saiz-Ruiz. 1996. "Pathological Gambling and Platelet MAO Activity: A Psychobiological Study." *American Journal of Psychiatry* 153: 119–21.

Blaszczynski, A., Z. Steel, and N. McConaghy. 1997. "Impulsivity in Pathological Gambling: The Antisocial Impulsivist." *Addiction* 92: 75–87.

Blum, Kenneth, John G. Cull, Eric R. Braverman, and David E. Comings. 1996a. "Reward Deficiency Syndrome." *American Scientist* 84: 132–45.

Blum, Kenneth, Ernest Noble, Peter J. Sheridan, Anne Montgomery, Terry Ritchie, Pudun Jagadeeswaran, Hanou Nogami, Arthur H. Briggs, and Jay B. Cohn. 1990. "Allelic Association of Human Dopamine D2 Receptor Gene in Alcoholism." *Journal of the American Medical Association* 263: 2055–60.

Blum, Kenneth, Peter J. Sheridan, R. C. Wood, Eric R. Braverman, T. J. Chen, and David E. Comings. 1995. "Dopamine D2 Receptor Gene Variants: Association and Linkage Studies in Impulsive-Addictive-Compulsive Behaviour." *Pharmacogenetics* 5: 121–41.

Blum, Kenneth, Peter J. Sheridan, R. C. Wood, Eric R. Braverman, T. J. Chen, John G. Cull, and David E. Comings. 1996b. "The D2 Dopamine Receptor Gene as a Determinant of Reward Deficiency Syndrome." *Journal of the Royal Society of Medicine* 89: 396–400.

Bolos, A. M., M. Dean, S. Lucas-Derse, M. Ramsburg, G. L. Brown, and D. Goldman. 1990. "Population and Pedigree Studies Reveal a Lack of Association Between the Dopamine D2 Receptor Gene and Alcoholism." *Journal of the American Medical Association* 264: 3156–60.

Boudikova, Blanka, Carol Szumlanski, Bonnie Maidak, and Richard M. Weinshilboum. 1990. "Human Liver Catecholamine-O-Methyltransferase Pharmacogenetics." *Clinical Pharmacology and Therapeutics* 48: 381–89.

Bozarth, Michael A. 1987. "Conditioned Place Preference: A Parametric Analysis Using Systemic Heroin Injections." In *Methods of Assessing the Reinforcing Properties of Abused Drugs,* edited by Michael A. Bozarth. New York: Springer-Verlag.

———. 1994. "Physical Dependence Produced by Central Morphine Infusions: An Anatomical Mapping Study." *Neuroscience and Biobehavioral Reviews* 18: 373–83.

Bozarth, Michael A., and Roy A. Wise. 1981a. "Intracranial Self-Administration of Morphine into the Ventral Tegmental Area in Rats." *Life Sciences* 28: 551–55.
———. 1981b. "Heroin Reward Is Dependent on a Dopaminergic Substrate." *Life Sciences* 29: 1881–86.
———. 1984. "Anatomically Distinct Opiate Receptor Fields Mediate Reward and Physical Dependence." *Science* 244: 516–17.
Bradberry, Charles W., Rand J. Gruen, Craig W. Berridge, and Robert H. Roth. 1991. "Individual Differences in Behavioral Measures: Correlations with Nucleus Accumbens Dopamine Measured by Microdialysis." *Pharmacology Biochemistry and Behavior* 39: 877–82.
Brock, John W., Jeffrey P. Ng, and Joseph B. Justice Jr. 1990. "Effect of Chronic Cocaine on Dopamine Synthesis in the Nucleus Accumbens as Determined by Microdialysis Perfusion with NSD-10." *Neuroscience Letters* 117: 234–39.
Broderick, Patricia A. 1985. "In Vivo Electrochemical Studies of Rat Striatal Dopamine and Serotonin Release After Morphine." *Life Sciences* 36: 2269–75.
Butler, Robert A. 1957a. "Discrimination Learning by Rhesus Monkeys to Auditory Incentives." *Journal of Comparative and Physiological Psychology* 50: 239–41.
———. 1957b. "The Effect of Deprivation of Visual Incentives on Visual Exploration Motivation in Monkeys." *Journal of Comparative and Physiological Psychology* 50: 177–79.
Cador, Martine, Trevor W. Robbins, and Barry J. Everitt. 1989. "Involvement of the Amygdala in Stimulus-Reward Associations: Interaction with the Ventral Striatum." *Neuroscience* 30: 77–86.
Cannon, Dale S., and Laura E. Carrell. 1987. "Rat Strain Differences in Ethanol Self-Administration and Taste Aversion." *Pharmacology Biochemistry and Behavior* 28: 57–63.
Carboni, Ezio, Assunta Imperato, Laura Perezzani, and Gaetano Di Chiara. 1989. "Amphetamine, Cocaine, Phencyclidine and Nomifensine Increase Extracellular Dopamine Concentrations Preferentially in the Nucleus Accumbens of Freely Moving Rats." *Neuroscience* 28: 653–61.
Carney, J. M., R. W. Landrum, M. S. Cheng, and T. W. Seale. 1991. "Establishment of Chronic Intravenous Drug Self-Administration in the C57BL/6J Mouse." *NeuroReport* 2: 477–80.
Carrasco, J. L., J. Saiz-Ruiz, E. Hollander, J. Cesar, and J. J. Lopez-Ibor. 1994. "Low Platelet Monoamine Oxidase Activity in Pathological Gambling." *Acta Physiologica Scandinavica* 90: 427–31.
Cassens, Geraldine, Carol Actor, Mitchel Kling, and Joseph J. Schildkraut. 1981. "Amphetamine Withdrawal: Effects on Threshold of Intracranial Reinforcement." *Psychopharmacology* 73: 318–22.
Cenci, M. Angela, Peter Kalen, Ronald J. Mandel, and Anders Bjorklund. 1992. "Regional Differences in the Regulation of Dopamine and Noradrenaline Release in Medial Prefrontal Cortex, Nucleus Accumbens, and Caudate-Putamen: A Microdialysis Study in the Rat." *Brain Research* 581: 217–28.
Chang, Jing Y., Steven F. Sawyer, Rong S. Lee, and Donald J. Woodward. 1994. "Electrophysiological and Pharmacological Evidence for the Role of the

Nucleus Accumbens in Cocaine Self-Administration in Freely Moving Rats." *Journal of Neuroscience* 14: 1224–44.

Chen, Jianping, William Paredes, and Eliot L. Gardner. 1993. "Effects of Acute Phencyclidine on In Vivo Efflux and Metabolism of Dopamine in Nucleus Accumbens, Caudate-Putamen, and Medial Prefrontal Cortex of the Awake, Freely Moving Rat." *Einstein Quarterly Journal of Biology and Medicine* 10: 78–86.

Chen, Jianping, William Paredes, Joyce H. Lowinson, and Eliot L. Gardner. 1991. "Strain-Specific Facilitation of Dopamine Efflux by Δ^9-Tetrahydrocannabinol in the Nucleus Accumbens of the Rat: An In Vivo Microdialysis Study." *Neuroscience Letters* 129: 136–40.

Chen, Jianping, Herman M. van Praag, and Eliot L. Gardner. 1991. "Activation of 5-HT$_3$ Receptor by 1-Phenylbiguanide Increases Dopamine Release in the Rat Nucleus Accumbens." *Brain Research* 543: 354–57.

Childress, Anna R., A. Thomas McLellan, Ronald Ehrman, and Charles P. O'Brien. 1988. "Classically Conditioned Responses in Opioid and Cocaine Dependence: A Role in Relapse?" *National Institute on Drug Abuse Research Monograph Series* 84: 25–43.

Childress, Anna R., A. Thomas McLellan, and Charles P. O'Brien. 1986. "Abstinent Opiate Abusers Exhibit Conditioned Craving, Conditioned Withdrawal, and Reductions in Both Through Extinction." *British Journal of Addiction* 81: 655–60.

Cloninger, C. Robert. 1987a. "Neurogenetic Adaptive Mechanisms in Alcoholism." *Science* 236: 410–16.

————. 1987b. "A Systematic Method for Clinical Description and Classification of Personality Variants." *Archives of General Psychiatry* 44: 573–88.

Cloninger, C. Robert, T. Pryzbeck, D. Svrakic, and R. Wetzel. 1994. *The Temperament and Character Inventory: A Guide to Its Development and Use.* St Louis: Center for the Psychobiology of Personality.

Comings, David E. 1995. "The Role of Genetic Factors in Conduct Disorder Based on Studies of Tourette Syndrome and Attention-Deficit Hyperactivity Disorder Probands and Their Relatives." *Journal of Developmental and Behavioral Pediatrics* 16: 142–57.

————. 1997. "Genetic Aspects of Childhood Behavioral Disorders." *Child Psychiatry and Human Development* 27: 139–50.

Comings, David E., Brenda G. Comings, Donn Muhleman, George Deitz, Bejan Shahbahrami, David Tast, Ellen Knell, Pat Kocsis, Rubin Baumgarten, Bruce W. Kovacs, Deborah L. Levy, Melissa Smith, Richard Borison, D. Durrell Evans, Daniel N. Klein, James MacMurray, Jeffrey Tosk, Jeffrey Sverd, Reinhard Gysin, and Steven Flanagan. 1991. "The Dopamine D2 Receptor Locus as a Modifying Gene in Neuropsychiatric Disorders." *Journal of the American Medical Association* 266: 1793–1800.

Comings, David E., L. Ferry, S. Bradshaw-Robinson, R. Burchette, C. Chiu, and Donn Muhleman. 1996a. "The Dopamine D2 Receptor (DRD2) Gene: A Genetic Risk Factor in Smoking." *Pharmacogenetics* 6: 73–79.

Comings, David E., Steven D. Flanagan, George Dietz, Donn Muhleman, Ellen Knell, and Reinhard Gysin. 1993. "The Dopamine D2 Receptor (DRD2) as a

Major Gene in Obesity and Height." *Biochemical Medicine and Metabolic Biology* 50: 176–85.

Comings, David E., Radhika Gade, S. Wu, Connie Chiu, George Dietz, Donn Muhleman, G. Saucier, L. Ferry, R. J. Rosenthal, H. R. LeSieur, L. J. Rugle, and P. MacMurray. 1997. "Studies of the Potential Role of the Dopamine D1 Receptor Gene in Addictive Behaviors." *Molecular Psychiatry* 2: 44–56.

Comings, David E., R. J. Rosenthal, H. R. Lesieur, L. J. Rugle, Donn Muhleman, Connie Chiu, George Dietz, and Radhika Gade. 1996b. "A Study of the Dopamine D2 Receptor Gene in Pathological Gambling." *Pharmacogenetics* 6: 223–34.

Comings, David E., S. Wu, Connie Chiu, Robert H. Ring, Radhika Gade, Chul Ahn, James P. MacMurray, George Dietz, and Donn Muhleman. 1996c. "Polygenic Inheritance of Tourette Syndrome, Stuttering, Attention Deficit Hyperactivity Conduct, and Oppositional Defiant Disorder: The Additive and Subtractive Effect of the Three Dopaminergic Genes: DRD2, D Beta H, and DAT1." *American Journal of Medical Genetics* 67: 264–88.

Cook, Edwin H., Mark A. Stein, Matthew D. Krasowski, Nancy J. Cox, Deborah M. Olken, John E. Kieffer, and Bennett L. Leventhal. 1995. "Association of Attention Deficit Disorder and the Dopamine Transporter Gene." *American Journal of Human Genetics* 56: 993–98.

Corbett, Dale, and Roy A. Wise. 1980. "Intracranial Self-Stimulation in Relation to the Ascending Dopaminergic Systems of the Midbrain: A Moveable Electrode Mapping Study." *Brain Research* 185: 1–15.

Crippens, Donita, and Terry E. Robinson. 1994. "Withdrawal from Morphine or Amphetamine: Different Effects on Dopamine in the Ventral-Medial Striatum Studied with Microdialysis." *Brain Research* 650: 56–62.

Crowley, Thomas J., Marilyn J. Macdonald, Elizabeth A. Whitmore, and Susan K. Mikulich. 1998. "Cannabis Dependence, Withdrawal, and Reinforcing Effects Among Adolescents with Conduct Symptoms and Substance Use Disorders." *Drug and Alcohol Dependence* 50: 27–37.

Dackis, Charles A., and Mark S. Gold. 1985. "New Concepts in Cocaine Addiction: The Dopamine Depletion Hypothesis." *Neuroscience and Biobehavioral Reviews* 9: 469–77.

Dackis, Charles A., Mark S. Gold, and Donald R. Sweeney. 1987. "The Physiology of Cocaine Craving and 'Crashing.'" *Archives of General Psychiatry* 44: 298–99.

Daghestani, Amin N., Eileen Elenz, and John W. Crayton. 1996. "Pathological Gambling in Hospitalized Substance Abusing Veterans." *Journal of Clinical Psychiatry* 57: 360–63.

Dai, Sefton, William A. Corrigall, Kathleen M. Coen, and Herbert Kalant. 1989. "Heroin Self-Administration by Rats: Influence of Dose and Physical Dependence." *Pharmacology Biochemistry and Behavior* 32: 1009–15.

Davis, Michael. 1992. "The Role of Amygdala in Fear and Anxiety." *Annual Review of Neuroscience* 15: 353–75.

Devine, Darragh P., Paola Leone, Dorothy Pocock, and Roy A. Wise. 1993. "Differential Involvement of Ventral Tegmental Mu, Delta, and Kappa Opioid Receptors in Modulation of Basal Mesolimbic Dopamine Release: In Vivo

Microdialysis Studies." *Journal of Pharmacology and Experimental Therapeutics* 266: 1236–46.

De Vry, Jean, Inge Donselaar, and Jan M. Van Ree. 1989. "Intraventricular Self-Administration of Heroin in the Rat: Reward Seems Dissociated from Analgesia and Physical Dependence." *European Journal of Pharmacology* 161: 19–25.

Dewey, Stephen L., Jonathan D. Brodie, Medina Gerasimov, Brian Horan, Eliot L. Gardner, and Charles R. Ashby Jr. 1999. "A Pharmacologic Strategy for the Treatment of Nicotine Addiction." *Synapse* 31: 76–86.

de Wit, Harriet, and Jane Stewart. 1981. "Reinstatement of Cocaine-Reinforced Responding in the Rat." *Psychopharmacology* 75: 134–43.

———. 1983. "Drug Reinstatement of Heroin-Reinforced Responding in the Rat." *Psychopharmacology* 79: 29–31.

De Witte, P., and M. F. Bada. 1983. "Self-Stimulation and Alcohol Administered Orally or Intraperitoneally." *Experimental Neurology* 82: 675–82.

Di Chiara, Gaetano, and Assunta Imperato. 1986. "Preferential Stimulation of Dopamine Release in the Nucleus Accumbens by Opiates, Alcohol, and Barbiturates: Studies with Transcerebral Dialysis in Freely Moving Rats." *Annals of the New York Academy of Sciences* 473: 367–81.

———. 1988. "Drugs Abused by Humans Preferentially Increase Synaptic Dopamine Concentrations in the Mesolimbic System of Freely Moving Rats." *Proceedings of the National Academy of Sciences of the United States of America* 85: 5274–78.

Dyr, W., W. J. McBride, T. K. Lumeng, and J. M. Murphy. 1993. "Effects of D1 and D2 Dopamine Receptor Agents on Ethanol Consumption in the High-Alcohol-Drinking (HAD) Line of Rats." *Alcohol* 10: 207–12.

Ebstein, Richard P., and Robert H. Belmaker. 1997. "Saga of an Adventure Gene: Novelty Seeking, Substance Abuse, and the Dopamine D4 Receptor (D4DR) Exon III Repeat Polymorphism." *Molecular Psychiatry* 2: 381–84.

Ebstein, Richard P, Lubov Nemanov, Ilya Klotz, Inga Gritsenko, and Robert H. Belmaker. 1997a. "Additional Evidence for an Association Between the Dopamine D4 Receptor (D4DR) Exon III Repeat Polymorphism and the Human Personality Trait of Novelty Seeking." *Molecular Psychiatry* 2: 417–19.

Ebstein, Richard P., Olga Novick, Roberto Umansky, Beatrice Priel, Yamina Osher, Damen Blaine, Estelle R. Bennett, Lubov Nemanov, Miri Katz, and Robert H. Belmaker. 1996. "Dopamine D4 Receptor (D4DR) Exon III Polymorphism Associated with the Human Personality Trait of Novelty Seeking." *Nature Genetics* 12: 78–80.

Ebstein, Richard P., Ronnen Segman, Jonathan Benjamin, Yamina Osher, Lubov Nemanov, and Robert H. Belmaker. 1997b. "5-HT2C (HTR2C) Serotonin Receptor Gene Polymorphism Associated with the Human Personality Trait of Reward Dependence: Interaction with Dopamine D4 Receptor (D4DR) and Dopamine D3 Receptor (D3DR) Polymorphisms." *American Journal of Medical Genetics* 74: 65–72.

Eichler, A. J., S. M. Antelman, and A. E. Fisher. 1976. "Self-Stimulation: Site-Specific Tolerance to Chronic Dopamine Receptor Blockade." *Society for Neuroscience Abstracts* 2: 440.

Elston, R. C. 1995. "Linkage and Association to Genetic Markers." *Experimental and Clinical Immunogenetics* 12: 129–40.

Emmett-Oglesby, Michael W., and John D. Lane. 1992. "Tolerance to the Reinforcing Effects of Cocaine." *Behavioral Pharmacology* 3: 193–200.

Engel, J., and L. Oreland, eds. 1987. *Brain Reward Systems and Abuse.* New York: Raven.

Epstein, J., and J. Gfroerer. 1998. "Changes Affecting NHSDA Estimates of Treatment Need for 1994–1996." In *Analyses of Substance Abuse and Treatment Need Issues.* Analytic Series A-7, DHHS Publication Number [SMA] 98-3227. Rockville, Md.: Substance Abuse and Mental Health Services Administration, Office of Applied Studies, U.S. Department of Health and Human Services.

Erb, Suzanne, and Linda A. Parker. 1994. "Individual Differences in Novelty-Induced Activity Do Not Predict Strength of Amphetamine-Induced Place Conditioning." *Pharmacology Biochemistry and Behavior* 48: 581–86.

Erb, Suzanne, Yavin Shaham, and Jane Stewart. 1996. "Stress Reinstates Cocaine-Seeking Behavior After Prolonged Extinction and a Drug-Free Period." *Psychopharmacology* 128: 408–12.

Esquirol, Jean E. D. 1838. *Des Maladies Mentales.* Paris: Bailliere.

Ettenberg, Aaron, and Roy A. Wise. 1976. "Nonselective Enhancement of Locus Coeruleus and Substantia Nigra Self-Stimulation After Termination of Chronic Dopaminergic Receptor Blockade with Pimozide in Rats." *Psychopharmacology Communications* 2: 117–24.

Everitt, Barry J., Martine Cador, and Trevor W. Robbins. 1989. "Interactions Between the Amygdala and Ventral Striatum in Stimulus-Reward Associations: Studies Using a Second-Order Schedule of Sexual Reinforcement." *Neuroscience* 30: 63–75.

Extein, Irl L., and Mark S. Gold. 1993. "Hypothesized Neurochemical Models for Psychiatric Syndromes in Alcohol and Drug Dependence." *Journal of Addictive Disease* 12: 29–43.

Extein, Irl L., David A. Gross, and Mark S. Gold. 1989. "Bromocriptine Treatment of Cocaine Withdrawal Symptoms." *American Journal of Psychiatry* 146:403.

Eysenck, Hans J. 1953. *The Structure of Human Personality.* New York: Wiley.

Fabre, Michele, Edmund T. Rolls, Jonathan P. Ashton, and Graham Williams. 1983. "Activity of Neurons in the Ventral Tegmental Region of the Behaving Monkey." *Behavioural Brain Research* 9: 213–35.

Feigelman, W., P. H. Kleinman, H. R. Lesieur, and Robert B. Millman. 1995. "Pathological Gambling Among Methadone Patients." *Drug and Alcohol Dependence* 39: 75–81.

Fibiger, Hans C., and Anthony G. Phillips. 1988. "Mesocorticolimbic Dopamine Systems and Reward." *Annals of the New York Academy of Sciences* 537: 206–15.

Fink, J. Stephen, and Gerard P. Smith. 1979a. "Decreased Locomotion and Investigatory Exploration After Denervation of Catecholamine Terminal Fields in the Forebrain of Rats." *Journal of Comparative and Physiological Psychology* 93: 34–65.

———. 1979b. "L-Dopa Repairs Deficits in Locomotor and Investigatory Exploration Produced by Denervation of Catecholamine Terminal Fields in the Forebrain of Rats." *Journal of Comparative and Physiological Psychology* 93: 66–73.

————. 1980. "Mesolimbic and Mesocortical Dopaminergic Neurons Are Necessary for Normal Exploratory Behavior in Rats." *Neuroscience Letters* 17: 61–65.

Fischman, Marian W., Charles R. Schuster, Javaid Javaid, Yoshio Hatano, and John Davis. 1985. "Acute Tolerance Development to the Cardiovascular and Subjective Effects of Cocaine." *Journal of Pharmacology and Experimental Therapeutics* 235: 677–82.

Fowler, C. J., L. von Knorring, and L. Oreland. 1980. "Platelet Monoamine Oxidase Activity in Sensation Seekers." *Psychiatry Research* 3: 273–79.

Fowler, Joanna S., Nora D. Volkow, Alfred P. Wolf, Stephen L. Dewey, David J. Schlyer, Robert R. Macgregor, Robert Hitzemann, Jean Logan, Bernard Bendriem, S. John Gatley, and David Christman. 1989. "Mapping Cocaine Binding Sites in Human and Baboon Brain in Vivo." *Synapse* 4: 371–77.

Frank, Robert A., Stacy Martz, and Thomas Pommering. 1988. "The Effect of Chronic Cocaine on Self-Stimulation Train-Duration Thresholds." *Pharmacology Biochemistry and Behavior* 29: 755–58.

Fray, Paul J., Stephen B. Dunnett, Susan D. Iversen, Anders Björklund and Ulf Stenevi. 1983. "Nigral Transplants Reinnervating the Dopamine-Depleted Neostriatum Can Sustain Intracranial Self-Stimulation." *Science* 219: 416–19.

Froimowitz, Mark, Kuo-Ming Wu, William Paredes, Charles R. Ashby Jr., Xinhe Liu, Marino Lepore, and Eliot L. Gardner. 1998. "Slow-Onset, Long-Lasting Prodrugs as Potential Medications for Cocaine Addiction: Binding, Reuptake, and Locomotor Assays." *Society for Neuroscience Abstracts* 24: 2169.

Froimowitz, Mark, Kuo-Ming Wu, William Paredes, Anthony Giordano, Jordan Spector, Xinhe Liu, Marino Lepore, and Eliot L. Gardner. 1997. "Effects of a Slow-Onset, Long-Acting Dopamine Reuptake Blocker on Cocaine Self-Administration and on Nucleus Accumbens Dopamine." *Society for Neuroscience Abstracts* 23: 1110.

Froimowitz, Mark, Kuo-Ming Wu, and Roger D. Spealman. 1996. "Slow Onset, Long-Lasting Dopamine Reuptake Blockers as Potential Medications for the Treatment of Cocaine Abuse." *Society for Neuroscience Abstracts* 22: 703.

Gaffan David. 1992. "Amygdala and the Memory of Reward." In *The Amygdala: Neurobiological Aspects of Emotion, Memory, and Mental Dysfunction*, edited by John P. Aggleton. New York: Wiley.

Gallistel, Charles R., Peter Shizgal, and John Yeomans. 1981. "A Portrait of the Substrate for Self-Stimulation." *Psychological Review* 88: 228–73.

Gardner, Eliot L. 1989. "Studies Reveal Findings in Brain Reward, Drug Addiction Relationship." *Psychiatric Times* 6: 12–16.

————. 1992. "Cannabinoid Interaction with Brain Reward Systems: The Neurobiological Basis of Cannabinoid Abuse." In *Marijuana/Cannabinoids: Neurobiology and Neurophysiology*, edited by Laura L. Murphy and Andrzej Bartke. Boca Raton, Fla.: CRC Press.

————. 1997. "Brain Reward Mechanisms." In *Substance Abuse: A Comprehensive Textbook*, edited by Joyce H. Lowinson, Pedro Ruiz, Robert B. Millman, and John G. Langrod. 3d ed. Baltimore: Williams and Wilkins.

Gardner, Eliot L., and Jianping Chen. 1992. "Ethanol Produces Naloxone-Blockable Enhancement of Extracellular Dopamine in Nucleus Accumbens of Lewis Rats." *Society for Neuroscience Abstracts* 18: 1431.

Gardner, Eliot L., Jainping Chen, and William Paredes. 1993. "Overview of Chemical Sampling Techniques." *Journal of Neuroscience Methods* 48: 173–97.

Gardner, Eliot L., and James David. 1999. "The Neurobiology of Chemical Addiction." In *Getting Hooked: Rationality and the Addictions*, edited by Jon Elster and Ole-Jørgen Skog. New York: Cambridge University Press.

Gardner, Eliot L., Xinhe Liu, William Paredes, Anthony Giordano, Jordan Spector, Marino Lepore, Kuo-Ming Wu, and Mark Froimowitz. 1998a. "Effects of a Slow-Onset, Long-Acting Dopamine Reuptake Blocker on Brain Reward Mechanisms." *National Institute for Drug Abuse Research Monograph Series* 178: 281.

Gardner, Eliot L., Mark Froimowitz, Kuo-Ming Wu, Xinhe Liu, William Paredes, Stephen Dewey, A. Morgan, Charles R. Ashby Jr., Robert Hayes, and Marino Lepore. 1998b. "Slow-Onset, Long-Lasting Prodrugs as Potential Medications for Cocaine Addiction: Electrical Brain Stimulation Reward and In Vivo Brain Microdialysis Studies." *Society for Neuroscience Abstracts* 24: 1484.

Gardner, Eliot L., Xinhe Liu, William Paredes, Marino Lepore, Charles R. Ashby Jr., Kuo-Ming Wu, and Mark Froimowitz. 1997. "Effects of a Slow-Onset, Long-Acting Dopamine Reuptake Blocker on Electrical Brain Stimulation Reward (BSR)." *Society for Neuroscience Abstracts* 23: 1110.

Gardner, Eliot L., and Joyce H. Lowinson. 1991. "Marijuana's Interaction with Brain Reward Systems: Update 1991." *Pharmacology Biochemistry and Behavior* 40: 571–80.

————. 1993. "Drug Craving and Positive/Negative Hedonic Brain Substrates Activated by Addicting Drugs." *Seminars in the Neurosciences* 5: 359–68.

Gardner, Eliot L., William Paredes, Diane Smith, Thomas Seeger, Amy Donner, Cassandra Milling, David Cohen, and David Morrison. 1988. "Strain-Specific Facilitation of Brain Stimulation Reward by Δ⁹-Tetrahydrocannabinol in Laboratory Rats." *Psychopharmacology* 96[suppl]: 365.

Gardner, Eliot L., Leslie S. Walker, and William Paredes. 1993. "Clozapine's Functional Mesolimbic Selectivity Is Not Duplicated by the Addition of Anticholinergic Action to Haloperidol: A Brain Stimulation Study in the Rat." *Psychopharmacology* 110: 119–24.

Gawin, Frank H., and Herbert D. Kleber. 1986. "Abstinence Symptomatology and Psychiatric Diagnosis in Cocaine Abusers." *Archives of General Psychiatry* 43: 107–13.

Gelernter, J., H. R. Kranzler, E. Coccaro, L. Siever, A. New, and C. L. Mulgrew. 1997. "D4 Dopamine-Receptor (DRD4) Alleles and Novelty Seeking in Substance-Dependent, Personality-Disorder, and Control Subjects." *American Journal of Human Genetics* 61: 1144–52.

Gelernter, J., H. R. Kranzler, S. L. Satel, and P. A. Rao. 1994. "Genetic Association Between Dopamine Transporter Protein Alleles and Cocaine-Induced Paranoia." *Neuropsychopharmacology* 11: 195–200.

George, Frank R. 1987. "Genetic and Environmental Factors in Ethanol Self-Administration." *Pharmacology Biochemistry and Behavior* 27: 379–84.

George, Frank R., and Steven R. Goldberg. 1989. "Genetic Approaches to the Analysis of Addiction Processes." *Trends in Pharmacological Sciences* 10: 78–83.

George, Frank R., and Richard A. Meisch. 1984. "Oral Narcotic Intake as a Reinforcer: Genotype X Environment Interaction." *Behavior Genetics* 14: 603.

Gerber, Gary J., and R. Stretch. 1975. "Drug-Induced Reinstatement of Extinguished Self-Administration Behavior in Monkeys." *Pharmacology Biochemistry and Behavior* 3: 1055–61.

Giros, Bruno, Mohamed Jaber, Sara R. Jones, R. Mark Wightman, and Marc G. Caron. 1996. "Hyperlocomotion and Indifference to Cocaine and Amphetamine in Mice Lacking the Dopamine Transporter." *Nature* 379: 606–12.

Goeders, Nick E., John D. Lane, and James E. Smith. 1984. "Self-Administration of Methionine Enkephalin into the Nucleus Accumbens." *Pharmacology Biochemistry and Behavior* 20: 451–55.

Goeders, Nick E., and James E. Smith. 1983. "Cortical Dopaminergic Involvement in Cocaine Reinforcement." *Science* 221: 773–75.

Gonon, François G. 1988. "Nonlinear Relationship Between Impulse Flow and Dopamine Released by Midbrain Dopaminergic Neurons as Studied by In Vivo Electrochemistry." *Neuroscience* 24: 19–28.

Gratton, Alain. 1996. "In Vivo Analysis of the Role of Dopamine in Stimulant and Opiate Self-Administration." *Journal of Psychiatry and Neuroscience* 21: 264–79.

Gratton, Alain, and Roy A. Wise. 1994. "Drug- and Behavior-Associated Changes in Dopamine-Related Electrochemical Signals During Intravenous Cocaine Self-Administration in Rats." *Journal of Neuroscience* 14: 4130–46.

Guitart, Xavier, Dana Beitner-Johnson, David W. Marby, Therese A. Kosten, and Eric J. Nestler. 1992. "Fischer and Lewis Rat Strains Differ in Basal Levels of Neurofilament Proteins and Their Regulation by Chronic Morphine in the Mesolimbic Dopamine System." *Synapse* 12: 242–53.

Guitart, Xavier, Jeffrey H. Kogan, Melissa Berhow, Rose Z. Terwilliger, George K. Aghajanian, and Eric J. Nestler. 1993. "Lewis and Fischer Rat Strains Display Differences in Biochemical, Electrophysiological, and Behavioral Parameters: Studies in the Nucleus Accumbens and Locus Coeruleus of Drug Naive and Morphine-Treated Animals." *Brain Research* 611: 7–17.

Gysling, Katia, and Rex Y. Wang. 1983. "Morphine-Induced Activation of A10 Dopamine Neurons in the Rat." *Brain Research* 277: 119–27.

Halikas, James A. 1997. "Craving." In *Substance Abuse: A Comprehensive Textbook*, edited by Joyce H. Lowinson, Pedro Ruiz, Robert B. Millman, and John G. Langrod. 3d ed. Baltimore: Williams and Wilkins.

Halikas, James A., Kenneth L. Kuhn, Ross D. Crosby, Gregory A. Carlson, and Frederick Crea. 1991. "The Measurement of Craving in Cocaine Patients Using the Minnesota Cocaine Craving Scale." *Comprehensive Psychiatry.* 32: 22–27.

Harlow, Harry F. 1950. "Learning and Satiation of Response in Intrinsically Motivated Complex Puzzle Performance by Monkeys." *Journal of Experimental Psychology* 40: 228–34.

Harris, Glenda C., and Gary Aston-Jones. 1993. "Beta-Adrenergic Antagonists Attenuate Somatic and Aversive Signs of Opiate Withdrawal." *Neuropsychopharmacology* 9: 303–11.

Hayes, Robert, Jordon Spector, Eliot L. Gardner, Mark Froimowitz, Kuo-Ming Wu, Xinhe Liu, William Paredes, Charles R. Ashby Jr., Marino Lepore, and Noboru Hiroi. 1998. "Slow-Onset, Long-Lasting Prodrugs as Potential Medications for Cocaine Addiction: Intravenous Cocaine Self-Administration Studies." *Society for Neuroscience Abstracts* 24: 2169.

Hernandez, Luis, and Bartley G. Hoebel. 1988. "Food Reward and Cocaine Increase Extracellular Dopamine in the Nucleus Accumbens as Measured by Microdialysis." *Life Sciences* 42: 1705–12.

Heyman, Gene M. 1998. "On 'The Science of Substance Abuse.'" *Science* 280: 807–8.

Higgins, Guy A., Peter Nguyen, Nanges Joharchi, and Edward M. Sellers. 1991. "Effects of 5-HT3 Receptor Antagonists on Behavioural Measures of Naloxone-Precipitated Opioid Withdrawal." *Psychopharmacology* 105: 322–28.

Higgins, Guy A., Peter Nguyen, and Edward M. Sellers. 1992. "The NMDA Antagonist Dizocilpine (MK801) Attenuates Motivational as Well as Somatic Aspects of Naloxone Precipitated Opioid Withdrawal." *Life Sciences [Pharmacology Letters]* 50: PL167–72.

Hiroi, Noboru. 1990. "A Pharmacological and Neuroanatomical Investigation of the Conditioned Place Preference Produced by Amphetamine." Ph.D. diss., McGill University.

Hiroi, Noboru, Robert J. McDonald, and Norman M. White. 1990. "Involvement of the Lateral Nucleus of the Amygdala in Amphetamine and Food Conditioned Place Preferences (CPP)." *Society for Neuroscience Abstracts* 16: 605.

Hiroi, Noboru, and Norman M. White. 1990. "The Reserpine-Sensitive Dopamine Pool Mediates (+)-Amphetamine-Conditioned Reward in the Place Preference Paradigm." *Brain Research* 510: 33–42.

———. 1991. "The Lateral Nucleus of the Amygdala Mediates Expression of the Amphetamine-Conditioned Place Preference." *Journal of Neuroscience* 11: 2107–16.

Hoebel, Bartley G., Anthony P. Monaco, Luis Hernandez, Edward F. Aulisi, B. Glenn Stanley, and Laslo Lenard. 1983. "Self-Injection of Amphetamine Directly into the Brain." *Psychopharmacology* 81: 158–63.

Hoffmann, Norman G., and Norman S. Miller. 1993. "Perspectives of Effective Treatment for Alcohol and Drug Disorders." *Psychiatric Clinics of North America* 16: 127–40.

Hoffmeister, Friedrich. 1979. "Progressive-Ratio Performance in the Rhesus Monkey Maintained by Opiate Infusions." *Psychopharmacologia* 62: 181–86.

Hollander, Eric, and Chenly M. Wong. 1995. "Body Dysmorphic Disorder, Pathological Gambling, and Sexual Compulsions." *Journal of Clinical Psychiatry* 56 [suppl. 4]: 7–12.

Hommer, Daniel W., and Agu Pert. 1983. "The Action of Opiates in the Rat Substantia Nigra: An Electrophysiological Analysis." *Peptides* 4: 603–8.

Hooks, M. Stacy, Alex C. Colvin, Jorge L. Juncos, and Joseph B. Justice Jr. 1992. "Individual Differences in Basal and Cocaine-Stimulated Extracellular Dopamine in the Nucleus Accumbens Using Quantitative Microdialysis." *Brain Research* 587: 306–12.

Hooks, M. Stacy, Patricia Duffy, Caryn Striplin, and Peter W. Kalivas. 1994. "Behavioral and Neurochemical Sensitization Following Cocaine Self-Administration." *Psychopharmacology* 115:265–72.

Hooks, M. Stacy, and Peter W. Kalivas. 1995. "The Role of Mesoaccumbens-Pallidal Circuitry in Novelty-Induced Behavioral Activation." *Neuroscience* 64:587–97.

Horger, Brian A., Albert Valadez, Paul J. Wellman, and Susan Schenk. 1994. "Augmentation of the Neurochemical Effects of Cocaine in the Ventral Striatum and Medial Prefrontal Cortex Following Preexposure to Amphetamine, but not Nicotine: An In Vivo Microdialysis Study." *Life Sciences* 55: 1245–51.

Hubner, Carol B., George T. Bain, and Conan Kornetsky. 1987. "The Combined Effects of Morphine and D-Amphetamine on the Threshold for Brain Stimulation Reward." *Pharmacology Biochemistry and Behavior* 28: 311–15.

Hughes, R. N. 1968. "Behavior of Male and Female Rats with Free Choice of Two Environments Differing in Novelty." *Animal Behavior* 16: 92–96.

Hunt, William A., L. Walker Barnett, and Laurence G. Branch. 1971. "Relapse Rates in Addiction Programs." *Journal of Clinical Psychology* 27: 455–56.

Huston-Lyons, David, and Conan Kornetsky. 1992. "Effects of Nicotine on the Threshold for Rewarding Brain Stimulation in Rats." *Pharmacology Biochemistry and Behavior* 41: 755–59.

Huston-Lyons, David, Molly Sarkar, and Conan Kornetsky. 1993. "Nicotine and Brain Stimulation Reward: Interactions with Morphine, Amphetamine, and Pimozide." *Pharmacology Biochemistry and Behavior* 46: 453–57.

Imperato, Assunta, Luciano Angelucci, Paola Casolini, Alessandro Zocchi, and Stefano Puglisi-Allegra. 1992a. "Repeated Stressful Experiences Differently Affect Limbic Dopamine Release During and Following Stress." *Brain Research* 577: 194–99.

Imperato, Assunta, and Gaetano Di Chiara. 1986. "Preferential Stimulation of Dopamine Release in the Nucleus Accumbens of Freely Moving Rats by Ethanol." *Journal of Pharmacology and Experimental Therapeutics* 239: 219–28.

Imperato, Assunta, Andrea Mele, Maria G. Scrocco, and Stefano Puglisi-Allegra. 1992b. "Chronic Cocaine Alters Limbic Extracellular Dopamine: Neurochemical Basis for Addiction." *European Journal of Pharmacology* 212: 299–300.

Imperato, Assunta, Angelina Mulas, and Gaetano Di Chiara. 1986. "Nicotine Preferentially Stimulates Dopamine Release in the Limbic System of Freely Moving Rats." *European Journal of Pharmacology* 132: 337–38.

Jackson, William J., and Eliot L. Gardner. 1974. "Modulation of Hypothalamic ICSS by Concurrent Limbic Stimulation." *Physiology and Behavior* 12: 177–82.

Jaffe, Jerome H. 1992. "Current Concepts of Addiction." *Research Publications of the Association for Research in Nervous and Mental Disease* 70: 1–21.

Jaffe, Jerome H., Nicola G. Cascella, Karen M. Kumor, and Michael A. Sherer. 1989. "Cocaine-Induced Cocaine Craving." *Psychopharmacology* 97: 59–64.

Jaffe, Jerome H., and William R. Martin. 1985. "Opioid Analgesics and Antagonists." In *The Pharmacological Basis of Therapeutics*, edited by Alfred G. Gilman, Louis S. Goodman, Theodore W. Rall, and Ferid Murad. 7th ed. New York: Macmillan.

Jonsson, Erik G., Markus M. Nothen, J. Petter Gustavsson, Helge Neidt, Stefan Brene, Alexandra Tylec, Petter Propping, and Göran C. Sedvall. 1997. "Lack of Evidence for Allelic Association Between Personality Traits and the Dopamine D4 Receptor Gene Polymorphisms." *American Journal of Psychiatry* 154: 697–99.

Kalant, Harold. 1977. "Comparative Aspects of Tolerance to, and Dependence on, Alcohol, Barbiturates, and Opiates." In *Alcohol Intoxication and Withdrawal*, edited by Milton M. Gross. New York: Plenum.

Kalivas, Peter W., and Patricia Duffy. 1993. "Time Course of Extracellular Dopamine and Behavioral Sensitization to Cocaine. I. Dopamine Axon Terminals." *Journal of Neuroscience* 13: 266–75.

———. 1995. "Selective Activation of Dopamine Transmission in the Shell of the Nucleus Accumbens by Stress." *Brain Research* 675: 325–28.

Kalivas, Peter W., Patricia Duffy, Roger Dilts, and Raymond Abhold. 1988. "Enkephalin Modulation of A10 Dopamine Neurons: A Role in Dopamine Sensitization." *Annals of the New York Academy of Sciences* 537: 405–14.

Kalivas, Peter W., Erik Widerlov, Donald Stanley, George Breese, and Arthur J. Prange. 1983. "Enkephalin Action on the Mesolimbic System: A Dopamine-Dependent and a Dopamine-Independent Increase in Locomotor Activity." *Journal of Pharmacology and Experimental Therapeutics* 227: 229–37.

Kelsey, John E., and Susan R. Arnold. 1994. "Lesions of the Dorsomedial Amygdala, but Not the Nucleus Accumbens, Reduce the Aversiveness of Morphine Withdrawal in Rats." *Behavioral Neuroscience* 108: 1119–27.

Khodzhagel'diev, T. 1986. "Formirovanie vlecheniia k nikotinu u myshei linii C57BL/6 i CBA [Development of Nicotine Preference in C57BL/6 and CBA Mice]." *Biulleten Eksperimentalnoi Biologii Meditsiny* 101: 48–50.

Kiyatkin, Eugene A., Roy A. Wise, and Alain Gratton. 1993. "Drug- and Behavior-Associated Changes in Dopamine-Related Electrochemical Signals During Intravenous Heroin Self-Administration in Rats." *Synapse* 14: 60–72.

Kleber, Herbert D. 1992. "Treatment of Cocaine Abuse: Pharmacotherapy." *Ciba Foundation Symposium* 166: 195–200.

———. 1994. "Our Current Approach to Drug Abuse: Progress, Problems, Proposals." *New England Journal of Medicine* 330: 361–65.

Klitenick, Mark A., Phillipe DeWitte, and Peter W. Kalivas. 1992. "Regulation of Somatodendritic Dopamine Release in the Ventral Tegmental Area by Opioids and GABA: An In Vivo Microdialysis Study." *Journal of Neuroscience* 12: 2623–32.

Knecht, T. 1995. "Joy Riding: Multiple 'Strolchenfahrten' in angetrunkenem Zustand bei einer dissozialen Persönlichkeit mit Suchtendenzen [Joy Riding: Multiple Criminal Car Rides in an Intoxicated State in Relation to Asocial Personality with Addictive Tendencies]." *Archiv fur Kriminologie* 196: 1–5.

Kogan, B. M., A. A. Tkachenko, A. Z. Drozdov, E. P. Andrianova, T. S. Filatova, I. V. Man'kovskaia, and I. A. Kovaleva. 1995. "Obmen monoaminov pri razlichnykh formakh parafilii [Monoamine Metabolism in Different Forms of Paraphilias]." *Zhurnal Nevropatologii Psikhiatrii Imeni SS Korsakova* 95: 52–56.

Kokkinidis, Larry, and Bryon D. McCarter. 1990. "Postcocaine Depression and Sensitization of Brain Stimulation Reward: Analysis of Reinforcement and Performance Effects." *Pharmacology Biochemistry and Behavior* 36: 463–71.

Kokkinidis, Larry, Robert M. Zacharko, and Patrick A. Predy. 1980. "Post-Amphetamine Depression of Self-Stimulation Responding from the Substantia Nigra: Reversal by Tricyclic Antidepressants." *Pharmacology Biochemistry and Behavior* 13: 379–83.

Koob, George F. 1982. "The Dopamine Anhedonia Hypothesis: A Pharmacological Phrenology." *Behavioral and Brain Sciences* 5: 63–64.

———. 1996. "Drug Addiction: The Yin and Yang of Hedonic Homeostasis." *Neuron* 16: 893–96.

Koob, George F., and Floyd E. Bloom. 1988. "Cellular and Molecular Mechanisms of Drug Dependence." *Science* 242: 715–23.

Koob, George F., Athina Markou, Friedbert Weiss, and Gery Schulteis. 1993. "Opponent Process and Drug Dependence: Neurobiological Mechanisms." *Seminars in the Neurosciences* 5: 351–58.

Koob, George F., Louis Stinus, Michel Le Moal, and Floyd E. Bloom. 1989a. "Opponent Process Theory of Motivation: Neurobiological Evidence from Studies of Opiate Dependence." *Neuroscience and Biobehavioral Reviews* 13: 135–40.

Koob, George F., Tamara L. Wall, and Floyd E. Bloom. 1989b. "Nucleus Accumbens as a Substrate for the Aversive Effects of Opiate Withdrawal." *Psychopharmacology* 98: 530–34.

Kornetsky, Conan. 1985. "Brain-Stimulation Reward: A Model for the Neuronal Bases for Drug-Induced Euphoria." *National Institute on Drug Abuse Research Monograph Series* 62: 30–50.

Kornetsky, Conan, and George Bain. 1992. "Brain-Stimulation Reward: A Model for the Study of the Rewarding Effects of Abused Drugs. *National Institute on Drug Abuse Research Monograph Series* 124: 73–93.

Kornetsky, Conan, George T. Bain, Ellen M. Unterwald, and Michael J. Lewis. 1988. "Brain Stimulation Reward: Effects of Ethanol." *Alcoholism Clinical and Experimental Research* 2: 609–16.

Kornetsky, Conan, and Christine Duvauchelle. 1994. "Dopamine, a Common Substrate for the Rewarding Effects of Brain Stimulation Reward, Cocaine, and Morphine." *National Institute on Drug Abuse Research Monograph Series* 145: 19–39.

Kornetsky, Conan, and Ralph U. Esposito. 1979. "Euphorigenic Drugs: Effects on the Reward Pathways of the Brain." *Federation Proceedings* 38: 2473–76.

Kornetsky, Conan, Ralph U. Esposito, Stafford McLean, and Joseph O. Jacobson. 1979. "Intracranial Self-Stimulation Thresholds: A Model for the Hedonic Effects of Drugs of Abuse." *Archives of General Psychiatry* 36: 289–92.

Kosten, Therese A. 1994. "Clonidine Attenuates Conditioned Aversion Produced by Naloxone-Precipitated Opiate Withdrawal." *European Journal of Pharmacology* 254: 59–63.

Kosten, Therese A., Mindy J. Miserendino, Sandra Chi, and Eric J. Nestler. 1994. "Fischer and Lewis Rat Strains Show Differential Cocaine Effects in Conditioned Place Preference and Behavioral Sensitization but Not in Locomotor Activity or Conditioned Taste Aversion." *Journal of Pharmacology and Experimental Therapeutics* 269: 137–44.

Kotler, M., H. Cohen, Ronnen Segman, I. Gritsenko, Lubov Nemanov, B. Lerer, I. Kramer, M. Zer-Zion, I. Kletz, and Richard P. Ebstein. 1997. "Excess Dopamine D4 Receptor (DRD4) Exon III Seven Repeat Allele in Opioid-Dependent Subjects." *Molecular Psychiatry* 2: 251–54.

Kreek, Mary J. 1992. "Rationale for Maintenance Pharmacotherapy of Opiate Dependence." *Research Publications of the Association for Research in Nervous and Mental Disease* 70: 205–30.

Krugylak, Leonid, and Eric S. Lander. 1995. "High-Resolution Genetic Mapping of Complex Traits." *American Journal of Human Genetics* 56: 1212–23.

Kruk, Zygmunt L., S. Cheeta, J. Milla, R. Muscat, J. E. Williams, and Paul Willner. 1998. "Real-Time Measurement of Stimulated Dopamine Release in the Conscious Rat Using Fast Cyclic Voltammetry: Dopamine Release Is Not Observed During Intracranial Self-Stimulation." *Journal of Neuroscience Methods* 79: 9–19.

Kupfermann, Irving. 1991. "Hypothalamus and Limbic System: Peptidergic Neurons, Homeostasis, and Emotional Behavior." In *Principles of Neural Science*, edited by Eric R. Kandel, James H. Schwartz, and Thomas M. Jessell. 3d ed. New York: Elsevier.

Kurata, K., Y. Tanii, R. Shibata, and M. Kurachi. 1993. "Differential Effects of Tight and Loose 2-hour Restraint Stress on Extracellular Concentrations of Dopamine in Nucleus Accumbens and Anteromedial Frontal Cortex." *Japanese Journal of Psychiatry and Neurology* 47: 57–61.

LaHoste, G. J., J. M. Swanson, S. B. Wigal, C. Glabe, T. Wigal, N. King, and J. L. Kennedy. 1996. "Dopamine D4 Receptor Gene Polymorphism Is Associated with Attention Deficit Hyperactivity Disorder." *Molecular Psychiatry* 1: 121–24.

Lander, Eric S., and Nicholas J. Schork. 1994. "Genetic Dissection of Complex Traits." *Science* 265: 2037–48.

Lannfelt, Lars, Pierre Sokoloff, Marie-Pascale Martres, Catherine Pilon, Bruno Giros, Erik Jonsson, Gran Sedvall, and Jean-Charles Schwartz. 1992. "Amino Acid Substitution in the Dopamine D3 Receptor as a Useful Polymorphism for Investigating Psychiatric Disorders." *Psychiatric Genetics* 2: 249–56.

Lawford, Bruce R., Ross M. Young, John Rowell, Joan Qualichefski, Barbara H. Fletcher, Karl Syndulko, Terry Ritchie, and Ernest P. Noble. 1995. "Bromocriptine in the Treatment of Alcoholics with the D2 Dopamine Receptor A1 Allele." *Nature Medicine* 1: 337–41.

LeDoux, Joseph E. 1989. "Cognitive-Emotional Interactions in the Brain." *Cognition and Emotion* 3: 267–89.

LeDoux, Joseph E., Jiro Iwata, Piera Cicchetti, and Donald J. Reis. 1988. "Different Projections of the Central Amygdaloid Nucleus Mediate Autonomic and Behavioral Correlates of Conditioned Fear." *Journal of Neuroscience* 8: 2517–29.

Leith, Nancy J., and Robert J. Barrett. 1976. "Amphetamine and the Reward System: Evidence for Tolerance and Postdrug Depression." *Psychopharmacology* 46: 19–25.

Lepore, Marino. 1993. "A Behavioral and Neurological Analysis of the Self-Administration of Brain-Stimulation Technique: A Model of Drug Self-Administration." Ph.D. diss., McGill University.

Lepore, Marino, and Keith B. J. Franklin. 1992. "Modelling Drug Kinetics with Brain Stimulation: Dopamine Antagonists Increase Self-Stimulation." *Pharmacology Biochemistry and Behavior* 41: 489–96.

Lepore, Marino, and Eliot L. Gardner. 1995. "Neurobiological Relationship Between Vulnerability to Depression and to Drug Abuse: In Vivo Microdialysis Studies." *Society for Neuroscience Abstracts* 21: 1955.

Lepore, Marino, Xinhe Liu, Virginia Savage, Daniel Matalon, and Eliot L. Gardner. 1996. "Genetic Differences in Δ^9-Tetrahydrocannabinol-Induced Facilitation of Brain Stimulation Reward as Measured by a Rate-Frequency Curve-Shift Electrical Brain Stimulation Paradigm in Three Different Rat Strains." *Life Sciences [Pharmacology Letters]* 25: PL365–72.

Lewis, Michael J., and Harry L. June. 1990. "Neurobehavioral Studies of Ethanol Reward and Activation." *Alcohol* 7: 213–19.

———. 1994. "Synergistic Effects of Ethanol and Cocaine on Brain Stimulation Reward." *Journal of the Experimental Analysis of Behavior* 61: 223–29.

Li, Ting K., and Lawrence Lumeng. 1984. "Alcohol Preference and Voluntary Alcohol Intakes of Inbred Rat Strains and the National Institutes of Health Heterogeneous Stock of Rats." *Alcoholism* 8: 485–86.

Ling, Geoffrey S., Jason Gari Umans, and Charles E. Inturrisi. 1981. "Methadone: Radioimmunoassay and Pharmacokinetics in the Rat." *Journal of Pharmacology and Experimental Therapeutics* 217: 147–51.

Lopez Viets, V. C., and W. R. Miller. 1997. "Treatment Approaches for Pathological Gamblers." *Clinical Psychology Review* 17: 689–702.

Lowinson, Joyce H., Pedro Ruiz, Robert B. Millman, and John G. Langrod, eds. 1997. *Substance Abuse: A Comprehensive Textbook.* 3rd ed. Baltimore: Williams and Wilkins.

Lundstrom, K., M. Salminen, A. Jalanko, R. Savolainen, and I. Ulmanen. 1991. "Cloning and Characterization of Human Placental Catechol-O-Methyltransferase cDNA." *DNA and Cell Biology* 10: 181–89.

MacLean Paul D. 1955. "The Limbic System ('Visceral Brain') and Emotional Behavior." *Archives of Neurology and Psychiatry* 73: 130–34.

Maisonneuve, Isabelle M., and Mary J. Kreek. 1994. "Acute Tolerance to the Dopamine Response Induced by a Binge Pattern of Cocaine Administration in Male Rats: An In Vivo Microdialysis Study." *Journal of Pharmacology and Experimental Therapeutics* 268: 916–21.

Malhotra, A. K., M. Virkkunen, W. Rooney, M. Eggert, Markku Linnoila, and D. Goldman. 1996. "The Association Between the Dopamine D4 Receptor (DRD4) 16 Amino Acid Repeat Polymorphism and Novelty Seeking." *Molecular Psychiatry* 1: 388–91.

Markou, Athina, and George F. Koob. 1991. "Postcocaine Anhedonia: An Animal Model of Cocaine Withdrawal." *Neuropsychopharmacology* 4: 17–26.

———. 1992. "Bromocriptine Reverses the Elevation in Intracranial Self-Stimulation Thresholds Observed in a Rat Model of Cocaine Withdrawal." *Neuropsychopharmacology* 7: 213–24.

Marlatt, G. Alan. 1985a. "Cognitive Factors in the Relapse Process." In *Relapse Prevention: Maintenance Strategies in the Treatment of Addictive Behaviors,* edited by G. Alan Marlatt and Judith R. Gordon. New York: Guildford.

————. 1985b. "Cognitive Assessment and Intervention Procedures for Relapse Prevention." In *Relapse Prevention: Maintenance Strategies in the Treatment of Addictive Behaviors*, edited by G. Alan Marlatt and Judith R. Gordon. New York: Guildford.

————. 1987. "Craving Notes." *British Journal of Addiction* 82: 42–44.

Matthews, Robert T., and Dwight C. German. 1984. "Electrophysiological Evidence for Excitation of Rat Ventral Tegmental Area Dopaminergic Neurons by Morphine." *Neuroscience* 11: 617–26.

McBride, W. J., J. M. Murphy, Gregory J. Gatto, A. D. Levy, K. Yashimoto, Lawrence Lumeng, and Ting K. Li. 1993a. "CNS Mechanisms of Alcohol Self-Administration." *Alcohol and Alcoholism* 2[suppl]: 463–67.

McBride, W. J., J. E. Chernet, W. Dyr, Lawrence Lumeng, and Ting K. Li. 1993b. "Densities of Dopamine D2 Receptors Are Reduced in CNS Regions of Alcohol Preferring P Rats." *Alcohol* 10: 387–90.

McCourt, William F., Ronald J. Gurrera, and Henry S. G. Cutter. 1993. "Sensation Seeking and Novelty Seeking: Are They the Same?" *Journal of Nervous and Mental Disease* 181: 309–12.

Meliska, Charles J., Andrzej Bartke, Geoffrey McGlacken, and Robert A. Jensen. 1995. "Ethanol, Nicotine, Amphetamine, and Aspartame Consumption and Preferences in C57BL/6 and DBA/2 Mice." *Pharmacology Biochemistry and Behavior* 50: 619–26.

Mendelson, Jack, S. Teoh, U. Lange, Nancy Mello, R. Weiss, and A. Skupny. 1987. "Hyperprolactinemia During Cocaine Withdrawal." *National Institute on Drug Abuse Research Monograph Series* 81: 67–73.

Merlo Pich, Emilio, Marge Lorang, Mark Yeganeh, Fernando Rodríguez de Fonseca, Jacob Raber, George F. Koob, and Friedbert Weiss. 1995. "Increase in Extracellular Corticotropin-Releasing Factor-Like Immunoreactivity Levels in the Amygdala of Awake Rats During Restraint Stress and Ethanol Withdrawal as Measured by Microdialysis." *Journal of Neuroscience* 15: 5439–47.

Minabe, Yoshio, Kenji Emori, and Charles R. Ashby Jr. 1995. "Significant Differences in the Activity of Midbrain Dopamine Neurons Between Male Fischer 344 (F344) and Lewis Rats: An In Vivo Electrophysiological Study." *Life Sciences [Pharmacology Letters]* 56: PL261–67.

Mirenowicz, Jacques, and Wolfram Schultz. 1994. "Importance of Unpredictability for Reward Responses in Primate Dopamine Neurons." *Journal of Neurophysiology* 72: 1024–27.

Misslin, René, and Philippe Ropartz. 1981. "Effects of Methamphetamine on Novelty-Seeking Behaviour by Mice." *Psychopharmacology* 75: 39–43.

Misslin, René, Philippe Ropartz, and L. Jung. 1984. "Impairment of Responses to Novelty by Apomorphine and Its Antagonism by Neuroleptics in Mice." *Psychopharmacology* 82: 113–17.

Moolten, Marjorie, and Conan Kornetsky. 1990. "Oral Self-Administration of Ethanol and Not Experimenter-Administered Ethanol Facilitates Rewarding Electrical Brain Stimulation." *Alcohol* 7: 221–25.

Moreton, J. Edward, Timothy Roehrs, and Naim Khazan. 1976. "Drug Self-Administration and Sleep-Wake Activity in Rats Dependent on Morphine, Methadone, or L-Alpha-Acetylmethadol." *Psychopharmacologia* 47: 237–41.

Mucha, Ronald F. 1987. "Is the Motivational Effect of Opiate Withdrawal Reflected by Common Somatic Indices of Precipitated Withdrawal? A Place-Conditioning Study in the Rat." *Brain Research* 418: 214–20.

Muramatsu, Taro, and Susumu Higuchi. 1995. "Dopamine Transporter Gene Polymorphism and Alcoholism." *Biochemical and Biophysical Research Communications* 211: 28–32.

Murphy, Dennis L., Robert H. Belmaker, Monte S. Buchsbaum, Neil F. Martin, Roland Ciaranello, and Richard J. Wyatt. 1977. "Biogenic Amine-Related Enzymes and Personality Variations in Normals." *Psychological Medicine* 7: 149–57.

Nader, Karim, Antoine Bechara, David C. Roberts, and Derek van der Kooy. 1994. "Neuroleptics Block High-but Not Low-Dose Heroin Place Preferences: Further Evidence for a Two-System Model of Motivation." *Behavioral Neuroscience* 108: 1128–38.

Nazzaro, Jules M., Thomas F. Seeger, and Eliot L. Gardner. 1980. "Naloxone Blocks Phencyclidine's Dose-Dependent Effects on Direct Brain Reward Thresholds." *Proceedings of World Conference on Clinical Pharmacology and Therapeutics*. London: British Pharmacological Society.

———. 1981. "Morphine Differentially Affects Ventral Tegmental and Substantia Nigra Brain Reward Thresholds." *Pharmacology Biochemistry and Behavior* 14: 325–31.

Nestler, Eric J. 1993. "Molecular Mechanisms of Drug Addiction in the Mesolimbic Dopamine Pathway." *Seminars in the Neurosciences* 5:369–76.

———. 1994. "Molecular Neurobiology of Drug Addiction." *Neuropsychopharmacology* 11: 77–87.

Nestler, Eric J., Xavier Guitart, Jordi Ortiz, and Louis Trevisan. 1994. "Second-Messenger and Protein Phosphorylation Mechanisms Underlying Possible Genetic Vulnerability to Alcoholism." *Annals of the New York Academy of Sciences* 708: 108–18.

Nisell, Magnus, George G. Nomikos, and Torgny H. Svensson. 1994a. "Systemic Nicotine-Induced Dopamine Release in the Rat Nucleus Accumbens Is Regulated by Nicotinic Receptors in the Ventral Tegmental Area." *Synapse* 16: 36–44.

———. 1994b. "Infusion of Nicotine in the Ventral Tegmental Area or the Nucleus Accumbens Differentially Affects Accumbal Dopamine Release." *Pharmacology and Toxicology* 75: 348–52.

Noble, Ernest P. 1993. "The D2 Dopamine Receptor Gene: A Review of Association Studies in Alcoholism." *Behavior Genetics* 23: 119–29.

Noble, Ernest P., Kenneth Blum, M. E. Khalsa, Terry Ritchie, Anne Montgomery, R. C. Wood, R. J. Fitch, T. Ozkaragoz, Peter J. Sheridan, M. D. Anglin, A. Paredes, L. J. Treiman, and R. S. Sparks. 1993. "Allelic Association of the D2 Dopamine Receptor Gene with Cocaine Dependence." *Drug and Alcohol Dependence* 33: 271–85.

Noble, Ernest P., Kenneth Blum, Terry Ritchie, Anne Montgomery, and Peter J. Sheridan. 1991. "Allelic Association of the D2 Receptor Gene with Receptor-Binding Characteristics in Alcoholism." *Archives of General Psychiatry* 48: 648–54.

Noble, Ernest P., S. T. St. Jeor, Terry Ritchie, K. Syndulko, S. C. St. Jeor, R. J. Fitch, R. L. Brunner, and R. S. Sparkes. 1994. "D2 Dopamine Receptor Gene and Cigarette Smoking: A Reward Gene?" *Medical Hypotheses* 4: 257–60.

O'Brien, Charles P. 1997. "A Range of Research-Based Pharmacotherapies for Addiction." *Science* 278: 66–70.

O'Brien, Charles P., Anna R. Childress, I. O. Arndt, A. Thomas McLellan, G. E. Woody, and I. Maany. 1988. "Pharmacological and Behavioral Treatments of Cocaine Dependence: Controlled Studies." *Journal of Clinical Psychiatry* 49 (suppl, February 1988): 17–22.

O'Brien, Charles P., Anna R. Childress, and A. Thomas McLellan. 1991. "Conditioning Factors May Help to Understand and Prevent Relapse in Patients Who Are Recovering from Drug Dependence." *National Institute on Drug Abuse Research Monograph Series* 106: 293–312.

O'Brien, Charles P., Anna R. Childress, Thomas McLellan, and Ronald Ehrman. 1990. "Integrating Systematic Cue Exposure with Standard Treatment in Recovering Drug-Dependent Patients." *Addictive Behaviors* 15: 355–65.

O'Brien, Charles P., Anna R. Childress, A. Thomas McLellan, and Ronald Ehrman. 1992. "A Learning Model of Addiction." *Research Publications of the Association for Research on Nervous and Mental Disease* 70: 157–77.

O'Brien, Charles P., and A. Thomas McLellan. 1998. "Myths About the Treatment of Addiction." In *Principles of Addiction Medicine,* edited by A. W. Graham, T. K. Schultz, and B. B. Wilford. Chevy Chase, Md.: American Society of Addiction Medicine.

O'Keefe, John, and Herman Bouma. 1969. "Complex Sensory Properties of Certain Amygdala Units in the Freely Moving Cat." *Experimental Neurology* 23: 384–98.

Ono, Yutaka, Hiroshi Manki, Kimio Yoshimura, Taro Muramatsu, Hiroko Mizushima, Susumu Higuchi, Gohei Yagi, Shigenobu Kanba, and Masahiro Asai. 1997. "Association Between Dopamine D4 (D4DR) Exon III Polymorphism and Novelty Seeking in Japanese Subjects." *American Journal of Medical Genetics* 74: 501–3.

Ostrowski, Nancy L., Cynthia B. Hatfield, and Anthony R. Caggiula. 1982. "The Effects of Low Doses of Morphine on the Activity of Dopamine-Containing Cells and on Behavior." *Life Sciences* 31: 2347–50.

Papez, James W. 1937. "A Proposed Mechanism of Emotion." *Archives of Neurology and Psychiatry* 38: 725–43.

Parsons, Loren H., and Joseph B. Justice Jr. 1993. "Serotonin and Dopamine Sensitization in the Nucleus Accumbens, Ventral Tegmental Area, and Dorsal Raphe Nucleus Following Repeated Cocaine Administration." *Journal of Neurochemistry* 61: 1611–19.

Parsons, Loren H., Amanda D. Smith, and Joseph B. Justice Jr. 1991. "Basal Extracellular Dopamine Is Decreased in the Rat Nucleus Accumbens During Abstinence from Chronic Cocaine." *Synapse* 9: 60–65.

Paulson, Pamela E., and Terry E. Robinson. 1995. "Amphetamine-Induced Time-Dependent Sensitization of Dopamine Neurotransmission in the Dorsal and Ventral Striatum: A Microdialysis Study in Behaving Rats." *Synapse* 19: 56–65.

Perez de Castro, I., A. Ibanez, P. Torres, J. Saiz-Ruiz, and J. Fernandez-Piqueras. 1997. "Genetic Association Between Pathological Gambling and a Functional DNA Polymorphism at the D4 Receptor Gene." *Pharmacogenetics* 7: 345–48.

Persico, Antonio M., Bruce F. O'Hara, Stacy Farmer, Robin Gysin, Steven D. Flanagan, and George R. Uhl. 1993. "Dopamine D2 Receptor Gene Taq I 'A' Locus Map Including 'A4' Variant: Relevance for Alcoholism and Drug Abuse." *Drug and Alcohol Dependence* 31: 229–34.

Persico, Antonio M., David J. Vandenbergh, Stevens S. Smith, and George R. Uhl. 1993. "Dopamine Transporter Gene Polymorphisms Are Not Associated with Polysubstance Abuse." *Biological Psychiatry* 34: 265–67.

Pettit, Hugh O., Hwai T. Pan, Loren H. Parsons, and Joseph B. Justice Jr. 1990. "Extracellular Concentrations of Cocaine and Dopamine Are Enhanced During Chronic Cocaine Administration." *Journal of Neurochemistry* 55: 798–804.

Pettit, Hugh O., and Audrey J. Pettit. 1994. "Disposition of Cocaine in Blood and Brain After a Single Pretreatment." *Brain Research* 651: 261–68.

Phillips, Anthony G., and Hans C. Fibiger. 1987. "Anatomical and Neurochemical Substrates of Drug Reward Determined by the Conditioned Place Preference Technique." In *Methods of Assessing the Reinforcing Properties of Abused Drugs*, edited by Michael A. Bozarth. New York: Springer-Verlag.

Phillips, Anthony G., and Fredrik G. LePiane. 1980. "Reinforcing Effects of Morphine Microinjection into the Ventral Tegmental Area." *Pharmacology Biochemistry and Behavior* 12: 965–68.

Piazza, Pier V., Jean M. Deminiere, Michel Le Moal, and Hervé Simon. 1989. "Factors that Predict Individual Vulnerability to Amphetamine Self-Administration." *Science* 245: 1511–13.

Pontieri, Francesco E., Gianluigi Tanda, Francesco Orzi, and Gaetano Di Chiara. 1997. "Effects of Nicotine on the Nucleus Accumbens and Similarity to Those of Addictive Drugs." *Nature* 382: 255–57.

Pothos, Emmanuel, Pedro Rada, Gregory P. Mark, and Bartley G. Hoebel. 1991. "Dopamine Microdialysis in the Nucleus Accumbens During Acute and Chronic Morphine, Naloxone-Precipitated Withdrawal and Clonidine Treatment." *Brain Research* 566: 348–50.

Puglisi-Allegra, Stephano, Assunta Imperato, Luciano Angelucci, and Simona Cabib. 1991. "Acute Stress Induces Time-Dependent Responses in Dopamine Mesolimbic System." *Brain Research* 554: 217–22.

Pulvirenti, Luigi, and George F. Koob. 1994. "Dopamine Receptor Agonists, Partial Agonists, and Psychostimulant Addiction." *Trends in Pharmacological Sciences* 15: 374–79.

Rebec, George V., Chad P. Grabner, Michael Johnson, Robert C. Pierce, and Michael T. Bardo. 1997a. "Transient Increases in Catecholaminergic Activity in Medial Prefrontal Cortex and Nucleus Accumbens Shell During Novelty." *Neuroscience* 76: 707–14.

Rebec, George V., John R. Christensen, Cristiano Guerra, and Michael T. Bardo. 1997b. "Regional and Temporal Differences in Real-Time Dopamine Efflux in the Nucleus Accumbens During Free-Choice Novelty." *Brain Research* 776: 61–67.

Richardson, Nicole R., and Alain Gratton. 1996. "Behavior-Relevant Changes in Nucleus Accumbens Dopamine Transmission Elicited by Food Reinforcement: An Electrochemical Study in the Rat." 1996. *Journal of Neuroscience* 16: 8160–69.

Rietschel Marcella, Markus M. Nöthen, Lars Lannfelt, Pierre Sokoloff, Jean-Charles Schwartz, Mario Lanczik, Jürgen Fritze, Sven Cichon, Rolf Fimmers, Judith Körner, Hans-Jürgen Möller, and Peter Propping. 1993. "A Serine to Glycine Substitution at Position 9 in the Extracellular N-Terminal Part of the Dopamine D3 Receptor Protein: No Role in the Genetic Predisposition to Bipolar Affective Disorder." *Psychiatry Research* 46: 253–59.

Ritz, Mary C., Frank R. George, Christopher M. DeFiebre, and Richard A. Meisch. 1986. "Genetic Differences in the Establishment of Ethanol as a Reinforcer." *Pharmacology Biochemistry and Behavior* 24: 1089–94.

Robertson, Matthew W., Catherine A. Leslie, and James P. Bennett. 1991. "Apparent Synaptic Dopamine Deficiency Induced by Withdrawal from Chronic Cocaine Treatment." *Brain Research* 538: 337–39.

Robinson, Terry E., Phillip A. Jurson, Julie A. Bennett, and Kris M. Bentgen. 1988. "Persistent Sensitization of Dopamine Neurotransmission in Ventral Striatum (Nucleus Accumbens) Produced by Prior Experience with (+)-Amphetamine: A Microdialysis Study in Freely Moving Rats." *Brain Research* 462: 211–22.

Rocha, Beatriz A., Fabio Fumagalli, Raul R. Gainetdinof, Sara R. Jones, Robert Ator, Bruno Giros, Gary W. Miller, and Marc G. Caron. 1998. "Cocaine Self-Administration in Dopamine Transporter Knockout Mice." *Nature Neuroscience* 1: 132–37.

Rossetti, Zvani L., Yousef Hmaidan, and Gian L. Gessa. 1992. "Marked Inhibition of Mesolimbic Dopamine Release: A Common Feature of Ethanol, Morphine, Cocaine, and Amphetamine Abstinence in Rats." *European Journal of Pharmacology* 221: 227–34.

Routtenberg, Aryeh. 1981. "Drugs of Abuse and the Endogenous Reinforcement System: The Resistance of Intracranial Self-Stimulation Behavior to the Inebriating Effects of Ethanol." *Annals of the New York Academy of Sciences* 362: 60–66.

Roy, S. N., A. K. Bhattacharyya, A. Pradhan, and S. N. Pradhan. 1978. "Behavioral and Neurochemical Effects of Repeated Administration of Cocaine in Rats." *Neuropharmacology* 17: 559–64.

Rupcich, N., G. R. Frisch, and R. Govoni. 1997. "Comorbidity of Pathological Gambling in Addiction Treatment Facilities." *Journal of Substance Abuse Treatment* 14: 573–74.

Scanlon, Paul D., Fredrick A. Raymond, and Richard A. Weinshilboum. 1979. "Catechol-O-Methyl Transferase: Thermolabile Enzyme in Erythrocytes of Subjects Homozygous for the Allele for Low Activity." *Science* 203: 63–65.

Schaefer, Gerald J., and Richard P. Michael. 1986. "Changes in Response Rates and Reinforcement Thresholds for Intracranial Self-Stimulation During Morphine Withdrawal." *Pharmacology Biochemistry and Behavior* 25: 1263–69.

Schilstrom, Bjorn, H. Martin Svensson, Torgny H. Svensson, and George G. Nomikos. 1998. "Nicotine and Food Induced Dopamine Release in the Nucleus

Accumbens of the Rat: Putative Role of α7 Nicotinic Receptors in the Ventral Tegmental Area." *Neuroscience* 85: 1005–9.

Schooler, Carmi, Theodore P. Zahn, Dennis L. Murphy, and Monte S. Buchsbaum. 1978. "Psychological Correlates of Monoamine Oxidase in Normals." *Journal of Nervous and Mental Disease* 166: 177–78.

Schrater, Paul A., Albert C. Russo, Toni L. Stanton, J. Robert Newman, Lynn M. Rodriguez, and Alexander L. Beckman. 1993. "Changes in Striatal Dopamine Metabolism During the Development of Morphine Physical Dependence in Rats: Observations Using In Vivo Microdialysis." *Life Sciences* 52: 1535–45.

Schuckitt, Marc A. 1994. "Low Level of Response to Alcohol as a Predictor of Future Alcoholism." *American Journal of Psychiatry* 151: 184–89.

Schulteis, Gery, Athina Markou, Lisa H. Gold, Luis Stinus, and George F. Koob. 1994. "Relative Sensitivity of Multiple Indices of Opiate Withdrawal: A Quantitative Dose-Response Analysis." *Journal of Pharmacology and Experimental Therapeutics* 271: 1391–98.

Schultz, Wolfram. 1994. "Behavior-Related Activity of Primate Dopamine Neurons." *Revue Neurologique* 150: 634–39.

Schultz, Wolfram, Paul Apicella, and Tomas Ljungberg. 1993. "Responses of Monkey Dopamine Neurons to Reward and Conditioned Stimuli During Successive Steps of Learning a Delayed Response Task." *Journal of Neuroscience* 13: 900–913.

Schultz, Wolfram, Paul Apicella, Tomas Ljungberg, Ranulfo Romo, and Eugenio Scarnati. 1993. "Reward-Related Activity in the Monkey Striatum and Substantia Nigra." *Progress in Brain Research* 99: 227–35.

Schultz, Wolfram, Paul Apicella, Eugenio Scarnati, and Tomas Ljungberg. 1992. "Neuronal Activity in Monkey Ventral Striatum Related to the Expectation of Reward." *Journal of Neuroscience* 12: 4595–4610.

Seeger, Thomas F., and Kristin R. Carlson. 1981. "Amphetamine and Morphine: Additive Effects on ICSS Threshold." *Society for Neuroscience Abstracts* 7: 974.

Seeger, Thomas F., and Eliot L. Gardner. 1979. "Enhancement of Self-Stimulation Behavior in Rats and Monkeys After Chronic Neuroleptic Treatment: Evidence for Mesolimbic Supersensitivity." *Brain Research* 175: 49–57.

Self, David W., and Eric J. Nestler. 1995. "Molecular Mechanisms of Drug Reinforcement and Addiction." *Annual Review of Neuroscience* 18: 463–95.

Self, David W., Rose Z. Terwilliger, Eric J. Nestler, and Larry Stein. 1994. "Inactivation of Gi and Go Proteins in Nucleus Accumbens Reduces Both Cocaine and Heroin Reinforcement." *Journal of Neuroscience* 14: 6239–47.

Sesack, Susan R., and Virginia M. Pickel. 1992. "Dual Ultrastructural Localization of Enkephalin and Tyrosine Hydroxylase Immunoreactivity in the Rat Ventral Tegmental Area: Multiple Substrates for Opiate-Dopamine Interactions." *Journal of Neuroscience* 12: 1335–50.

Shaham, Yavin. 1993. "Immobilization Stress-Induced Oral Opioid Self-Administration and Withdrawal in Rats: Role of Conditioning Factors and the Effect of Stress on 'Relapse' to Opioid Drugs." *Psychopharmacology* 111: 477–85.

Shaham, Yavin, Heshmat Rajabi, and Jane Stewart. 1996. "Relapse to Heroin-Seeking in Rats Under Opioid Maintenance: The Effects of Stress, Heroin Priming, and Withdrawal." *Journal of Neuroscience* 16: 1957–63.

Shaham, Yavin, and Jane Stewart. 1995. "Stress Reinstates Heroin-Seeking in Drug-Free Animals: An Effect Mimicking Heroin, Not Withdrawal." *Psychopharmacology* 119: 334–41.

———. 1996. "Effects of Opioid and Dopamine Receptor Antagonists on Relapse Induced by Stress and Reexposure to Heroin in Rats." *Psychopharmacology* 125: 385–91.

Shiffman, Saul. 1987. "Craving: Don't Let Us Throw the Baby out with the Bath Water." *British Journal of Addiction* 82: 37–38.

Shiffman, Saul, Mary Hickcox, Jean A. Paty, Mary Gnys, Tom Richards, and Jon D. Kassel. 1997. "Individual Differences in the Context of Smoking Lapse Episodes." *Addictive Behaviors* 22: 797–811.

Shizgal, Peter. 1997. "Neural Basis of Utility Estimation." *Current Opinion in Neurobiology* 7: 198–208.

Siegel, Ronald K. 1982. "Cocaine Smoking." *Journal of Psychoactive Drugs* 14: 321–37.

Simpson, D. M., and Zoltan Annau. 1977. "Behavioral Withdrawal Following Several Psychoactive Drugs." *Pharmacology Biochemistry and Behavior* 7: 59–64.

Smith, Stevens S., Bruce F. O'Hara, Antonio M. Persico, David A. Gorelick, David B. Newlin, David Vlahov, Liza Solomon, Roy Pickens, and George R. Uhl. 1992. "Genetic Vulnerability to Drug Abuse: The D2 Dopamine Receptor Taq I B1 Restriction Fragment Length Polymorphism Appears More Frequently in Polysubstance Abuse." *Archives of General Psychiatry* 49: 723–27.

Solomon, Richard L. 1980. "The Opponent Process Theory of Acquired Motivation." *American Psychologist* 35: 691–712.

Solomon, Richard L., and John D. Corbit. 1974. "An Opponent-Process Theory of Motivation: I. Temporal Dynamics of Affect." *Psychological Review* 81: 119–45.

Sora, Ichiro, Christine Wichems, Nobuyuki Takahashi, Xiao-Fei Li, Zhizhen Zeng, Randal Revay, Klaus-Peter Lesch, Dennis L. Murphy, and George R. Uhl. 1998. "Cocaine Reward Models: Conditioned Place Preference can be Established in Dopamine- and in Serotonin-Transporter Knockout Mice." *Proceedings of the National Academy of Sciences of the United States of America* 95: 7699–7704.

Spanagel, Rainer, Osborne F. Almeida, Christine Bartl, and Toni S. Shippenberg. 1994. "Endogenous Kappa-Opioid Systems in Opiate Withdrawal: Role in Aversion and Accompanying Changes in Mesolimbic Dopamine Release." *Psychopharmacology* 115: 121–27.

Spanagel, Rainer, and Toni S. Shippenberg. 1993. "Modulation of Morphine-Induced Sensitization by Endogenous Kappa-Opioid Systems in the Rat." *Neuroscience Letters* 153: 232–36.

Specker, S. M., G. A. Carlson, G. A. Chistenson, and M. Marcotte. 1995. "Impulse Control Disorders and Attention Deficit Disorder in Pathological Gamblers." *Annals of Clinical Psychiatry* 7: 175–79.

Spielman, Richard S., and Richard M. Weinshilboum. 1981. "Genetics of Red Cell COMT Activity: Analysis of Thermal Stability and Family Data." *American Journal of Medical Genetics* 10: 279–90.

Spunt, Barry, Henry Lesieur, Dana Hunt, and Leila Cahill. 1995. "Gambling Among Methadone Patients." *International Journal of the Addictions* 30: 929–62.

Spyraki, Christina, Hans C. Fibiger, and Anthony G. Phillips. 1983. "Attenuation of Heroin Reward in Rats by Disruption of the Mesolimbic Dopamine System." *Psychopharmacology* 79: 278–83.

Stewart, Jane. 1983. "Conditioned and Unconditioned Drug Effects in Relapse to Opiate and Stimulant Drug Self-Administration." *Progress in Neuropsychopharmacology and Biological Psychiatry* 7: 591–97.

———. 1984. "Reinstatement of Heroin and Cocaine Self-Administration Behavior in the Rat by Intracerebral Application of Morphine in the Ventral Tegmental Area." *Pharmacology Biochemistry and Behavior* 20: 917–23.

Stewart, Jane, and Harriet de Wit. 1987. "Reinstatement of Drug-Taking Behavior as a Method of Assessing Incentive Motivational Properties of Drugs." In *Methods of Assessing the Reinforcing Properties of Abused Drugs*, edited by Michael A. Bozarth. New York: Springer-Verlag.

Stewart, Jane, and Paul Vezina. 1988. "A Comparison of the Effects of Intra-Accumbens Injections of Amphetamine and Morphine on Reinstatement of Heroin Intravenous Self-Administration Behavior." *Brain Research* 457: 287–94.

Stewart, Jane, and Roy A. Wise. 1992. "Reinstatement of Heroin Self-Administration Habits: Morphine Prompts and Naltrexone Discourages Renewed Responding After Extinction." *Psychopharmacology* 108: 79–84.

Stinus, Louis, Michel Le Moal, and George F. Koob. 1990. "Nucleus Accumbens and Amygdala Are Possible Substrates for the Aversive Stimulus Effects of Opiate Withdrawal." *Neuroscience* 37: 767–73.

Suarez, B. K., A. Parsian, C. L. Hampe, R. D. Todd, T. Reich, and C. Robert Cloninger. 1994. "Linkage Disequilibria at the D2 Dopamine Receptor Locus (DRD2) in Alcoholics and Controls." *Genomics* 19: 12–20.

Suaud-Chagny, M. R., K. Chergui, G. Chouvet, and François Gonon. 1992. "Relationship Between Dopamine Release in the Rat Nucleus Accumbens and the Discharge Activity of Dopaminergic Neurons During Local In Vivo Application of Amino Acids in the Ventral Tegmental Area." *Neuroscience* 49: 63–72.

Suzuki, Tsutomu, Frank R. George, and Richard A. Meisch. 1988. "Differential Establishment and Maintenance of Oral Ethanol Reinforced Behavior in Lewis and Fischer 344 Inbred Rat Strains." *Journal of Pharmacology and Experimental Therapeutics* 245: 164–70.

Thombs, Dennis L. 1994. *Introduction to Addictive Behaviors*. New York: Guilford.

Tidey, Jennifer W., and Klaus A. Miczek. 1997. "Acquisition of Cocaine Self-Administration After Social Stress: Role of Accumbens Dopamine." *Psychopharmacology* 130: 203–12.

Tiffany, S. T., and B. L. Carter. 1998. "Is Craving the Source of Compulsive Drug Use?" *Journal of Psychopharmacology* 12: 23–30.

Tiitinen, H., P. May, K. Reinikainen, and R. Naatanen. 1994. "Acute Novelty Detection in Humans Is Governed by Preattentive Sensory Memory." *Nature* 372: 90–92.

Trulson, Michael E., John C. Joe, Susan Babb, and Joachim D. Raese. 1987. "Chronic Cocaine Administration Depletes Tyrosine Hydroxylase Immunoreactivity in the Mesolimbic Dopamine System in the Rat Brain: Quantitative Light Microscopic Studies." *Brain Research Bulletin* 19: 39–45.

Uhl, George, Kenneth Blum, Ernest Noble, and Stevens Smith. 1994. "Substance Abuse Vulnerability and D2 Receptor Gene." *Trends in Neurosciences* 16: 83–88.

Uhl, George R., Gregory I. Elmer, Michele C. LaBuda, and Roy W. Pickens. 1995. "Genetic Influences in Drug Abuse." In *Psychopharmacology: The Fourth Generation of Progress,* edited by Floyd E. Bloom and David J. Kupfer. New York: Raven.

Vaillant, George E. 1966. "A Twelve-Year Follow-up of New York Narcotic Addicts. I. The Relation of Treatment to Outcome." *American Journal of Psychiatry* 122: 727–37.

———. 1988. "What Can Long-Term Follow-up Teach Us About Relapse and Prevention of Relapse in Addiction?" *British Journal of Addiction* 83: 1147–57.

———. 1998. "Natural History of Addiction and Pathways to Recovery." In *Principles of Addiction Medicine,* edited by Allan W. Graham, Terry K. Schultz, and Bonnie B. Wilford. Chevy Chase, Md.: American Society of Addiction Medicine.

Vandenbergh, David. J., Antonio M. Persico, Anita L. Hawkins, Constance A. Griffin, Xiang Li, Ethylin W. Jabs, and George R. Uhl. 1992. "Human Dopamine Transporter Gene (DAT1) Maps to Chromosome 5p15.3 and Displays a VNTR." *Genomics* 14: 1104–6.

Vandenbergh, David J., Lawrence A. Rodriguez, Ivan T. Miller, George R. Uhl, and Herbert M. Lachman. 1997a. "High-Activity Catechol-O-Methyltransferase Allele Is More Prevalent in Polysubstance Abusers." *American Journal of Medical Genetics* 74: 439–42.

Vandenbergh, David J., Alan B. Zonderman, Jocelyn Wang, George R. Uhl, and Paul T. Costa. 1997b. "No Association Between Novelty Seeking and Dopamine D4 Receptor (DRD4) Exon III Seven Repeat Alleles in Baltimore Longitudinal Study of Aging Participants." *Molecular Psychiatry* 2: 417–19.

van der Kooy, Derek. 1987. "Place Conditioning: A Simple and Effective Method for Assessing the Motivational Properties of Drugs." In *Methods of Assessing the Reinforcing Properties of Abused Drugs,* edited by Michael A. Bozarth. New York: Springer-Verlag.

Van Tol, Hubert H. M., Caren M. Wu, Hong C. Guan, Koichi Ohara, James R. Bunzow, Olivier Civelli, James Kennedy, Phillip Seeman, Hyman B. Niznik, and Vera Jovanovic. 1992. "Multiple Dopamine D4 Receptor Variants in the Human Population." *Nature* 350: 610–14.

Vanyukov, Michael M., Howard B. Moss, Ling M. Yu, Ralph E. Tarter, and Ranjan Deka. 1995a. "Preliminary Evidence for an Association of a Dinucleotide Repeat Polymorphism at the MAO_A Gene with Early Onset Alcoholism/Substance Abuse." *American Journal of Medical Genetics* 60: 122–26.

Vanyukov, Michael M., Howard B. Moss, Ling M. Yu, and Ranjan Deka. 1995b. "A Dinucleotide Repeat Polymorphism at the Gene for Monoamine Oxidase A and Measures of Aggressiveness." *Psychiatry Research* 59: 35–41.

Volkow, Nora D., Gene-Jack Wang, Marian W. Fischman, Richard W. Foltin, Joanna S. Fowler, Naji N. Abumrad, Stephen Vitkun, Jean Logan, S. John Gatley, Naome Pappas, Robert Hitzemann, and Callen E. Shea. 1997. "Relationship Between Subjective Effects of Cocaine and Dopamine Transporter Occupancy." *Nature* 386: 827–30.

Volpicelli, Joseph R., Arthur I. Alterman, Motoi Hayashida, and Charles P. O'Brien. 1992. "Naltrexone in the Treatment of Alcohol Dependence." *Archives of General Psychiatry* 49: 876–80.

von Knorring, A., J. Hallman, L. von Knorring, and L. Oreland. 1991. "Platelet Monoamine Oxidase Activity in Type 1 and Type 2 Alcoholism." *Alcohol and Alcoholism* 26: 409–16.

Wei, Eddie, Horace H. Loh, and E. Leong Way. 1973. "Brain Sites of Precipitated Abstinence in Morphine Dependent Rats." *Journal of Pharmacology and Experimental Therapeutics* 185: 108–15.

Weinshilboum, Richard M., and Fredrick A. Raymond. 1977. "Inheritance of Low Erythrocyte Catechol-O-Methyl Transferase Activity in Man." *American Journal of Human Genetics* 29: 125–35.

Weiss, Friedbert, Martin P. Paulus, Marge T. Lorang, and George F. Koob. 1992a. "Increases in Extracellular Dopamine in the Nucleus Accumbens by Cocaine Are Inversely Related to Basal Levels: Effects of Acute and Repeated Administration." *Journal of Neuroscience* 12: 4372–80.

Weiss, Friedbert, Athina Markou, Marge T. Lorang, and George F. Koob. 1992b. "Basal Extracellular Dopamine Levels in the Nucleus Accumbens Are Decreased During Cocaine Withdrawal After Unlimited-Access Self-Administration." *Brain Research* 593: 314–18.

Werner, Toreen E., Stanley G. Smith, and W. Marvin Davis. 1976. "A Dose-Response Comparison Between Methadone and Morphine Self-Administration." *Psychopharmacologia* 47: 209–11.

Westerink, Ben H. C., Johan Tuntler, Geert Damsma, Hans Rollema, and Jan B. de Vries. 1987. "The Use of Tetrodotoxin for the Characterization of Drug-Enhanced Dopamine Release in Conscious Rats Studied by Brain Dialysis." *Naunyn-Schmiedeberg's Archives of Pharmacology* 336: 502–7.

White, Norman M., and Noboru Hiroi. 1993. "Amphetamine-Conditioned Cue Preference and the Neurobiology of Drug Seeking." *Seminars in the Neurosciences* 5: 329–36.

Whitmore, Elizabeth A., Susan K. Mikulich, Laetitia L. Thompson, Paula D. Riggs, Greg A. Aarons, and Thomas J. Crowley. 1997. "Influences on Adolescent Substance Dependence: Conduct Disorder, Depression, Attention Deficit Hyperactivity Disorder, and Gender." *Drug and Alcohol Dependence* 47: 87–97.

Wightman, R. Mark, and Paul A. Garris. 1996. "Dopamine Release and Intracranial Self-Stimulation." *Society for Neuroscience Abstracts* 22: 832.

Willick, Myrna L., and Larry Kokkinidis. 1995. "The Effects of Ventral Tegmental Administration of $GABA_A$, $GABA_B$ and NMDA Receptor Agonists on Medial Forebrain Bundle Self-Stimulation." *Behavioural Brain Research* 70: 31–36.

Wills, Thomas A., Michael Windle, and Sean D. Cleary. 1998. "Temperament and Novelty Seeking in Adolescent Substance Use: Convergence of Dimensions of

Temperament with Constructs from Cloninger's Theory." *Journal of Personality and Social Psychology* 74: 387–406.

Wise, Roy A. 1980. "Action of Drugs of Abuse on Brain Reward Systems." *Pharmacology Biochemistry and Behavior* 13 [suppl.1]: 213–23.

———. 1981. "Brain Dopamine and Reward." In *Theory in Psychopharmacology*, edited by Steven J. Cooper. Vol. 1. New York: Academic.

———. 1984. "Neural Mechanisms of the Reinforcing Action of Cocaine." *National Institute on Drug Abuse Research Monograph Series* 50: 15–33.

———. 1987a. "The Role of Reward Pathways in the Development of Drug Dependence." *Pharmacology and Therapeutics* 35: 227–63.

———. 1987b. "The Brain and Reward." In *The Neuropharmacological Basis of Reward*, edited by Jeffrey M. Liebman and Steven J. Cooper. Oxford: Clarendon.

———. 1993. "In Vivo Estimates of Extracellular Dopamine and Dopamine Metabolite Levels During Intravenous Cocaine or Heroin Self-Administration." *Seminars in the Neurosciences* 5: 337–42.

———. 1996. "Addictive Drugs and Brain Stimulation Reward." *Annual Review of Neuroscience* 19: 319–40.

Wise, Roy A., and Michael A. Bozarth. 1981. "Brain Substrates for Reinforcement and Drug Self-Administration." *Progress in Neuro-Psychopharmacology* 5: 467–74.

———. 1984. "Brain Reward Circuitry: Four Circuit Elements 'Wired' in Apparent Series." *Brain Research Bulletin* 12: 203–8.

Wise, Roy A., and Elizabeth Munn. 1995. "Withdrawal from Chronic Amphetamine Elevates Baseline Intracranial Self-Stimulation Thresholds." *Psychopharmacology* 117: 130–36.

Wise, Roy A., Aileen Murray, and Michael A. Bozarth. 1990. "Bromocriptine Self-Administration and Bromocriptine Reinstatement of Cocaine-Trained and Heroin-Trained Lever Pressing in Rats." *Psychopharmacology* 100: 355–60.

Wise, Roy A., Paola Leone, Robert Rivest, and Kina Leeb. 1995a. "Elevations of Nucleus Accumbens Dopamine and DOPAC Levels During Intravenous Heroin Self-Administration." *Synapse* 21: 140–48.

Wise, Roy A., Caterina Marcangione, and Pat Bauco. 1998. "Blockade of the Reward-Potentiating Effects of Nicotine on Lateral Hypothalamic Brain Stimulation by Chlorisondamine." *Synapse* 29: 72–79.

Wise, Roy A., Paige Newton, Kira Leeb, Bryan Burnette, Dorothy Pocock, and Joseph B. Justice Jr. 1995b. "Fluctuations in Nucleus Accumbens Dopamine Concentration During Intravenous Cocaine Self-Administration in Rats." *Psychopharmacology* 120: 10–20.

Wise, Roy A., and Pierre-Paul Rompré. 1989. "Brain Dopamine and Reward." *Annual Review of Psychology* 40: 191–225.

Wolf, Marina E., Francis J. White, and Xiu T. Hu. 1994. "MK-801 Prevents Alterations in the Mesoaccumbens Dopamine System Associated with Behavioral Sensitization to Amphetamine." *Journal of Neuroscience* 14: 1735–45.

Wolf, Marina E., Francis J. White, Richard Nassar, Richard J. Brooderson, and Mohamed R. Khansa. 1993. "Differential Development of Autoreceptor Subsensitivity and Enhanced Dopamine Release During Amphetamine

Sensitization." *Journal of Pharmacology and Experimental Therapeutics* 264: 249–55.

Woodward, Albert, Joan Epstein, Joseph Gfroerer, Daniel Melnick, Richard Thoreson, and Douglas Wilson. 1997. "The Drug Abuse Treatment Gap: Recent Estimates." *Health Care Financing Review* 18: 5–17.

Yeomans, John S. 1989. "Two Substrates for Medial Forebrain Bundle Self-Stimulation: Myelinated Axons and Dopamine Axons." *Neuroscience and Biobehavioral Reviews* 13: 91–98.

Yeomans, John S., and Marco Baptista. 1997. "Both Nicotinic and Muscarinic Receptors in Ventral Tegmental Area Contribute to Brain-Stimulation Reward." *Pharmacology Biochemistry and Behavior* 57: 915–21.

Young, Shelly D., and Adrian C. Michael. 1993. "Voltammetry of Extracellular Dopamine in Rat Striatum During ICSS-Like Electrical Stimulation of the Medial Forebrain Bundle." *Brain Research* 600: 305–7.

Young, Gerald A., J. Edward Moreton, Leonard T. Meltzer, and Naim Khazan. 1977. "L-Alpha-Acetylmethadol (LAAM), Methadone, and Morphine Abstinence in Dependent Rats: EEG and Behavioral Correlates." *Drug and Alcohol Dependence* 2: 141–48.

Young, Gerald A., George F. Steinfels, and Naim Khazan. 1978. "Transitional Patterns of Self-Administration Following Substitution of Methadone or L-Alpha-Acetylmethadol (LAAM) for Morphine in Dependent Rats." *Drug and Alcohol Dependence* 3: 273–79.

———. 1979. "Spontaneous vs. Naloxone-Induced Abstinence in Dependent Rats Self-Administering L-Alpha-Acetylmethadol (LAAM) or Morphine." *Pharmacology Biochemistry and Behavior* 10: 585–89.

Zuckerman, Marvin. 1979. *Sensation-Seeking: Beyond the Optimal Level of Arousal.* Hillsdale, N.J.: Erlbaum.

———. 1994. *Behavioral Expressions and Biosocial Bases of Sensation Seeking.* Cambridge: Cambridge University Press.

Chapter 4

Addiction as Impeded Rationality

HELGE WAAL AND JØRG MØRLAND

F ROM A CLINICAL point of view, drug taking is a complex behavior that involves consciousness and deliberate actions. The drug taker has to procure the drug or accept an offer. Consumption further involves a varied set of actions and procedures. This behavior clearly involves series of choices. The puzzling question is, therefore, why any individual continues to make what he or she—and certainly we—judge to be poor choices, choices of regret and poor net result.

The traditional explanation either leans on lack of norms and morals or rests the case on a disease concept. The former has ancient roots and is represented for instance by Plato: "From the moment of their birth men have a desire for food and drink. Every living creature has an instinctive love of satisfying this desire whenever it occurs, and the craving to do so can fill a man's whole being, so that he remains quite unmoved by the plea that he should do anything except satisfy his lust for the pleasures of the body, so as to make himself immune to all discomfort." (Plato 1970, 782). "Give a man correct education, and these instincts will lead him to virtue, but educate him badly and he'll end up at the other extreme," Plato states. Obviously lack of education is seen to be the core problem. Aristotle used the term *akrasia*, signifying the weakness of the will that makes man unable to resist temptations.

While the approaches of morals and norms dominated in the past, the disease concept arose to prominence during this century. One of its most prominent advocates, E. M. Jellinek (1960), emphasized that alcoholism is not caused by lack of moral knowledge or strength but by a bodily disease that deserves both medical attention and protection from moralistic condemnations. One consequence is the treatment concept and access to social security benefits. Another is the idea that addicted individuals cannot resist but have to do what the disease causes them to: They are guiltless.

Between these two polarities we find most modern views on addiction. Few would adhere to the extreme positions and explain addiction solely as lack of morals or completely excuse the addict, but the relative balance shifts. The U.S. policy of "war on drugs" draws some of its intensity from the moralistic approach, while the British system of health orientation is based on a view of addiction as primarily a health problem. Both systems accept some acts of addiction as punishable, however, and some as treatable.

In recent years, neurobiological research has created a view of addiction as an acquired brain disease due to long-term drug intake. At the same time, addiction is approached from the point of view of choice theory. In this chapter, we review some central clinical and neurobiological findings that pertain to addiction in general and to different substances of abuse. (For simplicity, we refer to all these substances, including nicotine and alcohol, as drugs). We also touch on some aspects of nonchemical addictions. Second, we survey some aspects of rational choice theory as well as the main choice-theoretical approaches to addiction. For each of these theories, the main propositions are confronted with the core neurobiological and clinical findings. The essence of our discussion is that it is fruitful to approach addicted behavior as a consequence of impeded choice competency because we face a type of goal-directed behavior that characteristically leads to suboptimal overall utility. Neurobiological research has come a long way explaining why the addict suffers from impeded choice competency in a way that renders the individual vulnerable to a poor net result. The choice theories prepare the ground for an understanding within the frame of broader theories on human behavior. While none of the choice theories seem to catch all the clinical aspects of addiction, each can be fruitfully used for aspects of the behavior.

What Is to Be Explained?

All explanations of addiction and policies on substances of abuse will have to confront the complex clinical realities. The development of addiction involves characteristic changes in motivation and self-control important both to the individual and to society. The frequency of drug taking is a central factor in this process but not the sole factor. Others relate to societal influences and others again to upbringing or biological dispositions. The clinical phenomenology is mostly described by concepts such as desire for drug effects, development of tolerance, abstinence reactions, and craving for drugs. The picture is modified by symptoms that reflect individuals who are trying to control their drug use as well as efforts by others in their environment to make them do so. The behavioral pattern is influenced both by the set and the setting, as noted by Norman Zinberg (1984) in his extensive research on controlled drug use.

In what is often referred to as an addictive career, it is common to distinguish several stages or states, with different characteristics. On one end we have the initial or experimental stages. There is a middle ground of use pattern often called recreational use, with overlap to harmful or symptomatic use. On the other end we find the stages of dependence, with addiction as the extreme consequence. In the initial stage, few deviant characteristics are typically found among users. It seems to be a "normal" phenomenon to try drugs regarded as exciting and acceptable in an adolescent peer group. Use should consequently be understood as responsive to the social setting, but along the stages in the career the picture changes. The experimenting adolescent is usually very different from the hard-core addict. The patient who seeks treatment for anxiety is far from the patient who is desperate for more benzodiazepines, and the recreational wine drinker very unlike the *clochard*, but there is no hard-and-fast distinction among these stages, which are mainly used for heuristic purposes. Addiction or dependence is not a fixed point but rather the extreme end of a spectrum of behaviors. In the intermediate stages of harmful use, abuse, or symptomatic use, the individual sometimes makes poor evaluations and slips out of control. In addictive use, lack of control is a more fundamental characteristic, but it is never absolute. Given sufficiently serious negative consequences, all addicts are able to abstain in a situation in which drugs are available.

Because there are no sharp distinctions, attempts to give a precise definition have so far ended in blind alleys. Expert groups in the World Health Organization (WHO) have proposed and revised definitions for decades. Because of the variety and context dependence of the clinical realities, the theoretical concept of addiction has been discarded in favor of the purely empirical diagnosis of psychoactive substance dependence used in ICD 10 (World Health Organization 1992) and DSM IV (American Psychiatric Association 1994). Dependence is said to exist when a cluster of cognitive, behavioral, and physiological features that indicate impaired control is present. These features can be operationalized to yield specific criteria, of which a certain number have to be present within a given time frame for the diagnosis to be justified. The criteria for dependence are given for each type of drug, even though most heavy users seem to have a multidrug use pattern.

Neurobiological Observations

One basic finding is that all drugs abused by humans also induce characteristic drug-related behaviors in animals. These include drug self-administration, drug-related place preference, drug discrimination, and reduced thresholds for intracranial self-stimulation. Obviously, drug use is related to biological mechanism shared by most or all higher animal species.

All drugs that influence the function of the brain appear to act at least partly by affecting communication between nerve cells, either by stimulating these processes or by inhibiting them. The acute action of any drug is often compensated for if the drug is present over a long period of time or taken repeatedly. These compensating processes are generated in the brain either in the affected neurons or in other systems and typically tend to counteract the acute effect of the drug (homeostatic neuroadaptation, or counteradaptation). It is a general phenomenon that, with some exceptions, the effects of acute and repeated drug intake are dramatically different. This is also the case for drugs of abuse. Hence, we first describe the neurobiology linked to the primary effect connected to the first times of use and then discuss the effects of repeated intake. (For fuller presentations see Goldstein 1994 or Gardner and David 1998.)

Primary Effects

Whether taken orally, by snorting, by smoking, or by injection, all psychoactive drugs are transported from the site of introduction to the brain by the bloodstream to act primarily on the communication between neurons. This communication works through transmitters released by the sending neuron and received by specialized proteins in the cell membrane of the receiving neuron, the receptors. A drug may change the activity of any type of neurotransmission in a number of ways. The sum of all changes caused by a single drug constitutes the total acute effect of that drug. Thus some drugs can influence billions of neurons through their action, others probably less than a million. While psychoactive drugs in general share this mechanism of action, the distinguishing feature of drugs of abuse is an activation of specific parts of the mesolimbic brain, the frontal cortex, amygdala, and hippocampus. These brain structures are involved in the integration of emotional and behavioral processes, often coupled with feelings of pleasure. They also appear to be essential in motivational learning. It seems to be a common feature of drugs of abuse that they are able to cause an increase in the amount of the neurotransmitter dopamine released in the nucleus accumbens and hence to activate these parts of the brain.

This feature does not in itself explain addictive behavior. Dopamine release in these structures is important for all types of motivated behavior and hence is not specific for drug use. It is nevertheless significant that these structures play a particularly important role with respect to exploratory, incentive, and early consummatory phases of thirst and hunger as well as sexual and nursing behavior, followed by reduced activity in late consummatory and satiety phases. In a simple and reductionist form, the neurobiological hypothesis states that, unlike other drugs that affect the central nervous system, drugs of abuse have the common ability to increase brain activities underlying motivation. This is thought to be experienced as rewarding, and if the reward is strong enough, the pulls of drug taking take on a dominant role in behavior regulation. These effects appear to be connected to reinforcement behavior, even though their coupling to reward can be discussed.

The hypothesis has substantial support from a vast amount of animal experiments with surgical lesions, drug antagonists and agonists (substances that block or mimic the drug effect on the receptor site), measurements of the synthesis, release, levels, and turnover of neurotransmitters. It is also supported by studies in humans, notably of imaging of brain structure and function. Yet the hypothesis may have to be somewhat modified and nuanced. Studies indicate that dopamine signals, rather than being directly linked to the subjective experience of reward, might serve the purpose of drawing attention to salient events (Horvitz, Stewart, and Jacobs 1997). It is also demonstrated that some animal strains lacking the dopamine transporter will show cocaine-conditioned place preference (Sora et al. 1998) and that animals with destroyed dopamine nerve terminals in midaccumbens will self-administer ethanol (Koob 1999). Further, the dopamine release following drug intake is not obvious in all types of drug. The bulk of evidence, however, favors the hypothesis that the ability to cause release of the relevant neurotransmitter in the motivational brain structures is a (but not the only) central feature of addicting drugs (Koob 1999).

Repeated Drug Taking

The basic principle of reinforcement is that positively experienced consequences of a certain type of behavior increase the frequency of that behavior. Obviously, this might be the prime cause for repeated drug intake; it is enjoyable or gives relief. Other causes might also be connected to the set and the setting, as drug taking is a social phenomenon. Regardless of cause, with a certain frequency over a certain time period, changes may occur in the motivational system. These changes represent the general phenomenon of neuroadaptation, which induces changes in neuronal function usually to the opposite effect of that caused by the single-dose stimulus (counteradaptations). There are several mechanisms of neuroadaptation, ranging from changes in the synthesis, transport, release, reuptake, and metabolism of neurotransmitters to increased or decreased number of receptors and changes in the processing of receptor signals in the receiving neurons. Of particular importance are adaptations that involve changes in the genome expression of the adapted cells of a more permanent type. Once established, these adaptations will express themselves fully when not counteracted by drug action, that is, in the withdrawal period after the last drug intake.

The simplest way in which these neuroadaptive processes can contribute to repeated drug intake has been outlined by George Koob (1992; Koob and Bloom 1988) and Eric Nestler (1992). They describe homeostatic adaptations in the reward systems that would require increased drug doses to achieve the same dopaminergic response as earlier (tolerance). After adaptation the drug-free state would also present a lower than normal dopamine level in the nucleus accumbens, probably coupled with reduced normal reward resulting in a state of anhedonia. In this way, an unpleasant situation is created that can be relieved by drug intake. Detoxified addicts often describe it as depression or boredom, a feeling that life is devoid of meaning and salience. They are often perceived by others as indifferent, lazy, or ambivalent. This is precisely what would be expected in a state of hypofunctioning motivational system. In such a state, abstaining addicts obviously would find it difficult to motivate themselves to do anything but take the drug that, in their experience, relieves this state of misery.

In addition, several other mechanisms operate in the brain of the individual who takes drugs repeatedly. Some processes appear to be facilitated or sensitized. Thus in some cases, smaller drug doses than before are needed to achieve a given feeling of reward (reverse tolerance). It also seems that patterns can be established in which slight stimulation of dopaminergic transmission (caused by small drug doses, stress, or various drug-linked cues and expectations) induces a strong desire for drug taking. The salience of drug taking for the addicted subject thus may be linked to another type of neuroadaptation causing sensitization of motivational systems. The mechanisms underlying these processes are now being intensively investigated. Among several factors involved, changes in dopamine systems and the level of endogenous opioids (produced by the body itself without drug intake) appear interesting. This sum of homeostatic neuroadaptation, sensitizing, and other long-term effects of drug intake might be considered the neurobiological basis for the phenomena of increased incentive salience and craving. As craving is frequently described by addicts as the main cause of their relapse, it is important in dealing with drug use to understand these processes. At present, however, we do not have a clear picture of the mechanisms involved or of the brain regions outside the reward system that might be responsible.

Contributory Effects

As emphasized earlier, most drugs of abuse affect neurons in several areas of the brain besides those in the reward system. Consequently, both direct effects and neuroadaptations to repeated drug intake will occur also in brain structures related to other types of mental functioning. The subjective experience of the immediate drug effect is therefore different from drug to drug, as is well known in clinical experience. Also, the consequences of repeated drug use will differ. One example is the adaptive changes underlying increased autonomic nervous system activity during benzodiazepine, alcohol, and opiate withdrawal experienced as cardiovascular symptoms, sleep disturbances, and increased smooth muscular tonus. Another is the increased sensitivity to pain (hyperalgesia) during opiate withdrawal.

Addiction and Specific Drugs

Several investigators have asked how drugs of abuse with very different chemical structures can lead to the same change, that is to say, increased dopaminergic transmission in the nucleus accumbens. Experimental work has revealed a number of mechanisms that may explain why different drugs of abuse share a common denominator. Some drugs, notably cocaine, amphetamine, and related drugs exert their main action directly at the synaptic level, on dopamine reuptake and to some on extent dopamine release. Others, such as ethanol, opiates, and tetrahydrocannabinol (the active ingredient in cannabis), seem to act in a more indirect way, by stimulating neurons located in the ventral tegmental area. These neurons connect to neurons in nucleus accumbens and release dopamine on activation. All drugs of abuse may therefore cause release of dopamine in the nucleus accumbens but may also to varying extents involve additional transmitters and additional brain regions. Consequently, subjective experience of drug use, abstinence reactions, and clinical patterns vary enormously across the various addictions because of contributory mechanisms and different modes of use. In the following, some aspects of these differences are highlighted to prepare the ground for discussion of the choice theories.

Addiction to Opioids

Clinically, the euphoria of the opioid user is characterized by a relaxed attitude toward both physical pain and mental worries. The subjective experience is mostly described as one of harmony and pleasure, with an element of indifference to the problems of this world. After repeated use, abstinent addicts experience both post-use anhedonia and symptoms of autonomic nervous systems dysfunctioning, such as sweating, diarrhea, muscle cramps, and intestinal pains. Addicted users often claim to be primarily motivated by the wish to avoid abstinence—to become "normal." The pattern of use is characteristically seven-days-a-week, steady use.

Neurobiological research has clarified many aspects of opioid use. Several types of opioid receptors have been found, and both their distribution and the mechanism through which the motivational areas are stimulated are well researched. Different adaptive changes in opioid systems are well established, and both the motive to avoid abstinence reactions and the postuse anhedonia can be explained. Through measurements of the concentration of the drug in addicts' blood serum, it can be demonstrated that chronic addicts (and animals in adequately designed experiments) seem to regulate the intake in a way that secure a level of opioid molecules sufficiently high to avoid negative experiences, more than they are seeking the high.

Addiction to Central Stimulants

Drugs that induce a feeling of energy and alertness are often called central stimulants. The effects of these drugs such as cocaine, amphetamines, and similar drugs—are very different from those of the opioids. The experiences are described as pleasurable feelings of satisfaction, and exhilaration. Signals of thirst, hunger, and tiredness are suppressed, and the user feels able to continue activity beyond usual limits with increased sense of competency. When addiction occurs, use typically develops in the direction of binges. During a binge, the user needs increasing stimulation to keep the high, while at the same time the signals of bodily disturbances reach higher levels. The episode ends with a crash, often a panic-stricken experience of extreme fatigue, threatening dysphoria, and pains. Afterward, the user will sleep, eat, drink, and engage in recreational activities, often firmly convinced that he or she will never more indulge in this type of utility-reducing behavior. Depression can be prominent; then the songs of the Sirens are heard again. At first as weak although luring voices but sooner or later—often triggered by cues in the environment—the music grows into an irresistible seduction. A preference reversal occurs, often very dramatically, as many case stories show. All types of elaborate precaution and self-binding measure are thrown aside. The typical cocaine addict does not, therefore, have the steady seven-days-a-week habit of the heroin user but is characterized instead by cyclical behavior: increasing frequency of consumption followed by a crash and a period of abstention.

In this area, too, neurobiological research has brought increasing knowledge. Cocaine and amphetamines act directly on synapses in the reward system to increase the amount of transmitter dopamine present. Several catecholamine transmitters are additionally involved in brain areas outside the reward system. This might explain the immediate effects, the euphoria produced, and the profile of the experiences.

The mechanisms of neuronal adaptation are less clear. The characteristic clinical picture is one of increasing doses within the binge episode. There is no marked long-term or between-episode tolerance but obviously a strong within-episode tolerance. It has been conjectured that some form of transmitter depletion is involved. According to Eliot Gardner and James David (1998), this explanation is either incomplete or wrong. Instead, the cause might be an imbalance between positive and negative reward systems.

Addiction to Alcohol and Tranquilizers

Clinically, these drugs have hypnotic and relaxant properties. The intoxication is characterized by impeded motor coordination, and the euphoria is not always obvious. To some extent, the attraction of use is more state dependent than in the case of opioids and central stimulants. Diazepam, for instance, is experienced as more rewarding in states of anxiety (negative reinforcement). It is also well known that expectancy factors have a significant role at low blood alcohol concentrations. The low-dose alcohol intake might be experienced as positive to a large extent by what one thinks will happen (Marlatt and Rohsenow 1980).

Addictive use patterns vary. For alcohol, Jellinek (1960) developed a typology with distinct patterns of use. Gamma alcoholics have excessive drinking bouts caused by strong longings for the effects of alcohol. Delta-type drinking is regular excessive drinking caused by inability to abstain, which is in turn explained by the desire to avoid withdrawal reactions. Other types included the regular high-level consumption without signs of physical dependency (the alpha type) and the reckless high-level use connected to psychological and social problems (the beta type). Jellinek's typology has not been validated by research, and in clinical practice one mostly observes mixed types. Use patterns differ according to situation and life period. Benzodiazepine use disorders also have varying patterns, with chronic low-level use dependency at one end and mixed dependency with alcoholic bouts and high-level use of benzodiazepines at the other. High-level intravenous use is sometimes concomitant with heroin use.

Of the extensive neurobiological research in this area, only a few aspects will be mentioned. Benzodiazepines and most other sedatives and hypnotics are known to exert their effect on GABA receptors by facilitating the action of the transmitter, with increased inhibitory effects as the result (Wesson, Smith, and Seymour 1992). Alcohol has similar effects and seems in addition, among other effects, to inhibit the NMDA receptors and thus to inhibit excitation of cells equipped with these receptors (Tabakoff and Hoffman 1992). It has been suggested that inhibition of NMDA receptors in nucleus accumbens or related brain areas could cause similar effects as those mediated by increased dopamine levels. There is also some evidence that increased GABA transmission by indirect means could lead to increased dopamine levels. Dependency states are dominated by neuroadaptation, with hypofunction in inhibitory neurons important in the regulation of anxiety, muscular tension, and autonomic functions. This hypofunctioning is unmasked when drug supplies are cut short. The typical benzodiazepine or alcohol dependent therefore experiences tense anxiety and depressive states when the drug concentration falls below a certain level. The feelings are unpleasant, and release from them obviously pleasurable.

Addiction to Nicotine

The subjective experience of smoking tobacco is commonly described as a mix of relaxant and stimulating feelings. Often, the cigarette smoker has a ritual of using his smoking habit to punctuate his daily routines. As noted by Thomas C. Schelling (1992), smoking is in addition influenced by taste to the extent that the user attaches particular importance to special brands of tobacco. Alcohol consumption also has several of these features. Use is compatible with most social activities, since smoking as such has modest behavioral consequences and only moderate effects on mood. There is no obvious smoking-induced high. The addiction pattern of nicotine is more socially influenced than many other addictions, and smoking often becomes part of an everyday lifestyle. Smokers who try to kick the habit have to change their personal lifestyles in order to master a life without smoking. After the sharp abstinence reactions of the first week, the prominent problems are hunger pangs, sorrow, and a lack of richness of life. Relapse may come very soon after exposure to environmental cues associated with smoking but occurs more often as a result of a kind of exhaustion. Ex-smokers find that, all things considered, life is better with smoking than without and reverse a set of hard-won premises and preferences. Their cognition changes, and they decide that after all it is not that disastrous to be dependent.

The basic neurobiological mechanism is well known. Nicotine functions as an acetylcholine agonist (interacts with acetylcholine receptors). Acetylcholine receptors have a wide distribution in the central nervous system. Dopamine release has been demonstrated consequent upon nicotine administration (Jarvik and Schneider 1992). It is relatively difficult to get animals to use nicotine, and only some species will develop self-administration. Smoking is nevertheless rapidly addicting in humans, and the habit is very hard to overcome. The attractive experiences that occur when the drug reaches the central nervous system seem to a significant degree to depend on adaptation caused by previous use. Both addicted research animals and humans seem to regulate use according to the level in the blood (serum measurements).

Addiction to Cannabis

The subjectively experienced effect of cannabis is a composite one but, broadly speaking, of two types. The first type is a sensation of changed perception, and this effect seems to be connected to low-level use. The second type is a general relaxant effect that offers a picture of sedation. The euphoria produced by cannabis is therefore complex, characterized partly by changes in perception of sensory input and partly by a relaxant effect. Upon repeated use, the experience changes, so that the effects on perception diminish and a low-energy, semidepressed state seems to dominate, along with indifference and a reduced capacity for social functioning. Cannabis use is not typically characterized by strong cravings, and it is not clear whether there is any typical time pattern of preferences. Some users prefer abstention for long periods, particularly those interested in the low-dose effects on perception. Regular users tend to have a daily use pattern, but it is not clear that consumption tends to be stable at high or low levels.

As users who run out of supply usually fail to experience serious abstinence reactions, it has often been denied that cannabis is addictive. Nevertheless, a relatively high proportion of users persist in continued use, often in spite of negative consequences. The persistence is often explained by a disinclination to face the world without the drug rather than by strong cannabis euphoria or fear of withdrawal reactions.

Cannabis also exerts its effects through activation of specific receptors (THC receptors). Increases of dopamine in the reward system have been demonstrated following stimulation (Gardner and Lowinson 1991). An effect meditated through endogenous opioids has also been found. The preference for THC is blocked by dopamine antagonists in the same way as with other dependence-producing drugs. As in the case of nicotine, it is difficult to trick animals into developing a chronic use of cannabis. It can be done with some rat strains, which in consequence develop typical behavioral changes. Cessation of use seldom causes strong reactions, although neuroadaption has been demonstrated.

Behavioral (Nonchemical) Addictions

Some types of behavior have important traits in common with addiction to drugs. Gambling is a particularly prominent example. As vividly described by Fyodor Dostoyevsky (1964), for instance, the path to addiction typically starts with seemingly innocent experimentation. The experience is exciting and attractive and induces repeat behavior. Gradually and insidiously, the gambling takes on compulsive overtones. Intentions to abstain from gambling are broken by diverse chance happenings, well assisted by self-deception. Then promises are broken to others as well, and the adverse consequences of gambling become more and more obvious. Addicted gamblers seem incapable both of abstaining from the lure of cards or the horse race and of controlling their use of money. The characteristic pattern of use, regret, and yielding to temptation has extensive phenomenological similarities with patterns of addictive drug use (see also Elster 1999). Abstinence reactions have also been described, although these are debatable. The DSM IV system for diagnosing pathological gambling mirrors that used for drug dependence.

In some eating disorders, notably bulimia, the unhappy sufferer tries in vain to control her—sometimes his—intake of calories, only to experience defeat and binges of eating. The path to the problem typically starts with an attempt to lose weight with starvation beyond the limits the body can integrate. The food—quite often some form of carbohydrate such as ice cream, chocolate, and cake—takes on the characteristics of a strongly wanted good. Self-control breaks down, with compulsive bingeing as the result. Once again, the phenomenology shows significant similarity with the drug addict. The behavior continues in spite of obvious negative effects. It is ridden with shame, broken promises, and periods of remorse and regret. Anorexia nervosa, in which the individual develops a pathologic experience of the body and an uncontrolled need to get slimmer beyond ordinary reason, has other characteristics. Intake of food is experienced as unpleasant and shameful and abstaining as rewarding.

Other forms of behavior have been shown to be similar to the classical addictions. Some people seem unable to control their use of credit cards or, more generally, to control their impulse to obtain goods in a pattern that is detrimental to their economy and, often, their social life. Others seem to be sexually insatiable or at least unable to abstain from the pursuit of new and ever more frequent sexual encounters. These types of behavior are often named manias, obviously to illustrate a state of mind characterized by impoverished self-insight and self-control. The common phenomenological feature of these cases—pathological gambling, eating disorders, credit card mania, erotomania—is that the person tries to control an impulse to satisfy some felt need or desire. The behavioral pattern has several characteristics in common with drug addiction, and society often responds in similar ways. The treatment of these conditions also shares important traits with substance abuse treatment models.

The neurobiological knowledge, however, is far less developed. As all motivated behavior is accompanied by release of dopamine in the mesolimbic structures, we would expect this also to occur in these cases. The assumption is confirmed by preliminary research, but the significance of the findings is far from clear. In addition, some types of eating disorder seem to involve serotonergic disturbances. Little is known about neuroadaptive mechanisms. Since these behaviors do not involve a chemical substance introduced into the nervous system, there must obviously be some paradigmatic differences. Nevertheless, a shared mechanism related to disturbances in the dopamine-mediated motivational areas is likely, whereas the contributory mechanisms in all probability are different.

Addictions, Choice, and Neurobiology

Addiction is by definition characterized by repeated acts with a total sum of negative consequences. This implies insufficient choice capacity. In our reading, these effects are largely understandable in light of present neurobiological knowledge of the motivational system and different types of neuroadaptation. Dependence-producing drugs obviously vary in their mechanisms and effectiveness, but three types of phenomenon are always of significance. One is the intensity and duration of dopamine release after drug intake. This influences the degree of attraction of use. Another is the concomitant effects in other brain areas. The third is neuroadaptations within and outside of the reward areas. Neuroadaptations linked to reward areas diminish the ability to appreciate alternative choices to repeated drug intake and to keep a long-term perspective. Addicts tend to develop myopic choice patterns. Neuroadaptations in other brain areas have different consequences, rendering the addict subject to disagreeable feelings characteristic of various types of drug. In this period, certain stimuli might induce strong longings for the drug. These phenomena are at present under neurobiological research.

Addictions, Choice, and Rationality

Our next question is whether these findings are reconcilable with choice theories to the extent that a combination will increase understanding of addictions. We consider three choice-theoretical approaches to addiction, in the order of descending emphasis on the rationality of addiction. According to Gary Becker's theory, addictive drug use is fully rational. In George Ainslie's theory, such behavior exhibits a specific type of time inconsistency that may be viewed as a form of irrationality. According to George Loewenstein's theory, addicts are subject to powerful visceral forces that can distort their cognition and induce strong temporary preferences for drugs. Yet even his theory leaves some room for choice.

Becker's Theory

As a background to Becker's view, we first consider the concept of rationality itself. According to Jon Elster (1999), an act is rational if it represents the best way to satisfy the desire that caused it, given agents' beliefs about the opportunities available to them and assuming that these beliefs are based on adequate information. The type of desire is irrelevant for an assessment of the rationality of the action. All that matters is whether it is instrumentally adequate as judged by agents' own beliefs. Consequently, rationality is subjective through and through. Although this idea of rationality has several features in common with the optimizing principles that govern simple biological systems, it differs from the latter in allowing a greater role for maximization over time and for strategic interaction.

From the clinical point of view, the irrelevance of type of desire detracts somewhat from the usefulness of this concept of rationality. Addict are not just people with a certain type of desire that they more or less successfully try to satisfy but people with a desire that—especially if satisfied—can create severe problems for those concerned and for society at large. Intense desire for drugs is often the effect of addiction rather than its cause. This being said, the idea of addiction as rational self-medication cannot be excluded. As argued by Kenneth Blum and colleagues (1990), some individuals may be born with a reward deficiency syndrome, which can make consumption of drugs seem to be a rational way to enhance an otherwise drab life. Others might be born with attention deficit disorder (ADHD/ADD). Stimulants are then experienced as improving the ability to concentrate and to relate in social settings. Schizophrenics treated by neuroleptics, which inhibit dopaminergic transmission, often experience anhedonia, and their drug taking might be seen as a way of diminishing side effects.

According to Becker's analysis (Becker and Murphy 1988), addiction is a specific type of consumer behavior and, as such, subject to the rational choice paradigm. Some goods are habit forming, that is, they involve a positive relationship between past and present behavior. The more that has been consumed in the past, the more is consumed in the present. If this process lowers the long-term utility of the consumer, the habit is negative, or "bad." If long-term utility is raised, the habit is "good." Here, we focus on bad habits, excluding such cases as habituation to classical music.

A good may have this habituating property without being addictive. "Technically, a habit becomes an addiction when the effects of past consumption on present consumption are sufficiently strong to be destabilizing" (Becker 1992, 329). The idea of destabilization is relative to a given level of consumption. An addiction may also be stable—but typically at a high level of consumption. At lower levels, there is a tendency for consumption to increase until the high-level stable state has been reached.

Becker is not very explicit concerning the properties a substance must have in order to induce this pattern. In his most precise statement, he asserts that "it is indeed necessary for greater past consumption to raise the marginal utility from present consumption—this corresponds to what is called 'reinforcement' in the addiction literature. Several other parameters are also important, including the rate of discount of future utilities and the rate of decay or depreciation in the contribution of past consumption to current utility" (Becker 1992, 329).

Becker seems to rest his case on four assumptions:

1. Beginning users anticipate correctly from the outset all the consequences of the various options, including those of becoming addicts.

2. Users make their decisions by discounting anticipated utilities to their present value. The discounting takes place at a constant rate, so that the relative importance of any two future periods, when seen from the perspective of the present, is the same. Those who attach low importance to future utility might do so either because they are intrinsically myopic or because their life chances are objectively poor.

3. The more users have used the drug in the past, the lower their total utility from drug consumption in the present. This assumption can be justified by the presence of homeostatic neuroadaptation as manifest in the phenomenon of tolerance.

4. The more that users have used the drug in the past, the higher the marginal utility from the good in the present. This assumption, too, could be supported by the presence of neuroadaptation, as manifest in withdrawal symptoms or sensitization.

A main weakness in the model is assumption 1. In the initial stages of an addicting career described above, few addicts have any clear idea of what they are embarking upon. Assumptions 3 and 4 are well instantiated by some drugs, heroin addiction being a particularly good illustration. As tolerance sets in, use increases, with diminishing return; also, users suffer increasing despair if supply grows short. Nicotine is also quite consistent with the model. Some patterns of alcoholism also fit the assumptions, but here there is more variation among consumers. Although many individuals develop a regular pattern of high-level drinking, others exhibit an erratic pattern of drinking bouts. The pattern of cocaine or amphetamine addiction is very different, however, with either erratic or cyclical patterns of use. For these drugs, the covariation between past and present consumption is less systematic. There is almost no long-term tolerance, even though within-episode tolerance may develop quite fast. The pattern described by Becker is therefore not typical. Assumption 1 is especially implausible in the case of these drugs.

The type of systematic covariation presupposed by Becker is typically found only in the use of drugs for which users seem to regulate use frequency according to blood serum levels to avoid abstinence reactions. This pattern is not related to the core effects but more typically to some of the secondary effects. This is also the case for drugs for which abstinence reactions are most prominent. In these types of drug use, the increased marginal utility is also dependent on level of former use.

Cannabis is another problematic case. Although cannabis use is often high level and regular, it is sometimes low level and irregular. High-level regular use does not seem to be motivated by increased marginal utility. Rather, the user seems motivated by lack of interest in other activities, by devaluation of other utilities. Low-level irregular use is motivated by the wish to retain the effects on sensory experiences.

Assumption 2 has the counterempirical implication of excluding preference reversals. It is a mystery why people who discount the future at a constant rate would change their relative evaluation of drug taking and abstention from one point in time to another. Becker does only allow for external life events to modify preferences, and this is often described as causation for relapses. But, preference reversals can also occur without any changes in the environment, through sheer passage of time. To the extent that external factors are involved, these may be mere environmental cues rather than, as in Becker's analysis, traumatic events such as divorce or induction into the army. Becker would also have problems explaining why addicts try to control their use by techniques of self-binding. Basically, the Becker approach relies heavily on the push factors—factors connected to the problems of abstention. The theory is less useful for other aspects.

Ainslie's Theory

According to George Ainslie (1992) animals as well as human beings tend to discount the future hyperbolically. The central idea is that, whereas utility in the present counts much more heavily than utility in the near future, utility in the near future counts only a little more than utility in the remote future. This form of discounting allows the possibility of preference reversal. When people move along in time so that what was period 2 becomes the current period 1, a reward in period 2 that was inferior to another reward in period 3 when evaluated in period 1, may be superior to the period-3 reward when both are evaluated in period 2. Although in period 1 users planned to choose the period-3 reward, they change their mind in period 2 and choose the reward available at that time. The period-2 reward is initially dominated by its competitor and then comes to dominate it.

Ainslie argues that individuals use personal rules to overcome this inconsistency and to be able to stick to past decisions. In following a personal rule, they treat one consumption instance as one in a series of similar acts and their present choice as a predictor of future choices: If I yield to temptation today, why wouldn't I do it again tomorrow? Ainslie shows that rule-bound rationality may enable individuals to adhere to their original decision even when instant rationality would suggest a revision. (For a fuller discussion, see Ole-Jørgen Skog's chapter in this volume.)

For Ainslie, then, rule-bound rationality enables individuals to coordinate their different utilities or interests in a consistent manner. Individuals have an internal marketplace in mind, in which a wide array of interests might be pursued. These interests compete to dominate choice, and just as in rational choice theory, individuals choose that which is perceived as bringing the largest utility. Because of time dependency, those interests particularly close at hand tend to dominate even though they in the immediate past were judged inferior. Following this reasoning, we are able to understand that ambivalence and preference reversals can be understood even if we see humans as led by conscious choices. To Ainslie, "even seemingly irrational and unwanted behaviors are goal directed" (Anslie 1992, xii). The relevance for addictive behavior is obvious.

One warning should be noted. Anslie does not seem particularly focused on chemical addictions. His ambition is to explain human behavior in a larger sense, and addiction is first of all used as an especially vivid example in which the pursuit of interests leads to inconsistent choices "that one does not feel that one wants to make, but nevertheless makes repeatedly" (Ainslie 1992, 5). Addiction is therefore a class of behaviors, and Ainslie's central explanatory approach is time-dependent, hyperbolic discounting of future utilities.

To understand this view, it is necessary to understand an interest as a mental representation of a utility. Interests have different properties, among them a "characteristic period of dominance; a length of time when an interest's discount curve rises above those of its competitors. The period will depend on the kinds of rewards the interest has arisen to exploit and on the intrinsic limitations of their particular modes of exploitation. This period, in turn, will have major effects on what behaviors particular interests typically favor" (Ainslie 1992, 96). In this perspective, he defines addictions as behavior caused by interests that dominate other interests in periods ranging from hours to days and states that addictions have a "clear phase of conscious though temporary preference, followed by an equally clear period of regret" (Ibid., 97). Other types of interest have other periods of dominance. The period of domination for pains is fractions of seconds, that for itches seconds to minutes, and that for sellouts months to years.

All such patterns of temporary preference are likely to be experienced as problems, since they tend to detract from overall utility in the long run. In the case of addictions, they usually emerge as a problem after a few years. At that point, people may try to stop but are unlikely to succeed unless they apply strong and efficient personal rules. According to Ainslie (1998), clinical addiction is a behavioral pattern that follows from futile attempts to control preference reversals, when the relevant interest dominates for periods ranging from a few hours to a few days. The goods or interests with the temporal preference pattern of addictions include not only drugs of abuse but also behaviors such as gambling, overeating, and exhibitionism.

As we did with Becker's analysis, we can ask what properties a substance would need to have in order to cause the pattern described by Ainslie. Ainslie does not focus on any chemical or biological property. His prime interest lies in the time period of dominance during which other possible utilities are overshadowed. One approach to explanation might be through the strength of the euphoric effect (or of the expected effect). Small utilities would not dominate over large delayed utilities even at close hand. If a stronger utility does have sufficient strength, this does not cause an addiction unless the dominance lasts the time period that characterizes addictions. There must therefore also be an enduring characteristic: The experience of reward must last longer than other types.

With regard to the characteristics of single-dose usage, some drugs fit well with Ainslie's model. Whereas for most people the delights of ice-cream eating diminish rapidly, the euphoria of a heroin injection lasts for hours. The wish for heroin dominates over other interests, whether close or distant in time. In this perspective, Ainslie's model seems to focus adequately on the euphoria, while Becker's approach seems to focus mostly on the increasing marginal utility caused by abstinence reactions.

Although delayed larger utilities are obviously discounted, the influence of the time factor is more complicated. While the initial heroin high lasts a certain period, the effects of repeated drug intake complicate the picture. Through homeostatic neuroadaptation, the utility of heroin use in itself diminishes. It is the state without heroin that seems unattractive. At first, this is caused by abstinence reactions through neuroadaptation to the secondary effects. After these have diminished, post-use anhedonia by adaptation to the primary, core effects might cause most utilities to be devalued, whether present or distant. The devaluation may persist not only for days but for months or years.

Another important problem is that preference reversal often seems to come quite suddenly, by some cue-dependent signaling followed by craving reactions. It is not that the possibility of consumption is necessarily immediately available; some cues or signals seem to have profound influence on the preference situation.

The patterns of the nicotine addict and the cannabis user also represent some problems. Smoking is characteristically a long-term behavior. Most addicts use nicotine for several years, perhaps with short periods of half-hearted regret but often with no serious intention to quit. If they try, they typically experience signs of neuroadaptation—cravings and dysphoria. Although other and future utilities are strongly discounted during these periods, the cravings are initially very short-lasting, usually a few minutes. The time period in the initial phase of abstention is therefore more like that of itches. After a few days the duration of this period increases to reach that of addictions. Cocaine addicts and bingeing alcoholics conform better to Ainslie's patterns. For a period of hours to days, addicts engage in conscious rational behavior to procure the drug and then consume it. Later, when addicts become overwhelmed by the complications of use, a period of regret follows. A period of abstention may ensue, until craving (cue dependent or spontaneous) or the complications of a drug-free life induce a new period of drug use.

Although the specific patterns of various drugs may not fit Ainslie's model in a natural way, it performs well in explaining the general phenomenon of preference reversal. It is not clear, however, that it offers a full account of this phenomenon. Consider an example told by a former addict and cited by Lewis Yablonski (1965). The subject's wife was about to have their first child, and he was to be present during delivery. As his wife was having increasing pains, he was assisting the midwife in comforting and supporting her. He then noticed that the midwife's equipment included some morphine ampoules, which soon came to monopolize his attention. Acting strategically to steal the morphine while the midwife was busy with the delivery, he completely missed the moment of birth.

In this example, the desire for opioid was rekindled by the presence of cues. The distinction between closer and delayed rewards does not seem to have played any role. Rather, the idea of opioid supply became dominant to the extent of leading the addict to ignore other interests *in the present*. The conflict was not between an early and a delayed reward but between procuring the drug—which for strategic reasons was most easily done at the moment of birth—and participating in the magic experience. This example suggests a more general lesson. Relapses do not only, perhaps not even primarily, happen when the perceived opportunity to consume approaches in time. Frequently, they are triggered by cue-dependent cravings, in which an appetite seems to color the evaluation of alternative goods—present or future—in such a way that preference reversals occur.

In the example just given, what motivates addiction is the pull from euphoria. It is clear from Ainslie's discussion (1992, 98–99) that he also allows the push from dysphoria to be a motivation. In such cases, too, one can offer alternative explanations to his account. If heroin addicts go "cold turkey"—stop their heroin use abruptly—they will undergo a crisis that lasts for several days, with strong abstinence reactions and intense craving for heroin to relieve their misery. In this state, they prefer heroin not only to future sources of reward but also to virtually all alternative sources. Smoking poses a somewhat different problem. Former nicotine addicts may stay abstinent for weeks, perhaps months and even years. Yet, as their lives begin to feel devoid of color and intensity, one day the thought arises, "Hell, it's not worth it," and they relapse into smoking. Here, the temporal pattern seems like that of a sellout rather than of an addiction.

It might be concluded that the understanding of addiction as mechanisms of conscious but inconsistent choices is a fruitful approach, but the insistence on time dependency seems inadequate, particularly so if one is to take a given time period dominance of hours to days literally. The pull factors of attractive drug experiences are well fitted to the theoretical approach, although the theory less well incorporates push factors and the sudden yearning of the craving. Overall, therefore, we may question whether most preference reversals that are actually observed can be explained by Ainslie's theory. Compared to Becker, Ainslie has the merit of recognizing the existence and importance of preference reversal. Yet he neglects or simplifies the phenomenon of neuroadaptation; and through his exclusive emphasis on hyperbolic discounting, he deprives himself of important explanatory tools.

Loewenstein's Theory

Like Ainslie, Loewenstein (1999) views addiction as behavior caused by a specific type of preference reversals. For him, however, the major explanatory factor is not hyperbolic discounting. Instead, he stages a major attack on all traditional choice theory as the brilliant but emotionally crippled child of two brilliant parents: cognitive psychology and economics. In his opinion, both are "detached from the emotional and visceral richness of life." He insists that the addict's decision making is not a rational process that conforms to the conventional paradigm of expected utility maximizing. Preference reversal is not the result of conscious thought processes or of temporal proximity of opportunities for consumption but of "visceral impulses."

By viscerality, Loewenstein seems to have in mind feelings or preferences caused by autonomous, noncognitive processes related to biological needs. As examples of visceral influences he cites drives like hunger, thirst, the need for sleep, and sexual desires; emotions such as anger, fear, and depression; and stimulus-dependent reactions such as pain. All these factors are capable of influencing preferences and evaluations and of inducing choices that people know to be contrary to their moral standards or long-term interests. Strength of deprivation or cue-dependent reactions can evoke overwhelming visceral reactions, as when a starving person grabs his neighbor's meal or a sexually aroused public official pursues an erotic encounter even though it might have disastrous consequences for his career. This would also explain the acts and regrets of the father cited in Yablonsky who missed the birth moment of his child as visceral impulses caused a shift of his attention from the happy event to the chance of procuring morphine.

One problem with this approach is that the category of visceral factors seems to be so broad as to include virtually all influences except for the thin air of pure intellectual reasoning. The dynamics and mechanisms of the various visceral factors are also so different that it is hard to see what their common core might be. Leaving these broader issues aside, however, let us focus on how visceral factors might influence addiction-relevant choice.

For Loewenstein, addicts are people under the influence of drug-induced visceral impulses. The typical behavior pattern of addiction arises from unsuccessful attempts to master these impulses. Although Loewenstein does relate the core phenomenon of addiction to the influence of drugs on the motivational system, he neglects experiences of euphoria linked to the acute effects of dopamine release in the reward centers. Instead, the dynamics of drug taking are explained mainly in terms of experiences of dysphoria, pains, and cravings caused by the lack of the relevant drug. To be addictive, a psychoactive substance must be capable of inducing these negative reactions in sufficient strength to hijack and take control of the motivational system. The evaluative and planning functions of the brain come under the domination of these pirates and are used to fulfill the corresponding desires.

The model also explains another feature of addiction. After yielding to temptation—an angry outburst, a relapse into drug taking, eating the calorie-rich cake—individuals often are filled with regret, saying, "I don't know what came over me." Although the action was done consciously and voluntarily, the actors may not be able to understand the feelings and noncognitive reactions that motivated them. According to Loewenstein, the explanation of this phenomenon is that the human brain is poorly equipped for the task of remembering visceral impulses. It is difficult or nearly impossible to remember, with full vividness, the sensations, longings, and evaluations of the appetitive state, just as it is difficult or nearly impossible for a woman who has given birth to remember how the pains felt at the time. If women could remember, few would voluntarily become pregnant again. In many ways, the central aspect in Loewenstein's theory is the clinical experience of craving. This sudden longing for the drug should be distinguished from drug liking, which is connected to conscious positive drug use remembrances.

Although insightful, Loewenstein's theory is not without problems. Not all addictions fit the visceral impulse model. Drugs such as nicotine or cannabis are not typically characterized by strong visceral factors. Another difficulty is caused by the neglect of positive motivations. The common denominator underlying motivations to seek acute drug effects is an activation of the motivational system experienced as a state of well-being that might be sought deliberately rather than impulsively. Nor does the model account well for drug taking induced by prolonged postuse anhedonia (the "Hell, it's not worth it" syndrome). Finally, it seems that the memory of positive drug experiences can be extremely vivid and play a major role in inducing drug-taking behavior.

A Comprehensive Theory of Addiction?

Neurobiological findings are often cited as the explanation of addiction, or at least of aspects of addiction. These findings also pertain to choice-oriented theories, which seem to try to answer the core question, What is addiction? Roy Wise and Michael Bozarth (1987) distinguish between homology and analogy as explanatory heuristics. Two structural or behavioral features are homologous if they have the same causal (that is, evolutionary) history. They are merely analogous if they present similarities not induced by a common history. Whereas both bats and birds can fly, their wings are analogous rather than homologous. The apparently identical ability to fly is the result of two different developmental processes. By contrast, the wings of bats and the flippers of whales stand in a relation of homology. Similarly, we can ask whether different types of addiction and different features of addiction are analogous or homologous. In the preceding discussions we present some material that is relevant to this question and that we summarize from this perspective. The thrust of our analysis is that, since a unified theory of addiction presupposes that the central addictive phenomena are homologous rather than analogous, and since many causally important features of addiction do in fact exhibit analogy rather than homology, the prospects for a unified theory are somewhat dim. It is not a question of a causal theory of the development of wings but different factors that influence the ability to fly in itself.

Clinically, the picture of addiction obviously varies with and is also dependent upon both the set and the setting. To some extent it might be said that addiction results when strong negative consequences are insufficient to stop drug intake. Neurobiological research points to four basic aspects of addiction with different causation: primary (core) effects on reward and motivational systems; primary contributory effects in other brain structures; core neuroadaptations to repeated use; and contributory neuroadaptations to repeated use.

1. The core mechanisms motivating single-dose use appear homologous for all types of drug and linked to increased levels of synaptic dopamine in the same type of neurons. Central stimulants exert a direct effect on dopamine levels, while the effect of other drugs arises more indirectly, through intermediate receptor mechanisms and neuron chains. It is also possible that the primary effects of non-drug-related addictions are motivated in the same way, although in this case the possible changes of dopamine levels might be influenced by even more indirect mechanisms.

2. In contrast, contributory mechanisms differ both in origin and in effect. To the extent that they enhance the drug experience, they contribute to the drug-taking pattern, yet the relation among them is one of analogy rather than homology. They concern different areas of the brain and generate qualitatively different subjective experiences. Little is known about the contributory primary mechanisms in nonchemical addictions.

3. The core neuroadaptations of drugs seem to some extent to be homologous. Most involve adaptation to increased amounts of dopamine. A common feature appears to be a decreased level of dopamine, accompanied by anhedonia. Yet since the mechanisms that increase the dopamine level for single-dose usage differ in various drugs, the neuroadaptive processes probably also differ. In addition it is not clear whether facilitating neuroadaptations are present for all types of drugs or how these phenomena are linked to craving. The differences are probably even greater for nonchemical addictions. Here, analogy might be more prominent than homology.

4. Contributory neuroadaptations exhibit a great deal of variation according to area of the brain and nature of the causal mechanism involved. Thus opiate use causes a range of physical abstinence symptoms not found in other addictions. Alcohol and tranquilizers also have their specific withdrawal symptoms, in addition to the anhedonia that seems to follow abstention after all types of intensive drug use. Because of the distribution of acetylcholine receptors, neuroadaptations involving nicotine can be expected to arise in the cortex and hence affect cognitive functions, whereas those that involve opiates arise in nerve cells more typically found in structures that are important for affect and emotion. Although all types of neuroadaptation can motivate continued use to relieve unpleasant and dysfunctional states of mind, the underlying mechanisms are clearly analogous rather than homologous.

As can be seen, both clinical observations and neurobiological research point to composite forces or causations involved in addicted behavior. In light of this multiplicity of causal pathways, one may be somewhat skeptical about the very possibility of a "comprehensive theory of addiction." At the levels of both single use and repeated use, extremely heterogeneous contributory mechanisms account for a great deal of the variation in subjective experience and observed behavior. We are far from a situation in which neurobiological research explains addiction. What is explained is aspects of behavior and neurobiological changes that would understandably influence choice processes. The brain of a long-term consumer, the addicted brain, will undergo a number of changes that can be assumed to persist for various periods of time after the drug has left the body. Clinical evidence indicates that some of these changes might last for months or even years. The extent to which the various parts of the brain are involved will depend on the drug used and its particular profile of neurotransmitters and receptors. Involvement of brain structures and processes that are critical to rational thinking might, for instance, create a fundamental obstacle to the application of rational choice theories of drug addiction.

A related but more general question concerns the interaction of motivational and reward systems with the integrative and calculating functions of the brain. There is some evidence that aspects of brain functioning are best explained through application of nonlinear models (chaos theory) (Skarda and Freeman 1987; Kosslyn et al. 1993; Elbert, Ray, and Kowalik 1993). If that is so, some barely conscious stimulus may quite suddenly result in different weighing of utilities or a change in the perceived significance of choice opportunities and relationships. These dramatic small cause, large effect phenomena may occur because an enormous number of interrelated neurons may be activated in a fraction of a second. Standard models may therefore have insufficient explanatory power in the analysis of complex mental phenomena such as addictions.

Obviously, there is a need for integrative theories that can encompass clinical findings and neurobiological research findings. As our examples attempt to demonstrate, the different choice theories all capture some aspects of addiction, but none offers a complete picture. Becker's theory is best adapted to the "push" aspects of addiction connected to abstinence problems related to homeostatic neuroadaptations, while Ainslie's approach is better suited to the "pull" factors of euphoric experiences. Loewenstein's visceral theory is particularly well suited to the craving phenomenon. In some ways, this theory is best supported by neurobiological findings, but it seems to overemphasize the importance of craving and drug-induced memory limitations. It does, however, give an understandable account of preference reversals and of the seemingly inconsistent behavior of addicts—as do the theories of Ainslie.

Nevertheless, some aspects of addictive behavior are quite rational, in Becker's sense. Drug taking is in reality often regulated through goal-directed, conscious choices that attempt to maximize total utility, and both drug therapy and drug policy ought to take account of that fact. This pertains in particular to use of drugs such as opioids and nicotine, in which neuroadaptations seem to play a more conspicuous role. However, the criteria of full overview of consequences and an insistence on a constant discount rate for future utilities are not realistic. The value of Ainslie's theory lies not so much in his account of drug taking—although hyperbolic discounting certainly plays some role. Particularly valuable is his analysis of the influence of preference reversal typically seen in addictive behavior and his account of the strategies used to overcome addiction.

Conclusions

Addicts are not people without willpower or people driven to act without making choices. The clinical picture is of people who too often make choices that, in the long term, reduce their long-term utility and their total well being and, in addition, often burden both their families and society. These choices are suboptimal to long-term utility and, therefore, in the meaning of rational choice theory, irrational. The core problem is one of impeded rationality, of insufficient choice capacity to integrate present and future consideration in a sufficiently consistent pattern.

Here, one obviously has to take into consideration societal factors. Addicts do not exist in a social vacuum (Moene 1999; Waal 1999). Some of the lures of drug taking are primarily social, involving peer pressure or rebellion against the older generation and are better explained as such than as experiences connected to the effects of drugs on the brain. Conversely, some of the negative effects of addiction are caused more by the punitive and restrictive attitudes of society than by the inherent effects of addiction. The inability to consider the long-term consequences of addiction might be due to drug taking itself as well as to social reactions to abuse and the demoralizing experiences of an addictive career. For the inner-city addict, Keynes's phrase, "In the long run, we are all dead," can be more than a truism. Addictions form a vicious circle in which the addict as well as society are trapped in a suboptimal state.

One should also keep in mind that long-term addicts undergo durable brain changes that seem to affect their capacity for making rational choices and, more generally, choices that will enhance their overall welfare. Clinical and neurobiological evidence suggest some kind of motivational deficit in long-term addicts, although we do not know whether it involves wishful thinking, weakness of will, increased discounting of the future, or simply lack of interest in other rewards.

The choice theories stand out in this connection, with conceptual frames that seem to offer fruitful approaches to the integration of clinical understandings and neurobiological findings in a broader theory of human behavior. The theories seem to be clinically useful and to offer integrative views on the problems of addiction. They should not, however, be used as unified theories. They are approaches to improved understanding of a world in which both analogue and homologue factors influence the ability to "fly"—to master the difficult art of attaining optimal long-term utility when the temptations of short-term utility often are the enemies of long-term maximization. Whether these handicaps should be termed disease is a matter of definition.

References

Ainslie, George. 1992. *Picoeconomics: The Strategic Interaction of Successive Motivational States within the Person.* Cambridge: Cambridge University Press.

———. 1999. "The Dangers of Willpower: A Picoeconomic Understanding of Addiction and Dissociation." In *Getting Hooked: Rationality and the Addictions,* edited by Jon Elster and Ole-Jørgen Skog. Cambridge: Cambridge University Press.

American Psychiatric Association. 1994. *Diagnostic and Statistical Manual of Mental Disorders.* 4th ed. Washington D.C.: American Psychiatric Press.

Becker, Gary. 1992. "Habits, Addictions, and Traditions." *Kyklos,* 45: 327–46.

Becker, Gary, and K. M. Murphy. 1988. "A Theory of Rational Addiction." *Journal of Political Economy,* 96: 675–700.

Blum, Kenneth, John G. Cull, Eric R. Braverman, and David E. Comings. 1990. "Reward Deficiency Syndrome." *American Scientist* 84: 132–45.

Elbert, Thomas, William J. Ray, and Zbignew J. Kowalik. 1993. "Chaos and Physiology: Deterministic Chaos in Excitable Cell Assemblies." *Physiological Reviews* 74: 1–45.

Elster, Jon. 1999. Introduction to *Getting Hooked: Rationality and the Addictions,* edited by Jon Elster and Ole-Jørgen Skog. Cambridge: Cambridge University Press.

Dostoyevsky, Fyodor. 1964. *The Gambler.* New York: Norton.

Gardner, Eliot L., and Joyce H. Lowinson. 1991. "Marijuana's Interaction with Brain Reward Systems: Update." *Pharmacology, Biochemistry, and Behavior,* 40: 571–80.

Gardner, Eliot L., and James David. 1998. "The Neurobiology of Chemical Addiction." Draft, June 25, 1995.

Goldstein, Avram. 1994. *Addiction: From Biology to Drug Policy.* New York: Freeman.

Horvitz, J. C., T. Stewart, and B. L. Jacobs. 1997. "Burst Activity of Ventral Segmental Dopamine Neuros Is Elicited by Sensory Stimuli in the Awake Cat." *Brain Research* 759: 251–60.

Jarvik, Murray E., and Nina G. Schneider. 1992. "Nicotine." In *Substance Abuse: A Comprehensive Textbook,* edited by Joyce H. Lowinson, Pedro Ruiz, Robert B. Millman, and J. G. Langrod. Baltimore: Williams and Wilkins.

Jellinek, E. M. 1960. *The Disease Concept of Alcoholism.* New Brunswick: Hillhouse, 1960.

Koob, George F. 1992. "Drugs of Abuse: Anatomy, Pharmacology, and Functions of the Reward Pathways: Trends in Psychopharmacology." *Science* 13: 177–84.

———. 1999. "Drug Reward and Addiction." In *Fundamental Neuroscience,* edited by Michael J. Zigmond, Floyd E. Bloom, Story C. Landis, James L. Roberts, and Larry R. Squire. San Diego: Academic.

Koob, George F., and Floyd Bloom. 1988. "Cellular and Molecular Mechanisms of Drug Dependence." *Science* 242: 715–23.

Koob, George F., F. J. Vaccarion, M. Amalric, and Floyd E. Bloom 1987. "Positive Reinforcement Properties of Drugs: Search for Neural Substrates." In *Brain Rewards Systems and Abuse*, edited by J. Engel and L. Oreland. New York: Raven.

Kosslyn, S., N. Albert, W. Thompson, V. Malijkovic, S. Weise, Christopher Chabris, S. Hamilton, S. Rauch, and F. Buanno. 1993. "Visual Mental Imagery Activates Topographically Organised Visual Cortex: PET Investigations." *Journal of Cognitive Neuroscience*, 5: 263–87.

Loewenstein, George. 1999. "A Visceral Account of Addiction." In *Getting Hooked: Rationality and the Addictions*, edited by Jon Elster and Ole-Jørgen Skog. Cambridge: Cambridge University Press.

Marlatt, G. Alan, and D. J. Rohsenow. 1980. "Cognitive Processes in Alcohol Use: Expectancy and the Balanced Placebo Design." In *Advances in Substance Abuse*, edited by Nancy K. Mello. Vol. 1. Greenwich: JAI.

Moene, Karl O. 1999. "Notes on Habit Formation and Addiction." In *Getting Hooked: Rationality and the Addictions*, edited by Jon Elster and Ole-Jørgen Skog. Cambridge: Cambridge University Press.

Nestler, Eric J. 1992. "Molecular Mechanisms of Drug Addiction." *Journal of Neuroscience* 12: 2439–50.

Plato. 1970. *The Laws*. London: Penguin.

Schelling, Thomas C. 1992. "Addictive Drugs: The Cigarette Experience." *Science* 255: 430–33.

Skarda, C. A., and W. J. Freeman. 1987. "How Brains Make Chaos in Order to Make Sense of the World." *Behavioural and Brain Sciences* 10: 161–95.

Sora, Ichiro, Christine Wichems, Noboyuki Takahashi, Xio-Fei Li, Zhizhen Zeng, Randal Revay, Klaus Peter Lesch, Dennis L. Murphy, and George R. Uhl. 1998. "Cocaine Reward Models: Conditioned Place Preference Can Be Established in Dopamine- and in Serotonin-Transporter Knockout Mice." *Proceedings of the National Academy of Sciences of the United States of America* 95: 13,7699–7704.

Tabakoff, B., and P. L. Hoffman. 1992. "Alcohol: Neurobiology." In *Substance Abuse: A Comprehensive Textbook*, edited by Joyce H. Lowinson, Pedro Ruiz, Robert B. Millman, and J. G. Langrod. Baltimore: Williams and Wilkins.

Waal, Helge. 1999. "To Legalize or Not Legalize: Is That the Question?" In *Getting Hooked: Rationality and the Addictions*, edited by Jon Elster and Ole-Jørgen Skog. Cambridge: Cambridge University Press.

Wesson, Donald R., D. E. Smith, and R. B. Seymour. 1992. "Sedative Hypnotics and Tricyclics." In *Substance Abuse: A Comprehensive Textbook*, edited by Joyce H. Lowinson, Pedro Ruiz, Robert B. Millman, and J. G. Langrod. Baltimore: Williams and Wilkins.

Wise, Roy A., and Michael A. Bozarth. 1987 "A Psychomotor Stimulant Theory of Addiction." *Psychological Review* 94: 469–92.

World Health Organization. 1992. *The ICD-10 Classification of Mental and Behavioural Disorders*. Geneva.

Yablonski, Lewis. 1965. *The Tunnel Back*. New York: Macmillan.

Zinberg, Norman E. 1984. *Drug, Set, and Setting: The Basis for Controlled Intoxicant Use*. New Haven: Yale University Press.

PART III

ADDICTION, CHOICE, AND SELF-CONTROL

Chapter 5

Hyperbolic Discounting, Willpower, and Addiction

OLE-JØRGEN SKOG

THEORIES of addiction have traditionally not analyzed very carefully the basic problems of choice that addicted people are faced with. Addicts are conceived as consumption robots, helpless victims of their environment or their vices. Under these circumstances, "addiction" is not much more than a label, a ghost in the machine, called upon to explain norm-violating, self-destructive consumption behavior. Unfortunately, the proof of addiction is the very same behavior, and the explanation therefore becomes circular. A proper understanding of addiction requires a theory of how people conceive their world, how they evaluate different options, and how they make their choices. Among other things, we need to understand the role of ambivalence and inconsistencies in their deliberations. In this chapter, I discuss and compare two attempts in this direction.

In standard rational choice theory, actors are assumed to have consistent preferences and to act according to their own better judgment. In particular, rational actors are assumed to be dynamically consistent planners: If actors prefer an early, small reward *A* to a later, bigger reward *B* at a certain point in time, they will do so at all times. Hence, rational actors do not suffer from weakness of the will, and they never give in to temptations that they later regret. Addictions are often mentioned as an example of behavior that violates rationality: Many addicts seem to act contrary to their own better judgment, as they claim that they would like to stop their self-destructive consumption behavior, but still they continue consuming the substance they are addicted to.

However, Gary Becker and Kevin Murphy (1988) demonstrate that even fully rational utility maximizers with foresight, who take the future consequences of present consumption choices into consideration, may end up in a state the authors identify as an addictive state. In particular, certain consumers, characterized by an intermediate level of discounting of the future (compare Skog 1999), may end up at a high consumption level that gives them a lower level of welfare than they could have obtained from a lower consumption level. They are unable to leave the inferior, high-consumption state, since this would give rise to a temporary setback in welfare, and this setback would be larger than the (discounted) increase in future welfare that could be obtained from reduced consumption. Therefore, due to myopia, the rational addict is unable to take one step backward in order to take two steps forward.

As originally laid out, Becker and Murphy's theory of rational addiction faces three major and several minor problems (see Skog 1999 for a full discussion). First, they fail to explain how the rational consumer ends up in the suboptimal, high-consumption state in the first place. A possible solution to this problem has been suggested by Athanasios Orphanides and David Zervos (1995)—by relaxing the assumption of full information about their vulnerability. (For a critique of this solution, see Elster 1999.) Second, Becker and Murphy's theory fails to explain why rational addicts struggle to get out of their addiction. It follows from the theory's basic assumptions that, given addicts' consumption history and their personal preferences, continued heavy consumption is the best alternative for them. They may know that life would have been better if they had acted differently in the past, but since they cannot change their past (that is, their consumption capital, in Becker and Murphy's terminology) continued heavy consumption is their rational choice. Why, then, should rational addicts struggle to get out of their addiction? Third, Becker and Murphy cannot explain why relapse is so common among the addicted. If addicts should somehow manage to stop (say, with the aid of compulsory treatment), abstention or low consumption would be their rational choice in the future. Relapse into heavy consumption should not occur. At this stage, reformed addicts have full information about their vulnerability, and Orphanides and Zervos's mechanism cannot explain relapse.

The two latter difficulties can be resolved by relaxing the assumption of stable preferences and full information about future mental states. In fact, if we allow actors' future orientation (that is, their discount function) to fluctuate over time, actors may move in and out of the high consumption mode (Skog 1997). However, according to George Ainslie (1992), the basic assumption of dynamic consistency in Becker and Murphy's theory is at variance with the empirical evidence. Ainslie claims that people

**Figure 5.1   Hyperbolic Discounting of a Positive Reward (A)
and a Delayed Negative Consequence (B)**

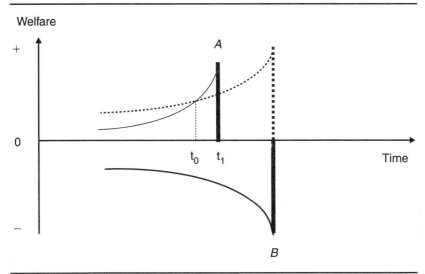

Note: For ease of comparison, a mirror image of the negative consequence is also shown (broken lines).

discount the future hyperbolically rather than recursively, as implied by standard theory. If this is so, the whole logic of Becker and Murphy's theory seems to break down.

Hyperbolic discounting implies that, long before actors have to make a choice—say, between a small, early reward and a bigger, delayed reward—actors prefer the bigger reward. Shortly before the choice has to be made, they change their mind and now consider the immediate, smaller reward better than the delayed, bigger reward. They give in to temptations. The same reversal occurs if they face a choice between abstention (valued as zero) and consumption of a good A, which carries a delayed punishment B, say, due to long-term negative consequences. This choice is illustrated in figure 5.1. Before time t_0, actors think the delayed punishment outweighs the positive reward, and they may form an intention of abstaining. However, in the time interval t_0 to t_1, their valuation is reversed, and the positive reward outweighs the punishment. Hence, at t_1, they will choose to do A.

George Ainslie's theory of addiction (Ainslie 1999) is centered on this dynamic inconsistency and its consequences. The temporary preference shift induced by hyperbolic discounting gives rise to regrets. As actors realize the inconsistencies in their mental bookkeeping, they will try to handle future temptations with different types of strategy. In picoeconomic theory, the strategy called personal rules plays a central role. Personal rules imply that actors choose to bunch together series of similar choice situations, making decisions over the entire set. They are shifting their mental bookkeeping from singular events to series of events, and this shift is a measure of willpower (Ainslie 1992, 161). Sometimes, but not always, this act of willpower may solve an addiction problem. However, as Ainslie points out, willpower is an awkward expedient, and personal rules may actually amplify the problem in certain cases.

The fundamental axiom in Ainslie's theory is motivational inconsistency and ambivalence, and the theory describes the strategies people may use to handle the resulting problems. The theory therefore allows for more complex interactions between conflicting motives within the person than do the conventional utility calculus that Becker and Murphy apply. However, as opposed to Becker and Murphy, Ainslie does not base his addiction theory on any explicit assumptions about the properties of potentially addictive substances. The phenomena Ainslie describes in his addiction theory are quite general and not restricted to the addictions. Since potentially addictive substances clearly do have specific properties that other substances do not have, it would be of interest to apply Ainslie's scheme to a consumption good with such properties.

The aim of this chapter is, therefore, to analyze from an Ainsliean point of view a consumption good with the same properties that Becker and Murphy analyze, in order to see how a hyperbolic discounter with willpower will tend to act. I continue as follows: In the next section, I discuss Ainslie's full theory of discounting, that is, hyperbolic discounting plus willpower. In the following section, I outline Becker and Murphy's consumption problem and analyze the Ainsliean discounter's choice in this type of situation. In the next section, the inconsistencies in the Ainsliean discounter's plans are analyzed, and in the last section I make a comparison between the two theories of addiction.

Ainslie's Theory of Discounting and Willpower

Ainslie's theory of discounting can be conceived as a two-tier theory, consisting of hard-wired hyperbolic discount curves and a cognitive element, namely willpower, in the form of personal rules.

According to Ainslie (1992), a single reward that is delayed by t time units is discounted by a factor

$$v(t) = \frac{1}{\beta + \alpha \cdot t}. \qquad (5.1)$$

As the discount factor at delay $t = 0$ should be equal to 1, we can—without loss of generality—set $\beta = 1$. Ainslie has no theory of interindividual or intraindividual variations in the parameter α and seems to conceive α as fixed. Obviously, α depends on the units of measurement for time. Hence, as long as we are not making interpersonal comparisons, we may choose the time unit so that a reward delayed one time unit is valued as half of its instantaneous value. This implies that $\alpha = 1$, and we obtain

$$v(t) = \frac{1}{1 + t}. \qquad (5.2)$$

This is the formula to be used in the calculations that follow.

When hyperbolic discounters experience preference reversals and give in to temptations enough times, they will come to see the choice between, say, abstention now and one cigarette now plus future penalties as a part of a larger package of similar choices in the future. At present, they value future abstention higher than future consumption while, at the same time, valuing present consumption higher than present abstention. However, according to Ainslie, they will come to see their present choice as a precedent for future choices, and therefore future choices have to be taken into consideration in relation to the present choice.[1] The alternatives are therefore a string of consumption events and a string of abstention events.

According to Ainslie, strings of choices are evaluated by adding together the discounted values of successive choices. Hence, the value of a string of N events, separated by τ time units and evaluated t time units before the first event, becomes

$$v_N(t) = \sum_{i=0}^{N-1} \frac{1}{1 + t + i \cdot \tau}. \qquad (5.3)$$

This function, which includes the cognitive element of willpower, represents Ainslie's complete discount function. It discounts the future less than the original hyperbolic function (Skog 1997) and is also less deeply bowed.

Immediately before the present choice has to be made, the immediate reward (A) from the first event is valued higher than the larger, delayed punishment. Hence, abstention (valued as zero) is less attractive than consumption. However, the discounted values of all later events go in favor of the abstention. Therefore, when the net value of the present consumption event is bunched together with the discounted values of later consumption events, it may very well turn out to be valued less than the sum of abstention events: Many small superiorities of distant abstention events may outweigh the clear superiority of the immediate consumption event. Hence, the change in bookkeeping may produce a switch in behavior.

Whether this switch actually takes place mainly depends on how many future choices actors decide to take into consideration. Consider the case in which actors evaluate the present and the next choice only. Then, the two consumption events will be considered worse than the two abstention events only if the discounted value of the punishment B at the first event is very close to the instantaneous value of the first consumption event A; that is, if the temptation is not very strong. However, strong temptations cannot be resisted by evaluating two events only. Strong temptations require a longer chain of successive choices and, hence, stricter personal rules.

In fact, in can be demonstrated that, with hyperbolic discounting, any temptation may in principle be resisted, provided that enough future events are taken into consideration (for a proof, see the appendix to this chapter). Hence, even if the instantaneous value of A is very much bigger than the discounted value of B, the temptation can be resisted if actors have formed a belief to the effect that their current choice is a precedent for numerous and very remote future events. In principle, willpower and personal rules could therefore solve all consumption problems of this type. The actual outcome would depend on actors' cognitive horizon, as measured by N. Ainslie does not offer a systematic theory of intraindividual and interindividual variations in the parameter N. I will not try to develop such a theory either. I instead focus on the consequences of variations in N.

It is sufficient at the present stage of the argument to note that the parameter N in the complete discount function obviously can be used as a measure of actors' willpower. People with low N are unable to take very many successive events into consideration and they may not be able to resist strong temptations. People with a large N will take even very distant events into consideration and may, therefore, be able to resist strong temptations. People with an N close to the critical level needed to overcome a certain choice problem may turn out to be very sensitive to the details of the circumstances under which the choice has to be made. Under stress, their horizon may be slightly shortened, enough for their personal rules to break down, although under normal circumstances they may be able to resist the temptation.

Becker and Murphy's Choice Problem with Ainsliean Discounting

In Becker and Murphy's theory, the potentially addictive drug has two distinct properties. $P1$ says that high consumption in the past has the effect of reducing present welfare levels. $P2$ says that the reduction in current welfare due to heavy consumption in the past, may to some extent be compensated by consuming much at present.[2] The causal mechanisms underlying the first property could be increased tolerance (more is needed to obtain the same pleasure), delayed harmful effects of past consumption, and so on. The second property could be due to increased salience of the drug, classical relief from withdrawal, or more generally suppression of any pain and discomfort addicts experience due to abuse in the past. Both properties $P1$ and $P2$ seem to be essential elements in the most important addictions.

Suppose actors are to choose between two options: consuming much or consuming little of a potentially addictive substance. They obtain more instantaneous pleasure from consuming much than from consuming only a little. However, there is a delayed punishment for consuming much: During the next time interval, actors will have a lower welfare level if they consume much during the present interval ($P1$). Now, this punishment for past heavy consumption is larger if actors choose to consume little than if they choose to consume much at present ($P2$). Hence, consuming much at present offers a kind of relief from displeasure. The instantaneous welfare levels associated with consuming little or much, given actors' past consumption, are illustrated in figure 5.2.

This reward structure is the starting point in Becker and Murphy's theory of rational addiction (Becker and Murphy 1988). Given their consumption history, consumers decide what to do next by adding together present and discounted future welfare levels for different future consumption careers, using an exponential discount function and choosing the consumption career with the highest overall welfare level. It can be demonstrated that myopic consumers will choose to consume much, whatever their consumption history. Very farsighted consumers will decide to consume only a little, whatever their consumption career. However, those with an intermediate discounting of the future will decide to continue as heavy consumers if they have consumed much in the past, although they will decide to consume a little if they have consumed only a little in the past (Skog 1999). The latter alternative gives them a higher overall welfare level than the former.

Hence, intermediate discounters can be trapped at a (globally) suboptimal high-consumption level: They will know that life would have

Figure 5.2   Instantaneous Utility of Present Consumption Choices for Persons with Different Consumption Histories

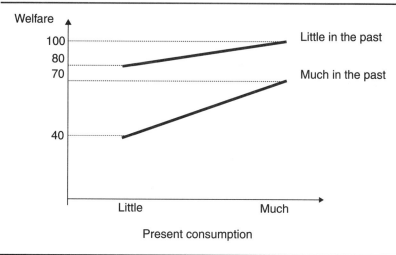

been better if they never had started consuming much, but according to their own utility calculus, they cannot leave the high-consumption career, since they discount the prospects of a higher future welfare too much. Therefore, it does not match up with the temporary setback they will experience by switching to low consumption.

We now consider hyperbolic discounters with willpower and personal rules to see how they will behave when they are faced with the same choice problem. Given their consumption history, we let the actors evaluate the two alternative consumption careers: consuming little now and in the future; and consuming much now and in the future. Actors have a fixed time horizon N, so they will consider the present and the next $(N-1)$ consecutive consumption events. The welfare levels associated with the different options are assumed to be the ones given in figure 5.2. We assume that the time intervals between consumption events are one time unit. We start by considering consumers immediately before the first choice has to be made, that is, at $t = 0$.

If the actors have time horizon $N = 1$, they will take only the current event into consideration. If they have consumed little in the past, they obtain one hundred by consuming much and eighty by consuming a little, so they will consume much. If they have consumed much in the past, they will obtain seventy by consuming much and forty by consuming little, so they will consume much even in this case.

With a time horizon of $N = 2$, they will take the present and the next event into consideration. If they have consumed little in the past, they obtain the following utility levels from the two alternatives:

little:

$$\frac{80}{1+0} + \frac{80}{1+1} = 120; \tag{5.4}$$

much:

$$\frac{100}{1+0} + \frac{70}{1+1} = 135. \tag{5.5}$$

Hence, they will choose to consume much; and if they have consumed much in the past, they obtain

little:

$$\frac{40}{1+0} + \frac{80}{1+1} = 80; \tag{5.6}$$

much:

$$\frac{70}{1+0} + \frac{70}{1+1} = 105. \tag{5.7}$$

Hence, even in this case, they will decide to consume much.

The overall welfare levels of the different consumption choices for persons with selected time horizons are reproduced in table 5.1. We observe that people with a time horizon less than eleven will choose to consume much, whatever they have done in the past. Those with a time horizon of thirty-one or larger will choose to consume little, whatever they have done in the past. However, those with an intermediate time horizon will choose to consume little if they have done so in the past, while they will choose to consume much if they have consumed much in the past.

In effect, hyperbolic discounters with only a little amount of willpower ($N < 11$) will not be able to quit their addiction, and if they have been abstaining for a while, they will quickly relapse to addiction. Hence, unless they are able to cultivate their willpower, they will continue their self-destructive lifestyle. These people are consonant addicts (Skog 1999): They are unable to quit and really do not wish to quit, as they consider life without the addictive substance to be even worse than life as a heavy consumer.

Table 5.1   Total Welfare of Two Consumption Careers for Consumers with Various Planning Horizons

Time Horizon (N)	Past Low Consumption		Past High Consumption	
	Continued low consumption	Switch to high consumption	Switch to low consumption	Continued high consumption
1	80.0	100.0	40.0	70.0
2	120.0	135.0	80.0	105.0
6	196.0	201.5	156.0	171.5
10	234.3	235.0	194.3	205.0
11	241.6	241.4	201.6	211.4
21	291.6	285.2	251.6	255.2
30	319.6	309.6	279.6	279.6
31	322.2	311.9	282.2	281.9
41	344.2	331.2	304.2	301.2

People with willpower at an intermediate level ($11 < N < 31$) will ordinarily not be able to get out of their spree with the aid of sheer willpower. When they are in the high-consumption mode, the way out is too troublesome. However, if someone or something has helped them to stop consuming excessively for a while, they would not immediately relapse. In the sober mode, life feels better without the addictive drug or with only normal, moderate amounts.

These people with intermediate willpower are dissonant addicts. When they are in the high-consumption mode, they prefer continued high consumption, but still they know that life would have been better (according to their own utility calculus) if they had been in the low-consumption mode. They can honestly say that they would not relapse if they somehow managed to get out of the high-consumption mode.

Last, strong-willed people will manage to overcome their addiction if, at some stage, they realize that they have ended up in a suboptimal consumption mode, and they will not relapse.

Consequently, when faced with a consumption choice of the same type as Becker and Murphy's rational consumer, hyperbolic discounters with willpower will act in a similar way. In particular, the asymmetry between stopping and starting, which is the defining characteristic of Becker and Murphy's rational addict, is reproduced in the hyperbolic case.

Inconsistent Plans

Exponential discounters are dynamically consistent. Hence, rational, dissonant addicts in the high-consumption mode will evaluate continued heavy consumption as better than discontinuation of heavy consumption, both when this evaluation is done immediately before the choice has to be made and well in advance of that time. If they happen to be in the low-consumption mode at a certain stage, they will plan for continued low consumption long before the actual decision has to be made, and they will stick to that plan afterward.

This is not true for hyperbolic discounters. Generally, they cannot be expected to come up with the same conclusion at all times. Although hyperbolic discounters with willpower and personal rules are less dynamically inconsistent than discounters without personal rules, they are not entirely consistent, and we cannot expect that their evaluation in advance is identical to their evaluation at the time of choice. In the preceding section we calculated their evaluations at the time of choice. Now we analyze their evaluations some time in advance.

Consider people with willpower $N = 10$. One time unit before they have to make the choice (at $t = 1$), they evaluate the two consumption alternatives as follows: If they have consumed little in the past, consuming little on the imminent event is valued at 161.6, while consuming much on the imminent event is valued at 156.4; therefore, they will opt for little. If they have consumed much in the past, consuming little in the imminent event is valued at 141.6, while consuming much in the imminent event is valued at 141.4, so even in this case they will opt for little.

It is easily verified that, for people with willpower $N = 10$, the same ordering applies at time distances greater than one time unit. Hence, well in advance of the actual choice, these people will plan to go for the low-consumption alternative in the future.

However, at $t = \frac{1}{2}$, their evaluation has changed. If they have consumed little in the past, they evaluate consuming little in the imminent event at 188.9 and consuming much at 185.3. Hence, they will plan to drink a little. If they have consumed much in the past, they evaluate consuming little on the imminent event at 162.3 and consuming much at 165.3. Therefore, at this point in time people with a high-consumption history will prefer to consume much, which violates their previous plan (at $t > 1$). However, people with a low-consumption history will not have changed their original plan.

At the time the actual choice has to be made (at $t = 0$), actors with willpower $N = 10$ will prefer to consume much, whatever their consumption history has been (see table 5.1). Therefore, at this stage, even people with a low-consumption history will have changed their mind, as they now value future low consumption at 234.3 and future high consumption at 235.0.

Figure 5.3   Preference Structures for People with Different Horizons (Willpower) at Different Times Before the Time of Choice

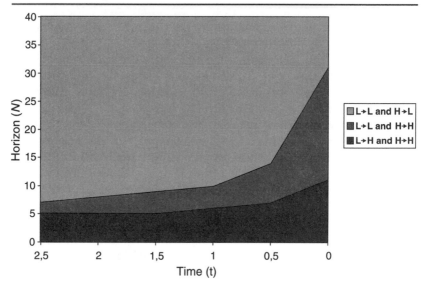

Note: $H \to L$ denotes persons who have had a high consumption in the past and who choose low consumption in the future, and so on.

This implies that dissonant addicts with hyperbolic discounting plus willpower may go to bed with the firm intention of not drinking tomorrow; nevertheless, they will end up drinking again the next day. Even consonant addicts may occasionally experience doubts as to whether they really wish to go on with their heavy-consumption lifestyle. Thus, the distinction between consonant and dissonant addicts is not as clear-cut within the Ainsliean framework as within the dynamically consistent framework of the rational consumer.

The changes in valuation for persons with different degrees of willpower as they approach the actual time of choice are displayed in figure 5.3. The figure shows the consumption plans of consumers with different horizons at different delays. For instance, those with horizon $N = 15$ will intend to consume little whatever their current consumption state ($L \to$ or L and $H \to$ or L) at all points in time before $t = 0.5$. Thereafter, they will be in the dissonant mode, intending to consume little if they are already consuming little and intending to consume much if they are already consuming much ($L \to$ or L and $H \to$ or H).

We observe that the crossover, or instability, will occur for most consumers with a weak or moderate willpower. Only strong-willed individuals ($N > 30$) will have highly consistent plans. People with less willpower will experience that their personal rules offer protection against temptations at a certain time distance while failing to support their longterm intention during the more critical phase. This failure may occur only when they are in the high-consumption mode, or irrespective of their consumption mode. The latter phenomenon will be most common among the weak willed (low N), while the former, more limited failure will be found only among people with moderately strong willpower.

This discrepancy between long-term plans and actual choices among consumers with a weak or moderately strong willpower may give rise to intraperson strategic battles between the "planner" and the "doer." Ainslie distinguishes four strategies planners may use to achieve self-control: extrapsychic mechanisms (public side bets or other causal mechanisms), personal rules (private side bets), attention control, and preparation of emotions. To this list, one could also add the present self's threats toward future selves (Skog 1997).

In particular, actors could try to increase their own cognitive horizon or willpower during the phase when they actually evaluate future low consumption higher than future heavy consumption. If they succeed, they may have solved their addiction problem (although the solution may be fragile). If they fail to do it, they may realize that this failure may erode their willpower in other life areas as well. To prevent this from happening, they may try to separate the life area in question from other life areas in their mental bookkeeping, in which case it may form a so-called vice (or lapse) district, in Ainslie's terminology. In that case, they will not be able to get out of their addiction.

Conclusion

A reasonable theory of addiction needs to explain at least three distinct phenomena: why people struggle hard but find it difficult to leave the addictive stage; why and how they entered this stage in the first place; and why relapse is so common. On these accounts, the Becker-Murphy and Ainslie theories can be summarized as in table 5.2.

The Becker and Murphy theory could easily be improved and made more realistic on the second issue (Skog 1999), and the same applies to Ainslie's theory. The two theories might actually turn out to be quite similar on this account.

Even with respect to the first issue, there seems to be a fair amount of overlap between the two theories. Admittedly, these theories are quite different in important respects. Still, there is also a common core, and this core comes into sight when we let the actors face the same consumption problem. In most of his work, Ainslie tends to analyze quite

Table 5.2   Comparison of the Ainslie and the Becker-Murphy Theories, on Three Measures

Theory	Struggle to Get Out	How Problem Started	Relapse
Ainslie	Explain difficulty by insufficient willpower. Explain struggle by dynamic inconsistency.	No systematic theory as yet. Could be based on too short cognitive horizon or insufficient information about risk and vulnerability.	Explained by erosion of willpower.
Becker-Murphy	Explain difficulty by myopia. No explanation of the struggle.	Explained by extraordinary circumstances or insufficient information and calculated risks (Orphanides and Zervos 1995).	No explanation.

simple problems of choice, and this affects the focus in his characterization of addiction. In the preceding sections, I demonstrate that when we address more complex choice problems (that carry the typical features of addictive substances) from an Ainslien point of view, we obtain a characterization of addiction that is fairly similar to Becker and Murphy's, at least with respect to the theories' explanations of why addicts find it difficult to quit.

The main difference between Becker and Murphy's standard rational choice theory and Ainslie's picoeconomic theory is dynamic consistency versus inconsistency. The congenital inconsistency that forms the starting in Ainslie's theory allows Ainslien addicts to struggle to get out of their addiction, and relapse may be explained within the Ainslien framework by erosion of personal rules and willpower. Hence, an addiction theory based on Ainslie's theory of motivation can handle the phenomena that are left unexplained by Becker and Murphy's theory of addiction.

However, even a less radical theory of discounting than the hyperbolic theory can solve the difficulties of Becker and Murphy's addiction theory. It is sufficient to assume that people's rate of discounting typically fluctuate unsystematically over time and that people are therefore not always equally farsighted. The theory of fluctuating discount functions postulate that people discount the future recursively and that they base their judgments on realistic expectations about their own future mental states. Hence, this theory can be seen as a straightforward extension of classical rational choice theory. Still, these consumers would act very much like Ainsliean discounters (Skog 1997). This theory predicts that addicts who get off the hook will easily relapse, and it also predicts that many addicts will struggle to get out of their addiction. Moreover, this theory allows many types of intraperson strategic battle similar to those described by Ainslie's theory.

Hence, the picoeconomic theory of addiction and the modified version of the rational choice theory of addiction obtained by allowing for fluctuations in discount functions do in fact have a fairly large common core.

Appendix

Let A be a small, early reward and B a larger, delayed reward. At a certain point in time subjects have to choose between them, and they will then obtain A immediately or B delayed one time unit. The same choice is repeated at time intervals equal to τ. The crossover takes place t_0 time units before the choice has to be made. The situation is depicted in figure 5A.1.

At t time units before the first choice has to be made, a string of N A choices and a string of N B choices are valued as

$$V_A(t) = \sum_{i=0}^{N-1} \frac{A}{1+\alpha(t+i\cdot\tau)};$$

(5.8)

$$V_B(t) = \sum_{i=0}^{N-1} \frac{B}{1+\alpha(t+1+i\cdot\tau)}.$$

(5.9)

We will prove that at the time the first choice has to be made, V_B can always be made larger than V_A by choosing an N large enough—that is, if N is large, then

$$V_B(0) > V_A(0).$$

(5.10)

Hence, by bringing in enough future choices, the large, delayed reward can always beat the small, immediate reward.
Proof: Let

$$f(x) = \frac{a}{b+c\cdot x},$$

(5.11)

where a, b, and c are all positive. From figure 5A.2 it is easily verified that the following inequalities hold:

**Figure 5A.1   Repeated Choices Between an Early, Small Reward (*A*)
and a Delayed, Bigger Reward (*B*)**

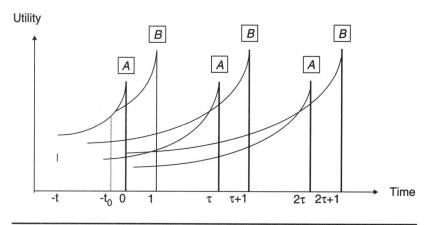

$$\sum_{x=0}^{N-1} f(x) > \int_0^N f(x)\,dx > \sum_{x=1}^{N} f(x).$$ (5.12)

On the basis of these inequalities we obtain

$$\sum_{i=0}^{N-1} \frac{B}{(1+\alpha)+\alpha \cdot i \cdot \tau} > \int_0^N \frac{B}{(1+\alpha)+\alpha \cdot x \cdot \tau}\,dx\,;$$ (5.13)

$$\sum_{i=0}^{N-1} \frac{A}{1+\alpha \cdot i \cdot \tau} = \sum_{i=1}^{N} \frac{A}{1+\alpha \cdot i \cdot \tau} + A - \frac{A}{1+\alpha \cdot N \cdot \tau}$$

$$< \int_0^N \frac{A}{1+\alpha \cdot x \cdot \tau}\,dx + \frac{A \cdot \alpha \cdot N \cdot \tau}{1+\alpha \cdot N \cdot \tau}.$$ (5.14)

Hence,

$$V_B(0) - V_A(0) = \sum_{i=0}^{N-1} \frac{B}{1+\alpha+\alpha \cdot i \cdot \tau} - \sum_{i=0}^{N-1} \frac{A}{1+\alpha \cdot i \cdot \tau}$$

$$> \int_0^N \left\{ \frac{B}{(1+\alpha)+\alpha \cdot x \cdot \tau} - \frac{A}{1+\alpha \cdot x \cdot \tau} \right\} dx - \frac{A \cdot \alpha \cdot N \cdot \tau}{1+\alpha \cdot N \cdot \tau}.$$ (5.15)

Figure 5A.2

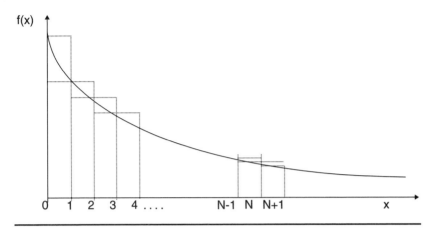

Integrating, simplifying, and substituting $k = B/A$ (note that $k > 1$), one obtains

$$V_B(0) - V_A(0) > \frac{A}{\alpha \cdot \tau} \cdot \ln\left\{ \frac{(1+\alpha+\alpha \cdot \tau \cdot N)^k}{(1+\alpha \cdot \tau \cdot N)} \right\} - \frac{B}{\alpha \cdot \tau}$$

$$\cdot \ln(1+\alpha) - \frac{\alpha \cdot N \cdot \tau \cdot A}{1+\alpha \cdot N \cdot \tau}. \qquad (5.16)$$

Now,

$$\frac{(1+\alpha+\alpha \cdot \tau \cdot N)^k}{(1+\alpha \cdot \tau \cdot N)} \to \infty \qquad \text{as} \qquad N \to \infty, \qquad (5.17)$$

while

$$\frac{\alpha \cdot N \cdot \tau \cdot A}{1+\alpha \cdot N \cdot \tau} \to A \qquad \text{as} \qquad N \to \infty. \qquad (5.18)$$

Hence, there must exist an N_0 so that $V_B(0) - V_A(0) > 0$, when $N > N_0$ (Q.E.D.).

It should be noted that this conclusion remains valid whatever the spacing of the choices (as measured by the parameter τ) and whatever the relative difference between the two rewards (as measured by the parameter k).

A previous version of this chapter has been discussed at the seminar on analytical and formalized approaches to social issues, University of Oslo, and the seminar on addiction, Russell Sage Foundation, New York. I am grateful to the participants for their comments.

Notes

1. For a critique of this assumption, see Bratman (1995). A further discussion of this issue can be found in Mele (1996) and Skog (1997).

2. More accurately, Becker and Murphy take care of past consumption by a measure called consumption capital and assume that ($P1$), overall utility, is a decreasing function of consumption capital, while ($P2$), the marginal utility of present consumption, is an increasing function of consumption capital.

References

Ainslie, George. 1992. *Picoeconomics: The Strategic Interaction of Successive Motivational States within the Person*. Cambridge: Cambridge University Press.

———. 1999. "The Dangers of Willpower. A Picoeconomic Understanding of Addiction and Dissociation." In *Getting Hooked: Rationality and the Addictions*, edited by Jon Elster and Ole-Jørgen Skog. Cambridge: Cambridge University Press.

Becker, Gary, and Kevin Murphy. 1988. "A Theory of Rational Addiction." *Journal of Political Economy* 96: 675–700.

Bratman, Michael E. 1995. "Planning and Temptation." In *Mind and Morals*, edited by Larry May, Marilyn Friedman, and Andy Clark. Bradford, Mass.: MIT Press.

Elster, Jon. 1999. *Strong Feelings: Emotion, Addiction, and Human Behavior*. Bradford, Mass.: MIT Press.

Mele, Alfred. 1996. "Addiction and Self-Control." *Behavior and Philosophy* 24: 99–117.

Orphanides, Athanasios, and David Zervos 1995. "Rational Addiction with Learning and Regret." *Journal of Political Economy* 103: 739–58.

Skog, Ole-Jørgen. 1997. "The Strength of Weak Will." *Rationality and Society* 9: 245–71.

———. 1999. "Rationality, Irrationality, and Addiction: Notes on Becker and Murphy's Theory of Addiction." In *Getting Hooked: Rationality and the Addictions*, edited by Jon Elster and Ole-Jørgen Skog. Cambridge: Cambridge University Press.

Chapter 6

Addiction and Self-Control

TED O'DONOGHUE AND MATTHEW RABIN

MANY OBSERVERS suspect that self-control problems and related time inconsistencies play an important role in the consumption of addictive products, leading people to develop and maintain addictions against their long-run interests. People often consume addictive products despite an expressed desire to quit. For many people, it would appear that the long-run harm caused by an addiction outweighs its short-run benefits. In extreme cases, people destroy their lives with harmful addictions. Our goal in this chapter is to carefully explore the role that self-control problems—and people's awareness of those problems—play in harmful addictions. To do so, we develop a formal model of the decision to consume addictive products that explicitly incorporates a time-inconsistent taste for immediate gratification.

Economists have proposed rational choice models of addictive behavior (Becker and Murphy 1988; Becker, Grossman and Murphy 1991, 1994). These models characterize how consuming harmful addictive products can decrease future well-being while at the same time increasing the desire for those products in the future. Because these models consider only time-consistent agents, however, they a priori rule out the possibility of self-control problems.

Like the rational choice models of addiction, our model assumes that the choice to consume an addictive product is volitional, in the sense that people balance their current desire for the addictive product against their perceptions of the future consequences of current consumption. Our model is quite different, and less extreme, than rational choice models, however, because it assumes that people may be overattentive to their immediate gratification (that is, they may have self-control problems) and may have incorrect beliefs about their future behavior (that is, they may not anticipate future self-control problems).

In the next section, we lay out our formal model. We assume that in each period people can either take a hit or not take a hit.[1] We incorporate two crucial characteristics of harmful addictive products. First, they involve *habit formation:* The more of the product people have consumed in the past, the more they desire that product now. Second, they involve *negative internalities:* The more of the product people have consumed in the past, the lower is their overall well-being now (regardless of current behavior).[2] The combination of habit formation and negative internalities implies that as people consume more and more of an addictive product, they get less and less pleasure from its consumption, yet they may continue to consume the product because refraining becomes more and more painful.

We incorporate self-control problems into the model by assuming that people have time-inconsistent intertemporal preferences. We apply a simple model of time-inconsistent preferences, originally proposed by Edmund S. Phelps and Robert A. Pollak (1968) in the context of intergenerational altruism, and later employed by David Laibson (1994a) to capture self-control problems within individuals: Relative to time-consistent preferences, people always give extra weight to well-being *now* over well-being at any future moment. These preferences give rise to self-control problems because at any moment people pursue immediate gratification more than they would have preferred if asked at any previous moment.

In addition to the implications of having self-control problems, we also focus on the implications of whether people are aware of their own future self-control problems. We examine two extreme assumptions: *Sophisticated* people are fully aware of their future self-control problems and therefore know exactly how they will behave in the future; and *naive* people are fully *un*aware of their future self-control problems and therefore believe they will behave in the future exactly as they currently would like themselves to behave. By systematically comparing *sophisticates, naifs,* and time-consistent agents (whom we refer to as *TCs*), we can examine the role of self-control problems in addiction and delineate how predictions depend both on self-control problems per se and on assumptions about foresight.

We begin with a stationary model of addiction, in which the temptation to hit can depend on the addiction level but otherwise remains constant over time, which allows us to identify some basic insights. We first ask what is the direct implication of self-control problems by comparing *TCs* and naifs. In the stationary model, naifs are always more likely to hit than *TCs*. Since naifs are unaware of future self-control problems, they perceive that they will behave exactly like *TCs* in the future and therefore perceive the same future consequences of current indulgence as do *TCs*. Given their overattentiveness to immediate gratification, however, naifs are more likely to hit than *TCs*. Clearly, this intuition is far more general than the model of stationary preferences: In essentially any model of addiction, self-control problems combined with an unawareness of future self-control problems will cause people to consume more of an addictive product than they would like to consume from a long-run perspective.

We next ask what are the implications of being aware of future self-control problems by comparing naifs and sophisticates. We identify two effects. First, sophistication about future self-control problems can make people pessimistic about future behavior (that is, they believe in general that they will hit more often than they would if they had no self-control problem). We refer to this phenomenon as the *pessimism effect*. Second, sophistication about future self-control problems may make people realize that they will resist future temptations only if they resist temptation today. We refer to this phenomenon as the *incentive effect*. Because the habit formation property of addictive products implies that current indulgence has larger future costs the more people expect to refrain in the future, pessimism about future behavior tends to exacerbate overconsumption due to self-control problems. The incentive effect, in contrast, tends to mitigate overconsumption due to self-control problems. Hence, whether sophisticates hit more or less often than naifs depends on the relative magnitudes of the pessimism and incentive effects.

Of course, since the incentive effect is driven by future restraint, it can be operative only if there is some future period where people would refrain in the face of pure pessimism. Consider the implications of this point in a stationary model. If in period 1 people would hit when "unhooked" in the face of pure pessimism, then in all periods they would hit when unhooked in the face of pure pessimism, and therefore the incentive effect cannot be operative. In contrast, if in period 1 people would refrain when unhooked in the face of pure pessimism, then in all periods they would do so, and therefore the incentive effect can be operative. This logic implies that if people are initially unhooked, the incentive effect can be operative if and only if people would refrain without it. Since the pessimism effect makes sophisticates more likely to hit than naifs, we can therefore conclude that sophisticates are more likely than naifs to become addicted starting from being unhooked.

This logic does not imply that sophisticates are more likely to hit than naifs once hooked. Even if people would hit when hooked in the face of pure pessimism, refraining may reduce their addiction level to a point at which they would refrain in the face of pure pessimism, in which case the incentive effect would be operative. Indeed, in our model sophisticates are always more likely than naifs to quit an established addiction.

We then consider nonstationary environments. First, we consider a model of youth, wherein the intrinsic temptation to hit is high early in life but declines as people get older. Second, we consider a weekend-weekday model, wherein the temptation to hit alternates between high (on weekends) and low (on weekdays). Third, we briefly discuss temporary temptations arising from traumatic events such as a divorce or a death of a loved one. Some examples in these nonstationary environments illustrate that the result that naivete helps people avoid harmful addictions is very special to the stationary environment. There are two reasons for this reversal. First, sophisticates may consume less in nonstationary environments because the incentive effect becomes operative in a broader array of circumstances. In particular, the incentive effect being operative merely requires that people refrain in the face of pure pessimism when the temptation to consume is lowest. For instance, in the youth model this means that people refrain when unhooked in the face of pure pessimism *in their old age;* and in the weekend-weekday model this means that people refrain when unhooked in the face of pure pessimism *on weekdays.* Second, naifs may consume more in nonstationary environments because of their aforementioned tendency not to quit an established addiction. When it is optimal to give in to high temptations and later quit, naifs often give in to high temptations and then never quit. Because we suspect nonstationary environments are more prevalent, we tentatively interpret such results to say that "sophisticated self-control problems" are not a major source of harmful addictions. If self-control problems help explain severely harmful addictions, we suspect they do so only in conjunction with some degree of naivete.

We extend our model to incorporate different types of "variable myopia." First, we consider *consumption-induced myopia*—we suppose that self-control problems may depend on recent consumption. When people are sober, they might have very mild self-control problems. Once they have had a few drinks, however, they may suddenly have significant self-control problems. Second, we consider exogenous variation in the taste for immediate gratification. These extensions allow us to further highlight the importance of fully understanding one's self-control problems. Consumption-induced myopia (in addition to basic self-control problems) always makes naifs consume more of an addictive product but may induce sophisticates—because of their fear of addiction—to consume even less of the addictive product than if they had no self-control problem. With an exogenously varying taste for immediate gratification, naifs—while consuming more than they would if they had no self-control problem—may consume *too little* relative to sophisticates, because they undertake repeated, costly, unsuccessful attempts to quit their addiction under the naive belief they can stay unhooked.

We conclude the chapter by comparing our model of addiction to time-consistent models of addiction. We feel that studying self-control as it relates to addiction is an obviously appropriate line of research because self-control problems seem to exist and seem to be important. We also conjecture that research on addiction might be improved if researchers choose to investigate self-control problems rather than solely investigating the extreme time-consistent model. We then conclude by discussing what we suspect is on most people's minds when studying addiction—the degree to which people hurt themselves by becoming addicted. Rational choice models do not and cannot address the question of when and how people systematically hurt themselves by becoming addicted—except to assume the question away a priori. Especially because we illustrate at the end of the chapter that even modest self-control problems can hurt people severely, we feel that formulating models as a means for understanding when and how people might hurt themselves is an important agenda.

The Basic Model

We consider a discrete-time model with periods 1, $\cdots$, T, wherein we consider both $T < \infty$ and $T = \infty$.[3] We vastly simplify the model by assuming that in each period, t, consumption of an addictive product, a_t, is either 0 or 1: Each period people can either take a hit or not take a hit, wherein $a_t = 1$ if they take a hit and $a_t = 0$ if they refrain. Furthermore, we assume that the good is free. Our focus on free products helps highlight the fact that people may avoid addictive products because they lead to unpleasant long-run consequences, rather than because of the purchase price per se. It also simplifies notation and analysis.

Each period, people merely choose whether to hit this period (and cannot commit to any future choices).[4] Choice is rational or volitional in the sense that people balance their current desire for the good against the future consequences of consumption, given their current beliefs about their future behavior. Hence, whenever people take a hit, they are doing what currently seems to them to be the best course of action, with the important caveat that they may be overweighting their current well-being relative to their future well-being. In this sense, our model does not abandon the economic paradigm of considering human choice as balancing the benefits and costs of a course of action. As discussed in the introduction, however, our model is quite different from the rational choice models of addiction because we allow people to have self-control problems and incorrect beliefs about their future behavior. As a result, our model does not necessarily imply that people will follow their most preferred lifetime path of behavior.

The crucial feature of addictive products is that past consumption affects current well-being. Gary S. Becker and Kevin M. Murphy (1988) provide a model of "instantaneous utility functions" to capture this feature, and we adopt (a translation of) their model. People's instantaneous utility for a given period represents how much pleasure they experience that period. Suppose that all effects of past consumption on period-t instantaneous utility can be captured in a single summary statistic, which we denote by k_t. We often refer to k_t as people's *addiction level* in period t. People's instantaneous utility in period t is given by $u_t(a_t, k_t)$—that is, how much pleasure they experience in period t depends both on whether they hit and on their addiction level.

In general, people's addiction level will be a function of their past consumption. Gary S. Becker and Kevin M. Murphy (1988) assume $k_t = \gamma k_{t-1} + a_{t-1}$ for some $\gamma \epsilon [0, 1]$. For simplicity, we limit attention here to the case $\gamma = 0$, which implies that $k_t = a_{t-1}$. If people hit last period (that is, $a_{t-1} = 1$), then they are hooked this period (that is, $k_t = 1$); and if people refrained last period (that is, $a_{t-1} = 0$), then they are unhooked this period (that is, $k_t = 0$). Limiting attention to the case $\gamma = 0$ is of course unrealistic. Assuming $\gamma = 0$ implies that there are only two addiction levels, being hooked and being unhooked. Moreover, it implies that a single period of restraint gets people completely unhooked and that a single period of indulgence gets people completely hooked. These assumptions make sense only if periods are somewhat lengthy. Even so, it turns out that our main results and intuitions will hold for any $\gamma \epsilon [0, 1]$. Hence, although the reader should not take our model too literally, we believe the model does reveal some more general insights.

Suppose the period-t instantaneous utility function takes the form shown in table 6.1. We often drop the subscript t from k_t and a_t when there is no danger of confusion. An important concept for the analysis will be the *current temptation to consume* the addictive product, by which we mean the instantaneous utility from taking a hit relative to that from not taking a hit. With the formulation in table 6.1, the temptation to consume in period t given addiction level k is $f_t(k) - g_t(k)$. Of course, the decision whether to hit relies on more than merely the current temptation to consume, since people care about how current consumption affects future instantaneous utilities. This trade-off between the current temptation to consume and the future costs of such consumption is the crux of the choice to become addicted.

We consider two characteristics of addictive products. The first is that they can be habit forming: The more people have consumed in the

Table 6.1   Instantaneous Utility Function I

Condition	Utility from Hitting: $u_t(1, k_t)$	Utility from Refraining: $u_t(0, k_t)$
When unhooked ($k_t = 0$)	$f_t(0)$	$g_t(0)$
When hooked ($k_t = 1$)	$f_t(1)$	$g_t(1)$

past, the larger is their current temptation to consume; for example, smoking cigarettes at age sixteen increases the temptation to smoke a cigarette at age seventeen. Formally:

DEFINITION 1   A product is *habit forming* if for all t, $f_t(1) - g_t(1) > f_t(0) - g_t(0)$.

In addition to being habit forming, addictive activities often generate negative internalities: The more people have consumed in the past, the smaller is their current well-being (no matter their current behavior); for example, smoking cigarettes at age sixteen reduces pleasure at age seventeen both from smoking and from not smoking.[5] Formally:

DEFINITION 2   A product has *negative internalities* if for all t, $f_t(1) < f_t(0)$ and $g_t(1) < g_t(0)$.

Negative internalities include health problems due to overeating or oversmoking, as well as the "tolerance" that is exhibited for many drugs.[6] Of course, activities can generate negative internalities without being habit forming (for example, eating cheesecake); and a habit-forming activity need not generate negative internalities (for example, jogging). "Addictive products" are usually considered both to be habit forming and to generate negative internalities, and that is the case we study in this chapter. Figure 6.1 illustrates what the instantaneous utility function might look like for such a good.

Our formulation allows for instantaneous utilities to vary across time. For simplicity, we assume that any nonstationarities arise from variations in the utility from hitting—that is, we assume $g_t(k)$ is independent of t. We can then without loss of generality express the period-t instantaneous utility function in terms of three parameters, as shown in table 6.2.

The formulation in table 6.2 normalizes the instantaneous utility from refraining when unhooked to be zero. Then f_t represents the temptation to hit when unhooked, ρ represents the magnitude of the negative internality, and $\sigma - \rho$ represents the magnitude of the habit formation. Any nonstationarities in the instantaneous utility function are captured by a

Figure 6.1   Instantaneous Utility

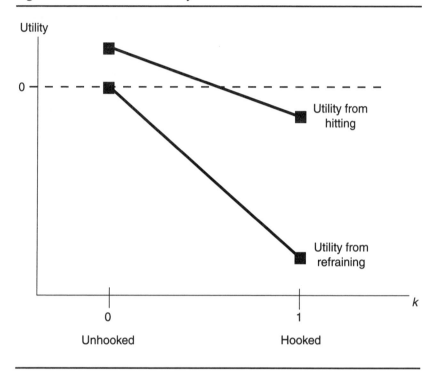

varying f_t. We should consider both the case of a stationary instantaneous utility function—so $f_t = f_o$ for all t—and the case of a nonstationary instantaneous utility function.

Throughout our analysis, we assume that people correctly predict how current consumption affects future instantaneous utility functions. Our analysis therefore ignores the possibility that people simply underestimate the addictive nature of products they consume. For the instantaneous utility function in table 6.2, this would mean that people underestimate ρ or σ. Although we suspect that this possibility might be quite important for addictive behavior—plausibly more important than self-control problems—our goal in this chapter is to study the implications of self-control problems alone.

Although the previous discussion characterizes instantaneous utilities for addictive products, in any given period people care not only about their current instantaneous utility but also about their future instantaneous utilities. This is captured by people's intertemporal preferences.

Table 6.2   Instantaneous Utility Function II

Condition	Utility from Hitting: $u_t(1, k)$	Utility from Refraining: $u_t(0, k)$
When unhooked ($k = 0$)	f_t	0
When hooked ($k = 1$)	$f_t - \rho$	$-\sigma$

Evidence suggests that people have self-control problems: People tend to pursue immediate gratification in a way that they do not appreciate from a long-run perspective. For example, suppose people are presented with a choice between doing seven hours of an unpleasant task on April 1 versus eight hours on April 15. We suspect that if asked on February 1 (that is, from a long-run perspective), virtually everyone would prefer the seven hours on April 1. Yet if given the same choice on April 1, most people would choose to put off the work until April 15.[7]

The standard economics model, in contrast, assumes that intertemporal preferences are *time consistent:* People's relative preference for well-being at an earlier date over a later date is the same no matter when they are asked. In the example above, such time consistency would require that, irrespective of the specific choice, people make the same choice on February 1 and April 1. The standard economics model therefore, a priori, rules out self-control problems.

A small set of economists and psychologists has over the years proposed formal models of time-inconsistent preferences and self-control problems.[8] Edmund S. Phelps and Robert A. Pollak (1968) put forward an elegant model of intertemporal preferences in the context of intergenerational altruism, which David Laibson (1994a) later used to capture self-control problems within individuals.[9] If u_τ is the instantaneous utility people get in period τ, then their intertemporal preferences at time t, U^t, can be represented by the following utility function:

For all t,

$$U^t(u_t, u_{t+1}, \cdots, u_T) \equiv \delta^t u_t + \beta \Sigma_{\tau=t+1}^{T} \delta^\tau u_\tau. \tag{6.1}$$

By assuming that both β and δ are greater than zero but no greater than one, these intertemporal preferences capture the idea that at each moment people care about their future well-being but typically less than they care about their current well-being. For $\beta = 1$, these preferences are time consistent, wherein the parameter δ represents "time-consistent" impatience. For $\beta < 1$, however, these preferences are time inconsistent, wherein the parameter β parsimoniously captures the degree to which people pursue immediate gratification: While β plays no role in determining people's willingness to trade off well-being among future periods, it determines how much more they care about their current well-being than their well-being in all future periods.

When people have self-control problems, an important issue arises: Are they aware of these self-control problems? Our analysis considers two extreme assumptions: *Sophisticated* people are fully aware of their future self-control problems and therefore know exactly how they will behave in the future; and *naive* people are fully *un*aware of their future self-control problems and therefore believe they will behave in the future exactly as they currently would like to behave in the future.[10] Since we wish to compare people with self-control problems to people without self-control problems, our analysis also examines time-consistent agents, whom we refer to as *TCs*.

To formalize our predictions about how the three types behave, we assume people follow "perception-perfect strategies," which in this environment implies that people choose to hit today if and only if hitting today is optimal given their current preferences and their current beliefs about how they will behave in the future.[11]

To capture people's beliefs about how they will behave in the future, we define a *strategy* α to be a function that specifies what people would do in all situations. In other words, for all k and t, $\alpha(k, t)$ is the action people would pursue in period t when their addiction level is k. For example, if $\alpha(0, t) = 0$ and $\alpha(1, t) = 1$, then people would refrain in period t if unhooked, and people would hit in period t if hooked.

Let $U_t(k_t, \alpha)$ be people's period-t continuation (long-run) utility as a function of their addiction level in period t, k_t, and their strategy, α. Long-run utility represents intertemporal preferences from some prior perspective, so that self-control problems (that is, β) are irrelevant. People's long-run preferences are represented by equation (6.1) when $\beta = 1$, and therefore TCs, naifs, and sophisticates have identical long-run utilities. A useful way to write $U_t(k, \alpha)$ is

$$U_t(k, \alpha) = \begin{cases} f_t(k) + \delta U_{t+1}(1, \alpha), & \text{if } \alpha(k, t) = 1 \\ g_t(k) + \delta U_{t+1}(0, \alpha), & \text{if } \alpha(k, t) = 0. \end{cases}$$

Consider people in period t who are contemplating the consequences of their current behavior on their future intertemporal utility. Suppose they perceive that they will follow strategy α^p beginning in period $t + 1$, in which case they believe that if they hit this period then their intertemporal utility beginning next period will be $U_{t+1}(1, \alpha^p)$, and they believe that if they refrain this period then their intertemporal utility beginning next period will be $U_{t+1}(0, \alpha^p)$. Hence, they perceive the (undiscounted) benefit of restraint to be $U_{t+1}(0, \alpha^p) - U_{t+1}(1, \alpha^p)$.

We now have a formalization of the choice of whether to hit today: People hit in period t if and only if, given their perceptions of future behavior α^p, the current temptation to hit $f_t(k) - g_t(k)$ is larger than the (discounted) future benefit from current restraint $U_{t+1}(0, \alpha^p) - U_{t+1}(1, \alpha^p)$. For simplicity, we assume people hit when indifferent. Notice that (given our very special assumptions) the benefit from restraint is independent of whether people are currently hooked, whereas the temptation to hit is higher if people are currently hooked. This means that for all three types, in any period people hit when unhooked only if they also hit when hooked.

TCs are time consistent, so for each (k, t) their continuation strategy maximizes their continuation utility. The implication of time consistency in the framework discussed in the preceding paragraph is that TCs correctly perceive their future behavior and that they discount the future benefit from current restraint by δ. Hence, we define perception-perfect strategies for TCs as:

DEFINITION 3   *A perception-perfect strategy for TCs* is a strategy α^{tc} that satisfies for all $k \geq 0$ and for all t, $\alpha^{tc}(k, t) = 1$ if and only if $f_t(k) - g_t(k) \geq \delta(U_{t+1}(0, \alpha^{tc}) - U_{t+1}(1, \alpha^{tc}))$.

At any point in time, naifs believe they will behave like TCs beginning with the next period. Hence, in any period, naifs perceive that they will follow strategy α^{tc} beginning with the next period. Since naifs discount the future benefit of current restraint by $\beta\delta$, we define perception-perfect strategies for naifs as:

DEFINITION 4   *A perception-perfect strategy for naifs* is a strategy α^n that satisfies for all $k \geq 0$ and for all t, $\alpha^n(k, t) = 1$ if and only if $f_t(k) - g_t(k) \geq \beta\delta (U_{t+1}(0, \alpha^{tc}) - U_{t+1}(1, \alpha^{tc}))$.

Sophisticates, like TCs, predict exactly how they will behave in the future. Sophisticates, like naifs, also discount the future benefit of current restraint by $\beta\delta$. Hence, we define perception-perfect strategies for sophisticates as

DEFINITION 5   *A perception-perfect strategy for sophisticates* is a strategy α^s that satisfies for all $k \geq 0$ and for all t, $\alpha^s(k, t) = 1$ if and only if $f_t(k) - g_t(k) \geq \beta\delta(U_{t+1}(0, \alpha^s) - U_{t+1}(1, \alpha^s))$.

In each period, TCs and naifs are really just choosing an optimal future consumption path. TCs will always stick to the behavior path chosen in the first period. Naifs, in contrast, will often revise their chosen behavior paths as their preferences change from period to period. Sophisticates are in a sense playing a game against their future selves. Hence, their behavior will partly reflect "strategic" reactions to bad behavior by future selves that they cannot directly control and partly reflect attempts to induce good behavior from future selves.

Stationary Preferences

In this section, we analyze a stationary model of addiction:

(A1) Assume that $f_t = f_o$ for all t.

Assumption A1 says that the instantaneous utility function $u_t(a, k)$ depends on the current level of addiction k but not on the specific period t. As we shall see, this assumption is rather important. In many cases it is quite unrealistic: It assumes, for instance, that the first hit of a cigarette or cocaine yields the same pleasure to a twenty-year-old as it does to a sixty-year-old. Nonetheless, as a base case and to clarify certain issues, we maintain this assumption for this section.

We begin with a three-period example that provides some intuition and also illustrates how to solve for the perception-perfect strategies for TCs, naifs, and sophisticates. Suppose people live for three periods, which we interpret as youth, middle age, and old age. In any given period, people are currently hooked if $k = 1$ (that is, because they hit last period) and unhooked if $k = 0$ (that is, because they refrained last period). Finally, suppose that people's preferences in each of the three periods can be represented with the following instantaneous utilities:

EXAMPLE 1: Suppose $f_o = 10$, $\rho = 18$, and $\sigma = 25$.

Table 6.3 displays example 1. Consider how TCs with $\delta = 1$ would behave. TCs hit no matter what in their old age, since the instantaneous utility from hitting is larger than the instantaneous utility from refraining whether hooked or unhooked. In their middle age, TCs decide whether to hit knowing they will hit no matter what in their old age. It is straightforward to show that they refrain no matter what in their middle age; for example, when hooked in middle age, refraining yields intertemporal utility $(-25) + 10 = -15$, while hitting yields utility $(-8) + (-8) = -16$. In their youth, TCs know they will refrain in their middle age and hit in their old age no matter what they do now, and they prefer to refrain (because refraining yields $0 + 0 + 10 = 10$ while hitting yields $10 + (-25) + 10 = -5$). Hence, TCs with $\delta = 1$ refrain in their youth and middle age but then hit in their old age.

Table 6.3   Example 1

Condition	Utility from Hitting: $u(1, k)$	Utility from Refraining: $u(0, k)$
When unhooked ($k = 0$)	10	0
When hooked ($k = 1$)	−8	−25

Consider next naifs with $\delta = 1$ and $\beta = \frac{1}{2}$. Naifs always believe they will behave like TCs in the future, and therefore in their youth naifs believe they will refrain in middle age and hit in old age no matter what they do now. Although having a self-control problem creates an increased desire to hit for naifs, with $\beta = \frac{1}{2}$ naifs manage to refrain while young, because they perceive that refraining yields $0 + (\frac{1}{2}) 0 + (\frac{1}{2}) 10 = 5$ while hitting yields $10 + (\frac{1}{2}) (-25) + (\frac{1}{2}) 10 = 2.5$. In their middle age, naifs are aware that they will hit no matter what in their old age. Now the self-control problem leads naifs to hit no matter what: Even when unhooked, hitting yields $10 + (\frac{1}{2}) (-8) = 6$ while refraining yields $0 + (\frac{1}{2})10 = 5$. Finally, in their old age, naifs, like TCs, hit no matter what. Hence, naifs refrain in their youth but hit in both their middle age and old age.

In this example, naifs indulge in the addictive activity more than TCs. This result turns out to be quite general: Self-control problems combined with a belief that in the future they will not have such problems always leads people to overconsume addictive products. Indeed, the following result follows directly from definitions 3 and 4: For any contingency, if TCs hit, then naifs hit, and therefore if naifs refrain, then TCs refrain.

LEMMA 1.   For any k and t, if $\alpha^{tc}(k, t) = 1$ then $\alpha^n(k, t) = 1$.

Now consider sophisticates with $\delta = 1$ and $\beta = \frac{1}{2}$. In their middle age, sophisticates correctly perceive that, like TCs, they will hit no matter what in their old age. Given this belief, it is in fact optimal to hit no matter what in their middle age (the comparison is identical to that for naifs). In their youth, sophisticates realize that they will hit for the rest of their lives no matter what they do now. As a result, it is optimal to hit during their youth as well, because hitting yields $10 + (\frac{1}{2}) (-8) + (\frac{1}{2}) (-8) = 2$, while refraining yields $0 + (\frac{1}{2}) 10 + (\frac{1}{2}) (-8) = 1$. Hence, sophisticates hit throughout their lives.

In this example, sophisticates indulge in the addictive activity more than naifs. Although this result may seem surprising, it reflects how sophisticates' correct pessimism about future behavior can lead to increased consumption in the realm of addiction. In their youth, sophisticates know they will hit no matter what during middle age, whereas naifs optimistically *and incorrectly* believe they will surely refrain during middle age. The habit-forming property of addictive goods implies, however, that the more people expect to hit in the future, the smaller is the future benefit of refraining now. As a result, having (correctly) pessimistic beliefs about future behavior can make sophisticates more likely to indulge than naifs.

Example 1 illustrates some basic intuitions of the stationary model. We now show that these intuitions hold more generally. To do so, we focus on the case where there is an infinite horizon ($T = \infty$). We do so for two reasons. First, it is expositionally easier to describe the results for an infinite horizon. Second, this assumption is closer in spirit to the rational choice models of addiction and yields more realistic results.

In an infinite-horizon model with stationary instantaneous utilities, TCs and naifs both follow a stationary strategy, wherein behavior depends only on the current addiction level k and not the specific period t. In any period, both TCs and naifs choose today's behavior by determining their optimal lifetime path of behavior beginning from today. Given an infinite horizon, stationary instantaneous utilities, and our assumption that people hit when indifferent, for any t there is a unique optimal lifetime path of behavior, and this path depends on the current addiction level k but not the current period t. This logic is summarized in the following lemma:

LEMMA 2. Under stationary instantaneous utilities and $T = \infty$, (1) there is a unique perception-perfect strategy for TCs, α^{tc}, and this strategy is stationary; and (2) there is a unique perception-perfect strategy for naifs, α^n, and this strategy is stationary.

Since there are only two addiction levels (that is, people can be hooked or unhooked), and since people would never hit when unhooked but refrain when hooked, there are three relevant stationary strategies that TCs and naifs might follow: They might hit no matter what; they might refrain no matter what; or they might refrain when unhooked but hit when hooked.

For sophisticates, there can be multiple perception-perfect strategies when there is an infinite horizon. However, there is a unique perception-perfect strategy for sophisticates when there is a finite horizon (given the assumption of hitting when indifferent). Throughout this chapter, we focus on perception-perfect strategies for an infinite horizon that correspond to the unique finite-horizon perception-perfect strategy as the horizon becomes long.[12] This restriction rules out a perpetual one-shot-is-all-I-get mentality, wherein people think to themselves, "If I can just refrain today then I'll refrain always, whereas if I hit today I'll hit forever after." More precisely, we rule out this mentality when it can be supported *only* by infinite-horizon reasoning (analogous to folk-theorem-type equilibria in infinitely repeated games), because a variant of such a mentality can arise in a stationary finite-horizon model.

When there is a long, finite horizon, the crucial question that determines the behavior of sophisticates is whether they would hit when unhooked in the second-to-last period while knowing that they would hit no matter what in the last period. If the answer is yes, then they will hit no matter what in the second-to-last period, and they face the same decision in the third-to-last period. As a result, everything unravels, and they hit no matter what in all periods. Suppose the answer is no, so that they refrain when unhooked in the second-to-last period. Since the benefit from restraint cannot be smaller than when they hit for sure next period, in this case sophisticates must always refrain when unhooked; that is, α^s satisfies $\alpha^s(0, t) = 0$ for all t. In this case, the behavior of sophisticates when hooked is unclear—they might hit when hooked in all periods, they might refrain when hooked in all periods, or they might hit when hooked every τ periods for some $\tau > 1$ (in which case, α^s is nonstationary). We summarize this logic in the following lemma:

LEMMA 3. Under stationary instantaneous utilities and $T = \infty$, α^s satisfies either (1) $\alpha^s(k,t) = 1$ for all k and t, or (2) $\alpha^s(0,t) = 0$ for all t.

Now consider observed behavior when people are initially unhooked (that is, $k_1 = 0$). Lemma 2 implies that both TCs and naifs either always hit or never hit, and lemma 3 implies that sophisticates also either always hit or never hit. To compare the three types, we must determine when each type always hits. TCs are time consistent, and therefore they always hit if and only if they prefer always hitting to never hitting. Since (it can be shown by calculating some infinite sums) always hitting yields intertemporal utility $f_o/(1 - \delta) - \delta\rho/(1 - \delta)$, and never hitting yields intertemporal utility 0, TCs always hit if and only if $f_o \geq \delta\rho$. For naifs, we must determine beliefs about future behavior. If $f_o + \sigma - \rho < \delta\sigma$, then TCs would refrain forever even if they were currently hooked. Naifs who are unhooked therefore consider taking a single hit, thinking they will never hit again. The single hit is worthwhile if and only if $f_o \geq \beta\delta\sigma$, in which case naifs always hit. If $f_o + \sigma - \rho \geq \delta\sigma$, then TCs would hit forever if they were currently hooked, and hence naifs who are unhooked believe (correctly) that they are choosing between never hitting and always hitting. In this case, naifs always hit if and only if $f_o \geq \beta\delta\rho / (1 - \delta + \beta\delta)$. Finally, sophisticates always hit when initially unhooked if and only if they prefer hitting today given that they will hit for sure tomorrow. Hence, sophisticates always hit if and only if $f_o \geq \beta\delta\rho$. Summarizing,

TCs always hit if and only if

$$f_o \geq \delta\rho.$$

Naifs always hit if and only if

$$f_o \geq \beta\delta\sigma, \text{ when } f_o < \rho - (1-\delta)\sigma.$$

$$f_o \geq \beta\delta\,\rho/(1 - \delta + \beta\delta), \text{ when } f_o \geq \rho - (1-\delta)\sigma.$$

Sophisticates always hit if and only if

$$f_o \geq \beta\delta\rho.$$

Given $\beta < 1, f_o > 0$, and $\sigma > \rho > 0$, the following proposition derives from the above equations:

PROPOSITION 1. Under stationary instantaneous utilities and $T = \infty$, if $k_1 = 0$ (that is, people are initially unhooked): (1) if TCs always hit, then naifs always hit; and (2) if naifs always hit, then sophisticates always hit.

Part 1 of proposition 1 merely restates lemma 1: Naifs are always more likely to hit than TCs. Part 2 of proposition 1 establishes that the surprising outcome of example 1—that sophisticates consume more of the addictive product than naifs—always holds in a stationary model when people are initially unhooked.

The result that sophisticates are more likely to hit than naifs, however, very much relies on people being initially unhooked. To illustrate, consider behavior in example 1 when $\beta = 2/3$ and $k_1 = 1$. With $\beta = 2/3$, both sophisticates and naifs hit in middle age if they are hooked but refrain in middle age if they are unhooked. Sophisticates correctly predict this behavior and, as a result, find it optimal to refrain while young even with $k_1 = 1$ in order to induce good behavior in middle age. Naifs, in contrast, believe they will refrain no matter what in middle age and therefore choose to hit while young for $k_1 = 1$. Hence, for $\beta = 2/3$ and $k_1 = 1$, sophisticates refrain in both youth and middle age, whereas naifs hit throughout their lives. (Proposition 1 is not violated, since for $\beta = 2/3$ and $k_1 = 0$, both sophisticates and naifs refrain in youth and in middle age.)

Hence, the example illustrates that, when initially hooked, sophisticates can be more prone to quit than naifs. In fact, this result holds more generally:

PROPOSITION 2. Under stationary instantaneous utilities and T-∞, if $k_1 = 1$ (that is, people are initially hooked): (1) If TCs always hit, then sophisticates always hit; (2) if sophisticates always hit, then naifs always hit.

The different results in propositions 1 and 2 highlight the complex role of awareness about future self-control problems. In fact, there are two ways in which sophistication about future self-control problems can influence people's behavior. First, sophistication about future self-control problems can make people pessimistic about future behavior (that is, they believe that in general that they will hit more often than they would if they had no self-control problem). We refer to this phenomenon as the *pessimism effect*. Second, sophistication about future self-control problems may make people realize that they will resist future temptations only if they resist current temptation. We refer to this phenomenon as the *incentive effect*.

With some oversimplification, figure 6.2 illustrates the distinction between the pessimism effect and the incentive effect. Figure 6.2 shows the future benefit of current restraint as a function of three possible beliefs about future behavior: People might believe they will always hit in the future no matter what they do now; people might believe they will refrain always in the future no matter what they do now; and people might believe they will always hit in the future if they hit now but refrain always in the future if they refrain now. The figure assumes parameters such that TCs refrain in all contingencies.[13] This implies that naifs and TCs both perceive that in the future they will refrain no matter what, and therefore according to figure 6.2 the future benefit from current restraint is σ.

Pure pessimism reflects that while TCs and naifs perceive that they will refrain no matter what in the future, sophisticates may perceive that they will hit no matter what in the future, in which case, according to figure 6.2, the benefit from current restraint is ρ. Hence, pure pessimism about future behavior implies that sophisticates are more likely to hit than TCs or naifs (because the perceived benefit from restraint is smaller). Figure 6.2 makes clear that this result is driven by the habit-forming property of addictive products (that is, σ > ρ is exactly equivalent to the product being habit forming). When a product is habit forming, the more often people will hit in the future, the less costly is hitting now.

Sophisticates may not be purely pessimistic; rather, they might be pessimistic about their future behavior when hooked but optimistic

Figure 6.2   Future Benefit of Current Restraint

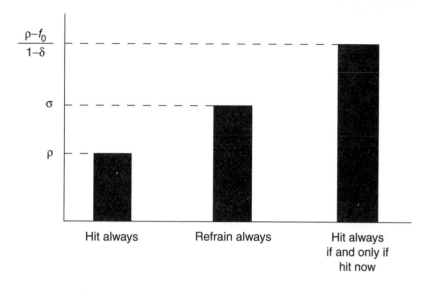

Perceived Future Behavior

about their future behavior when unhooked, in which case they perceive a need to refrain now in order to induce good behavior in the future. This is when the incentive effect is operative, and according to figure 6.2, in this case the benefit from current restraint is $(\rho - f_o)^0 / (1 - \delta) > \sigma$.[14] Hence, the incentive effect can imply that sophisticates are less likely to hit than *TCs* or naifs. This result is driven by sophisticates' concern about *improper* future overconsumption (a concern that neither *TCs* nor naifs would ever have). That is, sophisticates refrain when naifs or *TCs* do not only if sophisticates are refraining to prevent improper future behavior.

The crucial question then is when does the incentive effect become operative; and since the incentive effect is driven by future restraint, the answer is, only if there is some future period where sophisticates will refrain when unhooked *in the absence of the incentive effect*.[15] It is this intuition that drives the different results in propositions 1 and 2 (and that we build on in our discussion of nonstationary preferences and variable myopia). In the stationary model, if in period 1 people would hit when unhooked in the face of pure pessimism, then in all periods they would hit when unhooked in the face of pure pessimism, and therefore the incentive effect cannot be operative. This means that whenever sophisticates *need* the incentive effect to refrain when unhooked, it is inoperative. It follows that sophisticates are more likely than naifs to hit when unhooked (proposition 1). When people are initially hooked, in contrast, the incentive effect can be operative even when they would hit in the face of pure pessimism because refraining now will get them unhooked. It turns out that naifs refrain when hooked only if sophisticates refrain when unhooked, but then the incentive effect is operative and sophisticates are more likely to refrain when hooked than naifs (proposition 2).

Throughout this section, we explicitly and implicitly state that both sophisticates and naifs are "hurting" themselves with their behavior. Indeed, this notion can be formalized. Of course, in an environment in which people have different preferences at different times, we must specify what we are using for a welfare criterion. A conservative approach is to assume there are no true preferences and to consider Pareto comparisons (see, for example, Goldman 1979, 1980, and Laibson 1994a). Alternatively, Ted O'Donoghue and Matthew Rabin (1999) employ a less conservative approach, deeming the long-run preferences (that ignore any taste for immediate gratification) to be the true preferences, relevant for welfare analysis. In the examples of this section and throughout the rest of the chapter, however, sophisticates and naifs can hurt themselves by any criterion. Intuitively, if people get *inappropriately* addicted to a product, they are generating dissatisfaction in almost every period of their lives, and hence from all points of view addiction is perceived as undesirable. We return to this issue at the end of this chapter.

Nonstationary Preferences

Although the stationary model provides insight into how self-control problems and awareness of future self-control problems might affect addictive behavior, some of the results depend on the unrealistic assumption that the instantaneous utility function is constant over time. This assumption rules out the possibility that the desire to consume addictive products decreases as people get older. It also rules out the possibility of day-to-day fluctuations in the desire to consume addictive products—for example, the desire to consume may be greater on weekends than it is on weekdays, or the desire may be greater in response to certain traumatic events (as when abstaining alcoholics resume drinking during a crisis). In this section, we consider these possibilities in order to get a more complete picture of how self-control problems affect addictive behaviors.

As discussed earlier in the chapter, we model nonstationary instantaneous utilities by introducing variations in the utility from hitting.

Table 6.4.   Example 2

Condition	Utility from Hitting: $u_t(1, k)$	Utility from Refraining: $u_t(0, k)$
In youth when unhooked	14	0
In youth when hooked	−4	−25
In middle age when unhooked	10	0
In middle age when hooked	−8	−25
In old age when unhooked	−5	0
In old age when hooked	−23	−25

In other words, we assume there is a sequence $(f_1, f_2, \ldots, f_T)$ such that $f_t(k) = f_t - \rho k$, and we assume that $g_t(k) = -\sigma k$ for all t. The stationary case assumes $f_t = f_o$ for all t. In this section, we consider various ways in which f_t may depend on t.

For many addictive products, the temptation to consume declines over the course of one's life. For example, if a twenty-year-old and a sixty-year-old have both never taken cocaine, it seems likely that the temptation to take a first hit is larger for the twenty-year-old. This difference might arise from forces such as peer pressure, or the young body's physical resilience, or merely the fact that an older person tends to lose interest in novel activities. Consider the following model of addiction:

(A2) Assume that $f_1 \geq f_2 \geq \ldots \geq f_T$.

To illustrate how this new assumption can change the results, consider the following variant of example 1:

EXAMPLE 2: Suppose $(f_1, f_2, f_3) = (14, 10, -5)$, $\rho = 18$, and $\sigma = 25$.

Table 6.4 illustrates example 2. Examples 1 and 2 have the same levels of habit formation and negative internalities—that is, ρ and σ are the same in the two examples. Moreover, examples 1 and 2 have identical instantaneous utilities for middle age. In example 2, however, people have a larger temptation to hit in their youth and a smaller temptation to hit in their old age. Indeed, the crucial feature of example 2 is that people hit in their old age if and only if they are hooked (in example 1, people hit in their old age no matter what).

In example 2, it is straightforward to show that TCs with $\delta = 1$ refrain throughout their lives; sophisticates with $\delta = 1$ and $\beta = \frac{1}{2}$ also refrain throughout their lives; and naifs with $\delta = 1$ and $\beta = \frac{1}{2}$ hit throughout their lives. (The calculations are left to the reader.) Of particular interest is how modifying example 1 so as to incorporate a decreasing temptation over one's lifetime affects sophisticates and naifs in opposite directions. Sophisticates indulge less in example 2 than in example 1—in example 2 they never hit, whereas in example 1 they always hit—and naifs indulge more in example 2 than in example 1—in example 2 they always hit, whereas in example 1 they refrained in their youth.

That sophisticates indulge less in example 2 than in example 1 reflects the increased power of the incentive effect in the youth environment. In example 2, sophisticates hit in old age if and only if they are hooked. Knowing this, they hit in middle age if and only if they are hooked. In their youth, sophisticates correctly recognize that hitting now means also hitting in both middle age and old age, whereas refraining now means also refraining in both middle age and old age. Since even in their youth they perceive always hitting to be *worse* than always refraining, sophisticates choose to refrain in their youth. In their youth sophisticates would most like to hit now and refrain thereafter; but they choose to refrain in their youth in order to induce good behavior in the future (that is, because of the incentive effect).

That naifs indulge more in example 2 than in example 1 reflects how the youth environment can be problematic for naifs, who give in to large youthful temptations under the false belief that they will later quit. In example 2, in their youth, naifs (like sophisticates) would most like to hit in their youth and refrain thereafter. Since naifs do not foresee future self-control problems, they choose to follow this path in their youth; but they end up never quitting and, therefore, suffer a lifetime of addiction.

We now describe behavior more generally in the youth environment. The interesting case is that in which people have an increased temptation to hit while young but eventually the temptation falls to a more normal level. We refer to this phenomenon as people maturing:

DEFINITION 6   Suppose there exists some $\tau \geq 2$ such that $f_1 \geq f_2 \geq \ldots \geq f_\tau = f_{\tau+1} = \ldots = f_T$. Then we say people become mature in period τ.

With this definition in hand, we can state a general proposition regarding youth models:

PROPOSITION 3. Suppose that once a person becomes mature, she will refrain even in the face of pure pessimism. Then (1) in all situations, sophisticates hit only if naifs hit; and (2) sophisticates always hit only if they prefer (from a period-1 perspective) to always hit rather than never to hit.

The crucial condition in proposition 3 is that *there is eventually some period* in which people will refrain when unhooked even in the face of pure pessimism. We feel that this is a realistic condition for many addictive products—eventually people will lose interest in the product as long as they are unhooked at that time. The results in proposition 3 reflect that this condition is exactly the condition for when the incentive effect is operative in the youth environment. Part 1 states that in this case sophisticates are less likely to hit than naifs in all situations. Part 2 states that in this case sophisticates cannot suffer a *costly* lifelong addiction, because they choose to hit throughout their lives only if that is optimal from a period-1 perspective.

These results stand in stark contrast to the results in the stationary model. In the stationary model, the incentive effect is operative if and only if *in the first period* people would refrain when unhooked in the face of pure pessimism, and as a result sophisticates can suffer a very harmful lifelong addiction because of a feeling that addiction is inevitable. In the youth model, in contrast, as long as the temptation to consume eventually falls to the point at which people would choose to refrain even in the face of pure pessimism, the inevitability of addiction vanishes, and as a result sophisticates are less likely to hit than naifs and unlikely to suffer harmful lifelong addictions.

Although proposition 3 suggests that sophisticates will not suffer a lifelong addiction when doing so is particularly costly, sophisticates may engage in costly misbehavior in their youth (provided they will indeed quit once mature). For example, suppose people are sure they will quit drinking as soon as they graduate from college (that is, when they become mature). Knowing this, they may drink no matter what in the last semester at college, which can lead them to drink no matter what in the second-to-last semester of college, and so on. As a result, they may start drinking in the first semester of college knowing full well that they will drink throughout college and then quit, even though from the perspective of the first semester of college they would prefer not to drink at all in college. Two comments about such youthful misbehavior are in order. First, it can clearly be quite costly if maturity comes late in life. Even so, we feel that for many addictive products maturity does set in at a reasonable age. Second, whether such youthful misbehavior occurs depends critically on whether people would quit if hooked once mature. If not, then misbehavior during youth is quite dangerous and therefore unlikely. If so (for example, the college example above), then misbehavior during youth is quite safe and therefore likely.[16]

Finally, we note that although we have no formal results concerning the behavior of naifs, there is reason to believe that naifs are likely to do quite poorly in the youth environment. Recall that in the stationary model

Table 6.5   Example 3

Condition	Utility from Hitting	Utility from Refraining
On weekend when unhooked	13	0
On weekend when hooked	−2	−18
On weekday when unhooked	10	0
On weekday when hooked	−5	−18

naifs have a tendency not to quit once hooked *even when it is well worth their while*. In the youth environment this becomes a real problem whenever the optimal plan is to hit in one's youth and later quit. Indeed, even in cases in which naifs would refrain forever after reaching maturity unhooked, naifs may form a very harmful lifelong addiction. For example, naifs may indulge in some addictive activity every week during college, planning to quit as soon as they graduate, and then indulge every week after graduation for the rest of their lives, each week planning to quit *next* week.

In addition to generally declining over one's lifetime, the temptation to engage in addictive activities may also fluctuate from day to day. The temptation to consume alcohol, for instance, may be larger on weekends than it is on weekdays. Consider the following model of addiction:

(A3) Assume that $f_t = f_o + X$ for $t \in \{1, 3, 5, \ldots\}$ and that $f_t = f_o$ for $t \in \{2, 4, 6, \ldots\}$.

This assumption says that each period is either a weekend (odd-numbered periods) or a weekday (even-numbered periods), and the temptation to hit is larger on weekends. Consider the following example:

EXAMPLE 3: Suppose $f_o = 10$, $\rho = 15$, $\sigma = 18$, and $X = 3$.

Table 6.5 illustrates example 3. Given the instantaneous utilities in example 3, TCs never hit when $T = \infty$ and $\delta = .99$.[17] For δ close to one, TCs choose the behavior that maximizes their long-run per-week payoff. If TCs choose to always hit, then they have payoff −2 on weekends and −5 on weekdays for a per-week payoff of −7. If they choose to never hit, their per-week payoff is zero. If they choose to hit on weekends and refrain on weekdays (that is, to consume in moderation), then they have payoff 13 on weekends and −18 on weekdays for a per-week payoff of −5. Hence, TCs choose to never hit.

Next consider how naifs and sophisticates behave, now assuming that $\beta = .7$. Naifs choose to hit in all periods. For naifs (and sophisticates), on any specific weekend the optimal lifetime plan of behavior is to hit today and never again, regardless of whether they are currently hooked. On any specific weekday, the optimal lifetime plan is to hit today and never again if they are currently hooked and never to hit if they are currently unhooked. Naifs therefore hit on weekends whether or not they are hooked and hit on weekdays when they are hooked. As a result, naifs hit in all periods. Sophisticates, in contrast, only hit every other weekend (that is, sophisticates follow the behavior path: Hit, refrain, refrain, refrain, hit, refrain, refrain, refrain, hit, . . .). In other words, sophisticates consume the addictive good in much smaller amounts than naifs. This example is precisely the type of situation where the incentive effect helps out sophisticates. Naifs hit on the first weekend planning to get unhooked during the upcoming weekday, but once hooked they are not able to resist even the weekday temptation. Sophisticates realize that for certain weekdays they will be able to control themselves only if they are unhooked, and thus they have an extra incentive to refrain even in the face of a larger temptation the preceding weekend.

To understand the specific cycle that sophisticates follow, we must ask when the incentive effect will be particularly strong. Suppose there is some weekend when sophisticates hit whether or not they are hooked.[18] On the preceding weekday, there is no incentive effect. Even so, given the smaller weekday temptation, sophisticates hit if and only if they are hooked. The incentive effect is therefore operative on the preceding weekend, and as a result they are able to resist the higher weekend temptation when unhooked. Since they hit when hooked on that weekend, the incentive effect is even stronger on the preceding weekday: Restraint induces further restraint in each of the next two periods, whereas hitting induces further hits in each of the next two periods. For this particular example, the incentive effect is now strong enough that sophisticates refrain on that weekday whether or not they are hooked. However, this means there is no incentive effect to overcome the larger temptation on the preceding weekend, so sophisticates hit on that weekend whether or not they are hooked, restarting the cycle.

Example 3 and other similar examples further highlight our main theme in this section: Restricting attention to stationary instantaneous utilities is very misleading, because it ignores a number of realistic situations wherein sophistication is likely to help people with self-control problems and wherein naivete can really hurt people with self-control problems. Indeed, in a more general model of periodically changing utilities we hypothesize that sophisticates may consume even less than TCs. (In example 3, we have made assumptions such that TCs refrain altogether.)

Gary S. Becker and Kevin M. Murphy (1988) and Gary S. Becker, Michael Grossman, and Kevin M. Murphy (1991, 1994) discuss the role of traumatic events (such as divorce, the death of a loved one, being fired) in causing people to consume addictive products. Within their stationary model, however, they are limited to formalizing traumatic events as discrete shocks to people's addiction level. By allowing for nonstationary instantaneous utilities, we can better endogenize traumatic events, formalizing them as short-term increases in the temptation to consume. Indeed, a model with traumatic events might be qualitatively similar to the youth model and the weekend-weekday model. For instance, we can reinterpret youth as the period of time directly following the traumatic event in which the temptation to consume an addictive good is high and maturity as the point at which the person has "recovered" from the traumatic event. Alternatively, we can imagine life as being full of traumatic events, in which case the weekend-weekday model could be interpreted as capturing the repeated fluctuations between normal times (that is, weekdays) and traumatic times (that is, weekends).

Predicting the effects of traumatic events in light of our other nonstationary models suggests that traumatic events are most likely to lead to severe addictions for naifs. Even when they do not want a lifelong addiction, naifs may end up with one because they consume when the temptation is high, thinking they will just quit once they recover. Of course, traumatic events can also cause TCs to get addicted when they would not in the absence of such events—but only if the shock is so severe that they prefer a lifelong addiction at the moment they first hit. We do not have a good empirical sense for how important such events are in inducing addiction (and, more likely, relapse), but if they *are* important, we suspect that any attempt to infer either the implicit discount rate or marginal utility of consuming the addictive product during such events would be more suggestive of naive self-control problems than a nonmyopic rational choice decision to begin a long-term addiction.[19]

Variable Myopia

In our discussions of stationary preferences and nonstationary preferences, we analyze behavior assuming that the extent of people's self-control problems does not vary at all over time. While observed propensity to succumb to temptation can vary because of changes in the scale of temptation—and indeed it is the role of habit formation in altering these trade-offs that is the crux of the role that self-control problems play in addiction—our examination of stationary and nonstationary preferences assumes that the degree of myopia itself is constant. We now consider two examples in which β varies over time. These examples further buttress our general impression that severely harmful addictive behavior is more likely to arise from naive self-control problems than from sophisticated self-control problems.

In the sections on stationary and nonstationary preferences we assume that past consumption of addictive products affects current behavior only through its effects on instantaneous utilities. For many addictive products—particularly mind-altering substances such as alcohol—there is a second mechanism through which past consumption can influence current behavior: Very recent consumption might in fact increase the magnitude of self-control problems. For example, sober people may have only modest self-control problems, but once they start drinking alcohol, they may develop severe self-control problems. When drunk, they may virtually ignore the long-run consequences of their behavior and just pursue immediate gratification. We refer to this phenomenon as *consumption-induced myopia*.

To introduce consumption-induced myopia into the model, suppose that if people refrained last period, then their intertemporal preferences are described by equation 6.1 with $\beta = \beta_0$; but if people hit last period, then their intertemporal preferences are described by equation 6.1 with $\beta = \beta_1 < \beta_0$. In other words, people are especially myopic when they have consumed in the preceding period and are currently hooked.[20] We assume that time-consistent people are unaffected by consumption-induced myopia, and therefore the behavior of *TC*s will again represent the benchmark of how naifs and sophisticates would like to behave from a long-run perspective.

The assumptions of naivete and sophistication are essentially the same in this environment as in the basic model. In any given period, naifs believe that they will behave like *TC*s in the future. Sophisticates, on the other hand, are completely aware of their self-control problems, including the effects of consumption-induced myopia, and they therefore correctly predict future behavior.[21]

To see how consumption-induced myopia might matter, consider a nonstationary weekend-weekday example:

EXAMPLE 4: Suppose $f_o = 10$, $\rho = 15$, $\sigma = 18$, and $X = 8$.

Table 6.6 displays example 4. Example 4 is identical to example 3 except that the weekend temptation is larger. For $T = \infty$ and $\delta = .99$, it is straightforward to show that *TC*s always hit on weekends and refrain on weekdays. For the case $\beta_0 = \beta_1 = .9$, it is straightforward to show that sophisticates and naifs both behave exactly like *TC*s, so naifs and sophisticates both consume in moderation: Hit on weekends and refrain on weekdays.

Table 6.6   Example 4

Condition	Utility from Hitting	Utility from Refraining
On weekend when unhooked	18	0
On weekend when hooked	3	–18
On weekday when unhooked	10	0
On weekday when hooked	–5	–18

Now consider $\beta_1 < \beta_0 = .9$. For simplicity, we focus on $\beta_1 = 0$, which means that the consumption-induced myopia is severe. For naifs, β_1 is irrelevant to their decision when unhooked since it affects neither their current preferences nor their predictions of future behavior. Given $\beta_0 = .9$, naifs hit on weekends when unhooked and refrain on weekdays when unhooked; but β_1 is very relevant for naifs' decisions when hooked because it is incorporated into their current preferences. For $\beta_1 = 0$, naifs hit when hooked on both weekends and weekdays. Hence, naifs with consumption-induced myopia always hit. Extrapolating from our model, we can interpret this example as naifs becoming alcoholics not because they immediately start out drinking every day but because they start out drinking immoderately on nights they had intended to drink moderately. Then, because they become more and more hooked on alcohol, eventually they will start drinking every day.

For sophisticates, unlike naifs, β_1 can influence behavior when unhooked, since sophisticates correctly predict how they will behave when hooked, and this prediction can influence current behavior. For $\beta_1 = 0$, sophisticates of course always hit once they start hitting, just like naifs.[22] When unhooked, however, sophisticates anticipate—and disapprove of—their future behavior resulting from hitting on a weekend and therefore *never* hit. Note that sophisticates consume less of the addictive product than *TCs*. We call such an outcome *preemptive abstinence*, and tautologically this abstinence is not ideal: It *would* be preferable to drink moderately, but sophisticates recognize that their true choice is between total abstinence and total addiction, and their choice of abstinence is preferable to the total addiction to which naifs succumb.[23]

A second noteworthy aspect of this example, related to the preemptive abstinence, concerns comparative statics on β_1. For sophisticates, lowering β_1 decreases consumption—it can move sophisticates from consuming in moderation to not consuming at all. This contrasts with both naif behavior in the consumption-induced myopia model and either naif or sophisticated behavior in the unitary myopia model. In both those cases, people always consume more on average in

Table 6.7   Example 5

Condition	Utility from Hitting: $u(1, k)$	Utility from Refraining: $u(0, k)$
When unhooked ($k = 0$)	2	0
When hooked ($k = 1$)	−1	−5

response to intensifying the average self-control problem. Naifs never try to preempt self-control problems and hence can only respond to increases in such problems by succumbing more often. In the unitary myopia model, for all examples with sophistication that we have investigated, the direct effect of a stronger taste for immediate gratification always swamps the indirect effect of preemptive abstinence.

While the previous example assumes myopia may depend on recent behavior, myopia might also depend on exogenous forces. A period of depression may induce a lack of concern for the future consequences of one's actions. Various cues in the environment—such as seeing somebody else smoke—may induce a temporary temptation to consume the product that does not necessarily correspond to the enjoyment one will derive from the activity. Finally, consumption-induced myopia for one addictive product might affect the level of myopia for another addictive product. Just as people who are drunk may lose inhibition in drinking more, they may also lose the inhibition to smoke. Hence, in studying addiction to cigarettes, the exogenous event of whether people are drunk may lead to variations in ability to refrain from smoking.[24]

Consider the following stationary example:

Example 5: Suppose $f_o = 2$, $\rho = 3$, and $\sigma = 5$.

Table 6.7 illustrates example 5. In example 5, consider an infinite horizon with $\delta = .99$. To model the time variance of myopia in a simple and extreme way, suppose that $\beta_t = 1$ for odd t and $\beta_t = 0$ for even t. TCs refrain always, since any other course of action yields a negative average utility. Hitting always yields utility profile $2, -1, -1, -1, \ldots$, and the cost of refraining when hooked (-5) outweighs the benefit of hitting when unhooked (2), so any pattern of moderate consumption also will not be attractive.

Naifs and sophisticates both hit in even periods, whether hooked or unhooked, since in these periods they do not attend at all to their future well-being. What do they do in odd periods?

Sophisticates refrain in the first period but then hit in all future odd periods. In every odd period after the first period, sophisticates will find themselves currently hooked. Since they realize they will hit in even periods, they correctly anticipate that their choice is between hitting every other period versus hitting every period. Hence, their choice of utility profiles in all odd periods after the first is between $(-5,2, -5,2, \ldots)$ from alternating and $(-1, -1, -1, \ldots)$ from always hitting. Hitting always is preferable to repeatedly suffering the pain of withdrawal—only to repeatedly become addicted again.

Naifs likewise refrain in the first period, but naifs *will* make the mistake of repeatedly trying to quit their habit because they naively think that they will stay unhooked, in which case they perceive it as worthwhile to pay the cost of withdrawal.[25]

While sophisticates consume more than naifs in this example, sophisticates are in fact behaving more in their long-term interest. Both are consuming more than is optimal, but the harm from consumption is very much not monotonic in consumption—if people simply will not be able to control themselves often enough, they may in fact be better off living with their addiction than trying to eliminate it.[26] The more general point is that in a world of variable myopia, misguided attempts to quit addictions, followed by relapse, may represent another significant problem for naifs.

Conclusion: Self-Control Versus Rational Choice

Our goal in this chapter has been to outline some simple models of the relationship between self-control problems and addictive behavior. Researchers who use mathematical models to study human choice—mostly economists—traditionally approach intertemporal choice problems by assuming time consistency. By focusing on self-control problems, therefore, we depart from this traditional approach. We conclude by discussing some of the advantages of our self-control model of addiction relative to rational choice models of addiction.

Throughout, we have not addressed the issue of whether self-control problems can lead to behaviors that cannot be explained with time-consistent preferences. In fact, such smoking guns—*qualitative* predictions that are inconsistent with rational choice theory—are difficult to come by in our highly stylized and simplified models. In these models, only a few types of behavior can arise, and most of these behaviors could arise from time-consistent preferences.[27] One might ask, then, why it is worthwhile to study a self-control model of addiction. We feel there are a number of reasons.

The most obvious reason is simple realism. The evidence overwhelmingly supports the existence of a time-inconsistent taste for immediate gratification, and we conjecture that almost all social scientists, policy makers, and humans in general believe in their hearts that people have self-control problems. It is true that time consistency is a simpler assumption (and more familiar to economists), and it is clearly warranted to investigate human behavior with simplifying assumptions—in a sense this is one of the strengths of economics. But, it is also clearly warranted to investigate human behavior with more realistic assumptions, particularly in arenas such as addiction wherein common intuition is that a facet of human nature ignored by economists may matter.

Related to the issue of realism, we predict that models incorporating self-control problems (especially, we conjecture, models that include an element of naivete) will be better calibrated than rational choice models and hence make sounder *quantitative* predictions. We do not have empirical evidence for this conjecture, but to illustrate our reasoning we present a simple calibration exercise within our framework: We demonstrate how very patient people with very small self-control problems can get addicted in situations in which time-consistent people would get addicted only if they were to discount the future at an implausibly heavy rate.

Formally, we ask what discount factor $\hat{\delta}$ would time-consistent people need to have to match the behavior in a given example of people with (β, δ) preferences. Consider a stationary infinite-horizon model with a period length of one week—for example, each week people decide whether to indulge in an addictive activity. Consider people who have a (long-run) *yearly* discount factor .95 (that is, $\delta^{52} = .95$), where δ is the weekly discount factor. In addition, these people have very small self-control problems: They have an extra bias for this week's well-being over next week's well-being of only 1 percent (that is, $\beta = .99$). If these people were to make a one-shot decision concerning well-being this week versus well-being during a week one year from now, they would look very patient: Their discount factor for this range would be .9405. But, suppose these people must decide each week whether to consume an addictive product characterized by the following instantaneous utilities:

EXAMPLE 6: Suppose $f_0 = 10$, $\rho = 10.1$, and $\sigma = 10.1$.

Table 6.8 illustrates example 6. It is straightforward to show that these people always hit in this situation, whether they are sophisticated or naive. How impatient would time-consistent people have to be to always hit in this situation? It can be shown that time-consistent people with discount factor $\hat{\delta}$ always hit only if $\hat{\delta} \leq .99$., and since $\hat{\delta}$ is the per-period

Table 6.8   Example 6

Condition	Utility From Hitting: $u(1, k)$	Utility from Refraining: $u(0, k)$
When unhooked ($k = 0$)	10	0
When hooked ($k = 1$)	−10.1	−10.1

discount factor, this implies that time-consistent people always hit only if they have a yearly discount factor ($\hat{\delta}^{52}$) smaller than .6. Hence, people with yearly discount factor .95 and very small self-control problems of $\beta = .99$ behave in a way that is consistent with a rational choice model of addiction but only for implausibly low yearly discount factors smaller than .6. Moreover, more extreme calibration results arise if we consider a smaller period length or larger self-control problems. For instance, consider $\delta^{52} = .95$ as before, but now suppose $\beta = .95$. In this case, there exist instantaneous utilities such that sophisticates or naifs always hit whereas time-consistent people would always hit only for a yearly discount factor smaller than .07, which is ludicrously small.

The crucial intuition driving these calibration results is the incremental nature of most addictive behavior. At each point in time, people choose whether to indulge now, and the cumulative effect of these decisions determines whether people get and remain addicted. With self-control problems, a sequence of incremental decisions can lead to behavior very different from how people would behave if committing up front to a lifetime path of behavior. In a rational choice model, in contrast, the incremental nature of addiction is irrelevant. If people know exactly what the future holds, and have no self-control problems, then people become addicted only if that is the optimal lifetime path of behavior.

Indeed, this incremental decision-making intuition suggests ways that our self-control model of addiction might yield qualitatively distinct predictions in more complicated environments. For example, consider the possibility of nonlinear pricing, such as having a yearly fee in conjunction with a per-unit price. Rational choice models would suggest, for instance, that a (monopolist) tobacco company could increase profits by using such a two-part tariff, since presumably consumers are getting some surplus. In contrast, our self-control model of addiction suggests that such two-part tariffs are very much the wrong pricing strategy. For sophisticates, the yearly fee may be the commitment device needed to not become addicted. For naifs, our model suggests that at any point in time they may expect to consume very little (because they are planning to quit soon), and therefore naifs also would be unwilling to pay the yearly fee. Hence, in richer models, allowing for self-control problems may in fact yield qualitatively distinct predictions.

The final—and in our view probably the most important—reason for studying self-control problems is that they predict very different *welfare* implications than the rational choice model. As discussed at the end of the section about stationary preferences, our model, unlike rational choice models, implies that people are hurting themselves with severe addictions.[28] To further illustrate this point, we reconsider the calibration example above. Suppose instantaneous utilities are as in example 6, but now consider a finite horizon ($T < \infty$) and $\delta = 1$. It can easily be shown that people with self-control problems (with magnitude $\beta = .99$), whether sophisticated or naive, will hit every period—irrespective of T. What is their stream of utilities for doing so? It is 10 in the first period, and $-.1$ for every period thereafter. For a one-shot instantaneous utility of 10, they experience a total negative utility for the last $T - 1$ periods of their lives of $(T - 1)$ (0.1). Obviously, if the number of periods in their lives becomes arbitrarily large, they suffer an arbitrarily large negative lifetime utility. Even from the period-1 perspective, where they receive their one-shot instantaneous utility of 10 and discount the future by $\beta = .99$, this outcome is clearly an unattractive option relative to never hitting. In other words, from *any* perspective self-control problems are causing severe harm.

It is perhaps unclear whether self-control problems will turn out, empirically, to be a major facet of cigarette and alcohol consumption, and other forms of addiction. Further investigation is required, extending and generalizing models such as those we present in this chapter (most notably, to allow for variable consumption levels and to consider the effects of prices) so as to make them testable. Models that investigate self-control problems are necessary, though, if economists or other researchers using formal models intend for their research to be deemed relevant by those who think it plausible that (on average) people are too addicted to harmful products for their own good.

We are grateful to David Laibson and other participants at the conference on addiction, and to an anonymous referee, for useful feedback; and to Doug Almond and especially Erik Eyster for research assistance. For financial support, we thank the National Science Foundation (Award 9709485), and Rabin thanks the Russell Sage and the Alfred P. Sloan Foundations. This project was started while the authors were visiting the Math Center at Northwestern University, and we are grateful for its hospitality and financial support. A draft of this chapter was completed while Rabin was a Fellow at the Center for Advanced Study in the Behavioral Sciences, supported by National Science Foundation Grant SBR-960123. He is extremely grateful for the center's hospitality and the NSF's support.

Notes

1. Although we assume that consumption each period is a binary choice (rather than a continuous choice), our model is essentially a simplified form of the Gary S. Becker and Kevin M. Murphy (1988) and Gary S. Becker, Michael Grossman, and Kevin M. Murphy (1991, 1994) models.

2. Negative internalities may include future health, career, or personal problems, as well as tolerance.

3. See Ted O'Donoghue and Matthew Rabin (1998) for a more general formulation and analysis of the model we develop in this chapter. Readers can also refer to that work for proofs of generalized versions of the results presented here, for which we have omitted proofs.

4. Conspicuously absent from our model is the ability to use external commitment devices. Alcoholics sophisticated about their self-control problems may, for instance, choose to check themselves into the Betty Ford Clinic. Note that naifs would not use external commitment devices since they always believe they will behave themselves in the future.

5. Products could also generate *positive internalities*, wherein past consumption increases current well-being (for example, jogging). We borrow the term internalities from Richard J. Herrnstein et al. (1993), who define an internality as a within-person externality. The temporal internality we consider is merely one possible type of internality. Since we assume people fully understand how current consumption affects future well-being, we are in fact assuming that people internalize the internality; more generally, this need not be the case.

6. Note that such tolerance can be dissociated from habit formation: If $f_t(1) < f_t(0)$ and $f_t(1) - g_t(1) < f_t(0) - g_t(0)$, then people get less pleasure from consuming *and* are less tempted to do so. While self-control still has a role to play in consuming such nonaddictive but harmful products, we conjecture that self-control problems are less costly in such contexts. In any event, we do not analyze such situations in this chapter.

7. For some recent discussions of empirical evidence of time inconsistency, see Richard H. Thaler (1991) and Richard H. Thaler and George Loewenstein (1992).

8. See George Ainslie (1991, 1992), George Ainslie and Nick Haslam (1992a, 1992b), George Ainslie and Richard Herrnstein (1981), Shin-Ho Chung and Richard Herrnstein (1967), Kris Kirby and Richard Herrnstein (1995), and George Loewenstein and Drazen Prelec (1992). For formal economic models of time-inconsistent preferences more generally, see for instance Robert H. Strotz (1956), Edmund S. Phelps and Robert A. Pollak (1968), Robert A. Pollak (1968), and Steven M. Goldman (1979, 1980).

9. This model has since been used by David Laibson (1995, 1997), Ted O'Donoghue and Matthew Rabin (1998, 1999, forthcoming), Carolyn Fischer (1997), and others.

10. These assumptions (and the labels) were originally laid out by Robert H. Strotz (1956) and Robert A. Pollak (1968). Most papers studying time-inconsistent preferences assume sophistication (for example, Laibson [1994a, 1995, 1997], Fischer [1997]). George Akerlof (1991) and Ted O'Donoghue and Matthew Rabin (1998, 1999, forthcoming) also consider naive beliefs.

11. The term "perfect" is a play on the standard game-theoretic notion of perfect equilibrium and here reflects that people believe that their future behavior will be rational. The term "perception" allows for people to have correct or incorrect beliefs about their own future behavior.

12. For both TCs and naifs, the unique infinite-horizon perception-perfect strategy corresponds to the unique finite-horizon perception-perfect strategy as the horizon becomes long.

13. This is the most interesting case, since if TCs hit in all contingencies then so do naifs and sophisticates, and if TCs hit when hooked then so do naifs and sophisticates.

14. This inequality follows from the assumption that TCs would refrain when hooked. If TCs would hit when hooked, the inequality would be reversed. Moreover, the discerning reader will notice that in that case the incentive effect being operative means that sophisticates perceive the same benefit from restraint as TCs and naifs (and they all hit when hooked).

15. This conclusion relies on our restricting our attention to infinite-horizon, perception-perfect strategies that correspond to a perception-perfect strategy for some long, finite horizon.

16. This intuition corresponds to the standard game-theoretic result that making outcomes worse in some contingencies can help people because they may now avoid getting into those contingencies.

17. We choose $\delta = .99$ for this example because of our interpretation of period length as half of a week. For such a period length, any time-consistent discount factor must be close to one. (Indeed, even $\delta = .99$ implies a somewhat small yearly discount factor of .59.)

18. Recall that we restrict attention to perception-perfect strategies corresponding to the unique perception-perfect strategy for a finite horizon as the horizon becomes long. For a finite horizon, we suppose the last period is a weekend, and of course people hit whether or not they are hooked on this weekend.

19. Gary S. Becker and Kevin M. Murphy (1988) invoke traumatic events such as divorce to explain how people might start consuming an addictive product, but do not present any formal analysis of that decision. Athanasios Orphanides and David Zervos (1995) and Ruqu Wang (1997) more directly consider the decision to become addicted. Both papers emphasize the case in which people are uncertain as to how addictive a product is and experiment to find out. The logic of this section suggests naifs could suffer severe addictions in that environment because they experiment with overopti-

mistic beliefs about ease of quitting an accidental addiction. Sophisticates may suffer from the reverse problem. They may underexperiment because of a fear of getting addicted. Our general theme arises again: Sophisticates are unlikely to suffer an unwanted severe lifelong addiction, whereas naifs are far more likely.

20. Here again we emphasize that the dichotomous weekend-weekday model should not be taken too literally, and also draw attention to the restrictiveness of our assumption that people become immediately unaddicted after one period of restraint. Both aspects of our model exaggerate the resemblance of consumption-induced myopia to habit formation, when in more general models they would be much more distinct. Consumption-induced myopia implies that very recent consumption leads to more consumption of the addictive product—well beyond the habit formation plausibly induced by the recent consumption. It also dissipates immediately upon short-term cessation of consumption. If people start drinking heavily at eight o'clock in the evening, by ten o'clock they may be binge drinking without any regard to consequences. This will be true despite the fact that the two hours of drinking has not in any way made them alcoholics (indeed, the myopia induced by two hours of heavy drinking is likely to be much more intense for a novice than an experienced—and alcoholic—drinker). Both our assumption of $\gamma = 0$ (that addiction depends solely on the previous periods consumption) and our use of two- and three-period models leads to an artificial conflation of the two phenomena. Even within this simplistic model, however, one important distinction *does* show up: The *welfare* implications of consumption are very different if it comes from intensified myopia rather than habit formation. In our model, and in life, an alcoholic often benefits enormously in terms of current well-being from taking another drink; persistent consumption by addicts can sometimes be rationalized by cost-benefit analysis. The hypothesis of consumption-induced myopia may be that people consume a product that brings them virtually no pleasure, even in the short run. Indeed, although we focus on the habit-forming aspect of addictive products, products that induce myopia by altering one's perspective may be vastly overconsumed even if they are not at all addictive.

21. In addition to naifs and sophisticates, there are some natural hybrids to consider in this modified environment; for example, people might know β_0 but incorrectly believe $\beta_1 = \beta_0$. We doubt the plausibility of a sophisticated drunk; but allowing sophisticates to be naive while drunk would not affect our example below and would probably yield qualitatively similar predictions in more general settings. What is crucial is that sophisticates *when sober* anticipate the loss of control when drunk.

22. For less extreme values of β_1, sophisticates may stop hitting for values that naifs do not.

23. Such preemptive abstinence does not require consumption-induced myopia. Indeed, preemptive abstinence can arise in nonstationary models of the type discussed earlier.

24. A number of important issues, beyond the scope of this chapter, are raised by examples described above. First, it is not clear that these examples all really correspond to variations in β rather than variations in the marginal instantaneous utility of consuming the product. Although our impression is that alcohol-induced propensity to smoke cigarettes is not about a change in the utility function, it is far less clear that cues that make some activity salient do not directly affect the experienced well-being from engaging in the activity. Similarly, smoking, eating, or taking mind-altering drugs may be more utility enhancing when people are depressed than when they are not. We have not analyzed the variant-utility case sufficiently to know its implications but suspect it would be similar in many ways to the variable-myopia model.

A second issue concerns the degree to which changes in myopia from some of these sources are genuinely exogenous; just as people (if sophisticated) may avoid drinking out of fear of drinking to excess, so too people may avoid it out of fear of smoking to excess. Similarly, people may sensibly try to avoid certain cues that might set off addictive behavior—avoiding being around other smokers if they are trying to quit smoking. For work that discusses some of these issues, and departures from the simple discounting model of self-control problems, see David Laibson (1994b) and George Loewenstein (1996).

25. If the taste for immediate gratification in even periods were sufficiently strong, of course, they would (fortunately for them) procrastinate in attempting to withdraw. This example does not rely on the extreme assumption that there is no self-control problem in even periods; so long as $\beta_t > .8$ for t even naifs would repeatedly try to quit.

26. This pattern, and the suspicion of its suboptimality, is well known in weight control: Huge numbers of people "successfully" lose weight on diets only to regain it. We do not know the extent to which this phenomenon results from the type of logic described in this simple example. Of course, none of our models apply per se to overconsumption of food. Although obesity resulting from overconsumption of food is clearly an example of a negative internality, the habit formation aspect of addiction that we emphasize in our model is not present—or at least it is far more subtle. Nonetheless, especially since we do not carefully formulate in this chapter which results come from habit formation and which come from the negative internality, we believe it would be useful to apply similar analysis to the case of eating and other nonaddictive activities.

27. It is also the case that rational choice models of addiction tend not to make qualitative predictions that are inconsistent with self-control models of addiction. Essentially all qualitative implications emphasized in rational choice models of addiction are also consistent with our self-control model of addiction. For instance, extensions of our model (and all other reasonable models we can imagine) would be consistent with the prediction that demand for addictive products decreases with the price of those products—

which is perhaps the main empirical finding of Gary S. Becker, Michael Grossman, and Kevin M. Murphy (1991,1994).

28. We remind the reader that it is not obvious what the welfare criterion should be (as noted in our discussion about stationary preferences). Although we do not formalize any of the welfare claims made in this section, we are confident that variants of all our claims can be articulated using any reasonable welfare criterion.

References

Ainslie, George. 1991. "Derivation of 'Rational' Economic Behavior from Hyperbolic Discount Curves." *American Economic Review* 81: 334–40.

———. (1992). *Picoeconomics: The Strategic Interaction of Successive Motivational States Within the Person.* New York: Cambridge University Press.

Ainslie, George, and Nick Haslam. 1992a. "Self-control." In *Choice Over Time,* edited by George Loewenstein and Jon Elster. New York: Russell Sage Foundation.

———. 1992b. "Hyperbolic Discounting." In *Choice Over Time,* edited by George Loewenstein and Jon Elster. New York: Russell Sage Foundation.

Ainslie, George, and Richard J. Herrnstein. 1981. "Preference Reversal and Delayed Reinforcement." *Animal Learning and Behavior* 9: 476–82.

Akerlof, George A. 1991. "Procrastination and Obedience." *American Economic Review* 81: 1–19.

Becker, Gary S., and Kevin M. Murphy. 1988. "A Theory of Rational Addiction." *Journal of Political Economy* 96: 675–700.

Becker, Gary S., Michael Grossman, and Kevin M. Murphy. 1991. "Rational Addiction and the Effect of Price on Consumption." *American Economic Review* 81: 237–41.

———. 1994. "An Empirical Analysis of Cigarette Addiction." *American Economic Review* 84: 396–418.

Chung, Shin-Ho, and Richard J. Herrnstein. 1967. "Choice and Delay of Reinforcement." *Journal of the Experimental Analysis of Behavior* 10: 67–74.

Fischer, Carolyn. 1997. "Read This Paper Even Later: Procrastination with Time-Inconsistent Preferences." University of Michigan.

Goldman, Steven M. 1979. "Intertemporally Inconsistent Preferences and the Rate of Consumption." *Econometrica* 47: 621–26.

———. 1980. "Consistent Plans." *Review of Economic Studies* 47: 533–37.

Herrnstein, Richard J., George Loewenstein, Drazen Prelec, and William Vaughan. 1993. "Utility Maximization and Melioration: Internalities in Individual Choice." *Journal of Behavioral Decision Making* 6: 149–85.

Kirby, Kris, and Richard J. Herrnstein. 1995. "Preference Reversals Due to Myopic Discounting of Delayed Reward." *Psychological Science* 6: 83–89.

Laibson, David. 1994a. "Essays in Hyperbolic Discounting." Department of Economics, Massachusetts Institute of Technology.

———. 1994b. "A Cue Theory of Consumption." Department of Economics, MIT.

———. 1995. "Hyperbolic Discount Functions, Undersaving, and Savings Policy." Harvard University.

———. 1997. "Golden Eggs and Hyperbolic Discounting." *Quarterly Journal of Economics* 112: 443–77.

Loewenstein, George. 1996. "Out of Control: Visceral Influences on Behavior." *Organizational Behavior and Human Decision Processes* 65: 272–92.

Loewenstein, George, and Drazen Prelec. 1992. "Anomalies in Intertemporal Choice: Evidence and an Interpretation." *Quarterly Journal of Economics* 107: 573–97.

O'Donoghue, Ted, and Matthew Rabin. 1998. "Addiction and Present-Biased Preferences." Cornell University and University of California, Berkeley.

———. 1999. "Doing It Now or Later." *American Economic Review* 89: 103–24.

———. Forthcoming. "Incentives for Procrastinators." *Quarterly Journal of Economics.*

Orphanides, Athanasios, and David Zervos. 1995. "Rational Addiction with Learning and Regret." *Journal of Political Economy* 103: 739–58.

Phelps, Edmund S., and Robert A. Pollak. 1968. "On Second-Best National Saving and Game-Equilibrium Growth." *Review of Economic Studies* 35: 185–99.

Pollak, Robert A. 1968. "Consistent Planning." *Review of Economic Studies* 35: 201–8.

Strotz, Robert H. 1956. "Myopia and Inconsistency in Dynamic Utility Maximization." *Review of Economic Studies* 23: 165–80.

Thaler, Richard H. 1991. "Some Empirical Evidence on Dynamic Inconsistency." In *Quasi Rational Economics.* New York: Russell Sage Foundation.

Thaler, Richard H., and George Loewenstein. 1992. *Intertemporal Choice."* In *The Winners Curse: Paradoxes and Anomalies of Economic Life*, edited by Richard H. Thaler. New York: Free Press.

Wang, Ruqu. 1997. "The Optimal Consumption and the Quitting of Harmful Addictive Goods," Queens University.

PART IV

ADDICTION AND MOTIVATION

Chapter 7

The Intuitive Explanation of Passionate Mistakes and Why It's Not Adequate

GEORGE AINSLIE

PEOPLE HAVE always been puzzled by their own propensity to do things that they will regret—often deliberately and in full knowledge that they will regret them. Intoxication has been an exemplar of this kind of choice, confronting us not only with a self-destructive behavior but with an urge to repeat it that grows more robust with every "bad" experience.

This pattern seems irrational. We have always had an idea that the things we choose have a consistent value and that normal choice making consists of detecting that value and comparing it with the value of the available alternatives. This view matches much everyday experience. It has often seemed that, if only addictions could be described in terms of the processes we ordinarily use to weigh options, we could put our finger on the aberrant step and correct it.

The great religions have defined the problem somewhat allegorically, on the model of human relationships. Demons or the devil tempt a person away from a relationship with God, for instance. The classical Greeks imagined this, too, but also cultivated a more modern taste for mechanisms with known properties—for instance, Ulysses and the Sirens and Plato's description of the function of reason: Reason's role was to estimate the relative weights of pleasures and pains, to gather together the pleasant things, gather together the painful, and weigh the near and the far in the balance, and say which are the more (*Protagoras,* section 356–7, p. 23).

209

However, Plato soon ran up against the vigor of seemingly unreasonable choices; in response, he and then Aristotle proposed another factor in evaluation, passion, a second elementary motivational force, which could override reason. Passion was involuntary and overwhelming. Reason could lose its strength through the action of passion on intellect (Aristotle, *Nicomachean Ethics* 3:1150b20, 1140b11–12). In particular, passion might prevent the intellect from referring one's immediate case to the universal principle that should govern it (ibid. 1147a24–b17).

Proposal of this second force led to an enduring split between two principles of choice, lawful and unlawful, rational and irrational, mine and not-mine. The "mine" are what fit the commonsense theory of ourselves that weighs things consistently; the "not-mine" is everything else, the rebellious processes that do not follow this scheme, the doings of Lucifer, who rebelled from heaven.

When motivation became the object of scientific study, the same kind of exceptions to rational choice soon became apparent. Pavlov came up with the most robust solution—conditioned behavior, refined to conditioned *motives*, stated definitively in O. H. Mowrer's two-factor theory (1947).[1] In this form, Plato's passions seemed discernible in parametric research, and the ancient dual model was perpetuated.

It remains robust, probably because it fits the experience of being swayed by passion. Starting anew from the phenomenological level, decision researcher George Loewenstein seems to confirm this picture (1996, 1999): Satisfaction of innate hungers creates associations with the stimuli that happen to have been present (factor 1). This pairing of hungers with stimuli is not itself goal directed but creates cravings, which are subsequently reproduced by the new stimulus. Cravings, like Plato's passions, weigh suddenly on a person's motivational process (factor 2) and produce abrupt reversals of preference in favor of their objects. Recovering addicts do fine until they see something that was associated with taking drugs; that association produces such a craving that they may suddenly relapse, an experience that is actually described by many addicts (O'Brien, Ehrman, and Ternes 1986).

Loewenstein covers the main tenets of two-factor theory and advances it; I use his recent work to represent this approach in my critique. He describes these properties:

1.   There is a special class of motivation—Loewenstein calls it visceral—that is separate from motivation in general.

2.   Visceral motivation is aversive at its onset; reward comes from reducing visceral motivation.

3.   Visceral motivation is imposed temporarily on a person by a process that does not itself respond to reward.

4. Visceral motives must be summoned by external cues.
5. Visceral motives cannot be well imagined in advance (this is his own addition).

As Lowenstein applies it to the addiction process, two-factor theory operates like this: People ingest an addictive substance and get a visceral reward from it. After repeated ingestions, they discover negative effects that outweigh the positive and decide rationally to stop ingesting the substance. However, cues associated with ingestion have come to induce a visceral response called craving, which is unpleasant; this is the first, or classical conditioning, factor. The craving changes the balance of motives—the second, or goal-directed learning, factor—and to get rid of this unpleasant experience they decide to go on ingesting. However, in the absence of these cues they prefer to abstain, since they cannot "remember" the visceral reward.

This model fits the self-reports of addicts and the common experience of people trying to give up bad habits generally. The model is certainly time-honored. However, close examination suggests that the dichotomies it rests on are only casual rules of thumb, which people use to decide how difficult certain experiences will be to control, rather than basic distinctions. I argue that modern behavioral research and simple logic demote this model from the explanatory to the merely descriptive. Let us look at the tenets of two-factor theory one by one:

Is There a Fundamental Difference Between Visceral Motives, or Emotions, and Motivation in General?

Presumably all of our behavior is motivated, but when we become exceptionally conscious of our motives we tend to apply one of two terms to them: emotions or hungers. As named in common speech, emotions are a vast and heterogeneous array of experiences, ranging from three or four basic processes that are governed by identifiable neuronal processes and are discernible in lower animals (the *core emotions;* Panksepp 1982), through perhaps a dozen characteristic processes that do not have an identified physiology but that are named in many cultures and are recognizable in photographs of faces from other cultures (call the additional processes *stereotyped* emotions; Ekman and Friesen 1986; Izard 1971), to potentially scores of subtle mood states that are identified mainly by describing the situations that elicit them and that are apt to be peculiar to one culture or historic period (call the additional processes *subtle emotions;* Elster 1999; Stearns 1986, 1994).

Hungers are fewer and are named by a stimulus that the hunger moves you to "consume"—food, warmth, a drug; sexual desire is usually identified as a hunger rather than an emotion.

The main difference between hungers and emotions has been that hungers are more obviously controlled by the deprivation or supply of specific concrete stimuli. Even so, hungers for specific objects are extensively influenced by learned processes called tastes, and thus have some of the cultural specificity typical of emotions. To develop a taste for yak butter or blubber you must learn to associate their fatty flavor with satisfaction; to develop a taste for an abused substance, you must come to associate the chemical taste of alcohol or the disgust and nausea of heroin injection with the euphoria of the high.

Hungers otherwise resemble emotions so extensively that an observer newly come to the topic would conclude that they are the same but for the happenstance of stimulus controllability. I speak of both together except when that particular distinction is important. *Appetite* might be an appropriately inclusive term, despite being spoken more about hungers than emotions. Loewenstein seems to bound "visceral" motives about as widely as this combined category, although the term implies a noticeable physical reaction ("to feel it in your viscera"), and emotions at the subtle end of the spectrum seem to be accompanied by no more somatic sensation than purely cognitive experiences are.

Not only is the line between emotions and hungers indistinct, so is the line between emotions-hungers (which I am now calling appetites), and other reasons to seek or avoid things. Experts' lists of emotions differ enormously in extent and shade into what most people would call ordinary motives. Acting *in* fear of imminent death is accompanied by different physiological processes than acting *for* fear of looking sloppy, but is there any distinct point on the continuum between them when the fear ceases to be an emotion and becomes just a figure of speech? Is envy a special mental process or just a particular category of perceived want? Loewenstein himself counts curiosity as a visceral motive, though there are few more intellectual appetites than that.

The word emotion merely implies something that moves us, as if some of our behaviors were unmoved. On systematic scrutiny, however, almost all behaviors are motivated—another word meaning moved. The only exceptions are innate reflexes and those behaviors, if any, that can be driven solely by conditioned stimuli. I discuss presently the question of whether any behaviors are so driven. My point here is that the only distinction between emotions, hungers, and other motives seems to be their conspicuousness—some intensity or regularity that makes us notice them often enough to give them names. It looks as though the word emotion is to motivational science what the word hill is to topography: an identifiable feature that stands out from a less prominent background but is made of the same stuff and may or may not be named as a unique feature, at the convenience of the observer. For purists, emotion is more like the word mountain; that is, purists demand greater contrast with ordinary motives before they use a special term. However, they face the same problem of where in the foothills to put the boundary.

David Hume noticed this essential continuity a quarter-millennium ago:

> Now it is certain there are certain calm desires and tendencies, which, though they be real passions, produce little emotion in the mind, and are more known by their effects than by the immediate feeling or sensation. . . . When any of these passions are calm, and cause no disorder in the soul, they are very readily taken for the determinations of reason. (*A Treatise of Human Nature*, 2:3,3, quoted in Gosling 1990, 93)

The absence of a line separating visceral motives from others is one argument against their having a separate class of properties. However, there will be more compelling arguments.

Do Visceral Motives Have to Be Aversive, and Do They Have to Aim at Drive Reduction?

The greatest pleasures are associated with the satisfaction of cravings, which implies the satiation of drives. This has to be so, since great pleasure without satiation would lead to long-term preoccupation with the activity. It has been natural to extend this model to less vivid experiences: Perhaps all pleasure depends on reducing associated drives, and perhaps all drives, by simple symmetry, are aversive. This was the standard view of motivation in the nineteenth century: Drives were something hydraulic, like water in a reservoir or steam in a boiler, which accumulated inevitably through unmotivated processes, creating dysphoria when present and pleasure when released. Modern physiology has long since dispelled this notion as a literal theory, but its features remain in the more economic imagery of utility theory: Need is like debt, and reducing need is like income. It is implicit in Loewenstein's treatment; he assumes, for instance, that hunger is "largely aversive."

The symmetrical drive = pain/drive reduction = pleasure theory is an intuitively appealing way to imagine how Mother Nature gets work out of her creatures, and it does avoid the question of why people do not usually become absorbed in self-reward. If relief of craving or resolution of emotion is pleasurable, it seems only good balance that the onset should be aversive. If something is rewarding both in starting and stopping, what could be its homeostatic function? However, this theoretical symmetry contradicts much of common experience. Some hungers are indeed experienced as aversive, but some are welcome, which is the case when the term appetite is most apt to be used in everyday speech.[2] People commonly work up an appetite for dinner, boast of an appetite for sex, complain of a jaded appetite for entertainment, and so on. The exploitation of appetite is the art called savoring, in the study of which Loewenstein (1987) himself has done pioneering work.

The term drive implies no more than a potential to be rewarded in a particular modality. It is a physiological state that will support a hunger. The readiness to have an emotion is not usually spoken of as a drive—indeed, it is not usually spoken of at all—but the term fits as well as any. Whether or not a drive or the appetite (= hunger or emotion) it supports will be welcome depends not only on the modality (for example, painful cold versus pleasurable sexual arousal) but also on degree (mild versus severe hunger), the time course (hunger that is not ultimately satisfied generates painful pangs), and how it affects other opportunities for reward (the cycle of appetite and eating may be cultivated as entertainment or it may constitute an irritating distraction from a more satisfying activity).

Some appetites are rewarding without being followed by consumption. The effect of reward activity on level of appetite is also variable. Although words like consumption seem to imply that activity in the reward process uses up capacity for further reward, this is not always the case. The hungers, which have concrete substrates, are most apt to have separate phases: an increasing appetite that is proportional to deprivation of the substrate and a satisfaction that is proportional to consuming the substrate. The process of getting reward from food or drugs has an appetite phase that is markedly different from its consumption phase, and the appetite phase is not pleasurable in its own right. Appetite in these modalities becomes strongly aversive if it is not soon followed by consumption of its concrete object, and consumption of this object reduces capacity for reward in the near future. (Later, I comment on a complication, that sometimes consumption feeds back positively rather than negatively on appetite.)

The less a visceral process is limited by a concrete substrate, the less distinct do phases of appetite and satisfaction become. Sexual desire looks like a borderline case, a conventional hunger that acts somewhat like an emotion. That is, sexual experience entirely in fantasy can be robustly rewarding in the absence of any prospect of physical satisfaction. Sexual foreplay and fantasy do not use up drive; and sexual partners who cannot reach orgasm eventually tire of an episode without having been physiologically satiated. The cultivation of sexual appetite is by far the greatest factor in sexual satisfaction. For instance, people pay for a variety of sexually arousing stimuli even when they never lead to orgasm; even rats will work to copulate although prevented from ever ejaculating (Sheffield, Wulff, and Barker 1951).

It could be argued that the whole vast motivational economy of sexual stimulation is based entirely on managing appetite, since orgasm itself is available at will. Because sexual arousal without satiation leads to comparatively minor physical pangs—vesicle engorgement in males and unwanted secretions in females—it seems to be the converse of the appetite for food, which does not support fantasy well and which opens the person to far more intense physical pangs.[3]

Anger is positioned next to sex on the continuum of tangibility but on the other side of the conventional border between hungers and emotions. It, too, is robust in fantasy, a major component of action movies and a staple of many character-disordered patients who "nurse" it, not to mention the people who cherish opportunities for righteous indignation. It, too, is capable of physical consummation; although the object may be as arbitrary as a typewriter or a can in the street, there are said to be bars where men go for the express purpose of finding more satisfying objects to hit, "looking for a fight."

Fears may be next on the continuum. They are less tangible, in that they are "realized" less than hungers for food or even anger. There are, however, innate preparednesses for fear—of heights and snakes, for instance—and at least one concrete method of making chance stimuli occasions for fear is known: making these stimuli predictors of pain. Fear is usually classified as a negative emotion, but people buy fear in movies and roller-coaster rides and are drawn even to unwanted fears, as when they have an urge to look at a grisly scene that will give them nightmares. Even when there is no conscious attraction, as in phobias, people acquiesce in the kindling of fears and can learn to withhold this acquiescence. Behavior therapists have become quite effective at teaching how to do this (Clum 1989). Grief is similar in almost all of its aspects, supporting a market for the kind of stories called tearjerkers and, when grown to pathological proportions, responding to behavioral therapy.

In these cases, too, the boundary between hungers and emotions seems superficial. Furthermore, like the appetites for hunger-reducing activities, emotions range from welcome to unwelcome and pick up steam in a positively fed-back fashion early in their courses. This is most apt to be true of the emotions that have innate physiological expressions, like anger and fear, and least true of those that are merely appreciations of a situation, like irony or curiosity. Those that act like positively fed-back appetites differ from need-based hungers mainly in lacking distinct satiation processes; and as we have just seen, the satiation even of hungers is less distinct than convention would have it. Thus, visceral motives may or may not be aversive at their onset and "consumption" has a variable effect on drive reduction.

Are Visceral Processes Themselves Unmotivated?

Emotions themselves are commonly regarded as unmotivated; so, of course, are motivations in general. Naturally enough. For a motive itself to depend simply on motivation should lead to an explosive feedback reaction: If joy is both reward dependent and rewarding, people should neglect everything else and just generate joy until they keel over from exhaustion. The ability to self-reward like this would be like finding yourself in a drug house with a limitless supply of crack. Conversely, if fear is reward dependent and aversive, people should avoid generating it despite obvious evidence of danger. Thus it has seemed necessary to theorize that emotions are externally imposed, without regard to their rewarding properties: You respond to the site of an old auto accident with fear or to the sounds from a once-frequented bar with craving, despite the fact that these responses are unpleasant; therefore, conventional theory assumes, these responses must be reflexlike processes that have been transferred from their natural stimuli by some mechanism that does not respond to your motives.

That mechanism was supposed to be classical conditioning. In the early part of the twentieth century, there seemed to be a special class of responses that could not be emitted deliberately or shaped by reward or punishment but had to be triggered reflexively. The hardwired triggers were called unconditioned stimuli, but stimuli that had been paired with them (conditioned stimuli) could also become triggers. The unmotivatable responses were supposed to be smooth muscle or glandular activity—the domain of the autonomic nervous system—and, mostly by implication, the emotions. Some overlap was always recognized between motivatable and unmotivatable responses; some conditioned patterns seemed to occur in the "voluntary" muscles, for instance, and voluntary urination was known to be controlled by smooth muscle. Furthermore, the class of potential unconditioned stimuli was found to be identical with the class of motivating stimuli (Miller 1969). Nevertheless, the theoretical dichotomy was maintained until subtler experiments were done in the 1970s.

These experiments showed that the responses previously thought unmotivatable can be shaped by incentives if these are delivered soon enough after the response and, thus, that "involuntary" responses in humans can be made voluntary by delivery of the right biofeedback

(Basmajian et al. 1989); that the effect of conditioned stimuli can even be overridden by contrary incentives (Ainslie and Engel 1974); and perhaps most important, that conditioned responses are not just copies of unconditioned responses emitted to a new stimulus, like Windows icons dragged to a new part of the screen, but are different responses that must have been shaped anew (Rescorla 1988). Researchers in the area of conditioning concluded that only *information* can be linked by simple pairing—that all *responses* depend on adequate motivation (Atnip 1977; Dickinson 1980; Hearst 1975, 181–223; Herrnstein, 1969; discussion in Ainslie 1992, 39–48). Computer modeling of the common behavioral experiments has indeed shown that a single process can explain selection of both classical and goal-directed responses (Donahoe, Burgos, and Palmer 1993).

Thus the problem is not the nonexistence of classical conditioning, either in the laboratory or in creating ordinary appetites. On the contrary, conditioning is a familiar phenomenon. The problem is that conditioning per se connects only information—one stimulus to another—and does not transfer responses. Responses certainly arise to conditioned stimuli, and these responses often closely resemble the responses elicited by unconditioned stimuli, but the evidence is that they occur only insofar as they are motivated.

Motivated does not mean deliberate, however, or even pleasurable. Indeed, to say that all responses depend on their consequences, but that some unpleasant consequences reinforce responses, is to require some distinction between pleasure and whatever this reinforcement is. For instance, it is now well known that you can be trained to resist an urge to panic, or grieve, or entertain obsessions, or even to respond to painful stimuli like dental work or childbirth with aversion (Clum 1989; Licklider, 1959; Melzack, Weisz, and Sprague 1963); but even after this training, something draws you toward these negatively valued responses. Draws, not pushes. Obedience to an urge must be rewarding in some sense, but sometimes it is obviously not pleasurable.

The best intuitive illustration of the relationship of reward and pleasure occurs at the borders of overindulgence in addictive habits. For instance, I recently heard two smokers talk about how they continued to smoke even after they got no pleasure from it. Then one of them said that he had strictly cut down to ten cigarettes a day and experienced a marked return of the pleasure of smoking; the other replied with a similar experience. Cigarette smoking was obviously a *reward* at both times, since it maintained a behavior; but when near satiation reduced this reward, it ceased to be experienced as *pleasurable* at a level at which it was nevertheless effective enough to get chosen over the alternative of not smoking.

Behaviors that are necessarily rewarding but not pleasurable are familiar enough. People often work to avoid the opportunity for them: A nail-biter coats her nails with something bitter; a phobic person rehearses mental exercises to avoid inviting panic; a hiker who did not bring enough food tries to avoid thoughts that might provoke appetite. Such strategies are anomalies for conventional utility theory. In conventional theory, biting your nails is either worth it or not, and if panic is a choice, then panic is either worth it or not. There is no role for self-control. The possibility of rewards that are not pleasurable gets swept under the rug, and the choice of unpleasure is explained away by invoking classical conditioning: "It's not really a choice, it's a transferred reflex."

Here is where the finding that conditioning is only an informational process provokes a crisis. If conditioned responses must ultimately be based on rewards, how can aversive responses get conditioned? Not far behind is the question, What keeps people from short-circuiting their quest for pleasurable conditioned responses and just learning to emit these responses voluntarily? Once we discard conditioning as a mechanism for imposing and limiting appetites, we have to replace it with something else. That is, when we recognize that responses are conditioned only insofar as they promise more reward than their alternatives, we have to supply a mechanism for how organisms come to accept aversive experiences and avoid total absorption in those pleasant ones that are at their free disposal.

How does reward perform the job that two-factor theory depended on classical conditioning for: getting organisms to pay attention to aversive events and constraining them from overindulging in the positive ones? What makes people open themselves to grief and pain? What keeps them from consuming joy and sex like crack? What makes appetites so hard to shape that they are usually thought to be unresponsive to reward? Why, indeed, if appetites are reward-dependent responses, do people usually not experience their arousal as deliberate?

For those appetites that have tangible consumption objects (food, drugs), the question of limits might be easy to answer: Generating the appetite without consuming the objects eventually invites painful pangs or cravings, and it probably turns out to be easier to avoid the appetite itself than to disregard the subsequent pangs. The incentives that govern the appetite would be much the same as those that govern a deliberate decision, for example, to daydream about food (or drug highs) or not. The only obvious difference is that whatever balance of timing or motivation there is that permits deliberation is not present. By the time you have deliberated about whether to entertain the appetite, you have already entertained it.

For appetites that do not carry the threat of pangs for nonconsumption—and that includes all of the emotions, per se, as well as the pangs themselves—these questions are harder. Fortunately, a theoretical possibility that can handle both unpleasurable rewards and restricted self-pleasuring—namely, the hyperbolic discounting of rewards—turns out also to be a robust empirical finding. Hyperbolic discount curves for future events produce temporary preferences for smaller, earlier over larger, later rewards when the smaller, earlier rewards are imminently available. I describe this finding and its implications elsewhere (Ainslie 1992) and only summarize them here.

There is ample evidence that both animals and people discount prospective rewards in hyperbolic curves over a wide range of delays, ranging, in various studies, from seconds to decades (reviewed in Ainslie 1992, 63–80; see also Green, Fry, and Myerson 1994; Harvey, 1994; Kirby and Herrnstein, 1995). Furthermore, truly immediate rewards are almost irresistible: A rat that chooses between an immediate, short, electrical pulse in a rewarding brain center and a pulse twice as long at delays as little as one second strongly prefers the short, immediate pulse (Ainslie and Monterosso, unpublished data). A hyperbolic discounting pattern predicts robust temporary preferences, which can explain the familiar patterns of both negative and positive appetites.

When appetites are aversive—fear, grief, pangs, cravings, pain itself—their ability to attract the organism's participation (roughly, "attention") can be explained by a briefly rewarded aspect that obligates a subsequent, greater fall in reward. Such a recurrent spike of reward would underlie the vivid part of the appetite, the hard-to-resist undertow of panic, or anguish over a lost love, or dental or labor pain, powerful urges that nevertheless can be resisted by the well-timed counterposition of other motives—showing, as I argue above, that aversion is not just a reflex (see Ainslie 1987, 1992, 101–14). As with the experience of smoking while nearly satiated, the reward for these processes would be attenuated to the point where it no longer feels pleasurable; however, the attenuation would be of the reward's aggregate duration rather than its intensity (a horizontal narrowing rather than a vertical one on a graph of intensity over time), allowing the urge for the momentary initial reward to be temporarily preferred because of hyperbolic discounting.

It is not useful to ask whether pain feels like reward; that question refers intuitively to reward as a synonym of pleasure. The influence of reward has to be inferred from the experience that pain and negative emotions feel irresistible—or, better, very difficult to resist, a difficulty that measures the amount of reward that has to be bid against them and, hence, their own rewardingness. There is little direct evidence on how aversive stimuli reward attention; however, among the cells in the nucleus accumbens that respond to rewarding stimuli, there are some that respond to both rewarding and aversive stimuli—which at least suggests that they may have part of their mechanism in common (Mirenowicz and Schultz 1996).[4]

When appetites are mainly pleasurable and their rewards are available at will—joy, thrill, sexual arousal, the fruits of daydreams generally—a person learns great efficiency at getting them, just like the crack addict or brain self-stimulator. However, most pleasurable emotions do not renew their own appetites, as crack and direct brain stimulation evidently do. Greater efficiency at consumption means increasing triviality. Once we are familiar with a pleasurable pattern, we cannot stop ourselves from anticipating its imminent course, even though we thereby harvest its reward prematurely. That is, we stop building appetite—the suspense, longing, and so on—to its optimal level, since doing so defers reward; because of hyperbolic discounting, we temporarily prefer the smaller but earlier satisfaction. Children grow away from fantasy games not because they are punished for them but because they get too good at anticipating the turnings these games can take.[5]

Since these mechanisms are available for imposing and constraining processes that are themselves motivating, nothing prevents us from concluding that appetites depend on reward rather than on some other kind of determinant: Because the kinds of responses that can be conditioned can also be shaped by reward in the laboratory, it seems likely that this is happening also in nature and that appetites occur to the extent that there is reward for them to do so. That is, appetites are behaviors (operants, in behavioristic terminology) that are emitted only insofar as they either make the consumption of another reward more likely or increase its rewarding effect—unless, of course, they produce reward in their own right. This means that conditioned stimuli for appetites are not automatic triggers but rather cues that convey information that emitting the appetite will be more rewarding than not emitting it. They do not *release* appetite, they *occasion* it.

There remains the appearance that appetites are independent of motivation—that you "can't help" laughing or crying or salivating or getting an erection. After all, this is why emotions are called passions as opposed to actions; emotions are things that "come over you" uninvited. However, it is hard experientially to tell processes that need no motivation, like reflexes, from ones that are so strongly motivated that they always prevail; besides, emotions seem to be on a continuum as to how automatically they occur. Although sometimes you cannot help a gut reaction, sometimes you can.

There are certainly many cases in common experience in which motives feel like they govern emotions. People are commonly aware of nursing anger, courting fear, resisting hope, wallowing in sadness, yielding to jealousy, and otherwise finding ways of encouraging or discouraging an emotional process. The craft of acting involves learning how to deliberately summon emotionality; conversely, emotions and even pains that become chronic problems for people are known to respond to the self-control techniques of behavior therapy, as I note above. If irresistible emotions are governed by some other process than differential reward, then this process can at least be overcome by the prospect of differential reward—anger by the demand of a boss, fear by a perception of necessity, joy by a sense of duty, and so on. There must be a crucial element in common between reward and whatever kind of determinant does not require reward, because they trade in the same marketplace.

It is certainly hard to think of appetites as goal-directed behaviors, when they may fail to extinguish after hundreds of occurrences when they are not followed by their object. However, the incentives are probably no different than for a dog that wants to be fed. Begging is cheap compared to the value of the actual reward and seems to be worth it to the dog even if food is almost never forthcoming in a particular circumstance. Similarly, it is beyond most people's patience to convert an outdoor pet to an indoor pet: The sight of someone going out arouses it even after months of failures. So it seems to be with appetites as slight hopes appear.

To clarify the relationship I am suggesting between acts of consumption and the appetites for these acts: Appetites are reward-dependent behaviors in their own right and can have much the same properties whether or not they prepare for a more rewarding act of consumption. Reward-dependent behaviors include both a high from cocaine, which pays off within seconds to minutes and leaves the person depleted in a matter of hours, and the imagining of the high, which pays off within fractions of a second and produces dysphoric cravings in seconds.

I discuss elsewhere how a person learns intertemporal bargaining techniques to avoid addictive highs (Ainslie 1992). Learning to avoid imagining highs is apt to be harder, since bargaining techniques are unlikely to work well on rewards that are as rapidly available as imagination. Avoidance may be possible through attention-controlling techniques but will be harder to the extent that imagining the high is a step to obtaining the actual high. By itself, imagining a high is only one of a vast number of possible memories that habituate through repetition until they are only daydreams. However, insofar as imagining the high has been instrumental in actually getting high, it is supported by that additional reward.

The more an appetite is rewarding in its own right, the harder it will be to discourage by avoiding its object. Anger is usually experienced as a fairly unsatisfactory pleasure, despite the urge to nurse grudges—a poor substitute for something else by which a person has been disappointed. By contrast, sex supports fiction and fantasy in abundance. Thus it is not surprising to find Galen's second-century description of the greater difficulty in bringing the latter, "concupiscible," appetite under control:

> Unlike the irascible power, I represented this power as not suited to horses and dogs but befitting the wild boar and goat and any of the wild beasts which cannot be domesticated. . . . The chastisement of the concupiscible power consists in not furnishing it with the enjoyment of the things it desires. If it does not attain to this enjoyment, it becomes small and weak. The result is that the concupiscible power does not follow reason because it is obedient but because it is weak (Harkins 1963, 47).

Thus I would argue that a model of visceral factors as entirely motivated is consistent with our present knowledge. The discovery of hyperbolic discounting makes sense of the apparent difference between pleasure and reward and suggests that this distinction may allow us to account for the behavioral selection of subjectively unwelcome behaviors. Furthermore, the model that makes visceral factors out to be transferred reflexes is *not* consistent with our present knowledge. If my way of building aversion out of a temporal pattern of reward and nonreward turns out not to be viable, some other way will have to be discovered. This does not necessarily mean, however, that the familiar pattern of arousing appetite that has been called conditioning is not a factor in addictive choices; it just cannot be a basic mechanism. An explanation in terms of reward itself is obviously more direct.

Must Visceral Motives Be Elicited by External Cues?

In two-factor theory, hungers and other appetites must be elicited by stimuli that are outside of the person's control. If the theory's other assumptions were true, this tenet would be both possible and necessary. It would be possible because two-factor theory holds appetites to be special kinds of processes that initially depend on innate releasing stimuli but that can come to be elicited by arbitrary cues through pairing alone. It would be necessary in the case of aversive appetites, because, with conventional exponential discounting, there is no other mechanism to make a person generate them. The easiest cure for fear would be to dismiss it—to stick your head in the sand—unless fear had peremptory control of your attention. Conversely, if appetites were pleasurable and accessible at will, conventional exponential discounting implies that they would become preoccupying unless they were rationed by releasing stimuli that could be obtained only from outside.

However, we have reviewed evidence that conditioned behavior is only a special case of reward-dependent choice and that a wide range of appetites—both conventional hungers and emotions—lack discernible boundaries separating them either from acts of consumption or from other motives. Appetites seem to serve as a preliminary stage for some consumption modalities like food, sex, and drugs; appetite is arguably the only stage in emotions like grief and joy, which lack a subsequent consumption phase. Two-factor theory fails because the first factor is just as reward dependent as the second factor.

Furthermore, both people and animals have a robust tendency to discount the future hyperbolically. In that case, external stimuli should not be needed to either impose or release emotions. A small amount of immediate reward will be enough to lure someone into a process that is quite unrewarding over time and that is thus experienced as unpleasurable. External cues will not be turnkeys to switch on the unpleasurable emotion but will either create drive (as in pain) or give information that responding to an ongoing drive will be immediately rewarding (as when a familiar occasion for fear or anger comes into view).

Conversely, ready access extinguishes the common ruck of self-generated emotionality. Hyperbolically motivated impatience will habituate the pleasurable emotions that you entertain entirely at will, turning them essentially into daydreams. Those emotional patterns that keep their vigor have to have some property that makes them inaccessible to arbitrary entertainment; that property is apt to involve pacing by external occasions.

These considerations suggest that visceral motives (appetites) do not physically require outside stimuli to govern them. However, an organism will learn to avoid at a distance any circumstances that lure it into briefly rewarded processes. These circumstances will appear to impose negative appetites. Conversely, pleasure-seeking processes will compete for long-range survival on the basis of how well their cues for generating emotion defy voluntary control. Thus positive appetites, too, will seem to be governed by events that are themselves unmotivated.

That is, motivational economics rather than a duel of conditioned cues governs the competition among potential appetites. Ultimately, it is the prospect of reward rather than the happenstance of turnkeys that selects them. However, the best competitors are not the paths to reward that are most efficient; they are gambles, which generate occasions for appetite both intermittently and unpredictably. The most emotionally productive gambles in the long run seem to be commitments to personal relationships (for example, Elster 1999, 214), but there are many less subtle games that pay off faster: races, fights, puzzles, and the activity to which gambling most commonly refers. Actors learn to access interpersonal emotions without the occasions by which most people pace them but under conditions that are also constraining: within the limited context of their assigned roles. As with the negative appetites, hyperbolic discount curves predict the temporary preferences needed by this model, in this case for smaller, earlier versus larger, later emotional satisfactions.

Although there are wide variations in the equilibria people find between gratification at will and strict dependence on external occasions—the fantasy-prone seem to have emotions that are more robust despite free access, while sociopaths can usually imagine very little—everyone learns limits to their self-induction of positive emotions. By a similar logic, people avoid entertaining the horrible, and if they cannot—for example, in cases of overwhelming trauma, like posttraumatic stress syndrome—they dissociate the recollection into a circumscribed experience, just as if it were a binge or other major lapse of control (see Ainslie 1999). People wind up experiencing as emotion only those patterns that have escaped the habituation of free access by a selective process analogous to that described by Robert Frank (1988) for the social recognition of "authentic" emotions: Expressions that are known to be deliberately controllable are disregarded. By this process of selection, emotion is left with its familiar guise as passion, something that has to come over you.

Are Appetites Unpredictable?

Unpredictability has not been a feature of previous two-factor theories, but it is actually necessary if this kind of theory is going to account for temporary changes of preference, such as drug craving. Otherwise, people would be motivated just by their expectation of reward, discounted for delay and uncertainty, whether or not craving was an intermediate step. Even taking classical conditioning at face value, there is nothing in being conditioned per se that should keep a motive from coming into equilibrium with other motives. Without unpredictability, individuals should simply balance conditioned motives against all other kinds, if indeed they have any other kinds; conditioning should not make their valuation of future events inconsistent over time.

However, Loewenstein proposes that memory for visceral factors can be accessed only by what amount to conditioned stimuli, which would make these factors unpredictable. In support of this model, he points out an important property of appetites: their explosive growth

Figure 7.1   The Effect of Appetite in an Exponentially Discounted Model

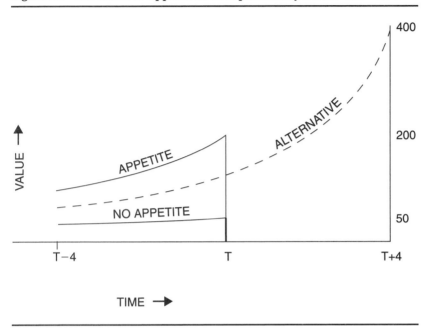

Note: Appetite may cause a smaller, earlier reward to be preferred to a larger, later alternative.

on seemingly arbitrary occasions, like seeing a dessert cart or an old drug haunt.

Many of the activities that get named as hungers, emotions, or appetites do have this property, which may catch an inexperienced person by surprise. Early in their satisfaction, these appetites do not decrease but increase. Scratching an itch initially makes it more intense, for instance; the finger foods that your host serves before dinner are called appetizers; and "first the man takes a drink, then the drink takes a drink."[6] That is, gratifying the appetite initially increases rather than decreases its force; early stages of these appetitive activities make their later stages more attractive. Up to a point, the appetites perpetuate themselves: Grief begets more grief, anger more anger, and craving more craving. It is reasonable to ask what the existence of such a positive feedback system implies about the reinforcement of appetites.

Surprise-based two-factor theory is diagramed in the discount curves of figure 7.1. Say that an event at time $t = T$ (food, the opportunity for sex, an occasion for anger, and so on) makes available a reward that will have magnitude = 50 if subjects have not previously developed an appetite, and

**Figure 7.2   The Effect of Conditioned Appetite in an Exponentially
Discounted, Two-Factor Model**

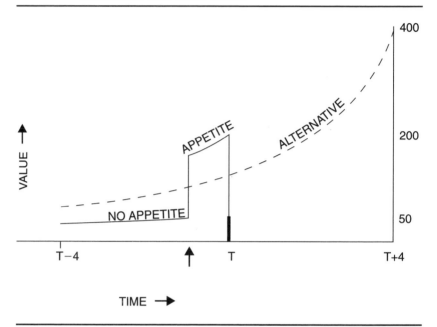

Notes: A conditioned stimulus for appetite at the arrow increases the value of the smaller,
earlier reward until it is temporarily preferred; but anticipation of this change would not
lead to avoidance, but rather make the figure approach figure 7.1.

200 if they have. Alternative to this event is (are) alternative reward
(rewards), with some value between 50 and 200 at time T, that will become
unavailable as of T if the first reward is chosen. The value of the alternative reward (rewards) could be depicted as the complex sum of various
future prospects but will be summarized here as a single event of reward
value 400 occurring at $T + 4$. Assuming that rewards are discounted in conventional exponential curves at value = amount × $(.75)^{(T-t)}$, subjects who
do not develop appetites for the index reward will never value it more
than the alternative reward (rewards) and will never expect to. The value
of the alternative reward will be 126 at T and will always have been higher
than the value of the index reward. However, if a conditioned stimulus at
some point before T causes the value of the index reward as of T to jump
to 200 (figure 7.2), there will be a change of preference toward the reward
at T, the very phenomenon we have been trying to explain.

The trouble with this mechanism is that, if this change of preference
occurs regularly, subjects should come to expect that the index reward

will occur—and *with* appetite; they should thus discount its value from 200 rather than 50. The upward step in figure 7.2 should occur at the outset or, if the learning process is gradual, earlier and earlier, until subjects' valuations are described simply by the upper curve. If the change of preference does not occur regularly, subjects' prospects may waver—but even then, with exponential discounting there will be no reason that they should try to avoid the sequence of appetite and index reward. When they foresee that they will find the index reward preferable at time $T - 1$ or 2, they should also find it preferable at the moment they foresee this and, conversely, for when they foresee that they will not find it preferable. Exponential curves allow no difference between foreseeing and approving of a future preference.

Thus continuing surprise is necessary for this version of the two-factor theory; and even surprising changes of preference would not be avoided in advance. Furthermore, the hypothetical mechanism of continuing surprise—failure of effective memory for the raw impact of incentives—does not regularly occur. Loewenstein cites examples of people who say that they cannot remember visceral experiences, but we should be careful about taking this as a basic property of appetites. Appetites are not always forgotten, nor are they entirely unpredictable even when they seem forgotten. People who face the prospect of a dessert cart or obstetrical pain remember that their preference is apt to reverse, and they can be seen to plan accordingly, as Loewenstein acknowledges. To take the case to its logical extreme, food-satiated rats that get appetite-inducing brain stimulation at a food cup at the end of a runway will learn to run to the food cup without being hungry—having learned, obviously, to expect the hunger as well as the food and being motivated by that expectation (Mendelsohn and Chorover 1965). In the case of pain specifically, even animals seem to be able to recall it with great precision, efficiently shifting between shock-avoidance schedules as small changes make one or another a little less punishing (Herrnstein 1969).

It is true that people sometimes say they cannot remember their painful experiences; but some people cannot *stop* remembering them, the curse of posttraumatic stress disorder. The crucial factor in remembering appetites is probably the consequence of their free availability that I note above: To remember them fully is to experience them and, possibly, to be drawn into the positively fed-back phase of their reward-ingness. This creates an incentive for people to keep their aversive memories at a distance, perhaps entertaining them only in the form of factual correlates (Morley 1993). The inability to remember them may be like the inability to touch a sore; similarly, the *urge* to remember them may be like the urge to touch a sore. The issue is not cognitive availability but motivation.

That is, what Loewenstein calls memory is actually a picturing, an entertainment of the appetites themselves. This effort is constrained by the fact that a vicarious trial of an appetite involves its real excitation; thinking about it in the abstract can set off its positively fed-back phase. Recovering addicts who think about their drug to test how far they have escaped its hold on them may find themselves dealing with a serious craving. In that case, the differential reward for ingesting the drug ceases to be what it was, the value of *Appetite followed by drug* versus the value of *No drug, given no appetite;* it becomes the value of *Drug, given appetite already present* versus the value of *No drug, given appetite already present.* Not only has the drug option increased in value by no longer needing an intervening appetite phase but also the no-drug option may have *decreased* even more in value because of the prospect of pangs if the drug is not ingested. Conversely, addicts who somehow arrange for thoughts about the drug to be sidetracked, so that they "can't" remember the high, both derive reassurance from this experience and avoid the pangs. People facing the possibility of strong appetites resemble less a dispassionate shopper than a woman in natural labor who is trying to escape the urge to panic at her pain stimuli. When an appetite is involved, remembering is not a neutral act.[7]

Figure 7.3 shows the way appetites should behave if discount curves are hyperbolic (value = amount$/[1 + \{T - t\}]$) rather than exponential. Without appetite, subjects will consistently prefer the alternative reward (rewards) and will be motivated to avoid the change of preference. However, they will not necessarily be motivated to avoid the appetite, if the appetite itself is rewarding. Say that subjects start developing an appetite at $t = T - 4$ and that this activity increases the reward available at T by 1.41 for every unit of time that it continues, pushing this value to 200 by time T.[8] The appetite alone does not preclude the alternative reward (rewards) and, in the early stages, does not lead to a change of expected choice—as long as the subjects have reason to believe that they can sample the appetite for a while and then quit. In the early stages, they may maximize expected reward by entertaining appetite and planning not to gratify it further. Indeed, when subjects can learn of their current potential for reward in a given modality only by trying out appetite, this sampling trick may be necessary.

Whether an appetite is desirable or undesirable, signs of its onset will be fed back in the same pattern that William James, C. G. Lange, and Charles Darwin describe for emotions generally:

> The free expression by outward signs of an emotion intensifies it. On the other hand, the repression, as far as this is possible, of all outward signs softens our emotions. He who gives way to violent gestures will increase

Figure 7.3   The Effect of Generating Appetite in a Hyperbolically Discounted Model

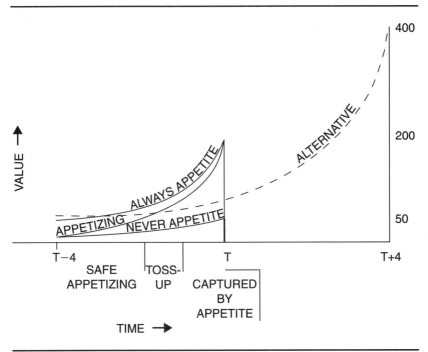

Notes: An organism that is motivated to avoid a smaller, earlier reward might still be motivated to generate some appetite, up to the point where the appetizing curve rises close to the discount curve from the preferred alternative; if it does not then stop generating appetite, its preference will reverse.

his rage; he who does not control the signs of fear will experience fear in greater degree (Darwin 1979, 366).

However, introspection of this process may be hampered both by its speed and by motives not to recognize it, as in J. M. Russell's example:

> I suspect that I may be getting seasick so I follow someone's advice to "keep your eyes on the horizon." . . . The effort to look at the horizon will fail if it amounts to a token made in a spirit of desperation. . . . I must look at it in the way one would for reasons other than those of getting over nausea . . . not with the despair of "I must look at the horizon or else I shall be sick!" To become well I must pretend I am well. (1978, 27–28)

Perhaps just assenting to see the dessert cart is a sign to yourself that you will give in, a sign that proves self-confirming. The observation of

Stanley Schachter, Brett Silverstein, and Deborah Perlick (1977) that orthodox Jews do not crave smoking on the Sabbath suggests that someone who never, really *never*, chooses from the dessert cart probably ceases to get a surge of appetite when it comes.[9]

The basic self-prediction in the quoted examples is an easier task than the self-prediction involved in willpower; willpower requires an individual to evaluate choices as precedents and thus is probably confined to humans. However, an animal could believably take part in these examples of predicting its own rage or sickness. The James-Lange-Darwin effect may be enough to create the explosiveness of appetites, even in animals, without our having to postulate any special hardwiring for it. Thus for an organism hovering around $T-3$ or -2 in figure 7.3, any event that presages a jump in appetite may reproduce that very jump and make the discount curve look like it does at the arrow in figure 7.2. Then the organism will not return to baseline but will give in to its urge.

It may be idle to ask why evolution would have rigged appetites with positive feedback systems, so that self-prediction becomes volatile. No one can say with certainty why rage, say, creates an incentive for more rage, facing an organism with a choice like *Do not augment your rage > calm down* versus *Augment your rage a little and thereby toss a coin between calming down and crossing the threshold to becoming furious.* However, it is reassuring to at least imagine a possibility.

Requiring an appetite phase before some kinds of reward-seeking activity may allow the activity to occur in a more all-or-none fashion than if not. To achieve an adaptive likelihood of sexual activity in a creature, for instance, nature might have found it best not to make it constantly rewarding. In most species this is regulated by making drive intermittent; but the drive is continuous in humans and some great apes, which might lead individuals to keep themselves close to satiation—say at a level like 50 in the figures, just below the competitive threshold. As soon as subjects raised their drive to 70 or 80, immediately available sex could again compete with only moderately delayed activities worth 400 or more. This could cause a maladaptive distribution of behavior; but with an appetite stage, nature could make sex usually rewarding at say, 10, with a provision to jump to 200 once the creature got "in the mood." Ten might be enough to reward fantasy but only mildly, in balance with many other activities that might be more useful most of the time. It would keep the organism observing, so that if an occasion associated with a prospective reward of 200 came along the organism would step up the rate of appetite generation until it reached the positive feedback threshold and then suddenly become occupied with sex to the exclusion of almost everything else until satiated. In modalities in which reward is not physically unavailable, a multiplier like appetite may permit organisms to act in a more focused and decisive manner than would a simple competition of drives.

The effect of such a configuration of incentives may be visible not only in subjectively involuntary processes like appetites but also in some deliberate choices. For instance, only the most primitive people habitually go naked. Insofar as clothes distance people from sexual stimuli, they may create in effect an (additional) appetite phase in consumption. Wearing clothes eliminates a relatively low-yield distraction from other activities; it moves the ordinary prospect of sexual reward from 50 or 70 to 10. Nudity, or provocative clothes, can then be chosen specifically in adequately rare circumstances to occasion a higher level of reward. The effect of the clothes is only slightly to lengthen the necessary delay before sex would be possible. Their main effect is to regulate the feedback of social and personal prediction: to provide information—both among people and to the wearer—about the wearer's likelihood of becoming interested in sex in the near future. By the same logic, an appetite phase in a reward-dependent activity may have been selected for in evolution as a buffer zone: to correct the overvaluation of the diminished returns from an activity that is always immediately available.

Conclusion: The Role of Craving in Loss of Control

A positively fed-back appetite phase does not mean that an organism is basing its choice on something other than expected reward. Naive individuals might indeed be surprised by a sudden surge of reward, but there is no reason why, with experience, they would not (hyperbolically) discount each outcome with which they were familiar and multiply it by its probability, whether or not some intermediate behavior of theirs affected this probability. If they wind up deciding in advance to gamble with drugs or dessert carts, it must be because the odds seem worth it at the time they make the choice. However, if they steer close to temptation, the recursive nature of their self-prediction will make the calculation of their prospects volatile. Whether or not they give in to gluttony, or intoxication, or anger, or panic, or seasickness may indeed turn on happenstances of what they see, including what they see in the behavior of their own appetites.

This one-factor theory has implications for the therapy of addiction and other self-destructive urges. Two-factor theory demands counterconditioning of the cues that give rise to craving, a method that has not worked well (Powell et al. 1990; Wilson 1978; Hunt and Matarazzo 1973; Lichtenstein and Danaher 1976; Clairborn, Lewis, and Humble 1972). The theory that I describe makes out the problem to be strategic.

Addicts trying to avoid self-destructive choices need to learn to navigate the pitfalls of intertemporal bargaining, particularly the effects of grouping prospective rewards into categories. The class of therapies called relapse prevention seems to do this best and is also among the most successful (Marlatt and Gordon, 1980). However, as with other strategies that depend on the timing of incentives, the possibilities are complex and the outcomes sometimes perverse (I discuss this at length in Ainslie 1999). Addicts whose recovery is shaky are certainly well advised to avoid predictable occasions for their cravings; but this avoidance does not fortify them against their addictions any more than the avoidance of phobic objects helps someone overcome a phobia.

Summary and Glossary

A two-factor theory requires appetites (or visceral factors) to be qualitatively distinct from reward-seeking mental processes, a distinction that does not stand up on close examination. Ultimately, there is no line that divides rewards from the stimuli that reinforce classical conditioning. The only reason that a separate conditioning principle has seemed necessary—to explain the imposition of negative visceral factors and the restraint of positive ones—can be removed by the hyperbolic shape of discounting the future.

Hyperbolic discounting implies a more parsimonious account of how visceral factors are generated, one that requires only one kind of reinforcement, here called reward. In this account, conditioned hungers and emotions (spoken of together as appetites) are just a special case of motivated behavior, kept from coming under the person's deliberate control by the extreme immediacy of reward either for generating the appetite (as in drug craving, pain, and panic) or for premature satiation (as in joy and thrill). Such a one-factor theory suggests the following relationships:

- Pleasures are outcomes that are subjectively desirable. They are a subcategory of reward.

- Rewards are whatever induce the mental process that selects a prior choice for repetition. Some short-range rewards lure people into participating in unpleasurable processes like grief or panic; conversely, some midrange pleasures like intoxication lure people into activities that are unrewarding (and unpleasurable) in the still longer run. Not all appetites are either pleasurable in themselves or lead to pleasurable experiences; but to survive, all must be rewarding.

- Deliberate behavior is a subcategory of reward-dependent behavior. It usually requires differential pleasure, not just reward, to maintain it. In the borderlands of this category like habituated smoking, rewards reported not to be pleasurable may maintain deliberate behavior.

- An individual's unlearned potential to be rewarded in a particular modality, which probably should be called drive for lack of a widely accepted alternative, forms the motivational basis for hungers, cravings, emotions, and appetites. Drives constrain what can be rewarding and do not themselves depend on reward.

- Hungers are motivated processes that in turn motivate seeking specific objects of consumption.

- Cravings are hungers.

- Emotions are those motivated processes that lack a specific object of consumption but that are conspicuous enough to get named. Depending on the observer's theory, they range from a core group with known physiological bases, through a broader group with stereotypic expressions, to the still broader, subtle group of any regular, noticeable motives.

- Appetites in common speech are hungers (except where used confusingly as a synonym for tastes), but I stretch the term to cover both hungers and emotions. Thus there may be appetites that are not "for" anything else. When appetites reward only briefly and undermine other sources of reward (panic, sometimes rage), they are avoided from a distance and experienced as aversive. Appetites lie on a continuum from those that are rewarding in their own right to those that demand a distinct phase of satisfaction, a phase that usually also involves satiation of the underlying drive. Those with more distinct satisfaction phases (thirst, drug craving) are more apt than those without them (joy, anger, panic) to have tangible objects of consumption.

- Visceral factors is Loewenstein's category. It seems to include hungers and core emotions but might include stereotyped or subtle emotions as well, for example, curiosity.

- Occasions are cues that an appetite will be rewarding; they may give information that the environment will support this reward, or they may be arbitrary pacing criteria that have their effect by preventing premature satiation.

- Tastes are learned dispositions toward generating particular appetites when drive and occasion are present.

- Addictions are tastes for particular pleasures that lead to greater unpleasure in the long run.

Addictive choices and other losses of self-control will often follow stimuli that occasion appetites for them, somewhat as Loewenstein describes. However, these appetites are better seen as reward-dependent processes that are part of the recursive self-prediction that Darwin and many others have elucidated rather than as the transferred reflexes of two-factor theory. Individuals can remember reward values with great accuracy but avoid rehearsing experiences like panic or drug craving lest they be lured back into them. Thus these experiences are often unreportable in practice. Once aroused, these processes function as self-confirming prophesies and, therefore, may seem both explosive and coercive.

A one-factor theory based on hyperbolic discounting does not negate the importance of appetites that are occasioned by cues but does avoid the empirical and theoretical problems of two-factor theory.

I thank John Monterosso for many helpful comments and thought experiments.

Notes

1. I think it is now safe to use conditioned to mean classically conditioned, although there was an old usage that made it mean simply learned.

2. It is better to speak of drive as the biological capacity for a modality to be rewarding and to speak of appetite as a goal-directed process that an organism sometimes bases on that capacity. In this nomenclature, starving people who are no longer hungry have high drive but no appetite (Carlson 1916).

3. The example of sex certainly bears out Loewenstein's observation that visceral arousal bears some resemblance to the actual consumption of reward.

4. Aversive appetites are not prominent under normal circumstances, probably because either they require an evoked drive, as with pain, or it is not hard to avoid getting within range of their very short rewards. This avoidance fails in the presence of occasions that used to be welcome and that the person has not learned to avoid—either because there has not been time enough for this learning (for example, the process of mourning) or because the person is ambivalent about avoiding them (for example, craving in the "dry drunk").

   However, some circumstances seem to expand the rewarding component of aversive appetites to the point at which they have the lure of addictions (that is, to the point at which they are not escaped or avoided even hours in advance); this can involve either entertaining forlorn wishes, for instance, until they foster pathological grief or paranoid jealousy, or succumbing to the urge to rehearse traumatic memories until they expand, via the Napalkov effect (Eysenck 1967) to become a posttraumatic stress syndrome. Such expansion is unaccounted for in classical conditioning models of emotionality. Of course, the temporary preference phenomenon that forms the whole basis for the seduction model of negative appetites makes no sense if discounting is exponential.

5. The hypothesis that a robust rewarding effect depends on continuing novelty is consistent with recent reports that reward-sensitive dopaminergic cells in a monkey's nucleus accumbens respond most when a rewarding stimulus occurs unpredictably (Hollerman, Tremblay, and Schultz 1998).

6. Even satiety does not seem to depend always on consumption of the hunger's object. Fantasy-prone individuals can induce the entire physiology of copulation by mental means and can also experience eating to satiation through mental means, although the satiety is brief (Wilson and Barber 1983). They are not preoccupied with sexual or eating fantasies because of this ability; some other constraints must be operating on their capacity for self-reward.

7. Pleasant emotional experiences are not as hard to remember but habituate—lose their juice—with repetition. This phenomenon, too, would be expected from our discussion in the last section.

8. Some probable complexities in the reward process are not diagramed. These include the reward for appetite itself and the reduction in alternative reward, which may be caused by some appetites themselves (for example, the pangs that an appetite for food commits you to if you do not eat).

9. It might be argued that people are consistent abstainers because their initial abstentions have extinguished the surge, but this is an unlikely direction of causality: Appetites are instant compared with motor behaviors. Like the begging of pets, they seem always to be on the edge of happening and seem to be maintained by even the least chance of a greater gratification to follow, despite the threat of the somewhat more delayed pangs they may entail.

References

Ainslie, George. 1987. "Aversion with Only One Factor." In *Quantitative Analysis of Behavior: The Effect of Delay and of Intervening Events on Reinforcement Value*, edited by Michael Commons, James Mazur, Anthony Nevin, and Howard Rachlin. Hillsdale, N.J.: Erlbaum.

———. 1992. *Picoeconomics: The Strategic Interaction of Successive Motivational States Within the Person*. Cambridge: Cambridge University Press.

———. 1999. "The Dangers of Willpower: A Picoeconomic Understanding of Addiction and Dissociation." In *Getting Hooked: Rationality and the Addictions*, edited by Jon Elster and Ole-Jørgen Skog. Cambridge: Cambridge University Press.

Ainslie, George, and Bernard T. Engel. 1974. "Alteration of Classically Conditioned Heart Rate by Operant Reinforcement in Monkeys." *Journal of Comparative and Physiological Psychology* 87: 373–83.

Aristotle. 1915. *Nicomachean Ethics.* In *Works of Aristotle,* vol. 9, edited by William Ross. London: Oxford University Press.

Atnip, G. 1977. "Stimulus and Response-Reinforcer Contingencies." In *Autoshaping, Operant, Classical, and Omission Training Procedures* 28: 59–69.

Basmajian, John, et al. 1989. *Biofeedback: Principles and Practice for Clinicians.* Baltimore: Williams & Wilkins.

Carlson, A. J. 1916. "The Relation of Hunger to Appetite." In *The Control of Hunger in Health and Disease.* Chicago: University of Chicago Press.

Clairborn, William, Philip Lewis, and Stephen Humble. 1972. "Stimulus Satiation and Smoking: A Revisit." *Journal of Clinical Psychology* 28: 416–19.

Clum, George A. 1989. "Psychological Interventions Versus Drugs in the Treatment of Panic." *Behavior Therapy* 20: 429–57.

Darwin, Charles. 1872/1979. *The Expressions of Emotions in Man and Animals.* London: Julian Friedman.

Dickinson, Anthony. 1980. *Contemporary Animal Learning Theory.* New York: Cambridge University Press.

Donahoe, John W., Jose E. Burgos, and David C. Palmer. 1993. "A Selectionist Approach to Reinforcement." *Journal of the Experimental Analysis of Behavior* 60: 17–40.

Ekman, Paul, and Wallace V. Friesen. 1986. "A New Pancultural Facial Expression of Emotion." *Motivation and Emotion* 10: 159–68.

Elster, Jon. 1999. "Gambling." In *Getting Hooked: Rationality and the Addictions,* edited by Jon Elster and Ole-Jørgen Skog. Cambridge: Cambridge University Press.

Eysenck, Hans J. 1967. "Single-Trial Conditioning, Neurosis, and the Napalkov Phenomenon." *Behavior Research and Therapy* 5: 63–65.

Frank, Robert H. 1988. *Passions Within Reason.* New York: Norton.

Gosling, Justin. 1990. *Weakness of Will.* London: Routledge.

Green, Leonard, Astrid Fry, and Joel Myerson. 1994. "Discounting of Delayed Rewards: A Life-Span Comparison." *Psychonomic Science* 5: 33–36.

Harkins, Paul W., trans. 1963. *Galen on the Passions and Errors of the Soul.* Columbus: Ohio State University Press.

Harvey, Charles M. 1994. "The Reasonableness of Nonconstant Discounting." *Journal of Public Economics* 53: 31–51.

Hearst, Eliot. 1975. "The Classical-Instrumental Distinction Reflexes, Voluntary Behavior, and Categories of Associative Learning." In *Handbook of Learning and Cognitive Processes,* edited by William Estes. New York: Erlbaum.

Herrnstein, Richard J. 1969. "Method and Theory in the Study of Avoidance." *Psychological Review* 76: 49–69.

Hollerman, Jeffrey R., Leon Tremblay, and Wolfram Schultz. 1998. "Influence of Reward Expectation on Behavior-Related Neuronal Activity in Primate Striatum." *Journal of Neurophysiology* 80: 947–63.

Hunt, William, and Joseph Matarazzo. 1973. "Three Years Later: Recent Developments in the Experimental Modifications of Smoking Behavior." *Journal of Abnormal Psychology* 81: 107–14.

Izard, Carroll E. 1971. *The Face of Emotion.* New York: Appleton-Century-Crofts.

Kirby, Kris N., and Richard J. Herrnstein. 1995. "Preference Reversals Due to Myopic Discounting of Delayed Reward." *Psychological Science* 6: 83–89.

Lichtenstein, Edward, and Brian G. Danaher. 1976. "Modification of Smoking Behavior: A Critical Analysis of Theory, Research, and Practice." In *Progress in Behavior Modification*, edited by Michel Hersen, Richard M. Eisler, and P. M. Miller. Vol. 3. New York: Academic.

Licklider, J. C. R. 1959. "On Psychophysiological Models." In *Sensory Communication*, edited by W. A. Rosenbluth. Cambridge: MIT Press.

Loewenstein, George. 1987. "Anticipation and the Valuation of Delayed Consumption." *Economic Journal* 97: 666–85.

———. 1996. "Out of Control: Visceral Influences on Behavior." *Organizational Behavior and Human Decision Processes* 35: 272–92.

———. 1999. "A Visceral Account of Addiction." In *Getting Hooked: Rationality and the Addictions*, edited by Jon Elster and Ole-Jørgen Skog. Cambridge: Cambridge University Press.

Marlatt, G. Allen, and Judith R. Gordon. 1980. "Determinants of Relapse: Implications for the Maintenance of Behavior Change." In *Behavioral Medicine: Changing Health Lifestyles*, edited by Park O. Davidson and Sheena M. Davidson. Elmsford, N.Y.: Pergamon.

Melzack, Ronald, A. Z. Weisz, and L. T. Sprague. 1963. "Strategems for Controlling Pain: Contributions of Auditory Stimulation and Suggestion." *Experimental Neurology* 8: 239–47.

Mendelsohn, Joseph, and Stephen L. Chorover. 1965. "Lateral Hypothalamic Stimulation in Satiated Rats: T-Maze Learning for Food." *Science* 149: 559–61.

Miller, Neal. 1969. "Learning of Visceral and Glandular Responses." *Science* 163: 434–45.

Mirenowicz, Jacques, and Wolfram Schultz. 1996. "Preferential Activation of Midbrain Dopamine Neurons by Appetitive Rather than Aversive Stimuli." *Nature* 379: 449–51.

Morley, Stephen. 1993. "Vivid Memory for 'Everyday' Pains." *Pain* 55: 55–62.

Mowrer, Orvil H. 1947. "On the Dual Nature of Learning: A Reinterpretation of 'Conditioning' and 'Problem Solving.'" *Harvard Educational Review* 17: 102–48.

O'Brien, Charles P., Ronald N. Ehrman, and J. W. Ternes. 1986. "Classical Conditioning in Human Dependence." In *Behavioral Analyses of Drug Dependence*, edited by Steven R. Goldberg and Ian P. Stolerman. Orlando: Academic.

Panksepp, Jaak. 1982. "Toward a General Psychobiological Theory of Emotions." *Behavioral and Brain Sciences* 5: 407–67.

Plato. 1988. *Protagoras.* In *Weakness of Will*, by William Charlton. Oxford, UK: Basil Blackwell.

Powell, Jane, Jeffery A. Gray, Brendan P. Bradley, Yainnis Kasvikis. 1990. "The Effects of Exposure to Drug-Related Cues in Detoxified Opiate Addicts: A Theoretical Review and Some New Data." *Addictive Behavior* 15: 339–54.

Rescorla, Robert A. 1988. "Pavlovian Conditioning: It's Not What You Think It Is." *American Psychologist* 43: 151–60.

Russell, J. Michael. 1978. "Saying, Feeling, and Self-Deception." *Behaviorism* 6: 27–43.

Schachter, Stanley, Brett Silverstein, and Deborah Perlick. 1977. "Psychological and Pharmacological Explanations of Smoking Under Stress." *Journal of Experimental Psychology: General* 106: 31–40.

Sheffield, Frederick, J. Wulff, and R. Barker. 1951. "Reward Value of Copulation Without Sex Drive Reduction." *Journal of Comparative and Physiological Psychology* 44: 3–8.

Stearns, Peter N. 1986. "Historical Analysis in the Study of Emotion." *Motivation and Emotion* 10: 185–93.

———. 1994. *American Cool: Constructing a Twentieth-Century Emotional Style.* New York: New York University Press.

Wilson, Sheryl C., and Theodore X. Barber. 1983. "The Fantasy-Prone Personality: Implications for Understanding Imagery, Hypnosis, and Parapsychological Phenomena." In *Imagery: Current Theory, Research, and Application,* edited by Anees A. Sheikh. New York: Wiley.

Wilson, T. G. 1978. "Alcoholism and Aversion Therapy: Issues, Ethics, and Evidence." In *Behavioral Approaches to Alcoholism,* edited by G. Allen Marlatt and P. E. Nathan. New Brunswick: Rutgers University Center on Alcohol Studies.

Wolpe, Joseph, G. Groves, and S. Fisher. 1980. "Treatment of Narcotic Addiction by Inhibition of Craving: Contending with a Cherished Habit." *Comprehensive Psychiatry* 21: 308–16.

Chapter 8

Emotion and Addiction: Neurobiology, Culture, and Choice

JON ELSTER

IN THIS CHAPTER I compare the phenomenon of addiction with that of emotion in the hope that the comparison may enhance our understanding of both. The discussion is methodological rather than substantive and, hence, has to cover a lot of ground very briefly. For fuller discussions I refer the reader to Elster (1999a, 1999b). Although included in a volume on addiction, the chapter treats the two phenomena symmetrically rather than merely using emotion as a foil for addiction. The value of the comparison is, I believe, enhanced by an evenhanded treatment.

I distinguish three main approaches to emotion and addiction: the neurobiological model, cultural or social constructivist models, and choice-theoretic models. Some references may be useful to give an idea of what I have in mind. Neurobiological approaches include Joseph LeDoux (1996) and Avram Goldstein (1994). Social constructivist studies include Catherine Lutz (1988) and Stanton Peele (1985). Rational choice analyses include Ronald de Sousa (1987) and Gary Becker (1996). An instance of an approach to both emotion and addiction that is choice-theoretic, although not based on rational choice theory, is George Ainslie (1992).

Emotion and addiction are special cases of what George Loewenstein (1996, 1999) calls visceral factors. In addition to emotions and cravings for addictive substances, these include what we might call primary visceral factors, such as hunger, thirst, pain, and drowsiness. These factors differ mainly with respect to their relation to cognition. Emotions have *cognitive antecedents* as well as *intentional objects*, at least in typical cases. Cravings are intentional, but they do not require any prior beliefs to be triggered. They may be importantly modified by beliefs, but that is another matter. Pain, hunger, thirst, and drowsiness are largely acognitive. If a brick falls on my head, I do not need to know it was a brick (or to have any other beliefs) in order to feel pain. Nor is my pain *about* anything. Although the desire to avoid withdrawal pains can be a component of cravings, the pain itself is not intentional. Whereas the primary visceral factors are relatively resistant to cultural and choice-theoretic explanations, these approaches have considerable force in trying to account for emotion and addiction.

Although I treat addiction and emotion mainly as two parallel and independent sets of phenomena, I also have occasion to mention some causal connections between them. The most important is that guilt and shame can be important factors in sustaining addictions as well as in providing a motivation to break the habit. More speculatively, we may wonder whether people can get addicted to emotional experiences. Michael Lewis (1992, 78), for instance, refers to the addictive potential of hubris, a feeling of exaggerated pride and self-confidence. It has also been claimed that it is possible to be addicted to love, either to love in general (Liebowitz 1983, 91–95) or to love for a specific person (Peele and Brodsky 1991). Similarly, casual observation suggests that some people are addicted to the feeling of righteous indignation and deliberately seek out situations in which they might experience that emotion. Whether it is useful for more theoretical purposes to refer to those phenomena as addictions is another matter.

In the following section, I explain what I mean by emotion and addiction and say something about the sources of what we know about these phenomena. In the next section, I discuss the relevance of culture for states of emotion and addiction. In the third section, I discuss the relation between emotion and addiction on the one hand and choice behavior on the other. In the fourth section, I discuss how neurobiology, culture, and choice interact in producing the phenomena of emotion and addiction. The final section offers some concluding comparisons between the two phenomena.

The Nature of Emotion and Addiction

We may characterize emotion and addiction in three ways. First, we may proceed by producing a simple list. We all have a pretty good idea about what counts as an emotion and at least a rough idea about which substances and behaviors have the potential for being addictive. We may call this the empirical approach. Second, we may proceed by enumerating the observable features that are common to all or most emotions or common to all or most addictive behaviors. This is the phenomenological approach. Third, we may proceed by identifying a common mechanism that generates all emotions or all addictions. This is the causal approach.

Figure 8.1

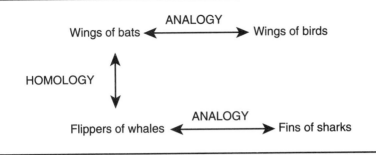

The distinction between the phenomenological and causal approaches corresponds to the distinction between analogy and homology in biology as shown in figure 8. 1. Sharks and whales are related by analogy, as are bats and birds. Whales and bats, by contrast, are related by homology, through a common causal history. In general, analogies have weaker predictive power than homologies. Two phenomena related by analogy need not have any further common features than those that define the analogy and those that are causally implicated by those features. There may be purposes for which the class of "creatures that fly"—including flying fish!—is a useful concept. Because all these creatures are subject to the same aerodynamic constraints, we can make some predictions about their form. The same is true for the class of organisms that live in the water. We cannot, however, make any predictions about their metabolism, reproductive system, and so on. Let me refer to the features that define an analogy as *primary* features and to those that are causally implicated by the primary features as *secondary* ones. A primary feature of a whale, in this perspective, is that it lives in water. A secondary feature is that it has a sleek shape that enables it to overcome resistance to moving in water.

Emotion and addiction *matter* because of their phenomenological properties. Yet to understand how they arise, maintain themselves over time, and decay, we may have to go beyond their observable features and look at the underlying causal mechanisms. In the study of addiction, this has been achieved to a considerable extent. In the study of the emotions, it has virtually not been achieved at all.

Emotion

Our knowledge about the emotions comes from a number of sources:

- Animal studies in the laboratory
- Animal studies in the wild, notably of primates

- Laboratory experiments with human subjects
- Historical and anthropological studies
- Introspection
- Fiction
- Philosophers and moralists

There are limits to what animal studies can tell us about human behavior. There are also limits on what we can learn from laboratory experiments with human subjects. Because of financial constraints one may not be able to create high-stake situations in the laboratory, unless one uses first-world research grants to study third-world subjects (Cameron 1995). Because of ethical constraints that were set up in the wake of Stanley Milgram's (1974) work, one cannot place subjects in situations that will induce strong negative emotions. Also, many of these studies rely on self-reports, which are a pretty fragile instrument. I believe, therefore, that to understand the subtler human emotions one has to turn to the last four sources, which is not to say that the first three have no value.

Mental states that seem to be uncontroversially emotional include regret, relief, hope, disappointment, shame, guilt, vanity, pride, envy, jealousy, malice, pity, indignation, anger, fear, disgust, hatred, contempt, joy, grief, parental love, and romantic love. Borderline or controversial cases include surprise, boredom, interest, curiosity, sexual desire, enjoyment, worry, and frustration. A complex special category is formed by the emotions induced by art. These include both the specifically aesthetic emotions generated by formal features of works of art and the nonaesthetic emotions that they can arouse in us. All these phenomena can be understood either in an occurrent sense, as emotional experiences, or in a dispositional sense, as tendencies to have occurrent emotions (anger versus irascibility). I deal mainly with occurrent emotions.

If we adopt the phenomenological approach, emotions are characterized by nine primary features (Frijda 1986; Ekman 1992):

- Sudden onset
- Unbidden occurrence
- Brief duration
- Triggered by a cognitive state
- Directed toward an intentional object
- Inducing physiological changes (arousal)

- Having physiological and physiognomic expressions
- Inducing specific action tendencies
- Accompanied by pleasure or pain (valence)

Not all the emotions listed have all the primary features. Some emotions arise slowly and gradually (love and sometimes anger). Others can have a very long duration (unrequited love, or anger when not relieved by revenge). The emotions induced by reading a good book need not trigger any specific arousal patterns or physiological expressions. The antecedent that triggers fear may be a perception rather than a cognition (LeDoux 1996). Anxiety need not have a specific intentional object. If a piece of music causes us to feel joy, the emotion seems to lack both antecedent and object (Budd 1995, chap. 4). Pride does not seem to have any specific action tendency (Hume 1960, 367). Mixed emotions such as nostalgia may have neutral valence.

The causal approach is undeveloped. Fear is the only emotion we are close to understanding at the neurophysiological level (LeDoux 1996). We do not know if other emotions have similar neural pathways. The relation between, say, parental love and fear may turn out to be like the relation between whales and sharks. Because of our lack of understanding of the core emotions, we should keep an open mind about the borderline cases. When more is known about the neurobiological substrates, some of the marginal cases may move to the center, and vice versa.

Addiction

Our knowledge about addiction comes from a number of sources:

- Animal studies in the laboratory
- Laboratory experiments with human subjects
- Clinical observations
- Observations of market behavior
- Historical and anthropological studies
- Introspection
- Fiction

The sources overlap with the sources of knowledge about the emotions, but there are some differences. There is no animal addiction in the wild. Conversely, testing theories of addiction by looking at how consumption responds to price changes or to changes in retail outlets has no analogue in the study of emotion. Although fiction is less indispensable in the study of addiction than in the study of emotions, fictional descriptions of gambling (Dostoyevsky 1964; Hamsun 1954) may help us understand the causal mechanisms underlying this phenomenon.

At the empirical level, the following substances appear to have the potential for inducing addictive behavior: caffeine, nicotine, alcohol and alcohol-related substances (including barbiturates and benzodiazepines, such as Valium), opiates, cocaine, amphetamine, cannabis, and hallucinogens. With a few exceptions, animals can be made to press levers furiously, even to the point at which they die, to get the rewards from these drugs. Borderline or controversial cases include overeating and various behavioral addictions such as compulsive gambling and addiction to television, to the internet, to video games, to relationships. As we distinguish occurrent emotions from emotional dispositions, we may also contrast within-episode and between-episode states of addiction. An alcoholic, for instance, may be defined as someone who tends to lose control over drinking once he has had one drink or as someone who finds it difficult to avoid having the first drink.

At the phenomenological level, the addictions can be characterized in terms of twelve features:

- Consumption-induced euphoria
- Withdrawal-induced dysphoria and discomfort
- Craving (for euphoria or for release from dysphoria)
- Tolerance
- Cue dependence (conditioned tolerance, withdrawal symptoms or cravings)
- Objective harm
- Crowding out (the search for the addictive experience dominates life)
- Mood alteration (over and above euphoria and dysphoria from use and abstinence)
- Desire to quit
- Inability to quit
- Denial
- Struggle for self-control (ambivalence)

Again, not all the putative addictions have all the phenomenological features. Whereas craving and cue dependence seem to be universal features of any candidate member of the group of addictive substances or behaviors, none of the other features is invariably observed. LSD does not involve tolerance or withdrawal. Coffee has only four of the enumerated properties: craving, withdrawal, tolerance, and cue dependence. Smoking does not tend to crowd out all other activities, nor is it mood altering.

At the causal level, all the substance-based addictions except alcohol have a common modus operandi in the dopaminergic system of the brain (Goldstein 1994). The euphoric effects of the drugs are caused by the release of large amounts of dopamine in the synaptic clefts (but see Robinson and Berridge 1993 for a different view of the role of dopamine in addiction). The dysphoric effects are caused by depletion of dopamine below normal levels. Roughly speaking, there are three molecular states or stages of addiction. In the first stage, the drug acts on receptors in the brain to release more dopamine. In the second stage, there is a process of neuroadaptation—a form of tolerance—by which the brain mechanisms adjust to the drug, for instance by reducing the number of receptors that are being stimulated. In the third stage, if a person stops taking the drug he or she will feel the bad effects of adaptation without the compensatory effect of the drug.

In the case of addiction, we know a great deal about the neurobiological substrate of the core cases. Some of the borderline cases are likely to prove very different. Yet there are some causal mechanisms common to chemical and behavioral addictions, notably those that are linked to the *awareness* of being addicted. These mechanisms generate secondary features of phenomena that are linked by analogy rather than by common causal mechanisms.

Culture, Emotion, and Addiction

What is culture? With an important qualification, I understand culture as any pattern of behavior, norms, values, beliefs, and concepts that is more than individual but less than universal. Culture is the realm of the particular.

I consider three sources of variation in behavior across societies. First, societies may exhibit different behaviors because for historical reasons they have ended up in different *coordination equilibria*. In theory, the United Kingdom and the United States could be identical in all respects except that people drive on the left in the first country and on the right in the second, together with features that flow directly from this difference. Differences in metric systems, number systems, and calendars can also generate differences in behavior that need not reflect anything but accidents of history. Second, behavioral differences may be due to different *norms and values.* I especially emphasize the importance of social norms in explaining cultural variation. Norms, in turn, are backed by emotions of shame and contempt (Elster 1999b). Although these emotions themselves seem to be culturally invariant, the norms they sustain can explain variations in other emotions. Third, differences in behavior may be due to different *beliefs and concepts*. An especially important category is constituted by beliefs about causality, notably those from which one can infer ends-means relations. Two groups might have the same values, norms, and coordination equilibria and yet show different behavioral patterns due to different beliefs about which means are likely to be efficient to realize specific ends.

The "important qualification" is that a mere commonality of behavior, norms, values, beliefs, or concepts in a certain group does not by itself constitute a pattern of culture. In addition to these shared characteristics I require, as Charles Taylor (1971) says in a different context, that the sharing itself be shared. I require, that is, that the members of the group are aware of the fact that others hold similar norms, values or beliefs or that they can be expected to behave in a similar manner. Whether or not one also makes it part of the definition that each member is aware that others are aware of this fact, and so on, these higher-order beliefs can usually be assumed to obtain.

Emotion and Culture

The emotions are very closely linked to some of the aspects of culture that I have outlined. I mainly emphasize two aspects. First, not all cultures recognize or conceptualize the same emotions. Even if (as I conjecture) the emotions themselves are universal, it does not follow that they are universally recognized. Second, when an emotion does belong to the conceptual repertoire of a culture, it can also become the target of prescriptive or proscriptive social norms, leading either to more or to less frequent occurrences than one would otherwise have observed.

To address the question of cultural variation in the emotions themselves, I need to consider two aspects of the relation between emotion and cognition that have been neglected so far. Earlier in the chapter, I argued that (1) complex human emotions are caused by cognition. In addition, (2) emotion may be the object of cognition, and (3) cognition may be the effect of emotion. It will turn out that in many important cases, all three relations obtain simultaneously and interact with each other.

An individual may be in the grip of an emotion and not be aware of it. We have all heard, and many of us have uttered, the angry utterance, "I am not angry!" Similarly, a person may be in love and not be aware of it; be envious of another's achievement and not be aware of it; and so on. Other people may have no difficulty in detecting the emotion, but the person concerned remains unaware of it. In many cases, the individual concerned is capable of becoming aware of the emotion. Once the emotion becomes the object of a cognition, the latter may in turn trigger new emotions, or meta-emotions. A person who consciously acknowledges love for an illicit partner may come to feel guilt or shame for the emotion. The relation between emotions and social norms is in fact a two-way street. Emotions regulate social norms but can also be the target of norms.

In other cases, the individual is prevented by idiosyncratic character traits from becoming aware of what he or she feels. Thus Michael Lewis (1992, 15–16) reports,

> I had a patient named John who received the news that a very dear aunt had died. At first, he reported experiencing great sadness at the loss. But then his sadness seemed to dissipate. Several weeks later, he felt agitated and experienced some trouble eating and sleeping. When I asked John how he felt, he replied that he felt tired. When I asked him whether he was depressed, he said that he did not feel depressed.

Lewis suggests two mechanisms that might explain why John did not acknowledge the fact that he was depressed: self-deception and socialization. The latter is spelled out as follows.

> As a child, John may have exhibited certain behaviors in situations of loss. When he did, his parents informed him that these behaviors means that he was tired, not sad. In other words, past experience may be capable of shaping people's self-awareness about an emotion, even to the extent of producing an awareness that is idiosyncratic in relation to the actual emotional state.

In still other cases, the obstacle to awareness is cultural rather than personal. Thus Robert Levy (1973) argues that in Tahiti, the misperception of depression as mere fatigue is the rule rather than an idiosyncratic exception. When a Tahitian,

> feeling strange after being separated from his *vahine,* interprets his feelings as illness and in so doing accepts a pervasive cultural pattern of playing down feelings of loss, it is evident that in some way and at some level he must know that he has suffered a significant loss. That is why his separation from his *vahine* made him feel sick or strange in the first place. That is, one "feels" considerably more than cultural forms may make consciously accessible. (324)

The emotion of depression does not belong to the conceptual repertoire of the Tahitians. Similarly, Bernard Williams (1993) argues that the emotion of guilt did not belong to the repertoire of the ancient Greeks;

Patricia Spacks (1995) notes that the conception of the emotion of boredom as an involuntary mental state rather than as a reprehensible sin did not exist until fairly recently; and C. S. Lewis (1936) says that the concept of romantic love did not arise until the European Middle Ages. Williams and Spacks also make the point (which Lewis overlooks) that the mental states themselves and their attendant expressions can exist even if there is no concept that captures them. They make the further crucial observation that when the emotion *is* conceptualized, it is also changed (Williams 1993, 91; Spacks 1995, 12–13). When a person has the conceptual wherewithal to say to himself, "God, I'm bored!" the state of boredom will typically become more acute and efforts to alleviate it more intense.

These examples show that an emotion may exist at the behavioral and physiological level even when it is not conceptualized as such. In these cases, we may say that the emotion exists as a *proto-emotion*. When the emotion is conceptualized, we may say that it exists as a *proper emotion*. It is tempting to say that the listed emotions exist in all human groups, either as proto-emotions or as proper emotions. One might even try to defend the stronger thesis, that any emotion that exists as a proper emotion in some group will be found in all groups, either as a proto-emotion or as a proper emotion. In that case, cultural variation would exist only at the level of conceptualization, not in the emotions themselves. Because of my lack of competence in the field of the anthropology of the emotions, I remain agnostic with respect to either thesis. Although some claims about the nonuniversality of emotion may rest on a confusion between the existence of an emotion and its presence in conceptualized form, I am in no position to assert that this fallacy underlies all claims of this kind.

When an emotion does exist as a proper emotion—that is, is part of the conscious cultural repertoire of a group—the awareness can affect the way the emotion is experienced as well as its role in social interaction. This effect may come about in several ways.

- The concept may embody beliefs about the nature of the phenomenon. Once a state is conceptualized as a depression, the person may think of it as long lasting and unamenable to intervention and sink more deeply into the state.

- The concept may change expectations about other people. Once a person can label his emotional state as love, he does not simply want to be with the other person, he wants to be loved in return.

- A proper emotion can become subject to social norms, which may change how it is experienced. In a (modified) example from Arlie Hochschild (1979, 567), a feminist mother who feels guilty about leaving her child in day care may feel ashamed of her guilt.

Figure 8.2

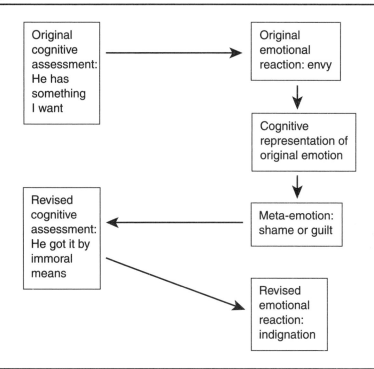

- An emotional state may also be viewed as violating a moral value. In a contrasting example from Hochschild, a traditionalist mother may think she feels too little guilt about leaving her child in day care and, in fact, feel guilty about her lack of guilt.

In the last two cases, the mothers would have to possess the concept of guilt, since otherwise the presence or absence of that emotion could not trigger the meta-emotions of shame or guilt.

A final link in the chain of mechanisms that may produce cultural variation in occurrent emotions turns on the capacity of emotion to modify and distort cognition. Figure 8.2 offers an example that, in fact, involves all three relations between emotion and cognition.

We assume (1) that the emotion of envy belongs to the repertoire of the group in question, (2) that social norms or moral values stigmatize feelings of envy, and (3) that on a given occasion the individual is aware that he or she is feeling envious. It follows that the individual will (4) feel a meta-emotion of shame or guilt.

Let me focus on the emotion of shame, which is generally agreed to be more intensely unpleasant and have stronger motivational power than that of guilt. The experience of envy and shame of envy may trigger various types of reaction. The individual might simply shrug his mental shoulders, think about something else, and forget the experience. Alternatively, he might defuse the emotion by the cognitive strategy of focusing on features that make the situation of the envied person less enviable. Looking at a rival, a woman might tell herself, "Yes, she is beautiful now, but think how miserable she will be when she loses her bloom." Finally, the envious person might use a more virulent cognitive strategy, that of rewriting the script to persuade himself that the envied person obtained his possession in an illegitimate way and perhaps at the expense of the envious person. The man who fails to get a promotion he hoped for may tell himself that his rival got it through obsequious behavior and malicious talk. This new way of looking at the situation triggers the intoxicating feeling of righteous indignation, which can be indulged in freely without any tinge of shame. The new emotion may also induce behavior, such as attempts to redress the injustice or to punish the undeserving rival.

The ability of emotion to shape cognition is, of course, a very general phenomenon. In the more specific mechanism described in figure 8.2, an emotionally modified cognition is capable of modifying emotion. Whether the mechanism is triggered depends both on the strength of the original emotion and on the strength of the meta-emotion. In the case of envy, the frequency and intensity with which it occurs may vary across groups. Small towns and villages seem to be breeding grounds for envy, whereas it may occur less frequently in groups characterized by greater anonymity and social mobility. Although envy is usually an object of disapproval, the condemnation can be stronger in some groups than in others. Contemporary Western societies are probably at one extreme on this scale. One rarely justifies aggressive behavior by saying "He's getting too big for his shoes," or "Who does he take himself for?" A more elaborate story is usually needed. In other societies, the story can be very thin indeed. Hence we would expect a great deal of envy whenever the conditions for the emotion to arise are present without there being strong norms against it. Conversely, envy would be rare either when it is repressed by strong norms or when there is little to repress in the first place.

Addiction and Culture

Emotions are universal, at least in the minimal sense that all human beings are subject to some emotions. Addiction, by contrast, is not a universal phenomenon. Although Norman Zinberg (1984, 27) states that "all known societies (with the possible exception of earlier Eskimo cultures) have used intoxicants for recreational purposes," this is not a claim about the near-universal nature of *addiction*. Substances with an addictive potential can be and often are consumed nonaddictively. In some societies, nonaddictive use appears in fact to be the main or even the only form of consumption. In a classic study, Craig MacAndrew and Robert Edgerton (1969) show that in many societies alcohol use has been regulated so that people could get drunk occasionally without turning into drunkards.

In still other societies, consumption is what *we* would call addictive, although members of the society in question do not think of it in that way. These societies exhibit what we may call—in an analogy with emotion—*proto-addiction*. Only in a few societies do we find *proper addiction*, that is, both the fact and the concept of addiction. Also, in societies that exhibit (what we call) addiction, the substances that sustain it differ greatly. The explanation of these variations lies in geography as well as in culture. People cannot get addicted to nicotine, cannabis, cocaine, or opium unless the relevant plants are available. Although alcoholic beverages can be made under a large variety of natural conditions, spontaneous fermentation of sugar-containing products cannot occur everywhere. In the modern world, these geographical factors have obviously lost much of their importance. It appears that one can also ignore genetic differences in the physiology of addiction. Although there are inborn racial variations in the rate at which different addictive substances are metabolized, they seem to play a marginal role in explaining addiction (Orford 1985, 156; Zhang 1995, 49; Hanson 1995, 311; Hall 1986, 168).

When people consume addictive substances, they often do so in public. The consumption takes place in the presence of other consumers and is causally linked to their consumption. The causal link can go in either direction. On the one hand, addicts may seek out fellow addicts to persuade themselves that their behavior is entirely normal. The alcoholic may "rationalize the need by assertions that he or she drinks no more than his or her friends. Accordingly, alcoholics tend to spend their time with other drinkers" (Goodwin and Gabrielli 1997, 143). On the other hand, people who might otherwise not have consumed may be induced to do so by the presence of fellow consumers. The sight of another person smoking, for example, may trigger the desire for a cigarette (cue-dependent craving). This effect is sometimes cited as an argument for a ban on smoking in public. Also, the presence of other consumers enters directly into the utility function. In a model offered by Karl O. Moene (1999), and with D and N indicating consumption and abstention,

> the pleasure of consumption is represented by an individual utility function, $v = v\,(x, y)$, where x indicates the person's own choice and y what the others choose. The temptation to drink or to take drugs is assumed to be social in character. Thus when the others drink the person prefers to drink as well, and when the others do not drink the person also prefers to abstain. Formally,

$$v(D,D) > v(N,D), \qquad\qquad (a.1)$$

$$v(N,N) > v(D,N), \qquad\qquad (a.2)$$

> which simply state that the individual does not like to deviate from what the others do. In addition, within a group of similar individuals a deviant behavior is assumed to impose a negative externality on the others. All else being equal, drinkers would rather interact with another drinker than with a nondrinker; and persons who like not to drink would rather like to interact with other nondrinkers than with drinkers. Stated formally, this can be expressed as

$$v(D,D) > v(D,N), \qquad\qquad (a.3)$$

$$v(N,N) > v(N,D). \qquad\qquad (a.4)$$

> The preferences indicated by (a.1)–(a.4) are conformist in two ways. On the one hand (a.1) and (a.2) state that people like to imitate what others do. On the other hand, (a.3) and (a.4) state that people would like others to imitate their behavior.

Moene shows that if potential drug consumers have conformist preferences of this kind, accidents of history can determine whether a society ends up in a high-use equilibrium or a low-use equilibrium. Beliefs and social norms are irrelevant for the outcome. Many other aspects of addiction are highly norm dependent, however, as is illustrated by variations in the use of alcohol. Drawing heavily on the essays in Dwight Heath (1995), I focus on this substance, although I occasionally touch on other substances and behaviors as well.

In almost all known societies throughout history, people have used beer, wine, or liquor for nutritional, medical, ritual, and recreational purposes—or just to get drunk. Moreover, the use of these beverages is embedded in a very dense network of social norms and sanctions. There is enormous variety in drinking behavior and drinking norms across cultures, at least with regard to moderate drinking. Alcoholics, by contrast, seem to be similar everywhere. "With the development of drunkenness and alcoholism in subpopulations, we observe the increase of psychic degradation and asocial behavior, and the loss of originality of alcohol customs and alcohol culture" (Sidorov 1995, 247).

For simplicity, we may distinguish three levels of alcohol consumption: zero (abstention), moderate, and heavy. On any given occasion, heavy drinking may have undesirable consequences of various kinds, such as traffic accidents caused by drunk driving or violent behavior due to the disinhibiting effects of alcohol. Sustained heavy drinking over time has a different range of undesirable consequences. Whereas some of the medical harms caused by regular heavy use take a long time to develop and may well go unnoticed altogether, others emerge more rapidly and are clearly visible. A person may drink so heavily that he is unable to keep his job, or his family life may go to pieces because of his heavy drinking.

If social norms were invariably utilitarian, we might expect them to be directed against heavy drinking that is perceived to have harmful short-term or long-term consequences for the drinking individual or for others. There are indeed many norms of this kind. Some of them, usually linked to religion, enjoin total abstention. Islam and certain Protestant sects, for instance, have absolute bans on alcohol. Secular norms, by contrast, often enjoin drinking in moderation. The Italian norm, to never drink between meals, has the dual effect of limiting total consumption and reducing the rate of absorption of alcohol into the body, thus buffering the short-term effect on the body. In Iceland, there are norms against drinking in the presence of the children and against drinking on fishing trips. Again, the norms have a dual function. In addition to reducing total consumption, they prevent undesirable effects on child rearing or work accidents.

Scandinavian countries more generally are governed by the following principles: "Drinking and working are kept strictly separate; drinking is still not integrated with everyday meals; and the main normative division tends to be one between non-drinking situations and situations where not only drinking but intoxication as well is culturally accepted" (Mäkelä 1986, 26). In these countries, there are also strong norms against drunken driving. Further norms regulate consumption of alcohol by providing narrow definitions of socially appropriate occasions for heavy drinking. MacAndrew and Edgerton (1969) give many examples to show how alcohol consumption and its effects may be regulated and limited by social norms. In some societies, there are norms that condemn heavy drinking on any occasion. Among Jews, especially in the Diaspora, drunkenness is often seen as characteristic of Gentiles. Similarly,

Spaniards hold a cultural prejudice against intoxication, drunkenness being a sort of ethnic boundary attributed to outsiders. In fact, Spaniards derived a sense of superiority over northern Europeans and over the natives they ruled in their colonies because of their "civilized" attitude toward drinking. In colonial Mexico . . . local Spanish officials saw excessive drinking as a custom that supported their view of Mexicans as "perpetual minors," incapable of conforming to Spanish standards of moderation. (Gamella 1995, 365)

In Italy there is also a strong opprobrium attached to being drunk in public, not so much because heavy drinking is seen as harmful as because it shows a deplorable lack of self-control.

Alcohol-related norms are not, however, always utilitarian. There are norms that condemn abstention as well as norms that enjoin people to drink heavily. Among the Mapuche Indians of Chile, drinking alone is criticized and so is abstention; such behavior is seen as showing lack of trust. The traditional French culture condemns both the teetotaler and the drunkard. In Italy, distrust of abstainers is expressed in a proverb: May God protect me from those who do not drink. In the American colonial period, abstainers were often suspect (but drinking problems were infrequent). In youth subcultures of many countries, abstainers are subject to heavy pressure and ridicule. Conversely, there are many societies in which heavy drinking is socially prescribed. In Mexico and Nigeria, the macho qualities shown in the ability to drink heavily are much admired. In prerevolutionary Russia, excessive drinking was obligatory in the subculture of young officers. Among the Polish gentry, "drinking was a manifestation of an idle lifestyle and wealth. Heavy drinking seemed to be not only a right but almost a duty of a nobleman. A host used to urge his guests to drink heavily and felt offended if they refused" (Moskalewicz and Zielinski 1995, 228).

When abstention is condemned or when heavy drinking is socially mandatory, would-be abstainers may have to resort to subterfuge. In Sweden, "a common question is, 'Do you want sherry, or are you driving?' It is so accepted that abstaining alcoholics often say they are driving because this relieves them of the social pressure that otherwise would certainly be exerted by the host to convince the guest to have a drink" (Nyberg and Allebeck 1995, 286–87). The norm of drinking can only be offset by another norm (against drunk driving). Similarly, it has been argued that conversions to Protestantism "provide an alternative for some Latin Americans who want to opt out of the costly and time-consuming civil-religious hierarchy of community governance in which even secular rituals often involve heavy drinking and drunkenness" (Heath 1995, 344). Again, the norm of drinking can only be overridden by another norm, which in this case has the backing of religion.

These are cases of the strategic use of norms. Conversely, people can behave strategically to get around the norms. Thus "some ancient Chinese considered alcohol itself to be sacred, and drank it only in sacrificial ceremonies; eventually, they would sacrifice whenever they wanted to drink" (Zhang 1995, 41). In Spain, "at certain hours, not to drink on an empty stomach is a tacit cultural prescription, and food, even a morsel, will be included with the drinking" (Gamella 1995, 261). In both cases, we observe a reverse of the original causal link: Rather than drinking when they are doing X, people do X whenever they want to have a drink. People who abide by the social norm of not drinking before dinner may find themselves moving dinner forward so as to drink more and still be able to tell themselves (and others) that the norm is respected. Although such strategies do not render the norms entirely ineffective, they can undermine them.

Moderate drinking reflects a delicate balance between the desire for alcohol and the social norms that keep it within bounds. Since behavior is more easily learned and imitated than norms, one might expect excessive drinking when a drinking and a nondrinking culture meet. The excessive drinking by natives in colonial Mexico may be due to this fact. The same mechanism applies to Israeli Arabs:

> Islam prohibits alcohol consumption; the Jewish religion does not but advocates moderation and warns against intoxication. These differences may explain why the incidence of daily drinking is higher among Arab men than Jewish men. The Arab who consumes alcoholic beverages separates himself from his religion and culture and loses his social-religious support. . . . He does not know how to drink and knows little about the nature of alcohol. These factors can contribute to his excessive drinking. (Weiss 1995, 150)

Alcohol-related norms may have counterproductive effects. Parental injunctions against drinking may have the opposite effect of the intended one, for one of several reasons. First, of course, young people very generally tend to oppose their parents. Second, the norms often convey the message that drinking is part of the adult world to which the adolescent desperately wants to belong. Third, people may form a desire to possess something simply because they are told they cannot have it (forbidden fruit) or, conversely, block their desire for it because they are told to consume it (Brehm 1966). Fourth, deliberate attempts to induce shame in others often induce anger and protest behavior rather than shame and avoidance behavior (Elster 1998). Shame is the correlate of spontaneous expressions of contempt, not of deliberate shaming behavior.

These are cases in which norms against drug taking induce drug taking in nonusers. Antidrug norms and values can also sustain the behavior at more advanced stages. Many who are subject to chemical or behavioral addictions incur strong feelings of shame (due to the perceived violation of a social norm) or guilt (due to a perceived violation of a moral norm). The need to blot out the awareness that one is making a mess of one's life can then be an important factor sustaining the behavior. The mechanism plays a role in sustaining not only alcoholism (Orford 1985, 138) but also overeating (Polivy and Herman 1993, 180), compulsive shopping (Baumeister, Heatherton, and Tice 1994, 227), compulsive gambling (Rosenthal and Rugle 1994, 33–34), and nicotine relapse (Lichtenstein and Brown 1980, 194).

Beliefs provide a final source of variation in the consumption of addictive substances. Many social norms are intertwined with beliefs about the effects of consumption. Again, alcohol provides a privileged example, although I also refer to other addictive substances.

The use of alcoholic beverages may be linked to various beliefs about their effects:

> In Nigeria, as in most African countries, alcohol is considered food, a necessary nutrient rich in vitamins, a stimulant and a disinfectant necessary to the body to fight against cold, fear, weariness, and intrusive microbes. . . . Alcohol is justifiedly considered a nutrient because Nigerian palm wine is reported to contain 145 milligrams of ascorbic acid and 100 grams of vitamin C per serving. (Oshodin 1995, 213)

In Italy, too, "wine is seen as nourishment. In the past, the nutritional aspects were particularly relevant in the alimentation of the lower classes, whose poor diet needed precisely those extra calories that wine could provide" (Cottino 1995, 157).

Alcohol has also been used for its superior hygienic properties. In the English Middle Ages, "alcoholic drinks were often safer to consume than water or milk, given the sanitary conditions of the time" (Plant 1995, 290). In contemporary rural Mexico, "good drinking water is less easily accessible than alcohol" (Rey 1995, 184). One may always ask, however, whether the effects of alcohol identified by modern observers are perceived by the consumers and motivate their drinking. Alcohol might simply have nutritional side effects while being consumed for its intoxicating properties.

Alcohol use and alcoholism can be iatrogenic when beer, wine, or liquor are taken or prescribed for their (alleged) medicinal properties:

> The amount of wine used for therapeutic purposes in the hospitals of pre-Revolutionary Russia exceeded its consumption per capita in the healthy population. The problems of alcohol therapy were most dramatic in pediatric practice; often [it] was the doctor who gave children their first wine. (Sidorov 1995, 244)

In France, well into the 1900s it was actually thought that wine could be used to cure alcoholism (Nahoum-Grappe 1995, 83). In French "medical lore from the 1500s to the 1700s, getting drunk was treated as a means of purging the body" (ibid., 80).

As these examples show, many beliefs about the benefits of alcohol are false or dubious. People have also formed various false beliefs about the harmful properties of alcohol and other substances. The great "absinthe scare" provides an example (Sournia 1986, 104–6). There is no scientific basis for believing that this drink, which remains forbidden in all European countries except Great Britain, has any damaging long-term effects over and above those caused by its ethanol content. There are several other cases in which the perception of long-term damage has been overstated, even wildly exaggerated. Zinberg (1984, 154) notes that

> although many controlled users feel that heroin can be used moderately, they regard it as more rapidly addicting than is warranted by the pharmacology of the drug. This attitude, of course, is understandable in view of the prevailing myths about heroin's power as well as the exposure of controlled users to addicts who have succumbed to the drug.

More radical examples are provided by the Victorian writer who describes the long-term effects of coffee as follows: "The sufferer is tremulous and loses his self-command; he is subject to fits of agitation and depression. He has a haggard appearance. As with other such agents, a renewed dose of the poison gives temporary relief, but at the cost of future misery." He describes the effects of tea in equally dramatic terms: "An hour or two after breakfast at which tea has been taken a grievous sinking feeling may seize upon the sufferer so that to speak is an effort. The speech may become weak and vague. By miseries such as these, the best years of life may be spoilt" (cited in Orford 1985, 73). Many beliefs about short-term harms are equally unfounded. Thus MacAndrew and Edgerton (1969) note that, although many modern writers argue that heavy drinking always causes disinhibition and loss of control, in many societies people do in fact drink heavily without any such consequences.

Conversely, harmful drugs may be seen as harmless. Whereas the misperception of short-term harm is unlikely, long-term damage may well go unnoticed. In some cases, it may essentially be unnoticeable. Asking why the skilled clinicians of antiquity failed to notice the organic lesions caused by alcohol, Jean-Charles Sournia (1986, 20) answers that the failure was

> linked to the average life span of people at the time, probably about forty years. Cirrhosis of the liver, lesions of the pancreas, and alcohol-induced cancers take several decades of intoxication before they manifest them-

selves, and even though some persons may be affected at a younger age the number of clinical cases was probably too small to attract the attention of doctors.

In other cases, the causal link is finally uncovered but only with some delay. Thus the rapid increase in lung cancer between 1920 and 1950 was initially imputed to pollution rather than to the true culprit, smoking (Goldstein 1994, 106–7). These examples concern only organic damage. There is much less uncertainty or ignorance attached to the often disastrous long-term effect of alcohol, heroin abuse, or compulsive gambling on the addict's financial and social situation. The addict himself may deny or deceive himself about these effects, but observers are unlikely to do so.

A particularly important set of beliefs is the idea that a given substance is addictive. Once a behavioral pattern is conceptualized as an addiction, with the concomitant causal beliefs, it may change dramatically. An especially important belief is that addiction is, if not irresistible, at least very hard to resist, almost amounting to compulsive desire. Hence, to the causal beliefs about the effects of drug taking on the addict's body and socioeconomic status, we must add causal beliefs about the effect of addiction on his will—specifically, on the ability to quit. Two opposite beliefs about this effect may have the same impact on behavior. Some addicts use their (usually self-deceptive) belief that they can quit at any time as an excuse for not quitting. Others use their (equally self-deceptive) belief that they are unable to quit as an excuse for not quitting. The belief that one is addicted may reinforce the addiction by the mechanism of dissonance reduction:

> Counter-attitudinal behaviour (e.g., continued smoking in spite of acknowledgement of dangers to health) is not necessarily dissonance-arousing for individuals who see their behaviour as beyond their voluntary control (e.g., who say "I can't help myself"), or who selectively reduce their self-esteem (e.g., who say "I haven't the will-power"). In terms of this interpretation, "dissonant" smokers are not in a state of unresolved dissonance, once they label themselves as addicted. It may well be, then, that many smokers are motivated to see themselves as addicts. . . . As more smokers come to acknowledge the health risks of smoking, it is to be expected that they will become non-smokers or, more probably, that they will seek extra justification for their continued behaviour. To label smoking as an addiction provides such a justification, and hence, in our view, this is not a theme that should be incorporated in health education aimed at the established smoker. (Eiser, Sutton, and Weber 1978, 100, 106)

The concept of addiction, with the concomitant belief that the craving for the drug is near irresistible, is relatively modern. Before 1800, what we would call alcoholism was often perceived as a form of excessive behavior, or gluttony. It was a vice, not a condition. In reality, of course, heavy drinkers were addicted. They died from cirrhosis of the liver, went to great lengths to find the next drink, looked for a drink the first thing in the morning, and so on. They just did not know they were addicted, any more than a young Tahitian whose girlfriend has left him knows that he is depressed. They were what we might call proto-alcoholics—easily recognized by modern observers but not conceptualized as such by those who were subject to it and by those around them. As in the analogous case of the emotions, when the phenomenon was conceptualized, it was also transformed. The idea that an alcohol addict can be cured only by total abstinence, for instance, entails a modification of the temporal pattern of drinking, with periods of abstinence alternating with bingeing. Once the would-be reformed alcoholic has had one drink, the belief that it will inevitably bring about total relapse becomes self-fulfilling. Conversely, of course, that very same belief may also prevent him from taking the first drink. The belief can change behavior for the better or for the worse.

The modern concept of addiction may give rise to iatrogenic forms of the condition, as suggested by the following passages:

It has generally been assumed by alcoholism treatment personnel in most industrialized countries that the disease-labeling process and the alcoholic's concomitant acceptance of the "sick" role would facilitate treatment and potentiate the chances of rehabilitation. Some writers . . . however, question the utility of indiscriminate application of the disease label, not only because it may not be appropriate for all varieties of alcohol-related problems, but also because *it may influence the very behavior it attempts to describe*. This could come about . . . by altering the cognitive expectancies held by alcoholics and by those in their immediate social environment, such that the drinker no longer is seen as responsible for his or her behavior. In this view, loss of control over drinking may result more from learned expectations than from physical predispositions, and chronic alcoholism more from a dependency role than from physiological dependence.

Another source of influence on alcoholics is the treatment process itself, since a major goal of treatment, especially in the U.S., is to convince the alcoholic of the validity of the disease concept, and to remove the personal stigma associated with the negative stereotype of the alcoholic. (Babor et al. 1986, 99, 107; my italics).

Choice, Emotion, and Addiction

Choice-oriented behavior is not the same as rational behavior. By the former, I simply mean behavior that is sensitive to rewards and punishments. By the latter, I mean behavior that fits into a complex pattern of optimization: The behavior must be optimal, given the desires and beliefs of the agent; the beliefs must be optimal, given the available evidence; and the investment in evidence acquisition must be optimal, given the beliefs and the desires.

Minimal and Rational Choice

We may think of behavior that is choice oriented but not rational as guided by *minimal choice*. Minimal choice is consistent with irrationality at each of the three levels of optimization. A person may be sensitive to the expected rewards from action even if the expectations are formed in an irrational manner or based on suboptimal investment in information. Moreover, reward sensitivity is consistent with failure to choose the best means to realize one's desires, given the beliefs. Suppose a person is tempted to embezzle money from his firm, although he believes that all things considered it is more prudent to abstain. We may imagine that he sticks to his decision until, one day, he finds himself in a position to embezzle a very large amount. He continues to believe that, all things considered, he should not do it, but the temptation is now so strong that it overrides his all-things-considered judgment. By construction, he is both reward sensitive and akratic—he conforms to the canons of minimal choice but not to those of rational choice.

We may ask whether there could be action that is not choice oriented or reward sensitive at all. For this to be the case, there would have to be a pair of options A and B such that the agent would choose A even if doing so would (be expected to) produce indefinitely large negative consequences, occurring with an indefinitely short delay and even if doing B would (be expected to) produce indefinitely large positive consequences occurring with an indefinitely short delay. Moreover, doing A would have to be an *action*—a deliberate bodily movement for the purpose of obtaining some goal—rather than a mere reflex behavior.

To illustrate this case, we may imagine a person in a lifeboat whose horrible thirst causes him to drink seawater. Although he knows that the seawater will cause him to die much more quickly than if he abstained, he is unable to abstain. In that case, we might want to say that his desire is irresistible and that he has no choice. The agent, we may assume, is disabled by thirst from paying attention to alternative actions and to long-term consequences of the action that is favored by the compulsive desire for water. The only thought in his mind is that an urgent discomfort will be relieved by drinking seawater. If the effect of a desire or a craving is to make some options and consequences disappear from the cognitive horizon of the agent, there is a real sense in which he has no choice. The agent is like a horse with blinkers, unable to detect and hence to react to dangers coming from outside his narrow field of attention.

Emotion and Choice

The relation between emotion and choice has several aspects (Elster 1998). Can one choose one's emotional experiences? Do the emotions detract from the rationality of choice or, on the contrary, enhance it? Can strong emotions preempt choice altogether, as in the case of the thirsty castaway?

It has been argued that emotions are chosen (Sartre 1936; Schafer 1976; Hochschild 1983; Solomon 1993), from which it would follow that they are capable of being assessed as rational or irrational (only Solomon draws this consequence). The argument goes against the traditional view that emotions are passively undergone (whence the word passion) rather than actively chosen. There is no doubt that some people can control their emotions or can call them up in themselves either by imagining situations in which they typically occur or by simulating their typical expressions, which may then induce the real emotion by feedback. (See also Ainslie, this volume.) Concerning the first mechanism, Hochschild (1983, 25) tells about how one air stewardess handles angry passengers without getting angry herself: "I pretend something traumatic has happened in their lives. Once I had an irate that was complaining about me, cursing at me, threatening to get my name and report me to the company. I later found out that his son had just died. Now when I meet an irate I think of that man." Concerning the second, Montaigne (1991, 638, 944) notes that preachers, professional mourners, and lawyers have the capacity to be moved by the words or expressions they are paid to produce. Yet in general, I believe the traditional view is right. The capacity to produce emotions at will is parasitic on their spontaneous occurrence. (For a fuller discussion, see Elster, 1999b.)

Another aspect of the traditional view is to oppose passion and reason and to argue that the former tends to subvert the latter. The conception of reason that we find in the ancient and modern moralists is not, however, the same as the modern idea of rationality. Roughly speaking, reason was seen as the ability to perceive and act on a conception of what is objectively good—for the individual or for the community. By contrast, rationality consists in the ability to act efficiently to realize the subjective desires of the agent. Emotion is an obstacle to reason if it enters into the formation of desires but is an obstacle to rationality only if it affects their implementation. Thus the person who pursues vengeance from an emotion of anger is acting contrary to reason but is not necessarily irrational, unless the anger makes him less efficient in pursuing his goal. No lengthy argument is needed to show that emotions can indeed detract from the instrumental efficacy of action. "Emotions can provide a meaning and a sense of direction to life but they also prevent us from going steadily in that direction" (Elster 1989b, 70).

There is, however, an emerging literature that argues that emotions can improve the quality of choice by serving as tiebreakers or, more generally, by enabling us to make decisions when the theory of rational choice fails to tell us what to do. This argument has been expounded in a book by Antonio Damasio (1994) and independently by other philosophers, psychologists, and neurobiologists (Sousa 1987; Johnson-Laird and Oatley 1992; LeDoux 1996). These writers argue that when there is an urgent need to make a decision, such as figuring out how to deal with a shape in the dark that might be a branch and might be a snake, rational choice theory is unhelpful. It tells us to scrutinize all available alternatives and all possible outcomes of each alternative and then apply the apparatus of utility maximization. Before you have completed this process, the snake, if there is one, may have gotten to you. Fortunately, they argue, our emotions help us to short-circuit this process. We freeze out of fear and thus gain the time we need to consider the process more carefully. As LeDoux (1996, 176) says, "In responding first with its most-likely-to-succeed behavior, the brain buys time."

These authors all assume that rationality amounts to what I elsewhere (Elster 1989a, 117) metaphorically call an *addiction to reason*. Some people do indeed have a craving to make all decisions on the basis of "just" or sufficient reasons (Shafir, Simonson, and Tversky 1993). That, however, makes them irrational rather than rational. A rational person would know that under certain conditions it is better to follow a simple mechanical decision rule than to use more elaborate procedures with higher opportunity costs. In many cases, the organism might cope perfectly well by adopting and following mechanical decision rules, such as *When you hear a sound you cannot identify, stand still,* or *When food tastes bitter, spit it out.* In reality, of course, that is not how we cope with novelty or bitter-tasting food—not because the program is unfeasible but because natural selection has wired us differently.

We may ask, finally, whether emotion can short-circuit the process of choice, altogether, by blocking the consideration of alternatives and consequences. Anger, fear, and sexual arousal (if we count that as an emotion) have all been cited as examples of emotions that can override considerations of self-interest and even survival. Yet the most striking example is perhaps provided by the capacity of shame to induce suicide. After a crackdown on pedophilia in France in 1997, for example, six accused individuals killed themselves. Intense feelings of shame tend to blot out any consideration of the future. In extreme cases, the person suffering from strong feelings of shame may not think beyond the present moment at all. All he wants is immediate release.

Addiction and Choice

We may distinguish two questions regarding addiction and choice. First, once individuals *are* addicted, does the condition affect their capacity for (rational) choice behavior? Second, do individuals *become* addicted as a result of (possibly rational) choice? Even assuming that addicts are irrational or reward insensitive, their state of addiction could still be the outcome of a rational choice, if the costs implied by irrationality or reward insensitivity were anticipated from the outset, on a par with medical risks and other harmful consequences of drug use.

As in the case of emotion, no lengthy argument is needed to conclude that individuals in a state of addiction often behave irrationally. This applies to within-episode as well as to between-episode behavior. When "under the influence," an alcoholic may discount the future more heavily (O'Donoghue and Rabin, this volume) as well as suffer other forms of "alcohol myopia" (Steele and Josephs 1990). In the middle of a binge, a cocaine addict may forget an earlier resolve to consume in moderation (Gardner and David 1999). Between episodes of consumption, addicts may engage in various forms of denial, rationalization, and self-deception to justify continued use. Even when fully aware of the dangers of drug use and determined to abstain, they may suffer weakness of will leading to relapse.

A more complicated issue is whether addiction can preempt choice altogether and induce "compulsive drug taking" (see Watson, this volume). Frank Gawin (1991, 1581) writes that "cocaine addicts report that virtually all thoughts are focused on cocaine during binges; nourishment, sleep, money, loved ones, responsibility and survival lose all significance." The passage from Benjamin Rush cited in the introduction to this volume makes the point even more vividly. If taken literally, these passages suggest that addicts can be insensitive to all other rewards than the drug. Needless to say, however, nobody has actually carried out an experiment in which, as in the example for Rush, an alcoholic has to expose himself to cannonballs criss-crossing the room. My hunch is that the capacity of addiction to blot out other considerations is less than that of strong emotions, because addiction affects a more superficial, or peripheral, part of the self.

Independently of the impact of addiction on rationality and reward sensitivity, we may ask whether the state may be the result of a choice— even a rational choice—to become addicted. Among the three choice-theoretic approaches to this issue, one assumes rational choice under certainty (Becker and Murphy 1988), another rational choice under risk (Orphanides and Zervos 1995), and a third that we may call "choice under

ignorance" (Herrnstein and Prelec 1992), which may or may not be rational, depending on whether the ignorance is rational or not. Each model
probably corresponds to some addictive careers, although none of them
in my opinion places enough weight on the cognitive distortions that facilitate the path to addiction. For the heavy drinker to become a problem
drinker and then an alcoholic, he usually has to persuade himself that his
problem is less serious than it actually is. Smokers tend to underestimate
the medical risks and gamblers to overestimate the chances of winning.
Whether these biases are exogenous and present from the beginning or
endogenous to the incipient addiction itself, they often play a decisive role
in the development of the full-blown addictive state.

Interaction of Neurobiology, Culture, and Choice

I now consider how these three explanatory factors may interact to generate some of the characteristic patterns of emotional and addictive phenomena in human beings.

Emotion

Because of the common neurobiological mechanisms and the different
levels of cognitive, moral, and social development, we would expect
similarities as well as differences between animal and human emotions.
There is a core of hard-wired emotions—anger, fear, parental love, sympathy, curiosity, surprise—that are common to humans and primates,
and at least some of these are also present in lower animals. By far the
most intensively studied of these emotions is fear (Marks 1987; Gray
1991; LeDoux 1996), the most striking finding being that this emotion
may be triggered by a mere perception without any cognitive processing. There are two pathways from the sensory apparatus in the thalamus to the amygdala, the part of the brain that causes visceral as well as
behavioral emotional responses. In accordance with the traditional view
that emotions are always preceded and triggered by a cognition, one
pathway goes from the thalamus to the neocortex, the thinking part of
the brain, and from the neocortex onward to the amygdala. The organism receives a signal, forms a belief about what it means, and then reacts
emotionally. There is also, however, a direct pathway from the thalamus
to the amygdala that bypasses the thinking part of the brain entirely.
Compared to the first pathway, the second is "quick and dirty." On the
one hand, it is faster. "In a rat it takes about twelve milliseconds (twelve
one-thousandths of a second) for an acoustic stimulus to reach the amygdala through the thalamic pathway, and almost twice as long through
the cortical pathway" (LeDoux 1996, 163). On the other hand, the sec-

ond pathway differentiates less finely among incoming signals. Whereas the cortex can figure out that a slender curved shape on a path through the wood is a curved stick rather than a snake, the amygdala cannot make this distinction.

In most humans in most contemporary societies, the quick and dirty path is relatively unimportant. Success and survival do not turn heavily on split-second decisions. Instead, decisions and the concomitant emotions depend crucially on prior cognitive processing of the situation. In animals other than humans, it is often difficult to decide whether what looks like an emotional reaction is triggered by a mental representation of the situation or whether it is merely a learned response. The apparent guilt of the dog that has shredded the newspaper in its owner's absence may simply be a conditioned fear of punishment, since the same response is produced when the owner himself shreds the newspaper and leaves it on the floor (Vollmer 1977).

In people, though, belief-induced emotions are certainly all-important. Moreover, many of the emotions that matter most in our lives are triggered by beliefs about mental states rather than by beliefs about observable phenomena. As far as I know, there is no conclusive evidence that animals other than humans are capable of forming beliefs about mental states, be it their own or those of other animals (or humans). To the extent that the beliefs are themselves about emotions—one's own or those of other people—culture plays an important mediating role by virtue of two main mechanisms. On the one hand, culture provides a cognitive label that enables us to identify the emotion in ourselves or others. On the other hand, culture provides the social norms and values that enter into our assessment of emotions as good or bad. We are supposed to be happy on our wedding day and to feel grief at funerals.

These normative expectations create a paradox. The emotions are largely outside our conscious control. There does not seem to be much point in social norms enjoining people to have or not to have certain emotions if they have no choice in the matter. Yet there is some room for choice even here. To some extent, we can call up emotions at will, by imagining situations in which they occur spontaneously or by simulating their expression. Also, in many cases all that is required is a reasonably credible simulation. To conform with the social norms regulating funerals, it is not necessary to make people believe that you are actually mourning—it is enough to put your face in the appropriately serious folds.

Addiction

Because of the common neurobiological mechanisms and the different levels of cognitive, moral, and social development, we would expect similarities as well as differences between animal and human addiction. Thus Eliot Gardner and James David (1999) write that "at the very outset and at late stages of recovery from drug addiction, humans are perhaps less similar to laboratory animals. But during the active addictive phase, and during both the acute and short-term withdrawal and abstinence phases, we are perhaps most similar to laboratory animals." Although I largely agree with this assessment, there are also some mechanisms sustaining the active addictive phase that are uniquely human.

Following the Gardner-David trichotomy of stages, let me begin with initiation. Because animals do not get addicted in the wild, their initiation into addiction is always forced by laboratory procedures. Humans, by contrast, can get hooked spontaneously. There are instances of people being manipulated into an addictive state, but they are exceptions. Although the pathways to addiction are numerous and varied, a few general categories stand out. Some individuals drift into addiction more or less by accident. This is the "primrose path" to addiction (Herrnstein and Prelec 1992). Some start consuming because of social pressure (conformism), others because they think consumption of a forbidden or discouraged substance is a sign of independence and adulthood (anticonformism). Some may try drugs out of curiosity, to see what these allegedly mind-blowing experiences really are like. A very general motivation is the need to distract oneself—to escape from a humdrum life or to avoid having to be alone with oneself. Pascal, for instance, explains gambling in terms of the need for "divertissement" (Elster 1999c).

In the second stage, that of active addiction, we find the various phenomenological features enumerated earlier. In the case of chemical addictions, some features are induced quite directly by the pharmacological effects of the drugs. Yet even in the second stage, addiction may be strengthened by cognitive mechanisms. I have already mentioned the very general fact that the knowledge that one is addicted may induce feelings of guilt and shame, which can be alleviated by indulging further in the addictive behavior. In addition, some individuals may be motivated to see themselves as addicts because that label provides a convenient excuse for continuing to engage in the addictive behavior. Animals that live in water have a sleek shape in common, regardless of their evolutionary history. Similarly, people who feel strong cravings to do something that they think they should not do may have certain behavioral patterns in common, regardless of the proximate or ultimate cause of the craving.

The third stage in the addictive career is that of fighting the addiction, trying to quit, and preventing relapse. Again, these activities presuppose awareness that one is addicted. Given this awareness, the mental and behavioral strategies deployed are largely the same for all addictions, be they chemical or behavioral. There is a limited repertoire of precommit-ment strategies that are used more or less across the board, with varia-tions, corresponding to the specific nature of the addictive behavior. Treatments, too, fall in a limited number of general categories, again with local variations. Even at this stage, neurobiology remains important. Gardner and David (1999) write that "a series of virtually insurmountable neurobiological hurdles are erected in the path of drug addicts wishing to stay abstinent," notably heightened vulnerability due to prior drug use, cross-vulnerability to other drugs, and cue-dependent cravings. The last obstacle arises for behavioral as well as for chemical addictions. The gam-bler or the binge eater is as vulnerable as the heroin addict to the condi-tioning effect of the environment associated with the addictive behavior.

In this story, neurobiology plays an important role in the second and third stages. The euphoria or dysphoria induced by consuming or abstaining are strongly motivating states with an indisputable physio-logical basis. Before the appearance of the negative effects of drug con-sumption, they provide positive and negative reinforcements that propel the addict forward on his path. Once these effects appear and he tries to quit, the physiological phenomena of conditioned craving, tolerance, and withdrawal can easily undermine his resolve.

Choice is especially important in the first and third stages. In the first stage, choices are often naive, in the sense that the user is unaware of the risks he is running. If he is "meliorating" rather than "maximizing" (Herrnstein and Prelec 1992), ignoring the "internalities" that one con-sumption decision may impose on the welfare derived from later con-sumption, we may or may not characterize him as irrational. To the extent that the tendency to meliorate is seen as a hardwired feature of the organism, the claim that it is irrational may seem unwarranted. On the other hand, the smoker—to take one example—has available to him all the information he needs to form the correct belief about the inter-nalities, and many people do in fact form the belief after a while. Failure to do so is a form of belief irrationality. Yet much hinges on the clause "after a while." If the smoker gets addicted so fast that he lacks the infor-mation he would need to understand the internality mechanism, he is subject to bad luck rather than to irrationality. This being said, given the amount of publicity about the effects of smoking, it is unlikely that a beginning smoker would have no idea about the danger of addiction. There may be cases in which it is rational to start on an addictive career even when one has full and accurate knowledge about the consequences, but I believe they are rare.

At the second stage, addicts obviously continue to make choices, yet they are increasingly vulnerable to irrational forces. In theory, one might argue that, while craving, tolerance, withdrawal, conditioning, and similar phenomena change the parameters of choice, they need not undermine the possibility of rational choice. One could see the addict as making optimal choices within the modified reward structure induced by the action of drugs. One view of the pharmacological action of drugs is that *they affect only the reward structure facing the individual, while leaving the capacity for making rational choices unaffected.* In an alternative and more plausible view, drugs *affect not only the reward structure facing the individual but also the capacity for making rational choices.* Because the action of drugs is intimately connected with volitional centers in the brain, it might give rise to one or several of the known forms of irrationality, notably weakness of will or wishful thinking. The effect might be so strong as to undermine the capacity to make choice altogether, notably during consumption binges.

At the third stage, choices are more sophisticated. Would-be quitters are subject to "imperfect rationality" (Elster 1984): They are weak and know it. Although some individuals may simply decide that quitting is the rational thing to do and then proceed to execute that decision, most people need to take precautions against their predictable tendency to relapse. They can notably

- Ask for treatment.
- Seek the help of others who are in the same predicament.
- Make access to the drug physically impossible or subject to delay.
- Impose costs on themselves for relapsing or reward themselves for not doing so.
- Avoid exposure to cues that might trigger conditioned craving.
- Try to extinguish the conditioning.
- Try to change preferences by aversion therapy or hypnosis.

Culture, finally, plays an important role in all stages. Again, it does so by virtue of two main mechanisms. On the one hand, culture provides the cognitive label of addiction, together with a number of concomitant causal prototheories. On the other hand, culture provides the values and norms that may label potentially addictive behaviors as desirable and actual addiction as undesirable. The peer pressure that causes a teenager to start consuming depends heavily on prevailing social norms. As one addict in El Barrio said about his school days, "Everybody was wild, and I wanted to be with the wild crowd, because I liked it. I didn't want to be a nerd, or nothing like that. I figured it was wise, so being wild became a habit" (Bourgois 1995, 194). Once a person has become addicted, the stigma that a given society attaches to the addiction, be it heavy drinking or smoking, may induce shame or guilt that the person tries to alleviate by engaging in the very activities that are stigmatized. Also, the addict may use the culturally provided label addiction as an excuse to persist in his behavior—he just cannot help it! At the third stage, culture may push him out of addiction, for instance by virtue of the stigma attached to smoking in affluent Western societies.

Conclusion

Many emotions and addictions involve strong feelings, characterized by physical arousal and negative or positive affect. They share these features with other states of the organism, such as pain or sexual arousal. As Loewenstein argues, these visceral states have many similar effects on cognition and behavior. Intense pain, intense shame, intense sexual arousal, or intense craving for cocaine have in common a capacity to derail the agent from his normal mode of functioning and to induce behaviors that go against what external observers and the agent himself, before and after the visceral experience, would deem to be in his best interest.

Some visceral states are essentially independent of, and impermeable to, external or internal influences. Nobody to my knowledge has attempted to argue that pain is a social construction. George Ainslie's claim (this volume) that pain and other "visceral factors" are *chosen* because of the short-term reward they offer to the agent, although intriguing, is not supported by direct evidence. The need to relieve a full bladder is similarly independent of culture or choice. Although these visceral disturbances can affect cognition and behavior, their origin is entirely physical. This statement does not imply that their impact on cognition and behavior is mind independent. The fact that some people refuse to talk under severe torture shows that the need to relieve intense pain need not be irresistible. The driver who feels an overwhelming drowsiness coming over him may be able to stay awake by pinching himself in the arm, thus using one visceral factor to counteract another. Visceral factors do not affect the capacity for purposive behavior in the manner of Alzheimer's disease, which acts on the core of the mind not merely on its periphery. These are metaphors, but the contrast should be clear.

Euphoric or dysphoric states associated with emotion are, by and large, triggered by beliefs. Euphoric or dysphoric states associated with addiction are, by and large, triggered by the injection of a chemical substance and by its disappearance from the body. Although extremely different in origin, the phenomenology of the states can be quite similar. The subjective effects of amphetamine and of love are quite similar—not only the hedonic aspects but nonhedonic aspects as well, such as reduced need for sleep or food. The difference is that the person who is in love can only think about one thing, whereas amphetamine can enhance concentration on any activity.

Beliefs can also have a role in the etiology of addictive states. Most obviously, beliefs matter for craving. A patient who has received morphine in the hospital and feels the typical withdrawal symptoms upon release will not crave the drug if he is unaware that his suffering is caused by drug abstinence and can be relieved by drug use. Beliefs can also matter for the state of dysphoria that generates the craving. Although I am unaware of systematic studies on the subject, casual observation and introspection suggest that when the agent believes that the substance is unavailable, or that its use will be subject to immediate sanctioning, the craving subsides. In addition to Goldstein's skier example cited in the introduction to this volume, one may cite the fact that some heavy smokers have little difficulty going without cigarettes on transatlantic flights if smoking is forbidden yet feel intense craving once they approach an area where they can smoke.

Whatever the importance of belief-dependent cravings, cue dependence is a very central and well-documented mechanism. By the mechanism of conditioned learning, addicts may experience euphoria, dysphoria, and craving at the mere sight or smell of an environment associated with their consumption. An ex-addict can go into relapse simply by watching a television program about addiction. The same mechanism—sensory cues invested with significance through associative learning—can also trigger emotion. As LeDoux shows, a conditioned stimulus may even trigger emotions such as fear when there is no conscious memory of the event that established the association. In fact, very traumatic events may have the dual effect of creating strong emotional or implicit memories that can recreate the emotion under the appropriate circumstances *and* of preventing the formation of conscious or explicit memories. If this hypothesis is verified, Freud will have been proved wrong: Lack of memory about traumatic events cannot be due to repression if the memory has not been formed in the first place.

The causal origin of the link between perception and emotion may also be found in evolution rather than in associative learning. A snakelike shape on the path may trigger an emotion of fear and a behavioral response of freezing because this is what evolution has programmed to happen. Cue-dependence cravings, by contrast, can arise only through learning. Cravings, unlike emotions, are artificial phenomena. For one thing, animal addiction does not occur spontaneously in the wild, and in some human groups addiction does not exist. For another, evolution has not produced a specialized neurophysiological machinery for responding to addictive substances. Instead, addiction occurs when and

Figure 8.3

	Emotions triggered by	Cravings triggered by
Cognition	Complex emotions	Belief-dependent cravings
Perception	Fear Aesthetic emotions	Cue-dependent cravings

because a chemical substance happens to fit into the brain reward system that evolved to ensure the motivation of the organism to satisfy basic needs of food, drink, and sex.

From a conceptual point of view, it is important to emphasize that emotions can be triggered by perception in which no cognitive content (in the form of propositional beliefs) is involved. In addition to fear and perhaps a few other very basic emotions, the aesthetic emotions also illustrate this idea. This being said, the more complex emotions are mostly triggered by beliefs rather than by perception. With cravings, it is the other way around. Whereas cue dependence is a massively important mechanism, belief dependence is probably marginal. The discussion is summarized in figure 8.3, with the most prominent cases circled.

This typology presupposes that the emotion or craving is initially absent and then is suddenly triggered by some external event. The states are characterized by sudden onset, unbidden occurrence, and brief duration. Yet *strong feelings are not necessarily transient*. Emotions such as love or wrath (the emotional desire for revenge) can persist for years or decades unless and until they are satisfied. An emotion can serve as the organizing principle of a life. Some addicts, too, are in a more or less constant state of craving. The life of the alcoholic, the heroin addict, or the compulsive gambler is organized around getting to the next drink, the next fix, or a source of gambling funds. Citing Herbert Fingarette and Francis Seeburger, Gary Watson (this volume) refers to this form of addiction as "existential dependence."

Addicts get their ideas about the nature of addiction and relapse from their environment. In addition to causal beliefs, the environment also provides them with norms and values. The beliefs, norms, and values differ across and within societies. The ordinary overweight person, for instance, will often be found in cultures and subcultures less concerned with body weight and slimness than is the case among professionals in contemporary Western societies. For many people in the past, for instance, the prospect of gaining weight as they grew older was seen as normal and (at least for men) even desirable. As values change and as people acquire ever more complex causal beliefs about the relationship among food intake, weight, and health, new patterns of weight change emerge. In addition to the serious eating disturbances of anorexia nervosa and bulimia, there are numerous off-on dieters whose weight pattern somewhat resembles that of bulimics. Charting drinking patterns before and after the "discovery of alcoholism" would probably yield qualitatively similar results. As in the case of eating disorders, the key explanatory variable is the emergence of *ambivalence* caused by the conflict between the craving to consume and the social disapproval of consumption.

Occurrent emotions as well as emotional dispositions are also very much the subject of normative assessments. Again, there is much cultural variation. A society that does not explicitly label and conceptualize a given emotion cannot harbor positive or negative attitudes toward it, either. In addition, even if the emotion is acknowledged as such, normative attitudes toward it may vary a great deal. What we would view as the overbearing and intolerable pride of Renaissance kings or princes was accepted as their due at the time. Whereas we tend to condemn an unbridled passion for revenge, other societies have condemned those who did not feel it on the appropriate occasion. In one society, people may feel and show contempt for disfigured or obese individuals, whereas in another that attitude itself would be met with contempt.

The common features of emotion and addiction must be seen against the background of two important differences. Emotions are natural and universal. Without asserting that there are some emotions that are found in all societies, it can be safely said that all societies feature some emotions. Addiction is artificial and nonuniversal, an accident of the interaction between brain reward machinery evolved for other purposes and certain chemical substances. At the same time, emotions are much more belief dependent than addictive cravings and drug-induced states. Because social life is embedded in an extraordinarily dense network of beliefs, emotions are central to all human activities. In comparison, the role of cognition and even perception in addiction is sharply limited.

Yet, some mysteries remain. Why is the amygdala centrally involved in addiction as well as in emotion (Gardner, this volume)? Why are love and amphetamine, so different in their causes, so similar in their effects?

How do guilt and shame from drug use interact with the dysphoria induced by withdrawal? Why do we sometimes have the impression that a person is addicted to the emotion of righteous indignation, seeking out or even creating occasions that will produce it? Beneath the differences, there may be further similarities that we do not yet understand.

References

Ainslie, George. 1992. *Picoeconomics: The Strategic Interaction of Successive Motivational States Within the Person.* Cambridge: Cambridge University Press.

Babor, Thomas F., et al. 1986. "Concepts of Alcoholism Among American, French-Canadian, and French Alcoholics." In *Alcohol and Culture: Comparative Perspectives from Europe and America,* edited by Thomas F. Babor. New York: New York Academy of Sciences.

Baumeister, Roy F., Todd F. Heatherton, and Diane M. Tice. 1994. *Losing Control: How and Why People Fail at Self-Regulation.* San Diego: Academic.

Becker, Gary. 1996. *Accounting for Tastes.* Cambridge: Harvard University Press.

Becker, Gary, and Kevin Murphy. 1988. "A Theory of Rational Addiction." *Journal of Political Economy* 96: 675–700.

Bourgois, Philippe. 1995. *In Search of Respect.* Cambridge University Press.

Brehm, Jack. 1966. *A Theory of Psychological Reactance.* New York: Academic.

Budd, Malcolm. 1995. *Values of Art.* London: Allen Lane.

Cameron, Lisa. 1995. "Raising the Stakes in the Ultimatum Game: Experimental Evidence from Indonesia." Working Paper 345. Princeton University, Industrial Relations Section.

Cottino, Amedo. 1995. "Italy." In *International Handbook on Alcohol and Culture,* edited by Dwight B. Heath. Westport, Conn.: Greenwood.

Damasio, Antonio. 1994. *Descartes' Error.* New York: Putnam.

Dostoyevsky, Fyodor. 1964. *The Gambler.* New York: Norton.

Eiser, Richard, Stephen Sutton, and Mallory Weber. 1978. "'Consonant' and 'Dissonant' Smokers and the Self-Attribution of Addiction." *Addictive Behaviors* 3: 99–106.

Ekman, Paul. 1992. "An Argument for Basic Emotions." *Cognition and Emotion* 6: 169–200.

Elster, Jon. 1984. *Ulysses and the Sirens.* Cambridge: Cambridge University Press.

———. 1989a. *Solomonic Judgments.* Cambridge: Cambridge University Press.

———. 1989b. *Nuts and Bolts for the Social Sciences.* Cambridge: Cambridge University Press.

———. 1998. "Emotions and Economic Theory." *Journal of Economic Literature* 36: 47–74.

———. 1999a. *Strong Feelings.* Cambridge: MIT Press.

———. 1999b. *Alchemies of the Mind.* Cambridge: Cambridge University Press.

———. 1999c. "Gambling and Addiction." In *Getting Hooked: Rationality and the Addictions,* edited by Jon Elster and Ole-Jørgen Skog. Cambridge: Cambridge University Press.

Frijda, Nico. 1986. *The Emotions.* Cambridge: Cambridge University Press.

Gamella, Juan F. 1995. "Spain." In *International Handbook on Alcohol and Culture*, edited by Dwight B. Heath. Westport, Conn.: Greenwood.

Gardner, Eliot, and James David. 1999. "The Neurobiology of Chemical Addiction." In *Getting Hooked: Rationality and the Addictions*, edited by Jon Elster and Ole-Jørgen Skog. Cambridge: Cambridge University Press.

Gawin, Frank. 1991. "Cocaine Addiction: Psychology and Neurophysiology." *Science* 251: 1580–86.

Goldstein, Avram. 1994. *Addiction*. New York: Freeman.

Goodwin, Donald W., and William F. Gabrielli. 1997. "Alcohol: Clinical Aspects." In *Substance Abuse: A Comprehensive Textbook*, edited by Joyce H. Lowinson, Pedro Ruiz, Robert B. Millman, and John G. Langrod. Baltimore: Williams and Wilkins.

Gray, Jeffrey A. 1991. *The Psychology of Fear and Stress*. Cambridge: Cambridge University Press.

Hall, Roberta L. 1986. "Alcohol Treatment in American Indian Populations." In *Alcohol and Culture: Comparative Perspectives from Europe and America*, edited by Thomas F. Babor. New York: New York Academy of Sciences.

Hamsun, Knut. 1954. "Far og sønn. En spillehistorie" (Father and Son: A Gambling Tale). In *Samlede Verker*, edited by Knut Hamsun. Vol. 4. Oslo: Gyldendal.

Hanson David J. 1995. "The United States of America." In *International Handbook on Alcohol and Culture*, edited by Dwight B. Heath. Westport, Conn.: Greenwood.

Heath, Dwight B. 1995. "An Anthropological View of Alcohol and Culture in International Perspective." In *International Handbook on Alcohol and Culture*, edited by Dwight B. Heath. Westport, Conn.: Greenwood.

Herrnstein, Richard, and Drazen Prelec. 1992. "Melioration." In *Choice over Time*, edited by George Loewenstein and Jon Elster. New York: Russell Sage Foundation.

Hochschild, Arlie R. 1979. "Emotion Work, Feeling Rules, and Social Structure." *American Journal of Sociology* 85: 551–75.

———. 1983. *The Managed Heart*. Berkeley: University of California Press.

Hume, David. 1960. *A Treatise on Human Nature*. Edited by Selby-Bigge. Oxford: Oxford University Press.

James, William. 1950. *The Principles of Psychology*. New York: Dover.

Johnson-Laird. Philip, and Keith Oatley. 1992. "Basic Emotions, Rationality, and Folk Theory." *Cognition and Emotion* 6: 201–23.

LeDoux, Joseph. 1996. *The Emotional Brain*. New York: Simon & Schuster.

Levine, Harry. 1978. "The Discovery of Addiction." *Journal of Studies on Alcohol* 39: 143–74.

Levy, Robert. 1973. *The Tahitians*. Chicago: University of Chicago Press.

Lewis, C. S. 1936. *The Allegory of Love*. Oxford: Oxford University Press.

Lewis, Michael. 1992. *Shame*. New York: Free Press.

Lichtenstein, Edward, and Richard A. Brown. 1980. "Smoking Cessation Methods: Review and Recommendations." In *The Addictive Behaviors*, edited by William R. Miller. Oxford: Pergamon.

Liebowitz, Michael. 1983. *The Chemistry of Love*. Boston: Little, Brown.

Loewenstein, George. 1996. "Out of Control: Visceral Influences on Behavior." *Organizational Behavior and Human Decision Processes* 65: 272–92.

————. 1999. "A Visceral Theory of Addiction." In *Getting Hooked: Rationality and the Addictions*, edited by Jon Elster and Ole-Jørgen Skog. Cambridge: Cambridge University Press.

Lutz, Catherine. 1988. *Unnatural Emotions*. Chicago: University of Chicago Press.

MacAndrew, Craig, and Robert Edgerton. 1969. *Drunken Comportment*. Chicago: Aldine.

Mäkelä, Klaus. 1986. "Attitudes Towards Drinking and Drunkenness in Four Scandinavian Countries." In *Alcohol and Culture: Comparative Perspectives from Europe and America*, edited by Thomas F. Babor. New York: New York Academy of Sciences.

Marks, Isaac M. 1987. *Fears, Phobias, and Rituals*. Oxford: Oxford University Press.

Milgram, Stanley. 1974. *Obedience to Authority*. New York: Harper and Row.

Moene, Karl O. 1999. "Addiction and Social Interaction." In *Getting Hooked: Rationality and the Addictions*, edited by Jon Elster and Ole-Jørgen Skog. Cambridge: Cambridge University Press.

Montaigne, Michel de. 1991. *The Complete Essays*. Translated by M. A. Screech. Harmondsworth: Penguin.

Moskalewicz, Jacek, and Antoni Zielinski. 1995. "Poland." In *International Handbook on Alcohol and Culture*, edited by Dwight B. Heath. Westport, Conn.: Greenwood.

Nahoum-Grappe, V. 1995. "France." In *International Handbook on Alcohol and Culture*, edited by Dwight B. Heath. Westport, Conn.: Greenwood.

Nyberg, Karin, and Peter Allebeck. 1995. "Sweden." In *International Handbook on Alcohol and Culture*, edited by Dwight B. Heath. Westport, Conn.: Greenwood.

Orford, Jim. 1985. *Excessive Appetites: A Psychological View of the Addictions*. Chichester: Wiley.

Orphanides, Athanasios, and David Zervos. 1995. "Rational Addiction with Learning and Regret." *Journal of Political Economy* 103: 739–58.

Oshodin, O. G. 1995. "Nigeria." In *International Handbook on Alcohol and Culture*, edited by Dwight B. Heath. Westport, Conn.: Greenwood.

Peele, Stanton. 1985. *The Meaning of Addiction*. Lexington, Mass.: Lexington Books.

Peele, Stanton, and Archie Brodsky. 1991. *Love and Addiction*. New York: Signet.

Plant, Martin A. 1995. "The United Kingdom." In *International Handbook on Alcohol and Culture*, edited by Dwight B. Heath. Westport, Conn.: Greenwood.

Polivy, Janet, and Peter Herman. 1993. "Etiology of Binge Eating: Psychological Mechanisms." In *Binge Eating*, edited by Christopher G. Fairburn and Terence Wilson. New York: Guilford.

Rey, Guillermina N. 1995. "Mexico." In *International Handbook on Alcohol and Culture*, edited by Dwight B. Heath. Westport, Conn.: Greenwood.

Robinson, Terry E., and Kent C. Berridge. 1993. "The Neural Basis of Drug Craving: An Incentive-Sensitization Theory of Addiction." *Brain Research Reviews* 18: 247–91.

Rosenthal, Richard J., and Loreen J. Rugle. 1994. "A Psychodynamic Approach to the Treatment of Pathological Gambling: Part I. Achieving Abstinence." *Journal of Gambling Studies* 10: 21–42.

Sartre, Jean-Paul. 1936. *Esquisse d'une théorie des émotions*. Paris: Hermann.

Schafer, Roy. 1976. *A New Language for Psychoanalysis*. New Haven: Yale University Press.

Shafir, Eldar, I. Simonson, and Amos Tversky. 1993. "Reason-Based Choice." *Cognition* 49: 11–36.

Sidorov, Pavel I. 1995. "Russia." In *International Handbook on Alcohol and Culture*, edited by Dwight B. Heath. Westport, Conn.: Greenwood.

Solomon, Robert C. 1993. *The Passions*. Indianapolis: Hackett.

Sournia, Jean-Charles. 1986. *L'alcoholisme*. Paris: Flammarion.

Sousa, Ronald de. 1987. *The Rationality of Emotion*. Cambridge: MIT Press.

Spacks, Patricia M. 1995. *Boredom*. Chicago: University of Chicago Press.

Steele, Claude M., and Robert A. Josephs. 1990. "Alcohol Myopia." *American Psychologist* 45: 921–33.

Taylor, Charles. 1971. "Interpretation and the Science of Man." *Review of Metaphysics* 3: 25–51.

Vollmer, P. J. 1977. "Do Mischievous Dogs Reveal Their 'Guilt'?" *Veterinary Medicine Small Animal Clinician* 72: 1002–5.

Weiss, Shoshana. 1995. "Israel." In *International Handbook on Alcohol and Culture*, edited by Dwight B. Heath. Westport, Conn.: Greenwood.

Williams, Bernard A. 1993. *Shame and Necessity*. Berkeley: University of California Press.

Zhang, Jiachen. 1995. "China." In *International Handbook on Alcohol and Culture*, edited by Dwight B. Heath. Westport, Conn.: Greenwood.

Zinberg, Norman. 1984. *Drug, Set, and Setting: The Basis for Controlled Intoxicant Use*. New Haven: Yale University Press.

PART V

ADDICTION AND CULTURE

Chapter 9

Addicts as Objects of Study: Clinical Encounters in the 1920s

CAROLINE JEAN ACKER

NLIKE many students of addiction, I do not seek to understand what addiction *is*. Rather, as a socially trained historian of medical and scientific disciplines, I am chiefly interested in how addiction is thought about in different disciplinary contexts—and why and how addiction becomes an interesting problem to a particular discipline in a particular time and place. For example, economists did not ponder the basis of addicts' behavior in the 1920s; they did in the 1990s.

Following Charles Rosenberg (1979), I use the concept of "ecology of knowledge" to characterize knowledge production in its disciplinary contexts and to situate disciplines, in turn, in their social contexts. Using such an approach, I examine the process whereby addiction posed new kinds of scientific and medical problems to American physicians, physiologists, pharmacologists, and sociologists in the early decades of the twentieth century (Acker 1993a). In this chapter, using clinical case records from the Narcotics Ward of Philadelphia General Hospital in the mid-1920s, I focus on the encounter between opiate addicts seeking treatment for their drug problem and a psychiatrist who reflects an emerging consensus that opiate addicts' defects of character made them virtually untreatable. These psychiatric interviews illuminate both the therapeutic dilemmas confronted by medical professionals seeking to help patients "get off the stuff" and the deepening stigma addicts encountered when they sought treatment for their addiction. They also reflect a moment in history when a set of research approaches to opiate addiction hardened into a constellation that prevailed through what David Courtwright (1989) calls the classic era of narcotic control.

Motives for practitioners of a discipline to take up a new problem vary. For economic and decision theorists seeking to understand the wellsprings of individual decision making, unraveling the nature of addiction promises to illuminate irrational influences on choice. The addict's dogged repetition of behavior that manifestly violates any rational calculus of self-interest poses a conundrum whose resolution may aid in understanding something fundamental about how humans act—as consumers, or more generally. That is, exploring the problem of addiction may contribute to resolving theoretical debates in the discipline.

In the 1920s in the United States, addiction posed different kinds of disciplinary opportunity, ones more closely linked to professional identity, to shifting patterns in science patronage, and to goals of infrastructure development than to advancement of theory. The groups most interested in opiate addiction as a scientific and medical problem in the 1920s included physicians engaged in the reform of their profession, psychiatrists seeking to broaden their professional purview, and pharmacologists working to build a pharmaceutical research and development infrastructure in the United States. In each case, these professional and disciplinary aspirations were consistent with, and in some cases were structurally linked to, the emerging federal policy apparatus that prohibited nonmedical use of opiates and incarcerated users. Seen together, these groups, their aims and activities, and their relations to each other and to the larger society constitute an institutional mosaic of complementary or interlocking interests.

As Courtwright (1982) shows, American prohibition of nonmedical opiate use occurred in part as a response to an emerging cohort of urban male opium, heroin, and morphine use in the context of the shifting entertainment venues and drug and sex markets in Progressive Era America (about 1890 to 1920). The typical addict of the late nineteenth century was a respectable, white, middle-aged woman who became addicted as a result of taking opiates for a medical complaint; this figure is most widely recognized in the character of Mary Tyrone in Eugene O'Neill's play *Long Day's Journey into Night*. By 1910, scores of teenage boys and young men were sniffing heroin in the pool halls and street hangouts of American downtowns, where restaurants, dance halls, and musical theaters were appearing in immigrant, working-class neighborhoods. In part, these emerging entertainment venues reflected a working-class, immigrant population shift toward more relaxed socializing between the sexes than that prescribed by Protestant middle-class groups (D'Emilio and Freedman 1988). These latter groups responded with concern to the larger challenges posed by new patterns of immigration from Southern and Eastern Europe and to such specific issues as the transmission of venereal diseases from prostitutes to middle-class families when married men infected their wives (Brandt 1987).

The political plank of Prohibition singled out the saloon as a site of damage to the working and earning capacities of the men who frequented them and the virtue of the women who spent time there. Thus, a whole range of entertainment institutions, from legitimate restaurants to outlawed (but often tolerated) brothels, seemed to Progressive Era reformers to pose serious threats to the moral, civic, and bodily health of the populace. By the 1920s, early impulses to study such problems and resolve them through legislation, regulation, and improvement of the urban environment hardened into sharper divisions between professionals, like physicians, and problematic groups, who were increasingly diagnosed as manifesting psychopathology in the form of failures of social adjustment.

Opiate addiction illustrates this trend. Widespread addiction to opiates was recognized as a serious problem by the 1890s; given the prevalence of women who had become addicted as a result of taking opiates for medical reasons, it is not surprising that both physicians and lay observers blamed the problem primarily on the prescribing practices of physicians. Progressive Era muckrakers also targeted the unregulated drug market, in which pharmacists could sell any medication to anyone who requested it (Adams 1906). The first federal legislation to regulate the drug trade, the 1906 Pure Food and Drugs Act, required any medication containing opiates to say so on the label. The American Medical Association (which reorganized in 1901 to become a more powerful agent for the interests of practicing physicians), as well as physicians writing therapeutics textbooks and others interested in reforming the profession, all counseled giving patients fewer opiates, in smaller doses, for shorter periods, for narrower indications (Acker 1995b).

For American physicians in the early twentieth century, concerns about opiates connected to a larger reform platform that transformed the overcrowded and splintered profession of the nineteenth century into the powerful elite that, by midcentury, had become emblematic of professional power (Parsons 1951; Starr 1982). At a time when physicians sought to recast medical knowledge in a scientific mold, opiates represented old-fashioned medicine, which treated symptoms, like pain or cough, rather than attacking the cause of disease. Physicians were eager to distance themselves from the widespread perception that they were responsible for most cases of addiction. Increasingly, this meant distancing themselves from addicts as patients (Acker 1995b). Thus, the AMA supported the 1914 passage of the Harrison Narcotic Act, the first federal legislation to restrict availability of any drug. The Harrison Act tracked sales of opiates and cocaine so as to prevent any sale or distribution except as administered or authorized by a physician. Most crucially for the fate of addicts, in 1919 the Supreme Court interpreted the Harrison Act to mean that physicians could not prescribe opiates on an ongoing basis to addicts to enable them to avoid withdrawal and craving or other dysphoric states, which made it difficult for them to sustain abstinence. The same year, the American Medical Association issued a resolution disapproving of ambulatory treatment of opiate addiction. In the 1920s, then, opiate addicts faced two alternatives: giving up their drug or using it in violation of law, social norms, and medical standards.

For many addicted individuals, however, abstinence was too difficult to sustain. Deprived of licit sources for their drug, they bought it on the illicit market. When their habits became too burdensome, or when family, employers, or legal authorities caught them and urged or forced them to seek treatment, they could rarely obtain help from private physicians. Many physicians were reluctant to treat addicts, since the hope of a lasting cure was dim and addicts increasingly gained a reputation for manufacturing medical complaints in an effort to secure morphine. Moreover, U.S. Treasury Department officials charged with enforcing the Harrison Narcotic Act zealously sought, indicted, and brought to trial physicians believed to be prescribing opiates in excessive quantities.

By the mid-1920s, for opiate addicts in the American Northeast, a few urban hospitals that still had "drug wards" remained the last place where they might seek a "cure"—a monitored and medicated ten days or so in which they went through withdrawal, ate three meals a day, rested, and achieved an abstinent state. Such a ward existed at the Philadelphia General Hospital since at least 1910. From 1926 to 1928, the Rockefeller-funded Bureau of Social Hygiene financed a comprehensive research effort at the hospital to improve understanding of addiction. In the research ward at Philadelphia General, researchers studied addicts in many ways: They watched the process of withdrawal carefully; they took a number of physiological measures while the patient was still taking opiates, during the course of withdrawal, and after withdrawal had been completed; they administered psychological tests and physical endurance tests. In addition, psychiatrist R. B. Richardson interviewed patients at length. The cases presented here are drawn from the transcripts of these wide-ranging interviews.[1]

These conversations record the experiences of the first cohort of American opiate addicts to confront managing their addiction in a legal climate of drug prohibition and to be treated as criminals because of their addiction. They also reveal the limited range of therapeutic tools available to helping these patients achieve a "cure."

Ralph Korlach's case (Case 8-GPG) illustrates well the social context of initiation as well as the skills and challenges involved in maintaining a habit at optimal doses that enabled him to be comfortable and functional. These challenges included maintaining reliable drug supplies from an illicit market, as the incident of his entering the hospital shows. Ralph was fifty years old when he entered the Men's Drug Ward at Philadelphia General Hospital on December 12, 1925, though the physician who examined him said he looked more like sixty-five. The peddler from whom Ralph regularly purchased heroin had been arrested, and Ralph had been unable to secure an alternate means of supply. After five days with no drug—and nearing the end of the roughest part of the withdrawal syndrome—Ralph contacted the local police and asked to be taken to the drug ward.

Ralph first used morphine in 1892, as a seventeen-year-old, the same year he left school, having reached the ninth grade. Ralph quit school to work as a painter's assistant, and he was a painter all his working life. The stenographer's clinical notes recount Ralph's first encounter with opiates:

Patient started at the age of 17 with morphine, which he continued for 20 years, always taking it by mouth. Morphine, when he first started, could be procured by going to the drug store and buying 10 grains for 10 cents. He states the reason he started was because he was associated with other fellows that used it. He states that these individuals seemed to have a good deal of pep and he wanted to see if he couldn't be the same way and be a good fellow. The most outstanding example of the effects was his association with a man who made balloon ascensions, and he was struck by the daredevilness of this individual. From the very beginning, the use of the drug was continuous, never being interrupted.

Ralph's drug-using career began in 1892, before heroin was available but when morphine was sold inexpensively in drugstores in a completely unregulated fashion. The practice of young men taking opiates as part of socializing with their age cohort in the context of the turbulent Northeastern American cities was in its early stages in 1892. At that time, nonmedical opiate use consisted largely of smoking opium in smoking dens in the Chinatowns of large East Coast and West Coast U.S. cities. Chinatowns possessed some of the characteristics typical of marginalized urban neighborhoods in nineteenth- and twentieth-century America. Whites' ethnic prejudice reinforced a tendency for Chinese to live in neighborhoods culturally isolated from surrounding neighborhoods peopled by non-Chinese. In part because they were excluded, by custom and at times by law, from many forms of wage labor, they engaged in entrepreneurial activities, some of which were illicit.

The Chinese and the neighborhoods they lived in were scapegoated as sources of urban problems; contagious illnesses were said to originate in Chinatown, and Chinese prostitutes were believed to be more depraved than white prostitutes, luring even young boys into sex for money (Trauner 1978; Acker 1988). In this context, opium dens were where male Chinese laborers, often working for low pay and separated from families who remained at home in China, sought relaxation. In the 1880s and 1890s, whites seeking adventure, novel drug experiences, and exoticism also frequented opium dens. Because skill was required to prepare opium for smoking, casual users rarely consumed the drug at home or at other social sites; they came to the dens where the cognoscenti would heat the opium to obtain the soft, gummy consistency that could be rolled into a small mass and inserted into a pipe for smoking.

The easy availability of morphine from any drugstore made it possible to pursue this drug experience in other settings besides opium dens. Morphine and, soon after its introduction to the market in 1898, heroin were used increasingly from about 1890 through World War I by young men in the turbulent urban neighborhoods of American cities, which were receiving tens of thousands of immigrants from Southern and Eastern Europe in the same period.

The oral method of administration that Ralph described, while it would produce powerfully pleasant sensations, would do so with a more gradual onset than the sniffing of heroin or subcutaneous injection of heroin or morphine, which within fifteen years would characterize much recreational use. Ralph himself shifted drugs and dosages over time. When passage of the Harrison Narcotic Act in 1914 made morphine harder to obtain, he began using heroin, which was easier to purchase in the growing street market for opiates. Ralph also found that he needed larger doses to achieve the effect he desired. For Ralph, despite his early attraction to "daredevilness," this meant maintaining a suitable level of functioning for his quiet life as a house painter. For example, he reported that "[t]he first year he worked he had to stop at times in the afternoon on account of the excessive dosage he used, but after he got to his accustomed dosage, and did not get sleepy, he was able to work above the average painter."

In other words, Ralph was not a thrill seeker, constantly raising his dose so that he could experience the rush that was available above his current tolerance level; rather, his pattern of use was one of maintenance, taking more or less the same doses over time so as to be able to work well and to avoid the discomforts of withdrawal. He worked for decades as a house painter and apparently lived much of his adult life in the home of his parents, coming home early in the evenings "on account of his mother." For most of the decades between his first drug use in 1892 and his hospital admission in 1925, he was able to secure drug supplies without serious difficulty. Besides switching to heroin after passage of the

Harrison Act, he was forced to change his behavior in response to market difficulties two other times. Once, unable to buy from his usual supplier during a police crackdown, he began taking paregoric. The final such episode was the one that brought him to the hospital; options for switching to another drug were not available, and after suffering through withdrawal as long as he felt able, he took the drastic step of turning himself in to the police for transport to the hospital.

Despite the relatively stable use pattern Ralph displayed, gently rising tolerance over the years did force him gradually to higher daily doses. The costs and risks associated with his habit had increased over the years, and the need to take larger amounts of drug was one factor heightening those costs.

Ralph's drug-using career illustrates a common pattern of opiate use. An individual consuming morphine or heroin on a steady basis begins to develop tolerance to the drug; that is, escalating doses are required to produce the desired acute effects of the drug. As the customary dose rises, however, the various costs associated with drug use also escalate. These include the monetary cost, as the individual must buy larger quantities of drugs, but also more intense side effects and diminished pleasure. So the addict often undertakes dose reduction or complete detoxification to get the situation back within more manageable limits, and this kind of habit management forms a frequent motive for seeking treatment. Since in the 1920s, "cure" was thought of fairly simply as achieving abstinence, and since this could be accomplished in any treatment regimen that ensured that the patient took no opiates for seven to ten days, the familiar revolving door of addicts in and out of treatment was a common pattern, then as now. Achieving abstinence meant reducing tolerance back to levels associated with the period before drug use, and so a comparatively small dose of heroin or morphine could pack a palpable kick. Thus, any recourse to drug use provided a powerful experience of the euphoric and calming effects of the drug.

However, tolerance quickly returned to earlier levels, and so the patient found himself on an accelerating roller coaster of euphoric use, rising tolerance, diminished pleasurable effects, dose reduction, and, again, resumed use. For Ralph, the oscillations of this roller-coaster pattern were fairly gentle, even though his dose levels were high. For others, tolerance escalated quickly as they sought to maximize the euphoric potentials of the drug. Repeated episodes of "cure"—or self-managed detoxification—periodically brought doses back to more manageable levels and then the up ride on the roller coaster began again.

Ralph's case illustrates that managing addiction, like managing a chronic disease, constitutes work and that the context of that work is powerfully shaped by the nature of the market in which the addict seeks his drug.[2] As both commonsense and expert views have consistently held, addiction can become the central organizing focus of one's life, displacing personal relationships, social obligations, pleasures, and the addict's own moral values. The extent to which this occurs varies widely, but it is not a function only of pharmacology or individual psychology. For example, in their classic ethnographic study of heroin acquisition patterns by young men in New York City, Edward Preble and John Casey (1969) trace changes in market patterns 1914 to 1969. As purity dropped and price rose in the illicit market for heroin, addicts were forced into more frequent retail purchases, and the time involved in both cash and drug acquisition expanded. At the same time, they argue, an addict identity formed as acquisition skills were honed and links were solidified with a social group of fellow heroin addicts. This identity, and the activities involved in it, gave coherence and a sense of meaning to a life on the margins of the legitimate economy and approved social roles. Thus, the nature of the market interacted synergistically with the socioeconomic situation and psychological needs of young men alienated from normative paths to adulthood to produce a pattern of activity centered on acquiring and using heroin.

In another ethnographic study of drug-using groups, Patricia Cleckner (1980) compares two groups of PCP users in Miami in the 1970s: a blue-collar working-class group and an affluent upper-middle-class group. The latter's substantial economic assets protected them from the vicissitudes of the illicit market: They could make large purchases when drugs were plentiful or of especially good quality, and these supplies could tide them over periods of scarcity or when a sample indicated a dealer's wares were substandard. Access to resources for managing drug problems, whether these arise from acute episodes or chronic patterns of use, also vary according to socioeconomic status (Acker 1993b). In these ways, individual decisions and actions involved in drug use are mediated by social context.

It is easy to sympathize with Ralph, a middle-aged man who had fallen into addiction at a time when opiates were widely available and social sanctions against use were few and who appeared to live a quiet and inoffensive life. At the same time, his case illustrates one of several ongoing frustrations for those attempting to treat opiate addiction. As addicts moved through phases of tolerance and desired to reduce their dose, they frequently presented themselves to physicians as patients seeking a "cure." As physicians gained experience with addicts who persisted in a pattern of renewed drug use after episodes of treatment, or who feigned pain in an effort to secure opiates, they became suspicious of addicts as patients. Such experiences, combined with intrusive scrutiny of prescribing practices by drug law enforcers and AMA blackballing if they were caught violating the Harrison Act, exacerbated an atmosphere of profound mutual distrust between addicts and physicians.

The case of Zachary Edwards (Case 26-25) illustrates the social and cultural tensions that underlay psychiatrist Richardson's attempts to return patients he saw as "constitutional inferiors" to mental health. As a thirty-year-old, Zachary belonged to a younger segment of the cohort of recreational drug users that emerged on the American scene beginning in the 1890s. In almost every aspect of his appearance, behavior, and life story, Zachary Edwards affronted the respectable middle-class norms that for psychiatrist Richardson were tokens of mental health and good character. Zachary was born in Newark, New Jersey, to parents who had immigrated from Belgium. In the home country, the family had relatives in the music world and the diamond business. Zachary's father had received some medical training and had worked as a medical intern but had died of pneumonia at age forty, leaving his mother as the sole parent of five children. She worked as a midwife for some years but, at some point, shifted to maintaining a wig-making business, and the family moved to New York. Zachary, the youngest child in the family, quit school at age thirteen to work with his mother. From wig making, he turned to hairdressing. For a while he owned his own beauty shop in Harlem. At the time he entered Philadelphia General for treatment of his drug addiction in 1926, he was working in someone else's shop as a marcel waver.

Zachary reported that he had begun using heroin in the company of a young woman who worked in show business and was apparently a customer who became a close friend. He became aware that she used drugs because he saw that she carried a syringe. She invited him to her apartment and gave him an injection of heroin. Although he complained that his drug-using friends should have informed him at the outset of the risks inherent in drug use, apparently Zachary was not entirely ignorant of them, as shown by his description of his earliest use episodes (as transcribed into the third person by the stenographer): "He used to sniff small quantities and then would [throw] the bottle away, desiring to quit. He would feel so bad, however, that he would go and buy more. Says his habit started two weeks after his first experience."

Thus, from his earliest contacts with the drug, Zachary appeared to engage in a struggle between desire for the drug sensation and desire to control his use. Zachary included heroin use in a life that included friendships with people in show business (he once aspired to enter show business himself), parties, travel to Paris and Bermuda, frequent visits to the theater and the Metropolitan Opera, and much reading. Although shaky on American history (as evidenced by his responses to questions in the Sensorium examination—such as "1776 was the fight between the North and the South"), he had read Dickens, Balzac, Hawthorne, and an author unfamiliar to both Richardson and the stenographer, to judge from the conversation and consistent misspellings in the transcript. The following exchange ironically reveals as much about Richardson as it does about Zachary, who had become adept in hiding aspects of his personality as necessary:

Richardson: What books have you read?

Zachary: Hedda Gabler.

Richardson: What was that about?

Zachary: Oh, about a girl who married a professor much older than herself and she gets into trouble with a younger man. Her husband studies all the time, and she has to find her own amusement.

Richardson: Was that the right thing for her to do?

Zachary: Well, he was much older and he studied all the time and would not take her out and all that. She was much younger than him and he should have been more considerate.

Richardson noted, after the last remark, "patient smiles."

On another day, Richardson again asked Zachary about his reading habits, and Zachary again responded with a reference to Ibsen:

Richardson: What other books have you been reading?

Zachary: One is Ibsen's, I can't recall the name of it.

Richardson: What was it about?

Zachary: It was also about a married woman getting into trouble with another man.

Richardson: Whose fault was that?

Zachary: Her husband's.

Richardson: When are you going to get married, Zach?

Zachary: Oh, I do not think ever.

Richardson: Where is your girl now?

Zachary: I do not know. She is just a friend that's all, she is not a real girl. She knows everything about me because I told her. I never went with her to get married. I would have to change a whole lot to get married.

Richardson's immediate segue from the fictional marriage (where he seems to blame Ibsen's unhappy heroine) to a question regarding

Zachary's marital intentions typifies his repeated urgings that patients adopt respectable middle-class lifestyles so as to have something to live for that might counteract the impulse to use drugs. Zachary's veiled hint that some fundamental change in himself would be necessary for him to be a marriage candidate is left unexplored. Between Zachary's freely given accounts of numerous relationships with women and Richardson's apparent inability to recognize the realities of the "gay" life Zachary describes himself as leading, there is no room to discuss the issues elicited in a brief interview conducted by hospital psychologist G. E. Partridge. Partridge summarized Zachary's sexual experiences as follows, beginning with a paraphrase of Zachary's own words: " 'Has seen enough of perverted relations.' Masturbation age of 12 or 14. Kind of afraid of it. Drugs keep the passion down." Richardson failed to sense that Zachary might find some of his sexual passions disturbing to himself and that opiate use might help him deal with them.

In reporting on his physical examination of Zachary, Richardson describes him as a heavy man with effeminate mannerisms who speaks with a lisp and polishes his fingernails. Such effeminacy for Richardson could only represent an inadequacy of manhood, not the basis for any positive form of identity. Zachary, in turn, had mastered various forms of passing, in the sense described by Erving Goffman (1963). He entered the hospital under an assumed name (he eventually admitted to Richardson that his real name was Jacques Artaud). He had adopted the name, perhaps because it sounded more American than his own, at a time when he contemplated going into show business, but the alias also served to conceal his identity when he entered the hospital.

In some ways, Zachary undoubtedly saw Richardson more clearly than Richardson saw Zachary. Because we can see Zachary only in this setting in which he undergoes professional examination, he remains somewhat opaque to us as well. However, it appears that Zachary inhabited a social world that Richardson could only glimpse through his contacts with some of the patients who appeared on his ward: a social world that embraced New York show business, an emerging gay subculture, fashion, brothels, restaurants, and night clubs. In contrast, Zachary repeatedly displays a thorough recognition of the kinds of standards Richardson embodies, as illustrated in the following responses (Richardson's questions are implied by Zachary's responses): "The girl I go with now works in the same place." "She is a respectable girl." "I guess I can tell a respectable girl." "You can talk to a girl and know she is one." "The others have different ways about them." "I can't describe it to you." Richardson's final verdict regarding Zachary was,

This expresses the rather uninteresting life of a hair dresser who works rather long hours, who appreciates that with a habit he is better working for some other person. His life is expressed in his story of playing around at different apartments, freely acknowledging that he goes to sporting houses. Remarks, "It is nature."

For Richardson, reading Balzac and Ibsen, frequenting the opera, and traveling to Paris and Bermuda added up to a drab, or at least an unproductive, life. More important to Richardson, Zachary indicated that a habit interfered with his ability to maintain his own hairdressing shop, and for Richardson this fall from entrepreneurship was another factor suggesting an overly self-indulgent personality whose only aims in life were to seek facile pleasures. Certainly Zachary himself agreed that his habit presented serious problems—his own repeated efforts at cure are also evidence—but for Richardson, the mental inferiority indicated by the heroin habit was inextricably linked to the mental inferiority indicated by effeminate behavior in a male and a lifestyle of practicing a trade connected to a social world of show business, fashion, and the arts.

In dealing with issues of gender and sexuality, Richardson consistently maintained a demeanor that allowed only a narrow range of possibilities. Men might be virile, and the types likely to be drug addicts often engaged in sexual relations with prostitutes or with unmarried girlfriends. Richardson affected language he thought of as typical in the sporting world that many of the addicts came from. Thus, in questioning men about whether they had ever contracted a venereal disease, he asked if they had "ever been set up." While he engaged men's confidence sufficiently to elicit many histories of casual, nonmarital sexual relationships, he also probed patients about the type of women they might consider marrying. He often urged marriage as a means of solidifying a way of life that would support drug abstinence. Thus, while he might seem superficially accepting of men's sexual exploits, he urged them to distinguish between respectable and unrespectable "girls."

Many patients remarked on the tendency of opiates to diminish sexual appetite, and for Richardson this fact seemed to be consistent with the lack of ambition and planning that he saw in many of the patients he interviewed. A few patients, like Zachary Edwards, were singled out as being particularly effeminate in appearance and manner. However, Richardson's reluctance to discuss homosexual behavior in any explicit way undoubtedly prevented patients from volunteering any such encounters.

Like marriage, plans for the future, and savings, heterosexual virility was for Richardson a touchstone of the mental health that could preclude addiction. He and his patients frequently discussed the need to "make a man of oneself" rather than relapse to the use of drugs. Both Richardson and his patients recognized that the hospital cure was intended to help the patient take on the attributes valued by a middle-class professional like Richardson himself. Richardson was also quick to invoke love of mother or wife as a motive to "stay off the stuff." For some patients, the failure to live up to such standards added to the sense of shame that surrounded their drug use. Others, even if they sincerely felt their habit to be a burden and wanted to end their habits, clearly parroted some of the answers they knew Richardson expected. In both situations, the effect was to compound the addict's distance from the figure of the physician. For Richardson, Zachary's failures of masculinity betokened a fundamental weakness, which was expected to prevent him from staying off drugs.

Just as Zachary Edwards, in appearance and behavior, violated Richardson's social norms, another patient, Robert Miller (Case 27-89), displayed tantalizing potential to live up to Richardson's expectations. Miller was admitted in August 1927. An unmarried sailor in port at Philadelphia, he had turned himself in to the police because he had run out of drugs and did not know where to buy any. The police had brought him to the narcotics ward. Miller indicated this had never happened to him before; in years of sailing, he had always been able to buy enough drugs ashore to last through voyages and renewed contact with suppliers. He also indicated, though, that he hoped to quit the habit:

Miller: After I left the ship I planned to see if I could break this habit, but I found out I could not do it very easily.

Richardson: Why do you want to break the habit?

Miller: Well, I don't want to be a wreck all my life.

Miller was the son of a mother who died giving birth to him and a father who abandoned him to the care of an aunt and uncle in Cripple Creek, Colorado. At the age of fifteen, he ran away because "I always wanted to see the world." He jumped freight trains and worked for short periods in Chicago and Milwaukee. In the latter city, while he was working as a pin boy in a bowling alley, he and some of his co-workers "all made it up to go to sea." Since then, he had worked as an oiler in ships' engine rooms and had traveled "all over the world." He saw his drug habit as blocking his hopes for advancement: "I would like to get a license for the engine room to work for myself but they would not issue me a license if they knew I was a drug addict."

Miller had begun his drug use sniffing heroin, but he quickly switched to subcutaneous injection on the advice of friends who said he was wasting drug by sniffing it. He also used cocaine occasionally, especially when in South America, where it was cheap and readily available. He also found he got "more of a thrill" from cocaine than from heroin. He had become adept at hiding his use even in the close shared quarters on shipboard:

Richardson: When you were aboard ship, how did you do it then?

Miller: Usually went to my room when my roommate was out and sometimes go in steerage room or some place like that.

He also learned how to acquire supplies in strange ports: "When I went ashore I usually go to drink and hang out with a bunch of fellows along the dock. There are a lot of dope fiends hanging around a waterfront." Despite his carousing, Miller also knew how to respect the rules of shipboard life:

Richardson: Do you respect your officers?

Miller: You got to when you are at sea.

Richardson: Do you complain much about things?

Miller: Not more than the average sailor about working conditions, grub and things like that. If you do things like that it gets all over the coast, so I decided they would never get me for [complaining].

Richardson: What do you consider your greatest experience?

Miller: I really never thought about it. Just what do you mean?

Richardson: What gave you the biggest thrill?

Miller: Well, the greatest moment in life was when the engineer told me I could be an oiler on one of those big boats. I really felt proud, threw out my chest and walked around with my head very high in the air.

Pleased with Miller's expression of ambition, Richardson probed his prospects for respectable family life. Miller had cut all ties with his relatives in Colorado: "I have no home. I do not know if my aunt and uncle are alive. I wrote them two or three times but did not get any answer. . . . I would not want any one to know about me in that town." Asked about girlfriends, Miller replied, "There was some one at one time," a young woman in Colorado whom Miller referred to as "the only decent person I know." Richardson elicited her name and address. Although this woman had since married someone else and borne two children, and although Miller was fifteen when he last saw her, Richardson pressed Miller to renew contact with her:

Richardson: Keep in touch with somebody who amounts to something, and if these people are decent I can see no harm in writing to both of them, do you?

Miller: I never thought about it in that light.

Further urging to think of an improved future prompted Miller to lament, "Who would have anything to do with a tramp like me? What have I got to live for? I would be ashamed to try to associate with any-body decent." The stenographer dryly and synoptically recorded the next portion of the interview: "Examiner gives patient advice as to how to live right. The patient is very co-operative and seems to take in the thoughts as they are presented to him, but he believes himself far from redemption and therefore does not see a clear road ahead of him, as is exemplified in his next remark: 'I would not want my sister to be in-troduced to any tramp like I am. I was always a wanderer and always, probably, will be. I am as low as a man can possibly go.'" Finally, Richardson prodded Miller to think about the distant future:

Richardson: What are you going to do when you get old?

Miller: Just what do you mean by that?

Richardson explained that "every one must provide for his old age when he is unable to work."

Richardson's own literary tastes are revealed in his recommendation of reading matter:

Richardson: Have you ever read "Lorna Doone"?

Miller: No sir.

Again, the stenographer summarized the psychiatrist's prescription: "Advice given to patient to read decent books and to make decent friends."

As with Edwards, Richardson also revealed much of himself in his physical description of Miller:

> Complexion is ruddy with dark-brown hair and blue eyes. His features are pleasing and his attitude is that of an individual who has known bet-ter days or who at least has been well raised. His language is such that might pass anywhere, and his reaction is prompt and he shows an accu-racy in making decisions and in his responses. Features are clean cut and his body is clean.

In his final summing up, Richardson expressed sympathy for Miller: "The patient is not asking for sympathy nor does he feel sorry for him-self, but his manner of expressing himself . . . makes one pity him and feel more kindly than ever towards this individual who apparently knows what is right and has the desire to do it but lacks opportunity."

Richardson responded with hope to Miller's personality, appearance, and respectable origins. His earnest lecture on how to live, following on his urgings that Miller read decent books and connect with decent people, appears to represent his best effort at therapeutic intervention for a patient he displays more than typical personal regard for. His admonitions to many patients that they muster the requisite willpower to "be a man" and "stay off the stuff" suggest that the patient was expected to muster resources of character in order to conquer his addiction. He does not address the complex of factors that would have made it difficult for Miller, even if not using drugs, to follow his advice; for example, the nomadic life of a sailor made it difficult to sustain close social contacts with people like the young woman who had remained in Cripple Creek and married someone else.

Richardson's conversations with his patients reflect a paradox in psychiatric thinking about addiction in the mid-1920s, one expressed in the work of U.S. Public Health Service psychiatrist Lawrence Kolb, who, in a series of landmark articles (1925a, 1925b, 1925c) solidified the view that, while any individual chronically consuming opiates could become addicted to them, only individuals with personality deficits predating any drug use would fall into the intractable pattern of chronic relapse that seemed to resist therapeutic effort. Kolb developed his ideas in the context of a reform movement to bring American psychiatry out of the isolation of the rural asylum and into the welter of urban life (Grob 1983; Rothman 1980). Influenced by the mental hygiene ideas of Adolf Meyer and trained in public health psychiatry by Thomas Salmon, Kolb had spent the years from 1913 to 1919 at Ellis Island screening prospective immigrants for mental conditions that might disqualify them for entry into the United States. The constellation of psychiatric ideas guiding this work included two that reflect psychiatrists' claims to utility in a rapidly urbanizing country absorbing hundreds of thousands of immigrants each year: The psychiatrist must be able to identify preclinical signs of latent mental illness (so as to turn away those who might later fall ill and become dependents of the state), and mental health was framed as appropriate adjustment to prevailing social norms (Acker 1993a).

Kolb (1925c) describes addicts in terms easily translatable into a language of misdirected class yearnings:

> They are struggling with a sense of inadequacy, imagined or real, or with unconscious pathological strivings . . . and the open make-up that so many of them show is not a normal expression of men at ease with the world, but a mechanism of inferiors who are striving to appear like normal men.

In the same article, Kolb compares addicts to "little men who endeavor to lift themselves into greatness by wearing 'loud' clothes or by otherwise making themselves conspicuous, when effacement would be more becoming."

Kolb developed a typology of addiction (framed in masculine terms despite the presence of women in the groups he studied) in which the most problematic kind of addict was the individual who lacked overt psychopathology but whose psychoneurotic engagement in pleasure seeking led him to try drugs; exposure to opiates brought this individual's latent psychopathology to the surface and condemned him to a life of futile amusements and empty craving. Because these people had the potential to live productive and marginally well-adjusted lives in the absence of drugs, Kolb believed in the 1920s that the laws banning importation of opiates would protect such people from their own predispositions to psychopathology. (Later in his career, Kolb became a prominent advocate of medical, rather than criminal justice, measures to combat addiction.)

Increasingly, though, and in spite of drug laws, addicts appeared to physicians as a group stubbornly resistant to treatment. Kolb's views, and Richardson's experiences, embody a paradox. One the one hand, addiction was believed to reflect a preexisting characterological deficit. On the other hand, the addiction, especially as it persisted through repeated treatment episodes, became a kind of diagnostic clincher that marked the individual as irredeemable. The failure to give up drugs was seen as a failure of character, and psychiatrists like Kolb and Richardson defined good character according to a narrow set of class and gender norms. Thus, the continuing addiction became a marker of the severity and untreatability of the underlying characterological disorder. Psychiatrists, and physicians in general, became increasingly pessimistic about possibilities of cure, and this pessimism left many of them unmotivated to challenge increasingly punitive federal policies toward addicts (Musto 1973).

By 1928, when the Bureau of Social Hygiene ceased funding the research at Philadelphia General Hospital, no licit options for maintenance therapy remained. Private practice physicians shunned addicts as patients, and the American Medical Association maintained close ties with enforcement bodies in the surveillance and professional banishment of physicians who overprescribed opiates or who themselves became addicted (Acker 1995b). In 1929, Congress passed legislation authorizing the U.S. Public Health Service to construct two federal "narcotic farms." The first of these, the Lexington (Kentucky) Narcotic Hospital, opened in 1935; the second, at Fort Worth, in 1938. These institutions were envisioned, and managed, as combined hospital-prisons for federal prisoners and probationers who were addicted to opiates as well as for voluntary patients. As alternative treatment options for addicts continued to dry up, stays at Lexington (which received patients from east of the Mississippi, while the Fort Worth institution took in patients from the West) became standard episodes in heroin addicts' using careers.

The Bureau of Social Hygiene's decision to stop funding the research at Philadelphia General Hospital occurred when, under new leadership, the bureau's Committee on Drug Addictions decided to shift all its research resources to the National Research Council for the funding of a single project: a search for a nonaddicting substitute for morphine so that physicians would no longer have to wrestle with the difficulties inherent in prescribing an addictive, but essential, medication. Besides fitting the aspirations of pharmacologists seeking to build a pharmaceutical research infrastructure in the United States, this project also furthered physicians' efforts to distance themselves from addicts as patients—whether as patients seeking treatment for their drug problem or as patients inadvertently addicted in efforts to manage pain. Project management by the National Research Council's Committee on Drug Addiction brought together federal drug policy makers, American Medical Association officials, as well as university-based organic chemists and pharmacologists. All agreed that finding a nonaddicting analgesic as powerful in controlling pain as morphine would relieve physicians of a nettlesome problem and, with appropriate border controls to exclude addicting opiates from the domestic market, resolve the social addiction problem as well (Acker 1995a).

However unrealistic the latter hope, the search for a nonaddicting opiate analgesic launched a decades-long research quest in which chemists and pharmacologists developed and tested thousands of compounds, hoping both to identify the sought-after analgesic and to further the science of predictive drug design. From its opening in 1935, the Lexington Narcotic Hospital was the designated clinical testing site for those compounds emerging from the National Research Council scientists' laboratories showing promise as analgesics. Public Health Service physician Clifton Himmelsbach was assigned to clinical testing for both the analgesic power and the addictive potential in humans of compounds of interest. At Lexington, the presence of prisoner-patients addicted to morphine enabled Himmelsbach to develop an addictiveness assay that, for the first time, provided a quick and reliable means of determining whether a new compound was addicting in the way morphine or heroin is (Acker 1995b). The most immediate utility of this assay was for pharmaceutical developers of analgesics who wanted to rule out addictiveness in test compounds.

By 1950, a number of follow-up studies of addicts following treatment seemed to establish that, consistently, 80 percent or more reverted to drug use within a few years (O'Donnell 1965). In 1951, Congress passed the Boggs Act, which introduced the first mandatory minimum sentencing requirements for drug trafficking. These penalties were further stiffened by the 1956 Narcotic Control Act. In the classic era of narcotic control, addicts became a potent symbol of the worst kind of malingerer and the worst kind of criminal.

The unraveling of the classic era consensus emerged in two realms, one professional and one grassroots. Alcoholics Anonymous, founded in the 1930s, based its methods of recovery on the experience and expertise of addicts themselves. In 1958, the American Medical Association and the American Bar Association jointly published a report urging more humane medical approaches to addiction and criticized overreliance on law enforcement. Enormous changes in the demographics of drug use in the 1960s and 1970s created a broader demand for treatment; in both the public and private sectors, a new infrastructure of treatment facilities was funded and built.

Definitions of addiction have changed dramatically since the 1920s. Addiction is now seen as a more general concept, applicable to nondrug behaviors as well as to drug-using behavior, though distinct pharmacological classes of drugs still display distinct patterns of addiction. A less stigmatizing focus on drugs and on patterns of use has replaced earlier conviction that only certain personality types were susceptible to addiction. An older physiological definition (tolerance and withdrawal) has been replaced by a behavioral one: In one formulation, addiction is characterized by compulsive use, use that is out of control, and continued use in spite of adverse consequences (Acker 1993b). The chasm that separated Alcoholics Anonymous and Narcotics Anonymous from physicians and other professional groups has been replaced by rapprochement and mutual support. Addicts' own knowledge of the experiences of addiction have informed current therapeutic practices. Addiction remains a deeply problematic condition, but the normalization of a disease concept of addiction, the existence of the National Institute on Drug Abuse, and the promising leads emerging from neuroscience research all betoken a commitment to continued progress in understanding addiction.

However, important legacies of the classic era remain. Organized medicine's virtual abandonment of addicts as patients for several decades represents a lost opportunity of clinical research and teaching. Many physicians remain reluctant to treat addicts as patients. Medical schools teach little about addiction, and practitioners may lack the education to screen routinely for alcohol and drug use during history taking. They may lack experience in incorporating treatment for addiction into general practice care, or they may have little understanding of the relationship of addiction to other medical conditions a patient may require treatment for. Social and economic factors may determine whether an addicted individual receives humane medical treatment or incarceration without treatment (Acker 1993b). In the public health realm, an isolated and marginalized population of injection drug users remain hard to reach with the means of preventing transmission of blood-borne infectious diseases (Des Jarlais et al. 1995). Policy at the federal level and in many states and localities makes it difficult in many places even to try to deliver such life-saving services.

Disciplinary approaches to addiction have shifted over the course of the twentieth century in response to a wide variety of factors. Historians have taken up addiction and drug use as new problems of interest, building on the groundbreaking work of David Musto in the 1970s (Musto 1973) and David Courtwright in the 1980s (Courtwright 1980, 1989). The new historical interest in drugs reflects in part a desire to understand the profound changes unleashed in the 1960s, including an explosion in new categories of drug use and users. Historians today benefit from several decades of social history and history of science and medicine. From these fields, they borrow tools that uncover voices formerly hidden, such as those of addicts in periods when they have been deeply stigmatized; that apply analysis of class, gender, and race to better understand the dynamics at play in conversations like those Richardson had with his patients; and they understand the production of knowledge as a social process in which disciplines interact dynamically with each other and with the worlds of politics, economics, and culture in which they are situated.

I am grateful to the Faculty Development Fund, College of Humanities and Social Sciences, Carnegie Mellon University, and to the Wood Institute for the History of Medicine, Philadelphia, for support of the research reported here. I am also grateful to the Russell Sage Foundation for enabling me to attend the addiction conferences held in Collioure, France, in June 1996 and New York in June 1997. Finally, I thank Jon Elster, conference organizer, and the other conferees for exposing me to new disciplinary approaches to addiction.

Notes

1. The case records used in this chapter are from the Records of the Philadelphia Committee for Clinical Study of Opium Addiction, housed at the College of Physicians of Philadelphia. Patient names have been changed. The stenographer's words are recorded here with misspellings corrected.

2. I am grateful to Chris Feudtner and Emily Abel, who, in separate discussions, introduced me to the idea that managing chronic illness is a form of work.

References

Acker, Caroline Jean. 1988. "White Labor and Chinese Exclusion in San Francisco in the 1870s." Unpublished manuscript.

———. 1993a. "Social Problems and Scientific Opportunities: The Case of Opiate Addiction in the United States, 1920–1940." Ph.D. diss. University of California, San Francisco.

———. 1993b. "Stigma or Legitimation? A Historical Examination of the Social Potentials of Addiction Disease Models." *Journal of Psychoactive Drugs* 25: 193–205.

———. 1995a. "Addiction and the Laboratory: The Work of the National Research Council's Committee on Drug Addiction, 1928–1939." *Isis* 86: 167–93.

———. 1995b. "From All-Purpose Anodyne to Marker of Deviance: Physicians' Attitudes Toward Opiates in the US from 1890 to 1940. In *Drugs and Narcotics in History*, edited by Roy Porter and Mikulas Teich. Cambridge: Cambridge University Press.

Adams, Samuel Hopkins. "The Great American Fraud." *Collier's* October 7 and 28, November 18, and December 2, 1905; January 13, 1906.

Brandt, Alan M. 1987. *No Magic Bullet: A Social History of Venereal Disease in the United States Since 1880.* Oxford: Oxford University Press.

Cleckner, Patricia. 1980. "Freaks and Cognoscenti: PCP Use in Miami." In *Angel Dust: An Ethnographic Study of PCP Users*, edited by H. W. Feldman, M. H. Agar, and G. M. Beschner. Lexington, Mass: Lexington Books.

Courtwright, David. 1982. *Dark Paradise: Opiate Addiction in America Before 1940.* Cambridge: Harvard University Press.

———. 1989. "The Era of Classic Narcotic Control." In *Addicts Who Survived: An Oral History of Narcotic Use in America, 1923–1965*, edited by David Courtwright, Herman Joseph, and Don Des Jarlais. Knoxville: University of Tennessee Press.

D'Emilio, John, and Estelle B. Freedman. 1988. *Intimate Matters: A History of Sexuality in America.* New York: Harper and Row.

Des Jarlais, Don, et al. 1995. "Maintaining Low HIV Seroprevalence." *Journal of the American Medical Association* 274: 1226–31.

Goffman, Erving. 1963. *Stigma: Notes on the Management of Spoiled Identity.* Englewood Cliffs, N.J.: Prentice-Hall.

Grob, Gerald N. 1983. *Mental Illness and American Society, 1875–1940.* Princeton: Princeton University Press.

Kolb, Lawrence. 1925a. "Drug Addiction in its Relation to Crime." *Mental Hygiene* 9: 74–89.

———. 1925b. "Relation of Intelligence to Etiology of Drug Addiction." *American Journal of Psychiatry* 5: 163–7.

———. 1925c. "Types and Characteristics of Drug Addicts." *Mental Hygiene* 9: 300–13.

Musto, David F. 1973. *The American Disease: Origins of Narcotic Control.* New Haven: Yale University Press.

O'Donnell, John A. 1965. "The Relapse Rate in Narcotic Addiction: A Critique of Follow-Up Studies." In *Narcotics*, edited by Daniel M. Wilner and Gene G. Kassebaum. New York: McGraw-Hill.

Parsons, Talcott. 1951. *The Social System*. New York: Free Press.

Preble, Edward, and John J. Casey Jr. 1969. "Taking Care of Business: The Heroin Addict's Life on the Street." *International Journal of the Addictions* 4: 1–24.

Rosenberg, Charles E. 1979. "Toward an Ecology of Knowledge: On Discipline, Context, and History." In *The Organization of Knowledge in Modern America*, edited by Alexandra Oleson and John Voss. Baltimore: Johns Hopkins University Press.

Rothman, David J. 1980. *Conscience and Convenience: The Asylum and Its Alternatives in Progressive America*. Boston: Little, Brown.

Starr, Paul. 1982. *The Social Transformation of American Medicine*. New York: Basic Books.

Trauner, Joan B. 1978. "The Chinese as Medical Scapegoats in San Francisco, 1870–1905." *California History* 57: 70–87.

Index